Children of Social W

Development in a Social Context

Edited by Martin Richards
and Paul Light

Polity Press

First published 1986 by
Polity Press, Cambridge, in association with Basil Blackwell, Oxford.
First published in paperback 1988.

Editorial Office:
Dales Brewery, Gwydir Street, Cambridge CB1 2LJ, UK.

Basil Blackwell Ltd
108, Cowley Road, Oxford OX4 1JF, UK

British Library Cataloguing in Publication Data

Children of social worlds.
  1. Child psychology
  I. Richards, Martin, *1940 Jan. 26–*   II. Light, Paul
  155.4   BF721

ISBN 0-7456-0099-9
ISBN 0-7456-0100-6 Pbk

Typeset by DMB (Typesetting), Oxford.

Printed in Great Britain by TJ Press, Padstow.

Contents

Contents

List of contributors

Robert Dingwall
Centre for Socio-Legal Studies, Oxford

Judy Dunn
College of Human Development, Pennsylvania State University

John Eekelaar
Pembroke College, Oxford

Rom Harré
Linacre College, Oxford

Chris Henshall
Health Promotion Research Trust, Cambridge

David Ingleby
Department of Development and Socialisation, University of Utrecht,
The Netherlands

Jean La Fontaine
London School of Economics

Jane Lewis
Department of Social Science and Administration, London School of Economics

Paul Light
School of Education, The Open University, Milton Keynes

Jacqueline McGuire
Department of Child Psychiatry, Institute of Child Health, University of London

Ann Oakley
Thomas Coram Research Unit, Institute of Education, University of London

Martin Richards
Child Care and Development Group, University of Cambridge

W. Peter Robinson
School of Education, University of Bristol

Professor Barbara Tizard
Thomas Coram Research Unit, Institute of Education, University of London

Cathy Urwin
Child Care and Development Group, University of Cambridge

List of contributors

Michael Wadsworth
Medical Research Council and the National Survey of Health and Development, Department of Community Medicine, University College, London

David Wood
Department of Psychology, University of Nottingham

Acknowledgements

The editors are grateful for the co-operation of the authors which made their task relatively painless. We would also like to thank Tanya Bascombe, Jill Brown, Dina Lew, Vivienne Light, Sally Roberts and Joan Shelton for their contributions to the preparation of the book.

Introduction

Martin Richards

This book is a collection of essays about children, their development and the social worlds of which they are part and in which they grow up. It represents the work of a group of social scientists who, while varying in their theoretical positions, all share a fundamental common belief that the development of children cannot be understood outside the social context in which it occurs. The influence of this context has often been treated as an 'optional extra' in relation to a universal asocial developmental process, rather as icing is to a cake. The basis of our argument is that social context is, at a variety of levels, intrinsic to the developmental process itself: rather than the icing of the cake it is as much a part of its structure as the flour or eggs that may be used to make it. It is, of course, a matter of great difficulty and complexity to construct a satisfactory theoretical perspective which adequately encompasses the subtleties of the relationships between people, what they do and the social worlds they inhabit, and, as the reader will discover, there are divergent views in the pages that follow. What is not at issue, however, is the need for such perspective.

   This book is in several senses a successor to an earlier co-operative effort, *The Integration of a Child into a Social World* (Richards, 1974). Both share the same basic theme as well as some of the same contributors. The earlier book was one of those happy accidents, which are, of course, not accidental, where the right people are in the right place at the right time. It appeared at a moment when developmental psychology was undergoing a considerable rejuvenation in Britain and elsewhere and when there had been a growing disenchantment with the prevailing view of development which either ignored the social world or trivialized it in the form of a series of 'social factors'. In a small way, it may immodestly be claimed, the earlier book provided a rallying point for those who accepted the criticisms and were committed to finding a better way forward. As time has passed since that book was published and research has proceeded, the question of some kind of revision of the book has been raised. To revise the text did not seem a very satisfactory answer, however, as the book was very much a product of its time. We felt that a better plan would be to start afresh and to provide some kind of commentary on the work of the last decade. And this is what we attempt here.

In this introduction, I wish to draw attention to some of the broad changes that have taken place over the last decade. The particular topics and themes which are developed in the various chapters are described in the brief introductions which appear at the beginning of each part of the book.

Perhaps the most striking change over recent years has been in the political and economic climate in which research and writing take place. In 1970 the atmosphere was still one of promise. Developmental psychology was expanding both in absolute terms and as the proportion it made up of the teaching and research effort within academic psychology. While cuts of one kind or another were not unheard of, it was not difficult for a new graduate to pursue Ph.D. work on a chosen topic, or for those with higher degrees to acquire both a permanent teaching position and a research grant. But perhaps more important than this relative freedom to conduct research, was the feeling of excitement and discovery that those involved felt at least from time to time. Work did seem to be moving in new directions and the horizons appeared very wide. As well as looking forward in new directions, there was the rediscovery of the past. What had passed for teaching in developmental psychology in most universities in the 1960s was sadly deficient but this had the unintended effect of making a visit to a library an exciting voyage of discovery. I still have a clear memory of the day when, as a relatively new Ph.D., I came across the work of G. H. Mead, a name previously unknown to me, by chance, while browsing in a library. On another occasion, about the same time, I have a memory of great excitement when reading the books of MacMurray for the first time. Of course, memory is very selective and it is easy to construct false pictures of Cider with Rosie days when the sun always shone and intellectual debate raged throughout the day and well into the night. But checking my memories with others I find I am not alone in remembering a very distinct atmosphere of excitement and enthusiasm in that period.

Today it is a very different world. Teaching and research continue, but the nature of both activities is not the same. Undergraduates have shown an increasing preference for subjects which hold out a better prospect of future employment than developmental psychology, and those who do come to us are usually more concerned about satisfying their examiners than uncovering the hidden curriculum in their subject. Researchers and teachers are on the defensive. It is not simply the lack of jobs and grants but a subtle change in stance which often seems to make intellectual work over solemn and unadventurous. Our subject has come of age, or at least some of the manifestations of the recent past have reached a kind of maturity, but has had the misfortune to do so at a point in history when anti-intellectualism seems to be in the ascendancy and government policies of divide and rule have placed the whole educational system under great stress. But this change in the political climate has by no means stifled all developmental work as this volume will attest. Indeed, it can be argued that the emergence of a more radical ideological position on the right of the political spectrum with its glorification of individuality has given a considerable spur to those psychologists who are seeking to articulate a fundamentally social account of individual development. The 'social constructionist' approaches have come increasingly under the spotlight of political attention, and these more or less explicitly underpin many of the chapters in this volume. In the final chapter David Ingleby traces the ways in which these theoretical arguments have developed and seeks to find common ground between the apparently rather heterogeneous solutions that are currently being advocated. In criticizing recent political changes and their effects on the educational system, however, we should not forget that the universities of a decade or so ago were hardly paragons of democracy and free intellectual expression. Indeed, the struggle against aspects of their institutional structure ('the university has lost control of its faculties') was part of the ideological shift that helped to create the rejuvenation of developmental psychology and many other fields at that time.

A central theme in the earlier volume was the criticism of a psychology based on universal laws that were supposed to hold good across all societies and at all historical times. It was argued that terms such as 'the mother' and 'the child' not only conveyed a meaningless generality but misrepresented the relationship between individuals and social worlds and portrayed social arrangements as if they were fixed laws of nature. The presence of historians and anthropologists among the authors in the present volume, and a concern with these issues in other chapters, indicates that this debate is by no means settled. At least if we use the well-known American journals as our yardstick, the basic position taken by the authors here and in the earlier volume still represents a minority view. In an analysis of the empirical papers published in *Child Development* in 1982 that were concerned with language, cognition and social development, it was found that only a small minority acknowledged that the findings might not hold beyond the boundaries of the culture in which the studies were carried out (Benigni and Valsiner, 1984). The authors comment that 160 of the 175 articles analysed 'failed to mention even the faintest possibility that the results could bear the mark of the cultural background of the subjects'.

It may be, however, that this result is unduly pessimistic. Leading national journals such as *Child Development* and *Developmental Psychology* impose a structure on published papers and have a selection process that does not encourage the publication of the new and innovative. Indeed, they could be said to represent the lowest common denominator of the developmental psychology enterprise and are more a product of the publish or perish career system than expressions of intellectual research and discovery. A rather different picture might have emerged had some of the newer and smaller journals or the collected volumes, which can often escape the dead hand of the editorial board and the formalized review process, been analysed. One of the recently founded journals drew attention to this by calling itself *New Ideas in Psychology*.

Benigni and Valsiner's analysis was published in the context of a debate about the lack of papers from abroad published in the major US developmental journals. They argued that the usual reasons given – that foreign authors do not understand submission procedures, have a poor command of English and so on – were not at the root of the problem and that it arises rather from differences in theoretical perspective. It would be quite inconsistent to exempt the work of psychologists from an analysis sensitive to cultural diversity. All the contributors to this volume work in Britain or have done so in the recent past. We hope that our choice of British authors does not arise from any mistaken chauvinism but is seen rather as an acknowledgement that there is cultural diversity in academic work and that we wanted to present the product of one academic community. It is clear, however, that there are plenty of authors on the continent of Europe, in North America and elsewhere whose work would fit easily within our perspective. Equally, that would not be true for all that goes by the name of developmental psychology in Britain. As was remarked in the introduction to the earlier volume, compared with North America, psychology in Britain and Europe represents a much smaller proportion of the academic community. This leads us into closer contact with colleagues in other disciplines which, in turn, may help to explain the lack of concern with disciplinary boundaries and the broad approach that is represented in this volume.

As far as topics are concerned, there have been some quite pronounced shifts in interest over the last decade. The analysis of mother-child or parent-child interaction has broadened its scope to encompass a much wider set of kinship and social relations. Infancy seems to have declined in interest as compared with later stages in life histories – perhaps our children are growing up. Another relative decline has been in work in language acquisition, which has had such an important influence on work on social and cognitive development. But part of this decline may be more apparent than real as at least some of the 'pure' language work has been subsumed into broader approaches to cognition and social development. One of the most obvious areas of growth has been in the field that has come to be known as social cognition – work which has developed out of the various criticisms of the way in which the social context was ignored in the Piagetian scheme of things. This active and lively field is well represented in the chapters that follow.

Ten or fifteen years ago a common complaint was that much psychology was unrelated to everyday concerns. With hindsight, and as the work on the ideological nature of psychology has made clear, it would have been more accurate to have been critical of the failure to make explicit the connections between psychological research and the social and political concerns of the societies in which it was carried out. No doubt encouraged by paymasters who have sought practical utility, researchers have moved into more practical spheres. Those who are concerned with learning are now much more likely to be found in a school class-room than an animal laboratory, for instance. Subjects such as divorce, unemployment, separation of parents and infants caused by medical practice, are but a few examples of topics that have received increasing concern in recent years. The old division between the pure and the applied is gradually disappearing as it is realized that work done in practical contexts may be just as 'basic' as that done in the laboratory or that with 'normal' samples outside. Indeed, in many areas such as the social cognition field, we have begun to realize what a curious and complex social situation is created in a laboratory experiment and the normal sample has been exposed for the ideological fiction that it is.

In many cases growing public concern about a problem leads to psychological research; so, for example, work on divorce has grown with the increasing divorce rate that occurred in most industrialized societies in the 1960s and early 1970s. So too, as Barbara Tizard (chapter 11) comments, has work on children and the nuclear threat paralleled rising and falling public perceptions of the probability of nuclear war. War has often dominated family life and is closely correlated with significant demographic variables – the marriage rate, for example – yet it has seldom received much attention from psychologists, at least from those who have an interest in the development of children rather than the techniques for the selection of recruits for the armed services. While we may wish that our children could grow without having to come to terms with the realization that nuclear war could end their lives, we cannot continue to avoid topics that may be politically or emotionally dangerous if we are going to provide a realistic account of human development.

References

Benigni, L. and Valsiner, J. 1984. Developmental psychology without the study of developmental processes. *Newsletter of the International Society for the Study of Behavioural Development*, no. 1, serial no. 7, 1–3.

Richards, M. P. M. (ed.) 1974. *The Integration of a Child into a Social World*. Cambridge: Cambridge University Press.

Part 1

Perspectives on the family

Introduction

'The family' is a central concern both in this part of the book and the next. The chapters making up this first part are not written from within the framework of developmental psychology, nor are they directly concerned with children or their development. Rather they offer perspectives on family life from the standpoints of social anthropology, social history, family law and feminism.

The key role of the family both as a social institution and as a context for child development is widely acknowledged. But it is often less than clear precisely what is meant by the term 'the family'. Jean La Fontaine explores the often confused and confusing usage of the term, and hints that the vagueness and imprecision of usage may reflect a latent ideological function. There is a widespread, if unanalysed, notion that the family is a natural unit, determined by the biological processes of bearing and rearing children. La Fontaine argues, by contrast, that the family should be regarded as a social construct denoting not so much an observable social entity as a culturally specific value.

La Fontaine explores distinctions drawn by social anthropologists between, for example, family as dwelling unit, as economic unit, and as reproductive unit, at the same time cautioning against considering any such unit in isolation from the wider society. The relations between the family and the wider society are taken up in the chapters that follow. Jane Lewis focuses on the interface between the family and the state. The family is today, as she remarks, high on the political agenda, with the ascendancy of 'New Right' ideas about getting the family to stand on its own feet by freeing it from intrusive interventions. Lewis examines present anxieties in the context of the history of earlier periods in which there was a similar concern about the breakdown of family life. In doing so she traces a developing relationship between the bourgeois ideal of family and the kinds of state intervention regarded as desirable or appropriate.

The circumstances of permissable intervention in the family are also the subject of Robert Dingwall and John Eekelaar's chapter. Here the specific focus is on family law, and the recurrent tension between the ideal of privacy and autonomy on the one hand and the need for regulation of events within the home on the other. The authors seek to temper the current swing towards emphasizing autonomy and freedom from interference, noting the argument that children are not free entrants into their family relationships. More radically, however, they seek to connect the issue of autonomy of families with the more general issue of individualism in developmental psychology – the analogy being to the way in which non-directive approaches to education have been bolstered by individualistic developmental theories such as those of Piaget. As Dingwall and Eekelaar point out, such libertarian notions assume the pre-existence of the individual, or of the family. But if – and here we meet one of the recurring themes of the present book – social practices are central to the formation and maintenance of the individual, or of the family, then there is not a pre-existing entity to liberate. In such circumstances, as Ingleby argues in his chapter in part 4, it can make no sense to condemn all forms of regulation.

Oakley, in the final chapter of part 1, seeks to disentangle the issue of motherhood from that of the family. She focuses on the tension between 'the public politics of feminism and the private politics of motherhood', examining her own and others' experiences and the clash between idealized motherhood and actuality. Here again, however, Oakley seeks to qualify the view of motherhood simply as an oppressive structure to be dismantled in the interests of individual liberation.

1

An anthropological perspective on children in social worlds

Jean La Fontaine

The inclusion of an article written by a social anthropologist in this volume is evidence of the changes in the course of the last ten years that have brought this subject much more to general attention. There has been an awareness of the usefulness of making cross-cultural comparisons in a variety of fields: medicine, law, art and music, to name but a few, besides, of course, psychology. For those who are interested in explaining an aspect of our own society, one convenient way of evaluating it is to compare it with similiar aspects in other societies. Anthropologists are known to study other parts of the world so, increasingly, people look to them for information on a wide variety of topics. However, as this chapter will hope to show, cross-cultural comparison is not merely a matter of placing the behaviour of peoples in different parts of the world beside our own, in order to understand either their behaviour or ours. The ideas behind comparison, the assumptions about other peoples and their place in the development of mankind are equally important. Because ideas take time to spread from the discipline in which they originated, it is probable that the views which are held outside anthropology are rather different from current thinking within it. As well as sketching the thinking behind modern anthropological approaches to the study of society in general and domestic life in particular, this chapter aims to show how assumptions which have been discarded in anthropology still appear elsewhere when cultural comparisons are made.

Social anthropology is, of course, centrally concerned with the understanding of different social worlds and their comparison. With a few notable exceptions (Raum, 1940; Read, 1959; Meyer, 1970; Middleton, 1970; Schildkrout, 1978), it has had much less interest in children. In general, anthropology has retained an outdated view of children as raw material, unfinished specimens of the social beings whose ideas and behaviour are the proper subject matter for a social science. The term that was used for the process of transforming children into the social actors who provide the data for anthropological analysis, socialization, implies a contrast between the 'natural human being' and the 'social person', an opposition which has been of central importance in Western views of society since at least the eighteenth century (see Ingleby, chapter 16).

Earlier in its development, however, during a period ending in roughly 1940, there had been an interest in socialization in anthropology, in which the dominant concept had been that of culture. The definition of culture used was that of E. B. Tylor, a nineteenth-century scholar, which makes it clear that culture is a set of skills and a body of knowledge that is handed on from generation to generation through a teaching process which transforms individuals into members of society. The culture of the past could be studied through the material remains which were the object of study of archaeologists, who, together with physical anthropologists interested in the physical nature of humanity, formed subdivisions within a discipline defined as the study of mankind. This was founded in the nineteenth century with the aim of discovering the laws of social evolution which would link the past with the present in terms of a development from 'savage' to 'civilized'. By the early twentieth century, when it had become clear that such an evolutionary approach was no longer tenable, the concept of culture survived the discarding of the theoretical apparatus for which it had been developed. The term was generally used in the plural, to indicate an interest in the comparison of contemporary variations in culture, rather than the evolution of a series of steps in the progress to civilization.

Early researchers had shown that all societies had institutionalized means of rearing their young to teach them, not merely necessary skills, but also a pattern of socially approved behaviour. Where specialized institutions for the education of the young seemed lacking, the same functions were performed by other institutions; in particular, parents were major agents of socialization in all societies. The interests of psychologists and psychoanalysts who studied the development of the personality and those of anthropologists interested in socialization appeared to be complementary. Interdisciplinary co-operation in the study of children was particularly close in the work of scholars in the United States where it gave rise to what was labelled the culture and personality school.

The proponents of this approach were largely students of Franz Boas, whose ideas dominated American anthropology during the early years of the twentieth century. He was a critic of evolutionists, pointing out the importance of the dissemination of ideas and practices from one people to another and making clear the lack of empirical foundation for the speculations of evolutionary theory. He perceived that 'cultural traits' or elements of a culture which were transmitted to another people were not taken over unchanged but adapted to fit in with the existing culture. For him, a culture consisted of an integrated assembly of traits which formed its own unique pattern. The organization of personality traits seemed to parallel this in its relation to the stereotyped modes of behaviour which were

characteristic of a particular people, and which were assumed to be the
result of training. The study of national character, or the relation between
culture and personality, appeared to be a key to the understanding of variations in such behaviour across cultures.

The best-known member of this school of thought is undoubtedly
Margaret Mead, whose books still enjoy a wide readership outside
anthropology. Her work on child-rearing and socialization in New Guinea
and Samoa, as well as the work of others such as Ruth Benedict, provoked
a strong and unfavourable reaction from anthropologists in Britain, where
it was heavily criticized from the start. Recently, a book by Derek Freeman
(1983), who also worked in Samoa, caused a furore in the United States
with its assertions that Mead's research was slipshod and superficial, that
she portrayed the Samoans as permissive in sexual matters and claimed
that they held ideas which were in fact quite contrary to their traditional
morality. His strictures, however, add little to the fundamental criticisms
of her theory and method that have been current in British social
anthropology for decades. Mead appeared to take for granted that behaviour
was simply an expression of personality and assumed a universal relevance
for psychological and psychoanalytic theories of individual behaviour
(Jahoda, 1970). She ignored the existence of standards of behaviour which
were maintained either by sanctions on non-conformity or the reciprocal
pressures of interaction. Her model is based on a far too simplistic set of
connections between social behaviour, personality and childhood experience, and virtually ignores all social life outside the domestic sphere.
Cultural variations in adult behaviour, the very stuff of anthropological
investigation, were, it seemed, to be reduced to differences in methods of
child-rearing. These different practices themselves were unexplained,
merely accepted as given.

The most damning criticism levelled at Mead, and the culture and
personality school in general, was one of method. The leading exponent of
a theory of culture in Britain was Malinowski (Firth, 1957) who held a position here very like that of Boas in the United States, although Malinowski
was much the younger man. He emphasized the function of a culture's
constituent institutions as the means of satisfying the basic needs for
food, shelter, reproduction and the maintenance of an orderly social life.
He argued vehemently that the first task of anthropologists was to eluci-
date the interconnection of institutions in a culture, rather than speculate
about its origins. Strangely, as Richards (1970) has noted, he did not list
socialization as a function, perhaps because he included it under 'reproduction' which he saw as the function of the family as an institution.
Malinowski's most lasting achievement was not his theory of culture but
his establishment of participant observation as the basic method of collecting data. Field-work in another society is still the basis of most anthropological work in Britain. Malinowski emphasized the need to learn the

language thoroughly, so as to be able to understand a people's way of thinking, and also to enable one to record conversations as they took place. Daily observation over an extended period permitted the observation of how disputes arose and were settled, as well as the pattern of everyday life. In short, the field-worker was expected to immerse him or herself in the life of a people, rather than relying on the answers of informants to questions which might be put through an interpreter. Malinowski's own field-work, which demonstrated the value of his method, became the model for others and British anthropologists, many of whom were Malinowski's students, came to regard this method as an essential preliminary and a distinctive feature of British anthropology. The fruitfulness of the method was immediately apparent and has remained largely unquestioned and has outlived Malinowski's theoretical contributions to the subject. Today it still provides a unifying framework for a discipline which has developed a wide range of divergent views and interests.

By British standards then, the research on which the culture and personality school based their conclusions was impressionistic and superficial. It led to a crude, inaccurate view of cultural differences and could not begin to explain variations in economic, political and legal institutions. Those aspects of social life which the culture and personality approach was least able to analyse became the main focus of anthropological interest. While Mead's ideas on the cultural rather than the biological origin of differences between the sexes were both stimulating and original, as the later feminist movement has come to realize, her influence in Britain was outside, rather than within, her own subject.

The lack of interest in socialization in British anthropology was caused by influences other than the reaction to the work of the culture and personality school. The publication of much of that work coincided with a shift in the dominant paradigm in anthropology in Britain. Under the influence of early sociological thinkers such as the Frenchman Durkheim and his English admirer, Radcliffe-Brown, the concept of society superseded that of culture as a means of defining the object of study. Regularities in behaviour, ideas and beliefs which were general among members of a group were to be classified as 'social facts' (Durkheim, 1895) and to be explained by their interconnections, not reduced to products of the biological or psychological nature of individual human beings. Society was to be understood as a structure of which the constituent units were not living individuals, but social groups, roles and relationships. While any individual might perform his or her role in a slightly different way and it was recognized that the personalities and circumstances of individuals affected their behaviour, a consideration of socialization was largely irrelevant to the analysis of such structures. The critical distinction described by Radcliffe-Brown was between the individual and the social role. He argued:

> Every human being living in society is two things: he is an individual and also
> a person. As an individual, he is a biological organism, a collection of a vast
> number of molecules organised in a complex structure within which, as long
> as it persists, there occur physiological and psychological processes and
> changes. *Human beings as individuals are objects of study for physiologists
> and psychologists.* The human being as a person is a complex of social
> relationships. He is a citizen of England [*sic*], a husband and a father, a
> bricklayer, a member of a particular Methodist congregation, a voter in a
> certain constituency, a member of his trade union, an adherent of the
> Labour party and so on. Note that each of these descriptions refers to a
> social relationship, or to a place in a social structure. *As a person, the human
> being is the object of study for the social anthropologist. We cannot study
> persons except in terms of social structure*, nor can we study social structure
> except in terms of the persons of which it is composed. (1940, 193–4, my
> emphasis)

This extended passage makes quite clear how the division of labour
between the social sciences, in which anthropology was now to be included,
and other related disciplines was to be achieved. It entails that distinction
between the individual and society referred to by Ingleby (chapter 14)
which remained fundamental to social anthropology for several decades.
In 1964 Gluckman still argued for the same division of labour that
Radcliffe-Brown had envisaged, claiming that anthropologists must make
do with what he called 'naive' models of psychological processes in order
to deepen their own specialist knowledge of social processes. While
subsequent developments, to which I will refer later, have modified the
concept of social structure and reintroduced a different version of that of
culture, the effect of Radcliffe-Brown's work was to put the focus of
anthropology on adults.

The isolationism of social anthropology was encouraged by relics of
nineteenth-century thinking which lingered on in other disciplines,
particularly in psychoanalytic theories. The identification of 'savages'
with children and the belief that other societies either represented earlier
stages in the evolution of the more advanced ones or manifested pre-
logical modes of thought prevented a dialogue between social anthropologists and psychologists. Few of the latter worked in other societies; those
that did were still inclined to see their members through the eyes of their
own culture and ignore the findings of anthropologists (Richards, 1970).
The years between the Second World War and the 1970s saw the establishment of social anthropology as a distinct discipline; this was no doubt due
to a concentration on a rather narrower definition of the subject than
is currently the case, and the establishment of a solid groundwork in the
form of a rich store of published ethnographic data on which to work.

In the United States, by contrast, the concept of social structure did not
alter the theoretical focus of anthropology which largely remained known

as cultural anthropology, linked to both archaeology and physical anthropology. The continued concern with the interrelation of cultural 'traits' and the influence of psychology led to a new, statistical approach. Yale University set up an indexing system, listing the cultural traits of as many societies as possible across the world. The Human Relations Area Files as it was called, was used to test a variety of hypotheses of which those of Whiting and his school are relevant to our present concerns. Whiting and his colleagues (1958) sought to explain the distribution of male initiation as a mechanism for socialization by relating it to domestic sleeping arrangements and the nature of the post-partum sexual taboo observed by spouses in many societies. He saw the last two traits as engendering both too close an association between boys and their mothers, and hostility between boys and their fathers. Initiation was the means devised to correct this, by separating boys from their mothers and reasserting the power of fathers. He showed a statistical correlation between the three traits but, as critics pointed out, the approach contained many flaws. The three cultural traits could not be established as independent variables and might well have been explained by their mutual dependence on some other social feature; secondly, no evidence was adduced that the emotions assumed to be engendered in the children were indeed present, or that initiation was in fact effective. Inaccuracies in the coding of information were also shown to exist and the whole study was vulnerable to the same type of objections as were made to that of Margaret Mead which it resembled.

The view of social institutions as the product of the interaction between child-rearing practices and the personalities of members of the group was so alien to the whole approach of British social anthropology that even Whiting's later work evoked little or no interest. Few of the papers given at a conference of the Association of Social Anthropologists on socialization in 1967 (Mayer, 1970) even referred to it. Subsequent work by the Whiting school is markedly more sophisticated in its use of the field-work techniques developed by anthropologists. However, work such as that of Konner (1977) on the Harvard !Kung project still contrasts rather sharply with that of anthropologists in two important ways.

There still seems to be an assumption that in studying hunting and gathering societies, the researcher is getting as close as possible to 'universal human characteristics'. Konner writes 'Since this [hunting and gathering] was the very subsistence pattern that characterised human adaptation during 99 per cent of the history of the genus Homo, it was deemed essential to pursue the study of modern hunting and gathering peoples as an adjunct to the study of human evolution' (Konner, 1977, 288). But the characteristics he lists as being typical of hunting-gathering societies are those of a particular modern type, often associated (as in the case of the !Kung) with symbiotic relations with settled, neighbouring peoples. There is no reason to assume that the rather simple society of the

!Kung resembles historically earlier social organization; this form of sub-sistence is known to have been associated recently with a great variety of social forms, some of them very complex, and there is no evidence that early man was any less varied. Simple forms of society are neither more primitive in the sense of being closer to the social life of early man, nor in the sense that they represent a simple common base on which other societies have been elaborated.

Secondly, observational studies undertaken by ethologists, both on a cross-cultural basis and more generally, ignore the vital element that behaviour is meaningful activity. The interaction of mothers and children in different societies relates directly to ideas about infants and children and about how they should be treated, and therefore cannot easily be compared without considering these cultural notions. Konner (1977) himself has to introduce a !Kung idea into his observations to explain why babies are rarely left to lie down when awake. But if one such explanation is necessary, then others might also be relevant; alternatively, if observation is not to include meanings, then this particular exception is not justified. Most anthropologists would consider that Konner pays far too little attention to !Kung ideas on the subject and how they affect behaviour. This general point will be considered again later in the chapter. Here it serves to demonstrate why British social anthropology continued to hold itself aloof from culture and personality studies and from its more recent ethological variants.

The 1967 conference on socialization, to which I referred (Mayer, 1970) did mark the beginning of a shift in social anthropologists' attitudes, which was the result of other developments in the discipline. To discuss them fully is beyond the scope of this chapter, but they can be seen to relate to the earlier history of anthropology, developing some of its basic themes.

Social anthropology still uses the notion of social relationships as a basic conceptual tool, although Radcliffe-Brown's concept of social structure has been found too inflexible to be useful. By social relationships, anthropologists still refer, not to patterns of interaction and feelings, but to a complex multi-stranded compound of assumptions about the world, moral values and ideas about behaviour, the distribution of resources, claims to authority and the exercise of power. A concern with individuals as agents, as shaping social life by exercising choices, has blurred the original distinction between the individual and the social person and awakened an interest in the relation between types of social behaviour and universal human characteristics. Feminist anthropologists have demonstrated how deeply held are the assumptions about gender roles and how widely they affect social life (see also Oakley, chapter 4). Statuses are seen to be claimed as well as conferred and the negotiation of claims to authority is recognized as one of the important processes to be understood.

The concept of structure has been, so to speak, intellectualized as a result of these ideas and the effect of the Marxist concept of ideology which has focused attention on the way in which socially held beliefs about the world perpetuate social forms. The analysis of economic and political systems in relation to systems of ideas has had the effect of focusing attention on the concepts used by social anthropologists themselves as examples of social products. The concentration on the interpretation of ritual actions and the interpretation of symbolism has led to a new interest in thought itself: systems of classification, perceptions of the world and the distribution of knowledge as a form of power.

The field-work method

How can all of this be of use in the understanding of the social worlds of children? Some consideration of field-work as a method is relevant, for 'studying the child in everyday life situations' (Ingleby, chapter 14) resembles what anthropologists do in collecting their data.

The understanding obtained by social anthropologists in research by participant observation in the field depends on the juxtaposition of the perceptions of the participant and the observer. Both elements are crucial. Social behaviour must be placed in the context of the meanings it has for the people concerned, which means eliciting, not only rules of conduct and moral issues, but the shared assumptions which are so taken for granted that they are rarely expressed. These are the 'self-evident truths' which are regarded as characterizations of the world as it is. They are rendered impervious to doubt or argument by this very quality of being a 'fact of life', which it is not within the capacity of human beings to alter. In studying other societies, one is brought up against these ideas by the mere fact of their difference from one's own; the obligation to study them provides a check on the tendency to make judgements and interpretations based on one's own assumptions, to be ethnocentric. Thus Korbin (1980) makes clear in her introduction to a collection of essays on child abuse in a variety of social settings the importance of distinguishing between normal behaviour which does not conform to Western values and that which violates the moral codes of the society concerned. She also points out, in a salutary passage, that many of the usual practices of Western societies may be judged cruel by the standards of other societies. The assumption that the meaning of behaviour cannot be taken for granted, and must be discovered for each society in order to make sense of people's behaviour, is crucial and marks social anthropologists off from their colleagues in ethology.

In studying sections of one's 'own' society, particularly when it is large and heterogeneous, the difficulties in avoiding ethnocentrically determined interpretations are great. Some anthropologists have argued, however (and see Richards, 1977), that only those who fully understand a society in all its complexity can really understand it and that these people are likely to be its own members. But Ingleby's discussion in this volume of how ideas of the relation between individual and society have influenced academic disciplines shows how influential culture can be: Western societies can be characterized by this particular concern which does not appear in the thought of other societies in the same form at all (Mauss, 1938–39; Dumont, 1970; Macfarlane, 1978). Of course, perfect objectivity is an impossible ideal, the Holy Grail of scholars; we are, after all, members of a particular society and subject to its influence on our thinking. However, the awareness that meanings which colour all social worlds must be determined by investigation, rather than assumed to be 'natural', is a direct result of cross-cultural comparison of the variety of guises such worlds may assume.

The observer must also document patterns in the distribution of resources, in the exercise of power and the attribution of authority. These may not be understood in the same way by members of the social group being studied or may not be perceived at all. Thus Whitehead (1981) shows that, despite a model of the household that assumes a common fund shared by all, the actual distribution of goods and services within a household reveals inequities which relate to the relative power of the men and women within it. The existence of an ideal of romantic love, as discussed by Sarsby (1983), seems quite at odds with the statistics of actual marriage choices, which show the influence of class, occupation and upward mobility (Heath, 1981). In this volume, the cases discussed by Dingwall and Eekelaar indicate how the power of the courts supports certain concepts of 'the family', but judges have the power to overrule parental rights where these conflict with the perceived interests of the child. Ultimately, there-fore, the structure of relations within what is thought of as an autonomous unit, sustained by 'natural' relations and affection, is deeply affected by the nature of the wider society.

The social representation of human development

Cross-cultural comparison reveals the variable social representation of the universal 'fact' of human development. In all societies the developmental process from birth to death receives social recognition. The conferring of a name on an infant is a recognition of its social identity at the start of its life. In many societies an unnamed infant is not a full social being; if it dies before being named it is not given a funeral, but the body is merely disposed of. In Britain, the pro- and anti-abortion lobbies hold different definitions of the point at which a human foetus becomes a human being but a stillbirth often does not receive the same funeral as a child that dies.

The life cycle is further broken up into stages, which are socially defined by reference to physical events, such as starting to walk, cutting teeth, learning to speak. Not all events are significant universally; some may be important milestones in one society, but ignored in another. However, Schildkrout (1978) is one of those who have pointed out that there are parallels in the stages recognized in Western and other societies, which would argue a universal reality that is being defined. What is more variable is the range of behaviour that is expected at the different stages through which individuals pass.

The definition of adult status, which entails a distinction between child and adult, is of prime significance in all societies, for adult status confers rights and responsibilities on the individual. It is always marked in some manner. Adulthood may be achieved through ritual, commonly at marriage, but initiation may mark the end of childhood and inaugurate an adult, or proto-adult, status. Alternatively there may be a gradual assumption of different rights and capabilities, as in Britain where 16 marks the assumption of sexual maturity, but the legal and political rights of citizenship are not achieved until the age of 18, and marriage confers a further increment in status. The chronological age at which adult status is reached may vary, between and within societies. Where it is marked by marriage, girls may become adult women at the age of 12 or 13, while boys remain children much longer. In some cases where the difference between the sexes is very marked in this respect, like that of the Samburu of Kenya (Spencer, 1965) the consequences may ramify widely. Among the Samburu, ranking by age is very important. Husbands are usually at least 15 and often up to 30 years older than their wives. The conjugal relationship is not expected to be one of equality between spouses and the age difference enhances a husband's authority. Even where husband and wife are seen as equal partners, as in Europe, differences in age, class and income may alter the balance of particular relationships.

Adulthood is always a matter of social definition rather than physical maturity. Slaves, however old, never acquire the full rights of social adults, nor do the mentally handicapped in many societies. The position of both may resemble that of children. Women's adult status may be less completely autonomous than that of men, if for example they remain dependent on father, brother or husband to exercise their legal and political rights. In Western society, it has been argued, adult status is defined by the requirements of a capitalist system (Aries, 1962).

All societies, in defining what is adult, also define what is not adult. Childhood is defined in contrast to the concepts which define adult status. It is not helpful to argue, as Aries (1962) seems to, that only one specific form of this definition, the modern Western one, is 'really' a concept of childhood. To take this approach is to carry relativism to the point where cross-cultural comparison becomes impossible, and the significance of the structural relation of responsibility/dependency, which is common to the variety of forms, is lost.

A more fruitful approach than the relegation of a concept of childhood to a dustbin labelled 'ideology' is to examine it more carefully. Like many value-laden concepts it reveals a certain ambiguity, referring at the same time to a state of physical being and a social position. Oakley's account of her relations with teenage children (chapter 4) shows how this ambiguity may result in conflict, which is familiar in both senses of the word.

In Britain the term 'child' has meaning in two distinct frames of reference. The first refers to stage of development and the biological, intellectual and social characteristics which are associated with it. It is in this sense that the term 'child' contrasts with 'adult' or 'baby'; the lack of a clearly recognized transition from one to the other may allow different, conflicting definitions of the same individual. The classification of individuals as adults or children affects their ability to assume social roles. According to the particular constitution of any particular institution, inherited positions may or may not devolve on children, they may or may not inherit property or titles. Some roles in institutional structures are so closely associated with the status of child that they may be used to define it: 'Oh she's still at school, just a child.' Recently a sixth-form girl who married her boyfriend was under threat of suspension from school, showing the incompatibility of the role of pupil with the status of adult; it was clear, too, that opinions were divided over the legitimacy of Oxford's admission of a 'mere child' to read for a degree in mathematics. Occasional anomalies such as this show up the way in which age, as an indicator of status as child, regulates the participation of children in society. However, it is the same social world as that of the adults, with whom the child has (socially defined) relationships. The child is neither confined to a children's world, nor to a domestic world; there is merely a range of relationships, assigned by convention, through which children participate in social life.

In its second sense, 'child' is one of a set of terms indicating a particular structure of such relations; it is one element in what anthropologists term a kinship system. In all societies, babies are born into an established network of social relations connecting them to other individuals as children, but also as siblings, nephews or nieces, and grandchildren. An important characteristic of these terms is that they are relational, that is, they indicate connections between roles, rather than individuals. One is a niece only in relation to an uncle or aunt, a child only in relation to a parent. In this sense an individual is always a child in relation to those recognized as its parents until their death. This strand lends a further ambiguity to the situation Oakely describes. The different terms of a kinship system form a classification of relatives, which establishes the identity of an infant as 'child of *X* and *Y*' but also as 'sibling of *A*', 'grandchild of *P*' and so on. They also influence the behaviour of individuals, through their concept of their relationship to the child.

Kinship relations are not established by the individuals concerned, they are conferred by birth into a particular social system. Individuals may choose to play their roles in different ways, allowing some relationships to remain inactive or ignoring others of their kin, but they are subject to pressures and sanctions if they depart too widely from the general patterns and they cannot change their kin: cousins may be unknown as individuals but they remain cousins. In all societies there is a bilateral spread of such ties, through ties to both parents, but in some societies one link also carries membership of significant social groups. The stigma which generally attaches to the illegitimate is largely because they lack the normal range of recognized kin; part of their social identity is missing.

The parent-child relationship is thus part of a system of kinship and the character of the system affects each element within it. Thus Bott (1957) shows how the nature of conjugal relationships in English families is related to the network of relations each spouse has with kin. Moreover the rights to, and responsibilities for, children may be distributed among kin, so that grandparents, mother's brother or father's sister may have the authority to make decisions affecting them or determine where they live. Adoption and fostering, baby-sitting and child-minding are elements of kinship behaviour and shape the child's social relations with adults (Goody, 1982). Such relationships may constitute a certain protection for a child's interests in that kin may provide a refuge from parents or support in a conflict with them. The role of the state, and the courts which are backed by the power of the state, discussed in chapter 3 by Dingwall and Eekelaar, is a further factor which affects the parent-child relationship. *Vis-à-vis* the state, however, the child is an individual citizen, albeit of less than adult status, and the state's action, apart from carrying greater power than that of individuals, is not that of a parent as much as an agency enforcing that part of social organization which is enshrined in law. The rights of political authorities in small-scale societies which lack modern state organization may limit the power and authority of parents but do not normally enforce an ideal of a child's rights as an individual, distinct from its relation to particular parents. The judgement of Solomon was concerned not with the interests of a child, but with the dispute between two women, both of whom claimed maternal rights.

The family

A characteristic of the societies which are loosely referred to as Western[1] is that some of their kinship terms have a very restricted referent; they apply to individuals and not to classes of kin. These terms (father, mother, brother, sister, son, daughter) and the relationships they designate, are collectively known as the 'family'. The assumption which underlies this key social value is one of genetic relatedness: the family is defined as founded on the bearing and rearing of children. It is thus seen as a 'natural unit' (Harris, 1981), a result of the 'facts of life'. Children share the physical substance of their parents and siblings are related by their common genetic endowment. 'Blood' relations are those who are related by the transmission of substance across the generations. Thus kinship relates ideas of reproduction to social relations and provides an image of interlocking families resulting from shared ancestry.

All societies base their ideas of kinship on similar notions of genetic connection, using concepts of 'bone', 'blood' or 'flesh', but these ideas are not identical. In some societies, a child's substance is shared only with its mother or, in others, the substance is derived from its father, nurtured in the womb. In the first case, a father is believed to have no genetic connection with his child, in the second the maternal role is reduced to feeding a being engendered by its father. A common reaction to such differences is to describe ideas which differ from the Western view as based on ignorance of the 'facts'; the Western view is held to be based on 'scientific knowledge'. Yet, as Barnes (1973) has shown, our theories of conception long pre-date the ability of science to demonstrate their validity, and folk notions may not coincide with the scientific theories of the time. There are other indications that 'the family' is founded not on biological but on social ties. An adopted child has the same social status as one begotten and borne by the individuals who are its parents, the paternal origin of adulterine children may be concealed, while a child born to an unmarried mother may be described as 'fatherless'. Women, and sometimes men, bring up children in what are termed 'one-parent familes' when divorce, death or separation has broken a former marriage tie.

The term 'family' defines no organized, easily identifiable group; it can also be applied to the whole range of recognized kin, as in the sentence: 'They have a family scattered over three continents.' The use of such terms as 'nuclear' or 'elementary family' for the narrower sense and 'extended family' for the wider meaning has not solved the problem of ambiguity in the word (Murray, 1981) which relates to the use of 'family' as synonymous with household. This usage has been the source of much confusion in the social sciences.

An important connotation of the word 'family' is the idea of a permanent association between a couple and their offspring, forming an autonomous unit. In this sense, it gives a moral value to a household based on the monogamous couple and their sole responsibility for their children. A particular form of the household becomes not only 'natural' but 'right' (Harris, 1981). This emphasis on the reproductive function of the family probably underlies the relative neglect of sibling relations, referred to elsewhere in this volume (Dunn, chapter 5), for it places the stress on relations between generations, rather than within a generation.

As with all such concepts, the family carries moral value rather than descriptive accuracy. It takes no account of the cycle of maturation, being a static definition. Individuals mature and marry. If spouses are to live together, one or both must leave their parents' home and render it incomplete as a family. It is this fact which indicates the limitation and ambiguity of the concept of the family, for whatever the pattern adopted in any society, and there are many different cultural norms of post-marital residence, the members of a mature family must be distributed among different households. The family can never represent social reality except for a proportion of households.

To cope with this difficulty, some sociologists have adopted another terminology referring to the family of orientation, in which the individual is a child, and to the family of procreation, in which he or she is a spouse and parent. This retains the emphasis on the reproductive function, and the links between successive generations, by focusing on the maturing individual, rather than on the family as a whole. The assumption that the family is a residential group is thus protected and the dogma of biological determination reaffirmed.

Indeed Parsons (1956) with whom this terminology is usually associated, argued that the nuclear family was a universal social group. In that all societies provide for the reproduction of both their human members and their social institutions, through the bearing and socialization of children, he asserted that the reproductive nucleus of parents and children was to be found in all societies. However, anthropological studies of other societies make it clear that domestic groups are very diverse and that there is considerable variation, both in the content of relationships between members of the so-called nuclear family, and in its relation to the kinship system as a whole. The classification of such different phenomena under a single term was clearly unsatisfactory. In order to pursue their long-term goal of explaining differences between societies, anthropologists were forced to consider the structure of households, thus making a distinction between family and household, which has now come into more general use (Rimmer, 1981).

In an attempt to solve the problem of providing a concept which might be used more fruitfully in comparative analysis, Fortes (1958) introduced a distinction between 'the family' and 'the domestic group'. He defined the family as the reproductive nucleus of the domestic group, which was a housekeeping and householding group. His colleague Jack Goody (1972), whose work has been very influential in the general field, sees 'the domestic group' as 'an overall term for three kinds of unit, namely the dwelling unit, the reproductive unit, the economic unit' (p. 106). The domestic group is an organization whose composition varies according to

the demands of subsistence production, the nature of property holding
and inheritance as well as the kinship system (Goody, 1958, 1976). This
approach has influenced historians, such as Laslett, as well as historical
demographers, all of whom have used it to illuminate the European past
and, in the process, to dispel some of the myths surrounding the nature of
the family in earlier times.

Yet this approach did not entirely solve the analytic problems inherent
in the use of this culturally specific term in cross-cultural comparison.
The distinction between 'family' and 'household' relies on separating the
reproductive (family) from the domestic (household) functions of the
Western concept. The connection between the two relies on the assumption that the reproductive function of the family entails the permanent
association of parents and children. Variations in household form were
held to be associated with stages in the developmental cycle of the
reproductive unit, rather than departure from a central norm which was
an advance on the view that all households which were not also nuclear
familes were somehow aberrant. But studies in the Caribbean (Morris,
1979; Spens, 1969; Smith, 1963, 1973), in Africa (Goody, 1973; Murray,
1981) and Australia (Sansom, 1978) have demonstrated the wide range of
conjugal association that results in the bearing of children and their
rearing by a variety of adults. In a particular society the children in any
one household may be the children of any one of the adults present, their
grandchildren, siblings' children, children of distant kin or adopted and
fostered children, pupils, apprentices, or domestic servants. The distribution of children among households for rearing has received relatively
little attention, despite the pioneering study by Esther Goody (1982) but it
is clear that parental responsibility may be delegated, not merely as a
necessity but as a positive strategy to maintain kinship links and/or to
offer the children special advantages. Western societies have had, in
addition, a number of specialized institutions such as children's homes
and boarding-schools, but wet-nurses, nannies, au pair girls, foster
parents, adoptive parents and kin have all undertaken the functions of
child care, whether in the same household or in different households from
the one in which the child was born.

The connection between family and household central to the Fortesian
concept is clearly not a matter of either the bearing or rearing of children.
It is rather that the idea of the family influenced the perception of the
arrangements of other societies and supported an analysis in terms of the
prevailing functional theory. Those anthropologists who have worked in
Europe have been equally influenced by the prevailing norms of their own
society (Harris, 1981). As Davis (1977) notes, they have failed to use the
systematic approach that has been developed in research outside Europe,
concentrating rather on household dynamics, patterns of inheritance, the
provision of dowry, residence, the contracting of marriages and inter-

personal kinship. In essence, they have been concerned with patterns of household structure. Social anthropologists have also worked in Great Britain but they too have tended to focus on family/household (Harris, 1983; Firth, Hubert and Forge, 1969), or on even more narrowly defined topics such as marriage (Leonard, 1980; Benson, 1981), romantic love (Sarsby, 1983), divorce (Hart, 1976) or conjugal relations (see also La Fontaine, 1985). Goody's study (1983) of the development of family and marriage in Europe is largely concerned with marriage prohibitions and inheritance of property. Important though these contributions have been, they have not contributed to a theoretical understanding of the relation between kinship systems and domestic structures.

The household

Concern with household structures, however, is directly relevant to the topic of this book since children are in their early years brought up largely within the household and even in later years it is the primary base with which they identify. The structure of the household is also a structure of social relations, a social world in which the children have their place. Its form is determined by a variety of factors: kinship, economic, political and legal. Membership of a household is normally assumed to be determined by residence; however, in many societies including those of Western Europe, this 'rule' is far too simple and does not adequately describe a much more fluid reality. Do students absent from home for the weeks of the university term count as members of the parents' households or not? Do au pairs or nannies? Some writers, interested in this question, have distinguished between 'household', meaning those who are legally domiciled in a particular household, and 'housefull', referring to those actually resident. However, the fluidity of many urban situations in the Third World is such that even such distinctions may not adequately represent the changing personnel of domestic groups, let alone the exchange of meals for labour or money on a regular basis, and other eating and sleeping arrangements which make it hard to decide just what is 'a' household (see La Fontaine, 1970; Wyer, 1984; Parry, 1979 for some examples). The account given by members of the society in question may schematize or give the 'normal' picture, so that observation is necessary to build up a fuller understanding of how such general views relate to the fluidity of daily events.

Households are economic units; even if, in industrialized societies, the members of a household do not produce their own food, the household is a part of the wider economy. It is significantly affected by the property rights of its members,[2] their income, whether in the forms of goods or cash, and the expenditure made to maintain its members. Members may or may not contribute to a common fund, but the distribution of resources within the unit is important for its structure (Morris, 1983; Pahl, 1983). Household organization also displays a characteristic division of labour; more has been published on the domestic labour of women than of that of men in industrial society but it is clear that despite variations within sub-groups or in particular households, a common pattern of activity demonstrates the divisions of age and gender which are a major feature of household structure. The control of resources is a source of power which supports the moral authority of parents and the position of the head of household, but which may also undermine authority, if the actual distribution of economic power is inconsistent with the expected norm. (See Goody, 1958, for a consideration of the relation between economy, property rights and the form of households.)

The activities of children must be included in any study of household organization for they are participants, not merely bystanders. While it is common to find that what children do is regarded as learning the skills of adults, a number of studies have shown that the tasks fulfilled by children may be essential to the household's economic viability. A pastoral economy means that a household needs herdboys and dairymaids (Stenning, 1958); without sons and daughters old enough to perform these tasks a couple cannot run an independent household and must join up with another one. Child-minding in very many societies, including those of modern Europe, is a task for older children, freeing the women for other tasks and sometimes earning the child pocket-money. Authority is delegated to older siblings for this task. The significance of children's labour is emphasized in Schildkrout's (1978) account of urban Kano. In this Muslim society, women must remain secluded within the compound; but an important part of the household income is derived from women's trade. There are no such restrictions on children, who market the goods, do the shopping and maintain the flow of information between households as they run their errands. The introduction of universal schooling has, in some societies, deprived women of their ability to undertake the traditional wide range of female tasks. A household draws on the resources of all its members, their labour, earnings and social relations outside it. Wallman's study of Eight London Households (1984) shows how significant the latter are in finding jobs, houses and services. Households are not autonomous units but are embedded in other institutions.

Household structure incorporates within it a distribution of power. Social anthropologists have been forced to take more account of this than other social scientists, since in many of the communities in which they have worked, household headship is a political office of some significance. While the writings of feminists have been largely concerned with power in the conjugal relationship, it must not be forgotten that parents and older siblings may exercise power over children, either in the forms of rewards and deprivations, or as physical force. The social problems of battered babies and wives, or of sexually abused children have drawn our attention to the misuse of this power, but its exercise in less dramatic ways is often ignored. Perelberg (1983) found that the committal to a mental hospital of wives, and, in particular, of grown children, could often be understood as an attempt by husbands or parents to hand over control to a stronger authority when they felt their own ability to control individuals had broken down. Their rights to demand compliance were no longer backed with force and were being ignored. The social world of children is structured by ideas of seniority and juniority, of legitimate authority and the locus of power. Richards (1939) observed that quite small Bemba children observed age precedence in their games and expected to give way to their seniors.

It is helpful to consider domestic life as consisting of several strands or layers. Fundamental cultural assumptions and moral axioms construct a view of the world within which relationships, expressed in explicit rules and generalizations, can be expressed. Much of the former must be elicited through the analysis of key terms and through casual remarks, stories, proverbs, myth and non-verbal behaviour; the latter can be formulated as answers to questions. The observer's understanding of the distribution of resources, and of the power structures, both through society at large and within the domestic group, and the influence of institutions which the participants consider quite distinct from their own concerns, form other strands. The regularities of observed behaviour are the product of all these factors, the pattern produced by their interweaving; the particularities of the behaviour of living individuals must include recognition of their emotions and the history of their interactions. The contribution that social anthropology can make to the understanding of the social aspect of child development is to draw attention to the assumptions which we take for granted. In distinguishing kinship as a system of relationship expressed in a biological idiom from the organized activities of a household, this chapter has attempted to focus on the weakness of the traditional concept of 'the family' and the falsity of seeing it in terms of the house shut off from the street, as a closed unit. It is, on the contrary, dependent on the wider society which shapes the characteristic form of the household and supports its internal relationships. Membership of this unit engages a child in social living from the moment of its birth.

Notes

1. These include the many different societies of Europe and North America but the eastern boundary of the area is rather ill-defined. Moreover, it should not be assumed that the kinship systems of this area are unique in all respects. There are bilateral systems of kinship reckoning in other parts of the world but I know

of no study which has compared them with 'western' systems in order to understand their similarities and differences.
2. By property rights, social anthropologists refer to all rights in resources, not merely the ownership of land, houses or other capital. See the article by Goody in *The Development Cycle in Domestic Groups* and his book *Production and Reproduction.*

References

Aries, P. 1962. *Centuries of Childhood.* London: Cape and Penguin Books, 1973.

Barnes, J. A. 1973. Genitor:genetrix :: nature:culture?, in J. Goody (ed.) *The Character of Kinship.* Cambridge: Cambridge University Press.

Benson, S. 1981. *Ambiguous Ethnicity: interracial families in London* (Changing Cultures Series). Cambridge: Cambridge University Press.

Bott, E. 1957. *Family and Social Network.* London: Tavistock.

Davis, J. 1977. *People of the Mediterranean: an essay in comparative social anthropology.* London: Routledge and Kegan Paul.

Dumont, L. 1966. *Homo Hierarchicus* (English edn, 1970). London: Wiedenfeld and Nicholson.

Dumont, L. 1970. The individual as impediment to sociological comparison and Indian history, in *Religion/Politics and History in India: collected papers in Indian sociology.* Paris and The Hague: Mouton.

Durkheim, E. 1895. *The Rules of Sociological Method* (edited and translated 1938 by G. E. G. Catlin). Glencoe, Illinois: The Free Press.

Firth, R. (ed.) 1957. *Man and Culture: an evaluation of the work of Bronislaw Malinowski.* London: Routledge and Kegan Paul.

Firth, R., Hubert, J. and Forge, J. A. 1969. *Families and Their Relatives in a Middle-Class Section of London.* London: Routledge and Kegan Paul.

Fortes, M. 1958. Introduction, in J. R. Goody (ed.), *The Development Cycle in Domestic Groups* (Cambridge Papers in Social Anthropology I). Cambridge: Cambridge University Press.

Freeman, D. 1983. *Margaret Mead and Samoa: the making and unmaking of an anthropological myth.* Cambridge, Mass.: Harvard University Press.

Gluckman, M. (ed.) 1964. *Closed Systems and Open Minds.* Edinburgh: Oliver and Boyd.

Goody, E. N. 1973. *The Contexts of Kinship.* Cambridge: Cambridge University Press.

Goody, E. N. 1982. *Parenthood and Social Reproduction.* Cambridge: Cambridge University Press.

Goody, J. R. (ed.) 1958. *The Development Cycle in Domestic Groups* (Cambridge Papers in Social Anthropology I). Cambridge: Cambridge University Press.

Goody, J. R. 1972. The evolution of the family, in P. Laslett and R. Wall (eds), *Household and Family in Past Time.* Cambridge: Cambridge University Press.

Goody, J. R. 1976. *Production and Reproduction: A comparative study of the domestic domain.* Cambridge Studies in Social Anthropology No. 17. Cambridge: Cambridge University Press.

Goody, J. R. 1983. *The Development of Family and Marriage in Europe.* Cambridge: Cambridge University Press.

Harris, C. C. 1983. *The Family and Industrial Society* (Studies in Sociology: 13). London: George Allen and Unwin.

Harris, O. 1981. Households as natural units, in K. Young, C. Wolkowitz and R. McCullagh (eds), *Of Marriage and the Market.* London: CSE Books.

Hart, N. 1976. *When Marriage Ends: a study in status passage.* London: Tavistock Press.

Heath, A. 1981. *Social Mobility.* London: Fontana.

Jahoda, G. 1970. A psychologist's perspective, in P. Mayer (ed.), *Socialisation: the approach from social anthropology* (ASA Monographs, 8). London: Tavistock Press.

Konner, M. 1977. Infancy among the Kalahari Desert San, in P. H. Leiderman, S. R. Tulkin and A. Rosenfeld (eds), *Culture and Infancy.* New York: Academic Press.

Korbin, J. 1980. *Child Abuse and Neglect: cross-cultural perspectives.* California: University of California Press.

La Fontaine, J. S. 1970. *City Politics. A Study of Leopoldville 1962–63.* Cambridge: Cambridge University Press.

La Fontaine, J. S. 1985. Anthropological perspectives on the family and social change. *The Quarterly Journal of Social Affairs,* I (1). *1,* 29–56.

Leonard, D. 1980. *Sex and Generation.* London: Tavistock Press.

Macfarlane, A. 1978. *The Origins of English Individualism.* Oxford: Basil Blackwell.

Malinowski, B. 1931. *Culture* (Encyclopaedia of the Social Sciences, IV). New York: Macmillan.

Mauss, M. 1938–9. Une Categorie de l'esprit humain: la notion de personne, celle de moi (Huxley Memorial Lecture, 1938, JRAI). *Journal of the Royal Anthropological Institute.*

Mead, M. 1928. *Coming of Age in Samoa.* London: Pelican Books.

Mead, M. 1930. *Growing Up in New Guinea.* London: Pelican Books.

Mead, M. 1950; 1962. *Male and Female.* London: Pelican Books.

Mayer, P. (ed.) 1970. *Socialisation: the approach from social anthropology* (ASA Monographs, 8). London: Tavistock Press.

Middleton, J. (ed.) 1970. *From Child to Adult: studies in the anthropology of education* (American Museum Source Books in Anthropology). New York: Natural History Press.

Morris, L. 1979. Women without men. *British Journal of Sociology,* **30,** 322–40.

Morris, L. 1983. Redundancy and patterns of household finance (paper presented at 1983 British Sociological Association).

Murray, C. 1981. *Families Divided: the impact of migrant labour in Lesotho.* Cambridge: Cambridge University Press.

Pahl, J. 1983. The allocation of money and the structuring of inequality within marriage. *Sociological Review,* **31.**

Parry, J. 1979. *Caste and Kinship in Kangra.* London: Routledge and Kegan Paul.

Parsons, T. 1940. *Essays in Sociological Theory, Pure and Applied.* Glencoe, Ill.: The Free Press.

Parsons, T. and Bates, R. 1956. *Family, Socialisation and Interaction.* London: Routledge and Kegan Paul.

Perelberg, R. J. 1983. *Family and mental illness in a London borough* (unpublished Ph.D. dissertion, London University).

Raum, O. F. 1940. *A Chaga Childhood*. Oxford: Oxford University Press.

Radcliffe-Brown, A. R. 1940. On social structure, reprinted in *Structure and Function in Primitive Society*, 1952. London: Cohen and West.

Read, M. 1959. *Children of Their Fathers: growing up among the Ngoni of Nyasaland*. London: Methuen.

Richards, A. I. 1939. *Land Labour and Diet in Northern Rhodesia*. Oxford: Oxford University Press for International African Institute.

Richards, A. I. 1970. Socialisation and contemporary British anthropology, in P. Meyer (ed.), *Socialisation: The approach from social anthropology* (ASA Monographs, 8). London: Tavistock Press.

Richards, M. P. M. 1977. An ecological study of infant development in an urban setting in Britain, in P. H. Leiderman, S. R. Tulkin and A. Rosenfeld (eds), *Culture and Infancy*. New York: Academic Press.

Rimmer, L. 1981. *Families in Focus: marriage, divorce and family patterns* (Study Commission on the Family Occasional Papers, 6). London.

Sansom, B. 1978. Sex, age and social control in mobs of the Darwin hinterland, in J. S. La Fontaine (ed.), *Sex and Age as Principles of Social Differentiation* (ASA Monographs, 17). London: Academic Press.

Sarsby, J. 1983. *Romantic Love and Society: its place in the modern world*. London: Penguin Books.

Schildkrout, E. 1978. Roles of children in urban Kano, in J. S. La Fontaine (ed.), *Sex and Age as Principles of Social Differentiation* (ASA Monographs, 17). London: Academic Press.

Smith, R. T. 1963. Culture and Social Structure in the Caribbean: some recent work on family and kinship studies. *Comparative Studies in Society and History*, 6.

Smith, R. T. 1973. The matrifocal family, in J. R. Goody (ed.), *The Character of Kinship*. Cambridge: Cambridge University Press.

Spencer, P. 1965. *The Samburu: a study of gerontocracy in a nomadic tribe*. London: Routledge and Kegan Paul.

Spens, T. 1969. Family structure in a Dominican village (unpublished Ph.D. dissertation, University of Cambridge).

Stenning, D. 1958. Household viability among the pastoral Fulani, in J. R. Goody (ed.), *The Developmental Cycle in Domestic Groups* (Cambridge Papers in Social Anthropology I). Cambridge: Cambridge University Press.

Tylor, E. B. 1871. *Primitive culture*. 2 vols. London: John Murray.

Wallman, S. 1984. *Eight London Households*. London: Tavistock Press.

Whitehead, A. 1981. I'm hungry, Mumu: the politics of domestic budgeting, in K. Young, C. Wolkowitz and R. McCullagh (eds), *Of Marriage and the Market*. London: CSE Books.

Whiting, J. J. W. M., Kluckholn, R. and Anthony, A. 1958. The function of male initiation ceremonies at puberty, in E. E. Maccoby et al., *Readings in Social Psychology*. New York: Holt.

Wyer, J. 1984. The ideology and economic organisation of migrants to an Amazonian city (unpublished Ph.D. dissertation, London University).

2

Anxieties about the family and the relationships between parents, children and the state in twentieth century England

Jane Lewis

In the twentieth-century literature and policy documents on the family, one theme predominates: the family is bedrock, for the quality of the nation depends on the quality of its homes. Yet it is also feared that the family is fragile and warnings that the family is 'disintegrating' have punctuated gatherings of political and religious leaders, professionals and academics at regular intervals since the late-nineteenth century (Wilson, 1977). The grim forecasts of the Moral Majority in the USA and leaked discussions of the British government's Family Policy Group early in 1983 (*Guardian*, 1983), are but the latest expressions of concern on this score.

Those expressing anxiety about the fate of the family may in effect be seen to be defending the bourgeois family ideal. Key elements of this ideal were identified by Victorian commentators who were convinced as to the superiority of the middle-class family and whose concern was focused on the apparent instability of the working-class family. Writers of domestic manuals stressed the importance of the home as a haven of peace and security:

> Peace must be preserved or happiness will be destroyed . . . Not only must an appearance of outward order and comfort be kept up, but around every domestic scene there must be a strong wall of confidence, which no external suspicion can undermine, no external enemy break through. (Banks and Banks, 1964, 54)

The late-Victorian businessman expected his wife to stay at home and provide 'comfort and inspiration and cleansing and rest' (Chorley, 1950, 268) on his return each day. By the end of the nineteenth century hearth and home had become the chief prop of a moral order no longer buttressed by religious belief. The image of peace and order a firm differentiation of roles between husband and wife were the key to a stable family life, and, implicitly, to the successful socialization of children and national stability.

In Parsons' (1955) classic formulation of the 1950s, this implicit link is made explicit. The bourgeois family with its bread-winning father and dependent wife, who performs the domestic labour for the household and cares for the young and the old, is seen as an harmonious organic unit successfully meeting the needs of an industrial society. (Unlike the majority of commentators on the family, Parsons remained optimistic that the bourgeois family would continue to survive and adapt to the calls made upon it.) For Parsonian functionalists the strategic importance of the bourgeois family lies in the way it mediates the needs of the larger society for the individual, particularly for the child. According to Goode (1980) the socialization of children provided the link between the biological survival of the species and the transmission of culture. Present-day crusaders for the bourgeois family ideal emphasize this idea of the crucial link between the private and public faces of the family, stressing the way in which it has successfully socialized individuals with personalities and values conducive to entrepreneurial capitalism and democracy: 'The family and specifically the bourgeois family is the necessary social context for the emergence of autonomous individuals who are the empirical foundation of political democracy' (Berger and Berger, 1983, 172).[1]

Politicians, policy-makers and most lobbyists for the family have assumed the bourgeois family to be the normal family form throughout the twentieth century, largely because it has been believed to be both 'natural' and the best way of securing stability in the public as well as the private spheres. Expressions of anxiety about its future have been episodic responses to perceptions of actual or incipient family failure during periods of military or economic crisis. Edwardian commentators were worried both about the physical welfare of children, because of the low quality of army recruits brought to light during the Boer War, and the economic instability of family, signalled by the increasing numbers of people coming onto poor relief. During the late 1940s, the social dislocation due to war, following hard on the 1930s Depression, was feared to have substantially destroyed family bonds, and both the decline in the birth rate and the increase in juvenile delinquency were cited as proof. It was this pessimism that sociologists in the 1950s and 1960s – Parsons and Goode in the USA, and Fletcher (1966) and Young and Wilmott (1957) in Britain – sought to dispel by their functionalist accounts of family change and development. In the 1980s anxiety has again been expressed about juvenile crime rates. Moreover, the rapid increase in the number of one-parent families (from 620,000 in 1971 to 920,000 in 1980, equivalent to about one in eight families – Rimmer, 1981, 38), appears to indicate a significant move away from the bourgeois family form and is feared to herald a further weakening of the family's capacity to care for its members. It is worth noting that a recurring feature of these moral panics has been the way in which they have been founded on inaccurate demographic and statistical assumptions.

The nature of the anxiety regarding the causes of family failure have changed over time, reflecting, in particular, the development of professional expertise and changing ideas about the nature of poverty, the role of women in society, and the importance of the mother-child relationship. Irrespective of the nature and strength of the pressure exerted by structural variables on the family, the analyses of family failure by those anxious about the family's future have been grounded at the level of individual behaviour, the aim being to ensure compliance with the bourgeois family ideal. During the late Victorian and Edwardian periods, social investigators and philanthropists regarded both male and female working-class parents with suspicion. Husbands were believed to be constitutionally lazy, and wives to be ignorant of the principles of household management and child care. By the 1940s, and the flood of literature on the need to 'rebuild' the family after the war, attention shifted entirely to the mother as the focus of both blame and hope for future improvement. In the recent 'New Right' literature faith in both parents is affirmed and the role of the state in 'policing' the family is castigated. Structural causes of family failure have been considered either secondary or non-existent. Nor has the perspective of those families who are the object of concern been considered.

These shifts in the focus of anxiety about the family, between parents' behaviour and the state's response, reflect changes in, first, the perception of how individual preferences on the part of husbands and wives conflict with the maintenance of the bourgeois family ideal and, second, how far it is believed that the essential privacy of the family may be invaded by agents external to it, as a means to fostering or policing the bourgeois family. This chapter will examine these themes in more detail, concentrating on the diagnosis of family disintegration in three main periods, the late nineteenth and early twentieth centuries, the 1940s, and the 1980s, and relating the diagnoses to the kinds of intervention into the family actually undertaken by the state or voluntary bodies in order either to bolster the family or deal with families who have been deemed to have failed.

Traditionally, the relationship between parents, children and the state has been analysed by the study of children coming into care and has focused on apparent swings between a policy of protection (prioritizing the welfare of the child) and one of prevention (prioritizing the family and treating the child's problems within the family), (Heywood, 1978; Packman, 1981; MacLeod, 1982). This approach depends on the analysis of legislative outcomes, whereas what follows focuses more on the social anxieties which produced a diagnosis of family failure. It is not the intention to make a causal connection between the diagnosis and the changing nature of intervention in the family. This would be to ignore the significance of the profound changes in the social, economic and political context over

time, and the complicated nature of policy-making, which in the area of
family policy may owe as much to cost constraints, inter-departmental
rivalries and responses to scandal as to the influence of ideas. But with 'the
family' now high on the political agenda, it is important to explore the way
in which it has been problematized in the past and to see how particular
diagnoses of family disintegration have structured policies and provided
legitimizing frameworks for particular interventionist strategies at particular points in time.

I The late nineteenth and early twentieth centuries: concern about
the working-class family

In 1906, Helen Bosanquet clearly described the characteristics of the stable
family. It required the firm authority of the father and the co-operative
industry of all its members, the wife working at home and the husband
wage-earning. She made the connection between the stable family and the
national importance of maintaining male work incentives particularly
forcefully:

> Nothing but the combined rights and responsibilities of family life will ever
> rouse the average man to his full degree of efficiency and induce him to
> continue working after he has earned sufficient to meet his own personal
> needs . . . The Family, in short, is from this point of view, the only known
> way of ensuring with any approach to success that one generation will exert
> itself in the interests and for the sake of another. (Bosanquet, 1906, 222)

She believed that the stable family sheltered young and old in one strong
bond of mutual helpfulness (making old age pensions, then under discussion, superfluous), and rendered the development of a political residuum
(an underclass) impossible, by training its young in the habits of labour
and obedience. Bosanquet made the point that families at both ends of the
social scale failed to conform to this model of family life. Much more
concern, however, was generally expressed about the working-class
family, and as much or more about the working-class father as the
working-class mother. Evidence of family failure was twofold: first, the
physical welfare of children measured by indices such as the incidence of
child neglect and the infant mortality rate, and, secondly, the number of
families seeking relief under the Poor Law.

Bosanquet was not alone in suspecting the working-class father of
unwillingness to shoulder his economic responsibilities. Other Edwardian
investigators firmly believed that married women's work provided
working-class men with the opportunity to idle. The economist F. Y.
Edgeworth (1922, 453) quoted approvingly the comment that a social
worker made in 1908, to the effect that 'if the husband got out of work,

the only thing the wife should do is sit down and cry, because if she did anything else he would remain out of work'. Mass unemployment modified this view somewhat and by 1937 J. C. Pringle, head of the Charity Organization Society, was prepared to admit that married women's employment did not necessarily adversely affect the work incentives of the husband, 'something that could not have been said with anything like the same confidence 25 years ago'.

In fact, there is considerable evidence that working-class families shared the bourgeois family ideal, but did not have the means to live according to its tenets. Booth's (1889) survey of London showed that 30 per cent of the population was unable to live on a man's wage alone. It was therefore inevitable that other family members, including the wife, would take paid labour. Yet by the Edwardian period it had become the hallmark of respectability for the skilled artisan that he should be able to 'keep a wife' (Stearns, 1973). At the 1877 Annual TUC Conference, Henry Broadhurst spoke of the duty of male unionists 'as men and husbands to use their utmost efforts to bring about a condition of things where their wives should be in their proper sphere at home, instead of being dragged into competition for livelihood against the great and strong men of the world' (Drake, 1920, 17). Women labour movement activists also considered that the withdrawal of female labour would benefit male wages and mean that working-class homes would be better ordered and managed (MacDonald, nd). As for women workers themselves, oral evidence has shown that those who worked full-time tended to be pitied by their neighbours. In view of the laborious nature of domestic work during the period this is not surprising (Roberts, 1978). Married women worked according to the dictates of the family economy, taking in homework, covering tennis balls, carding buttons, making brushes or shirts, or going out charring or hawking fruit as and when necessary. In some cases their husbands were neglectful, but mostly they were sick, out of work, or low paid. There is little evidence of women working for reasons relating to the need for personal fulfillment.

Commentators showed far more sympathy for working-class wives, regarding them for the most part as well-meaning but ignorant and often oppressed by selfish husbands. In 1870 the first Married Women's Property Act was passed primarily in order to give working-class women control over any earnings they might make. It was felt that they merited this protection as 'the great educators of the working classes' (PP, 1867–8, Q. 1154), and chancellors of the domestic exchequer. Vast effort was expended by philanthropists and the state, working through infant welfare centres and health visitors, to teach working-class mothers the principles of household management. Because the wife was seen as the 'pivot' (imagery which also marked the literature of the post-war period), any moral failure on her part was doubly serious. Charles Booth (1889, 147), for example, viewed drunkeness in wives as more serious a problem than in husbands.

Most philanthropists and hygienists considered it worth trying to educate working-class wives to better standards of housekeeping and child care. Nor were all their efforts resisted. Hannah Mitchell (1977), a working-class suffragist, recorded in her autobiography that she wished infant welfare centres had existed to give her advice when her children were young. Attempts to educate working-class women met with resistance chiefly when they threatened the privacy and domestic authority of the wife. Thus the health visitor was not as popular as the infant welfare centre. A film made in 1917 as part of the National Baby Week propaganda showed the health visitor, by this time a middle-class woman employed by the local authority, being led into a home by neighbours. This would, in fact, have been highly unlikely; health visitors did not on the whole enjoy the trust of working-class communities. Inside the house the young wife has fallen under the bad influence of a neighbour, is drinking heavily and neglecting her home. The health visitor saves the situation by taking the wife to the St Pancras School for Mothers, where she is instructed in child care and housewifery. The husband is thus able to fight for his country 'confident that the nation is looking after his home' (*Motherhood*, 1917).[2]

Philanthropists such as Bosanquet were in favour of educating wives, although they would have preferred that the responsibility for so doing remained in the hands of voluntary organizations. They were bitterly opposed to other measures of state intervention, such as the provision of school meals and medical inspection, which were introduced as a result of concern over child welfare in the wake of the Boer War, when so many working-class recruits to the army were found to be in poor physical health. Investigations into the heights and weights of children in the state elementary schools followed and provided an additional spur to medical officers of health and infant hygienists who had long been campaigning for improved child and maternal welfare (Lewis, 1980). To philanthropists and substantial numbers of politicians, however, school meals and medical inspection represented a threat to parental responsibility and both measures were made conditional for this reason. Parents were expected to contribute to the cost of school meals and the school attendance officer was usually given the task of assessing means. In the case of school medical inspection, parents (usually mothers) were advised what was wrong with their children but were not provided with access to treatment. National Health Insurance covered only wage earners, not dependants, which meant that parents (fathers) were being expected to exercise their obligation to maintain. Government was additionally concerned not to subvert private medical practice by the offer of free treatment in local authority clinics. Welfare was thus offered on terms that took little account of the realities of working-class income levels. In the political debate over school meals, which was dominated by the fear that the measure would destroy the father's incentive to provide, Keir Hardie commented:

> He did not think the Hon. Gentlemen who had spoken so often that afternoon knew what it meant to them [Labour MPs] to sit there and listen to their wives being described as slatterns and themselves as spendthrifts . . . It was absolutely untrue to say that they wanted their children to be quartered on the rates, but neither did they want children to be starved through the lack of ability on the part of parents through no fault of their own to provide them with food. (House of Commons, 1906)

The first demand of working-class men during the 1900s was for the 'Right to Work' (Brown, 1971). Secondly, both they and their wives wanted non-stigmatizing and non-intrusive welfare provisions to tide them over periods of misfortune (Thane, 1984). But fear of undermining male work incentives and a desire to educate working-class wives as to their domestic responsibilities made the offer of state assistance limited, conditional and intrusive. In many respects the brunt of the effort to bolster the bourgeois family ideal among working-class people was borne by the working-class wife. It was she who had to deal with the health visitor and the school attendance officer, attend the school medical inspections, and appear before the School Board Divisional Committee or the magistrate; the father was always summonsed but, to the chagrin of the authorities, rarely appeared. There, she had to explain the absence of the child, usually required for wage-earning if a boy, or baby-sitting while the mother worked if a girl. As one feminist philanthropist observed, mothers were 'being ordered by law to perform the impossible and punished if they failed' (Martin, 1911, 8).

Thus the conviction that the bourgeois ideal needed to be strengthened among working-class families, because of the manifest failure of husbands and wives to perform their roles, ignored the extent to which the ideal was in fact shared by working-class people and the structural problems which prevented it being achieved. In cases where the working-class family was deemed to have failed – the child being severely neglected, or the family coming onto the Poor Law – suspicion of the parents hardened into the belief that their case was hopeless and the child was often removed from the home both for protection and to stop the transmission of undesirable behaviour. As late as 1933, the Children and Young Persons Act made no provision to return the neglected child, who had been placed in care, to his parents. Samuel Smith (1883), a Liverpool cotton manufacturer, who played a leading role in the setting up of the Liverpool and London Societies for the Prevention of Cruelty of Children, wrote:

> The habits of the young are formed amid such depraving influences that they can scarcely grow up different from their parents and the conclusion has

gradually been forced upon me that we shall never break the hereditarian entail of pauperism and crime in this country until we take *far more stringent means to save the children.*[3]

Benjamin Waugh, the NSPCC's first Director, also believed that there was a strong link between neglect and delinquency, but unlike social investigators in the period after the Second World War, who saw a similar connection, his solution was to remove the neglected child from evil home influences. He also felt the parents should be punished. He had no patience with inspectors who showed sympathy for the parents and hesitated to prosecute. Waugh believed that by making examples of parents who had failed to care for their children the NSPCC would promote a higher ideal of family life among other working-class parents. In cases of neglect the border between the ignorant and hence educable, and the negligent and hence culpable often became blurred. NPSCC inspectors frequently interpreted dirt and poor housekeeping as evidence of neglect (Behlmer, 1982).

The tendency to include large numbers of parents in the ranks of those incapable of achieving the bourgeois family ideal, and whose influence on their children was therefore to be deplored, was reinforced by the common view that pauperism and vice were largely hereditary. Eugenicists were convinced that heredity was extremely important in explaining the incidence of infant mortality, illegitimacy, pauperism, disease and crime. For example, Karl Pearson, the Galton Professor of Eugenics at University College London, maintained that the health and habits of parents were 15 times as influential as many other factors causing infant deaths. The possession of good or bad habits was linked primarily to the health of the mother and both were considered to be in the main hereditary characteristics (Pearson, 1913; Karn and Pearson, 1922).

Both the Royal Commission on the Feeble Minded (PP, 1908) and on the Poor Laws (PP, 1909) were greatly concerned about the connection between pauperism, mental deficiency and illegitimacy. Destitute families forced to enter the workhouse were immediately split up, husbands from wives and children from parents. The treatment of single mothers is particularly revealing (Thane, 1978). Widows, deserted wives and unmarried mothers were usually able bodied and therefore capable of work but often had children to care for. Widows could for the most part be assumed to be deserving but if they proved unable to perform all the functions of the 'normal' family (i.e., caring and providing for their children), it was quite usual for the Poor Law authorities prior to the First World War to remove the children and put them in the workhouse rather than give the widow outdoor relief. The widow was then expected to work, sometimes being left the charge of one child, whom it was felt that she could reasonably be expected to maintain. The importance the early twentieth-century state attached to the belief that the family should take responsibility for its members made it usual for the role of the single mother to be defined as that of a worker rather than a mother, the state being reluctant to take the place of the male bread-winner. Deserted wives were still more likely to be refused outdoor relief because it was feared that they might collude with their ex-husbands to defraud the authorities. The harshest treatment was meted out to women who had shown no respect for the bourgeois family form and whose influence on their children was therefore considered to be inevitably harmful: the unmarried mothers. The majority of unmarried mothers was forced to enter the workhouse for the birth of their children and had great difficulty in keeping them thereafter. During the inter-war period, the enormous concern about the high birth rate of mental defectives, and the consequent decline in the 'national intelligence', resulted in the Poor Law authorities being given, in 1927, sweeping powers to detain girls classed as mentally defective who were in receipt of poor relief at the time of the birth (Cattell, 1937; Middleton, 1971; PP, 1974).[4]

Even in the late 1940s, when the cause of family failure was diagnosed firmly in terms of the strength or weakness of the mother-child bond, there was still some ambivalence over the desirability of any single mother devoting herself to full-time motherhood with the aid of the state. Professor Zweig still found National Assistance officials ready to label the widow with school age children who did not go out to work as an 'inferior type' and a 'professional widow' (Yudkin and Holme, 1963).

In the early twentieth century, the defence of the bourgeois family ideal was undertaken in the light of contemporary fear and suspicion of 'the submerged tenth' and in the firm conviction that middle-class ideals would have to be imposed on the working class. Some preventive, educational work was possible but, in cases of doubt, the parents were presumed beyond hope and the child was 'rescued'. Aid to the family as a whole would only further undermine the working-class father's sense of his economic responsibilities and permit people who were in all probability hereditarily tainted to reproduce further.

This attitude was strengthened during the inter-war years in respect to an ever more closely defined group of 'worthless' parents. Full employment during the Great War, followed by mass unemployment, went some way to destroying the notion of a class of 'unemployables' and the belief in moral failure as the cause of poverty, and state assistance to the unemployed and their families widened considerably during these years. Nevertheless, a large literature developed on the 'social problem group', which was identified as combining the following broad characteristics: 'insanity, epilepsy, occupational instability, inebriety and social dependency . . .' (Blacker, 1937, 4). The Mental Deficiency Committee appointed in 1924 emphasized that mental deficiency was primarily a question of heredity and raised the possibility of the existence of a social problem group comprising, essentially, the submerged tenth (Board of Education and Board of Control, 1927). In the wake of this, strenuous efforts were made to establish the precise size and characteristics of the group, with a view to segregating the members for the purposes of sterilization, if public opinion could be so persuaded. A Departmental Committee of the Ministry of Health recommended voluntary sterilization in 1934 (PP, 1933–4). In his *Social Survey of Merseyside*, Caradog Jones concluded: 'From the main discussion . . . a sub-normal type of family has emerged as the "villain of the peace", parading under one or more disguises sometimes under the cloak of unemployment, sometimes dependent on public assistance, sometimes living in overcrowded conditions, but all alike above the average in fertility' (Jones, 1934, 543).[5] This analysis and the solution, which involved some form of segregation and sterilization to stop the transmission of these undesirable characteristics, was in line with the idea that when a family failed – the measure being primarily one of social dependency – then nothing further could be done. The extreme solution of sterilization, which was seriously proposed, but not put into effect, resulted from the concomitant fear of inherited mental defect and a decline in the national intelligence. It may be suggested that Sir Keith Joseph's famous declaration of 1974, that the poor were reproducing to excess and leading to 'degeneration', should be seen as part of this tradition (Kevles, 1984).[6]

II   The 1940s: 'rebuilding' the family

In the wake of the Second World War there were substantial changes in approach to the problem of family failure. In his 1946 lecture on the family, J. C. Spence, a paediatrician who had organized the medico-social survey of some 1,000 Newcastle families, clearly defined the purpose of the family, relating it entirely to the welfare of children. The family should, he wrote, ensure growth and physical health, give the right scope for emotional experience, preserve the art of motherhood and teach behaviour (Spence, 1946). Thus the socialization of children rather than the importance of effective economic maintenance was now stressed, with more attention being paid to the role of the mother than to that of the father. Most commentators emphasized the need to 'rebuild' the family in the post-war period (Marchant, 1946). The dislocation caused by evacuation and intensive bombing, the consequent disruption to family life, and anxiety about both the rise in the illegitimacy rate and the fall in the birth rate took precedence over all other concerns. It was feared that family life had disintegrated during the war and in the face of this Spence felt the need to return to first principles, stressing the fundamental importance of the family unit and its profound 'biological significance'.

If the family unit was natural, then so also were separate roles for husband and wife within it and the primacy of the mother-child bond. Work by psychologists on children deprived of their parents during the war, either by death or as a result of evacuation, helped to bring home to a wider audience the idea that the mother was crucial to the child's normal development. The very idea of the 'normal child' had developed only with the increasing sophistication of the survey method during the inter-war years (Armstrong, 1983). Influential psychologists, many of whom acted as their own popularizers, saw the mother-child relationship as the key to the healthy development of the child and the 'adequacy' of the mother as the most important variable (Riley, 1983). In his radio broadcasts on motherhood during the late 1940s, Winnicott (1957, 4) stressed the natural quality of the relationship: 'Sometimes the urine trickled down your apron or wet right through and soaked you as if you yourself had let slip, and you didn't mind. In fact by these things you could have known that you were a woman, and an *ordinary devoted mother* [my ital.].' J. C. Spence (1946, 49) considered that women only achieved 'mature motherhood' with the sixth or seventh child. These ideas provided additional support for the bourgeois family ideal, itself assumed to be the natural way to organize family life.

Natural motherhood also meant full-time motherhood. Winnicott (1957, 88) told his listeners: 'Talk about women not wanting to be house-wives seems to me just nonsense because nowhere else but in her own home is a woman in such command.' The importance of continuous mothering received its most influential support from the work of Bowlby (1946), who made a direct connection between 'affectionlessness', or maternal deprivation, and delinquency, drawing on evidence from the experience of wartime evacuation. Women's work outside the home therefore stood condemned as likely to produce juvenile delinquency. This theme was picked up widely by social workers and guidance counsellors, and also by others not necessarily attracted to a psychological approach. For example, Basil Henriques (1955, 23), an East London magistrate, wrote:

> Quite simply it seems to me that by far the most far-reaching change in modern society is that the family is not considered to be so important as it used to be, and it is because of this that we have in our midst so many suffering, unhappy and delinquent children . . . legislation regulating the working hours of mothers of school age children is one of the most urgent reforms required for the creation of good homes.[7]

In many respects these arguments were not new. The NSPCC had drawn a direct link between child neglect (albeit in terms of physical welfare) and juvenile crime at the end of the nineteenth century, and early twentieth-century middle-class philanthropists had certainly stressed the importance of full-time motherhood. John Burns, the President of the Local Government Board had called for exactly the same reform as Henriques as a means of bringing down the infant mortality rate (Lewis, 1980). But the social and economic context of the 1940s was very different. The role of the mother was given priority because attention was focused on social dislocation as the primary cause of family failure and concern over the economic responsibility of the father did not bulk as large as formerly. Indeed, the literature of the 1940s gave little space to the role of the father. In a 1944 radio talk, entitled significantly 'What about Father?', Winnicott (1957) said that fathers were needed to help the mother feel well in body and happy in mind and to give her moral support especially in matters of discipline. Similarly, Spence (1946, 51) saw the father 'courteously and chivalrously providing shelter and protection and also sustenance for her [the mother's] mind and spirit'. The father's role was of secondary importance and his co-operation in performing it was, unlike earlier in the century, assumed. As Patricia Allatt (1981) has shown, wartime literature addressed to the forces also stressed the idea of responsible fatherhood and voluntary co-operation with the state.

There was in fact substantially greater sympathy with the father than previously. Spence (1946) felt actively uneasy about the father's position believing that the changes in the legal status of women, resulting in a movement towards an ideal of marriage that was companionate rather than patriarchal, posed a threat to the family, because it threatened to erode the authority of the father. The bourgeois family ideal required a strong paterfamilias, whose position in the nineteenth century was supported both by the law and a liberal political tradition, which appeared to talk about individuals as components of political systems, but which in fact referred only to male heads of families (Okin, 1980).

The growth in women's legal emancipation with respect to property, guardianship rights, political citizenship and grounds for divorce, combined with the move towards small families in all classes by the 1930s, appeared to many to threaten the institution of marriage and the family. For example, during the course of the Parliamentary debate over the 1925 Guardianship of Infants Act, which gave women equal guardianship rights over children, one MP declared:

> English Law, both Common Law and Equity, says if two people live together, as you cannot run a home by committee of two, one of them must have the deciding voice, and I think with wisdom it gives the husband a deciding voice. He has more experience of the world. In nine cases out of ten he makes the money which keeps the home going and as he pays he certainly ought to have a commanding voice in the decisions which are come to. (Davidoff, 1956, 105)

Bertrand Russell (1932) also deplored the decline in power of the father, seeing the paternalist state and the caring professions as having usurped the father's authority over his children via the school and the juvenile court, and having removed his *raison d'être* by providing his children with free school meals and medical attention. In fact, as has been seen, the issue of parental responsibility was never far from the minds of legislators and philanthropists and the main burden of state intervention was in fact borne by the wife, but as state provision widened, so this kind of argument has been further elaborated. In the recent work of Donzelot (1979), Russell's ideas have been taken one stage further and women, together with the state, are blamed for the decline of paternal authority. Donzelot maintains that in the late nineteenth and early twentieth centuries, women forged an alliance with professionals – doctors and philanthropists, and later social workers and psychologists – to protect and further the welfare of the child. He argues that it was this promotion of the woman as mother, educator and medical authority that was to serve as a point of support for the main feminist currents of the nineteenth century. Only such an alliance was 'capable of shaking paternal authority' (1979, 20). Thus women gained domestic authority and social status at the expense of men. Some middle-class women may have thus joined forces with child care experts, but there is little evidence of working-class mothers being regarded as anything but ignorant and hapless by medical men and philanthropists.[8] Nor have social investigators, other than Young and Willmott (1973), shown women to have gained domestic power, and their idea of the 'symmetrical family' has been subjected to searching and convincing criticism (Whitehead, 1976).

Writers in the 1940s viewed the issue of state provision with some ambivalence. Spence (1946, 50) echoed Eleanor Rathbone (1924) when he wrote that 'the core of the trouble is that our economic system is not based on a philosophy of human welfare which recognizes the right of every mother to possess the means of homemaking if she so desires it' and quoted William Beveridge to the effect that a large family remained the single largest cause of poverty. Nevertheless, on the same page he wrote that 'the tendency nowadays is to exaggerate the economic difficulties of motherhood, to depict its tribulations and to belittle its compensations and rewards'. Spence and others were prepared to countenance state assistance that would promote what they regarded as the key to re-establishing family life – full-time motherhood. In his Plan, which formed the basis for Social Security provision in the post-war period, Beveridge assumed that a married woman, regardless of whether she had children, would not engage in paid work and could therefore be classified as a dependant, her benefits being made payable through her husband's insurance. Unlike Spence, Beveridge welcomed the idea of companionate marriage, regarding it as a partnership. It was not an equal partnership, however, in that he also believed that husband and wife had strictly traditional, complementary roles to play, the husband as bread-winner (and the post-1945 Social

Security system went to some lengths to preserve male work incentives) and the wife as housewife and carer of young and old (Land, 1980, b; Lewis, 1983).

Any form of intervention, in the form of nursery provision, for example, which would relieve mothers of their responsibilities was resisted. Denise Riley (1983) has argued powerfully that the closure of nurseries after the Second World War was intimately related to inter-departmental tensions in Whitehall and was more the pragmatic result of central government's desire to transfer the cost of running nurseries to the local authorities than the outcome of ideas stressing the danger of maternal deprivation. As she points out, the latter were in any case common currency among psychologists well before the war and were also largely accepted by women. Certainly a source such as Nella Last's wartime diary shows that while she welcomed all sorts of changes in dress, manners, housework routines and in relations between husband and wife, she could not accept that women with small children might go out to work (Broad and Fleming, 1983). But while it is undoubtedly correct to stress the complexity of the decision-making surrounding nursery closure, it is nevertheless significant that ideas about the centrality of the mother-child relationship were so widely taken up in the 1940s. Local authorities in the early part of the century quickly discovered that it was cheaper to give outdoor relief than to take children into institutional care, and yet were hesitant to do so for fear of undermining the parental obligation to maintain. In the post-war years, Bowlby's ideas seem to have achieved the status of essential truth.[9] The Curtis Report (1945) on children in care strongly recommended fostering in preference to institutional care because of the importance of a mother substitute. In fact, such a recommendation highlighted an interesting underlying conflict between the belief in the importance of a family, even a foster family or one reconstituted (by remarriage), and the importance attached to the continuity of the mother-child relationship. In practice, the two have been held separate, so that the negative effects of remarriage, or of abuse from step and foster parents have tended to be glossed over, despite the Curtis Report's insistence on the importance of supervised and regulated foster placements.

Psychologists, paediatricians and policy-makers agreed that if mothers were to be assisted by the state they should be relieved of their chores, not their children. Beveridge (1948) was very concerned about the burden of domestic work falling on middle-class women in the absence, post-war, of domestic servants: 'A housewife's job with a large family is frankly impossible and will remain so unless some of what has now to be done separately in every home can be done economically outside the home.' In the event, little notice was taken of this aspect of his work. Rather, renewed calls were made for the education of girls in mothercraft. John Newsom (1948) advocated as separate a curriculum for girls – grounded in domestic subjects – as any advocated by early twentieth-century eugenicists and infant welfare experts.

The shift in diagnosis of the cause of family failure was also reflected in its treatment. Children were no longer likely to be immediately removed from their homes. Instead, more effort was made to rebuild the mother-child relationship. As Valerie MacLeod (1982, 29) has pointed out, the family became perceived as 'an institution which could best care for its members who were disturbed or ailing'. The Social Security system would meet economic need in the case of failure to maintain without resort to the Poor Law or the means test, leaving a new breed of professional social worker with more formal training in the latest psycho-social approaches to help the mother to achieve above all maternal 'adequacy', which is what Karl Pearson would have called 'maternal efficiency'. The concentration on the mother and on her importance as the chief agent of socialization was by no means new, but many more mothers were now considered capable of being educated to perform their role adequately.

In 1948 the Women's Group on Public Welfare, which had produced an influential report on the condition of child evacuees, *Our Towns* (1943), published a second report on *The Neglected Child and His Family*. While recognizing that middle-class parents may also neglect their children, the study concentrated on the 'problem family' and concluded that: 'In looking at these problem families there emerges one dominating feature – the capacity of the mother' (1948, 22). The report parted company from the pioneering studies of 'problem families' carried out in the mid-1940s by medical officers of health in conjunction with the Eugenics Society. As C. P. Blacker (1952, 12), the head of the Eugenics Society, explained, there had been renewed discussion of the social problem group as a result of the experience of evacuation, but the idea of a group was quickly displaced by the 'problem family', reflecting 'a transition from an impersonal, sociological to a personal and human approach'. This was an *ex post facto* rationalization. In fact, the studies published in the mid 1940s still firmly emphasized mental deficiency as the major cause of family failure and the crude use of animal imagery in many of the descriptions of the characteristics of problem families indicated that they were believed incapable of living a 'normal' family life (Savage, 1946; Brockington, 1949; Wofinden, 1950).

The Women's Group on Public Welfare criticized what they viewed as the confusion of intellectual with mental defect in these studies, pointing out that problem mothers were certainly appallingly ignorant, but that most appeared genuinely to love their children, who, whilst improperly cared for, seemed also to love their parents. These were not affectionless families as the efforts of mothers to reclaim their evacuated children proved. And where there was affection it should prove possible to educate mothers to a more mature understanding of their duties.

Titmuss (1962) attributed the contrast in the two approaches to the problem family to the difference between an essentially administrative and a psycho-social analysis. While it is true that by the late 1940s social workers were de-emphasizing the medical and eugenic passion for classifying and enumerating the characteristics of problem families, these families continued to be identified by their failure to function and were labelled as 'problems' only after they had come to the attention of more than one social service agency. But instead of punishing the parents for neglect or the failure to maintain, caseworkers did their best to respect their clients, helping them to achieve their full potential as parents and not imposing their (the caseworkers) own standards on them. This was not easy as Goldberg (1965) pointed out in a piece originally published in 1959:

Sometimes I envy those early pioneers who carried their values and ideals openly and proudly, who knew where they wanted to go and where they wanted their clients to go. We social workers of today, on the other hand, may or may not hold certain religious, moral social values. At any rate we claim that we do not impose them on our clients . . .

In fact, there is a good case to be made that while the post-war caseworkers' methods were very different, the aim remained essentially the same. For example, Tom Stephens (1962) defended the work of the Pacifist Service Units, which pioneered the family casework approach during the Second World War, by saying that while it might look as though PSU workers were relieving parents of their responsibility by painting rooms or even paying the rent, they were in fact exerting pressure on the parents, because the worker's own willingness to do the job brought home the responsibility to the parents. Pacifist Service Units and their successors, the Family Service Units, persevered with families who were not only considered inefficient, but who resisted the intervention of social services. If the family was broken up, the hope was that it would be temporary and sometimes mothers were sent away for rest and training rather than the child. Centres such as Brentwood Recuperative Centre in Cheshire provided rest for fatigued mothers and training in domestic skills. The Women's Group on Public Welfare (1948) reported approvingly that the Centre took for granted the fact that the women would have mending to do, and once every week the warden sat down with her work basket on 'the quiet assumption that this was usual', thus setting an example to the mothers.

The cause of family failure was still conceptualized at the individual level, not as moral failure leading to pauperism, but as personal failure to achieve mature personalities and relationships. In 1959 Barbara Wootton charged, first, that social workers were still failing to distinguish between personal inadequacy and simple economic misfortune, subscribing to the 'myth that poverty has been eliminated' under the welfare state, and, secondly, that 'the main difference between the social worker of today and that of yesterday lies less in the nature of its prescriptions than in the degree of their explicitness' (pp. 74 and 292). Some commentators have seen the restructuring of social service departments according to the 1968 Seebohm Report's recommendations as a move towards making social workers responsible for the provision of services rather than support for particular family relationships, in the manner advocated both by Wootton and Titmuss, reflecting a greater willingness at the end of the 1960s to use state welfare provision in the cause of keeping mother and child together.

III   The 1980s: the family versus the state?

The recent 'New Right' literature on the family has reacted forcefully against this expanded role of the state, and state interference in the family tends to be condemned. All previous diagnoses of family failure have stressed the need for parents to curb their personal preferences in order to conform to the bourgeois family ideal. But this runs counter to the logic of the 'New Right' theorists, who see the family as the primary agent of modernization, producing fully autonomous individuals, although the Bergers (1983, 118) allow that 'hyper-modernity' in the form of 'hyper-rationality and individualism' has tended to erode the family. Many 'New Right' authors bemoan the passing of the bourgeois family ideal among the middle classes since the liberal 1960s and tend to see the (respectable) working-class family as the only remaining repository of the ideal, defending its privacy and autonomy and showing concern about its children's achievement. Ferdinand Mount (1983, 162) writes of the family's 'permanent revolution against the state'. His condemnation of the erosion of parental (paternal) economic responsibility is not unlike that of Bosanquet but the focus of blame has shifted from the father to the state. As Rita Kramer (1983, 21) has put it:

> Here, then is the cliffhanger. Will society return control of children to the family . . . Can we return self assurance to mothers and fathers, along with confidence in how they raise their young? Or is it too late to stop the inexorable movement led by professionals, justified by academics, funded by the government, and publicized by the media, that claims society knows best – and is ready to tell mothers and fathers how to do it, and even to do it for them?

In many respects the case of the 'New Right' is persuasive. Mount (1983, 174), for example, writes of the health visitor:

> Our feelings are mixed even in the case of the most helpful of all public visitors. The District Health Visitor, who visits mothers with babies is often

sweet and sensitive and genuinely useful . . . But – and it remains an
inescapable, embarassing But – they cannot help being continuously aware
that she is there as an inspector as well as an advisor. Her eye roams the room
and the baby for evidence of dirt, neglect, even brutality. This kindly,
middle-aged body has at her ultimate disposal a stalinist array of powers . . .

Here Mount is trading on a long tradition of working-class suspicion of
the health visitor but he is wrong to deduce from this that working-class
mothers resented all state interference. A similar argument was made in
the 1920s by the conservative, Catholic, Mother's Defence League, led by
Cecil Chesterton's wife, Ada Jones. The League ignored working-class
demands for non-intrusive, non-stigmatizing welfare and insisted on the
right of the working-class family to be left alone (Durham, 1982). The
Bergers (1983) have also pointed out with some justification that as
the number and sophistication of professionals interested in the family
increased, more parents stood to be judged inadequate. The political Left
as well as the Right has rebelled against the idea of professional middle-
class agents of the state imposing essentially middle-class ideals on the
working-class family. Lasch (1977, pp. xvi–xviii), for example, has argued
that 'the same historical developments that have made it necessary to set
up private life – the family in particular – as a refuge from the cruel world
of politics and work, an emotional sanctuary, have invaded this sanctuary
and subjected it to outside control'. In his view capitalist control has
merely been extended through 'the agency of management, bureaucracy,
and professionalization'. The analysis of the 'New Right' has stressed,
correctly, the degree to which the bourgeois ideal has in fact been shared,
rendering the strenuous efforts to police it unnecessary. But this does not
mean that families do not require and desire help to overcome complex
problems of disadvantage which result from a mixture of familial and
socio-economic processes (Coffield, 1983). Both the Left and the Right
have over-romanticized the working-class family's ability to withstand
adversity.[10] It is not enough to do as Lasch or Mount do and deplore the
rise of the 'helping professions' because they have invaded the private
realm of family life and eroded its authority. Working-class men and
women have expressed distaste for the terms, conditions and methods of
the assistance they have been offered, but have not said that they want no
help at all. (See, for example, some of the 'consumer research' in social
work: Mayer and Timms, 1973, and Sainsbury, 1982.)

But in the case of the 'New Right', as Malcolm Wicks (1983) has pointed
out, proposals respecting family policy are 'at the centre of an inter-connected trinity of family, private market and the voluntary sector'. The end
is, as much as it was for Bosanquet or Spence, enforcement of the traditional bourgeois family ideal, but the strategy for achieving it is new.
Simple cuts in all state services, and tax and benefit 'incentives' will force
the family to stand on its own feet. This has particularly disastrous

implications for the 62 per cent of married women who now participate in the labour market. For example, the 1980 Education Act removed the responsibilities of local authorities to provide nursery education and provision has dwindled. The 'New Right' talks of helping the family to perform its tasks – particularly caring for the young and old – rather than relieving it of its burdens, not unlike Spence and Beveridge, but in the context of the 'inter-connected trinity' the policy implications are rather different. The Family Policy Group suggested that the ideas under discussion include adjusting 'tax and benefit allowances to see if families looking after their elderly might be better rewarded', and assessing whether 'present policies for supporting single parents strike the right balance between ensuring adequate child support to prevent poverty and encouraging responsible and self-reliant behaviour by parents' (Wicks, 1983; *Guardian*, 1983). In other words, indirect, negative policies are being considered as a means to encouraging the family to perform its functions, rather than the kind of positive, interventionist measures favoured in earlier periods.

Conclusion

It is always a problem to strike the right balance between continuity and change in an historical overview of this kind. It is important to note the regular reappearance of anxieties about the family over time and the similarities in the way in which such anxieties were expressed. In all three periods covered in this essay, concern was couched in moral terms, thus Mrs Bosanquet deplored the apparent lack of middle-class values of peace and order in the working-class family, J. C. Spence feared the moral effects of family disintegration, and the 'New Right' lobby talks about the decline in traditional family values. However, family success or failure has always been measured in functional terms based on the extent to which the family cares for its members. Anxiety about the family may thus be seen as a series of moral panics, firmly grounded in social and economic assumptions respecting the boundary between family and state responsibility.

Over time, the focus of anxiety within the family has shifted profoundly, from the role of the father to that of the mother and, finally, to that of the state. The first of these shifts was due, above all, to changes in ideas about poverty and attitudes towards the male bread-winner, and the increasing influence of psycho-social theories of family relationships, mediated by an increasing number of trained social workers. In both the early 1900s and the 1940s state intervention to deal with families deemed to have failed was countenanced as a means to fostering and policing the bourgeois family ideal, albeit the approach in the two periods was quite different, reflecting in part the changing diagnosis of family failure. The mood of the 1980s is again quite different and is bent on redrawing the boundary between the family and the state in such a way as to effect a substantial withdrawal by the latter.

In the light of the material considered in this essay, it does not seem that the needs of children have dictated policy at any given time. Policies towards children have never been formulated without a clear view as to the duties and failings of parents and it is these which have formed a major part of the framework of ideas within which policy has been decided. Perhaps the only strand of thinking and social action to prioritize the child has been that running through from Eleanor Rathbone to the Child Poverty Action Group, which has fought for a redistribution of income in favour of children, albeit in the case of Rathbone within the confines of the bourgeois family form (she did not want family allowances to go to unmarried mothers). The child poverty lobby has attended to the needs of children rather than the defence of the bourgeois family ideal. Those expressing anxiety about the family desired to shore up the bourgeois family in accordance with prescriptions of contemporary experts, philanthropists, social investigators and public health specialists in the early period, and paediatricians, psychologists and social workers after the Second World War. But in supporting particular sets of relationships with closely defined duties and obligations both the different needs of individual family members and the causes of family failure above and beyond those of the individual have been ignored.

Notes

1 Feminist social scientists have been developing a rather different analysis of the public and the private; see, for example, Gamarnikow et al. (1983).
2 I am grateful to Victoria Wegg Prosser for allowing me to preview this film, transmitted by Channel 4 in February 1984.
3 I am grateful to Christine Sherrington for allowing me access to her Ph.D. thesis (in progress), which analyses the NSPCC in detail.
4 Middleton (1971) and the Report of the Committee on One-Parent Families (PP, 1974) are agreed that the position of the unmarried mother showed little improvement during the inter-war years.
5 Chapters 12–18 of Jones (1934), *Social Survey of Merseyside* are devoted to the subject of subnormal types.
6 Kevles (1984) has no hesitation in categorizing Joseph's speech as part of the 'new eugenics'.
7 For a typical view of the educational psychologist, see Bowley (1948).
8 Barrett and McIntosh (1982) have effectively criticized Donzelot. I am also grateful to Katherine Arnup (1984) for access to her helpful unpublished critique.
9 Mackintosh (1965, 274) comments wryly on this: 'Pity the poor brat who has to be artificially fed, he is practically certain to be a nit-wit or a criminal. But there

is worse to come. Want of mother love . . . means the babe is deprived of something absolutely vital to its physiological and mental health.'
10 One of the classic examples from the Left is that of George Orwell (1937), *The
Road to Wigan Pier.*

References

Allatt, P. 1981. The family as seen through the Beveridge Report, forces education,
and popular magazines. A sociological study of the social reproduction of family
ideology in World War II (unpublished Ph.D. thesis, University of Keele).

Armstrong, D. 1983. *Political Anatomy of the Body: medical knowledge in Britain
in the twentieth century.* Cambridge: Cambridge University Press.

Arnup, K. 1984. The policing of families: a critical review (unpublished paper).

Banks, J. A. and Banks, O. 1964. *Feminism and Family Planning in Victorian
England.* Liverpool: Liverpool University Press.

Barrett, M. and McIntosh, M. 1982. *The Anti-Social Family.* London: Verso.

Behlmer, G. 1982. *Child Abuse and Moral Reform in England 1870–1908.*
Stanford: Stanford University Press.

Berger, B. and Berger, P. L. 1983. *The War Over the Family: capturing the middle
ground.* London: Hutchinson.

Beveridge, W. 1948. *Voluntary Action.* London: George Allen and Unwin.

Blacker, C. P. (ed.) 1937. *A Social Problem Group?* Oxford: Oxford University
Press.

Blacker, C. P. 1952. *Problem Families: five inquiries.* London: Eugenics Society.

Board of Education and Board of Control. 1927. *Report of the Mental Deficiency
Committee.* London: HMSO.

Booth, C. 1889. *London Life and Labour*, Vol. I. London: Williams and Norgate.

Bosanquet, H. 1906. *The Family.* London: Macmillan.

Bowlby, J. 1946. *Forty Four Juvenile Thieves: their characters and home life.*
London: Ballière, Tindall and Cox.

Bowley, A. 1948. *The Problems of Family Life: an environmental study.* Edinburgh:
E. S. Livingstone.

Broad, R. and Fleming, S. (eds) 1983. *Nella Last's War.* London: Sphere.

Brockington, C. F. 1949. *Problem Families* (Occasional Papers, 2, British Social
Hygiene Council).

Brown, K. D. 1971. *Labour and Unemployment 1910–1914.* Newton Abbott:
David and Charles.

Cattell, R. 1937. *The Fight for our National Intelligence.* London: P. S. King.

Chorley, K. 1950. *Manchester Made Them.* London: Faber.

Coffield, F. 1983. 'Like father, like son' – the family as potential transmitter of
deprivation, in N. Madge (ed.), *Families at Risk.* London: Heinemann.

Davidoff, L. 1956. The employment of married women in England, 1850–1950
(unpublished MA thesis, London School of Economics).

Donzelot, J. 1979. *The Policing of Families* (1st English edn, 1977). New York:
Pantheon.

Drake, B. 1920. *Women in Trade Unions.* London: Labour Research Department.

Durham, M. 1982. The Mother's Defence League 1920-1: a case study in class, patriarchy and the state (paper given at the History Workshop Conference, Sheffield).

Edgeworth, F. Y. 1922. Equal pay to men and women for equal work. *Economic Journal*, **32**, 453–57.

Fletcher, R. 1966. *The Family and Marriage in Britain: an analysis and moral assessment.* London: Penguin Books.

Gamarnikow, E., Morgan, D., Purvis, J. and Taylorson, D. 1983. *The Public and the Private.* London: Heinemann.

Goldberg, E. M. 1965. The normal family: myth and reality, in E. Younghusband (ed.), *Social Work with Families.* London: George Allen and Unwin.

Goode, W. J. 1980. *The Family* (1st edn, 1964). Englewood Cliffs, NJ: Prentice Hall.

Guardian. 1983. 17 February.

Henriques, B. 1955. *The Home Menders: the prevention of unhappiness in children.* London: George Harrap.

Heywood, J. S. 1978. *Children in Care: the development of the service for the deprived child* (1st edn, 1959). London: Routledge and Kegan Paul.

House of Commons. 1906. Debates. Hansard, Vol. 166, Col. 1385.

Jones, D. C. (ed.) 1934. *The Social Survey of Merseyside*, Vol. 3. Liverpool: Liverpool University Press and Hodder and Stoughton.

Karn, M. N. and Pearson, K. 1922. *Study of the Data Provided by a Baby Clinic in a Large Manufacturing Town* (Drapers Co. Research Memoires, Studies in National Deterioration). Cambridge: Cambridge University Press.

Kevles, D. J. 1984. Annals of eugenics, Pt. IV. *The New Yorker.* 29 October, 51–117.

Kramer, R. 1983. *In Defence of the Family.* New York: Basic Books.

Land, H. 1978. Who Cares for the Family? *Journal of Social Policy*, **9**, 257–84.

Land, H. 1980. The Family Wage. *Feminist Review*, **6**, 55–78.

Lasch, C. 1977. *Haven in a Heartless World: the family besieged.* New York: Basic Books.

Lewis, J. 1980. *The Politics of Motherhood: child and maternal welfare in England 1900–1939.* London: Croom Helm.

Lewis, J. 1983. Dealing with dependency: state practices and social realities, 1870–1945, in J. Lewis (ed.), *Women's Welfare/Women's Rights.* London: Croom Helm.

Lewis, J. 1984. *Women in England 1870–1950.* Brighton: Wheatsheaf.

MacDonald, Mrs J. R. nd. *Wage Earning Mothers.* London: Women's Labour League.

Mackintosh, J. M. 1965. *Topics in Public Health.* Edinburgh: E. S. Livingstone.

MacLeod, V. 1982. *Whose Child? The family in child care legislation and social work practice.* London: Study Commission on the Family, Occassional Paper 11.

Marchant, J. (ed.) 1946. *Rebuilding Family Life in the Post War World.* London: Odhams.

Martin, A. 1911. *Married Working Women.* London: National Union of Women's Suffrage Societies.

Mayer, J. E. and Timms, N. 1973. *The Client Speaks: working class impressions of casework.* London: Routledge and Kegan Paul.

Middleton, N. 1971. *When Family Failed.* London: Gollancz.

Mitchell, H. 1977. *The Hard Way Up* (1st edn, 1968). London: Virago.

Mount, F. 1983. *The Subversive Family: an alternative history of love and marriage* (1st edn, 1982). London: George Allen and Unwin.

Motherhood. 1917. Imperial War Museum F. Department.

Newsom, J. 1948. *The Education of Girls.* London: Faber.

Okin, S. M. 1980. *Women in Western Political Thought* (1st edn, 1979). London: Virago.

Orwell, G. 1937. *The Road to Wigan Pier.* London: Gollancz.

Packman, J. 1981. *The Child's Generation: child care policy in Britain* (1st edn, 1975). Oxford: Basil Blackwell and Martin Robertson.

Parsons, T. and Bales, R. F. 1955. *Family Socialization and Interaction Process.* Glencoe, Ill.: Free Press.

Pearson, K. 1913. The Chadwick Lecture. MS Pearson Papers. Item 73. D. B. Watson Library University College.

PP. 1867–8. Special Report from the Select Committee on the Married Women's Property Bill. Cmd. 441, VII, 339.

PP. 1908. Report of the Royal Commission on the Care and Control of the Feeble Minded. Cmd. 4202, XXIX, 159.

PP. 1909. Report of the Royal Commission on the Poor Laws and Relief of Distress. Cmd. 4499, XXXVII, 1.

PP. 1933–4. Report of the Departmental Committee on Sterilization. Cmd. 4495, XV, 611.

PP. 1945–6. Report of the Care of Children Committee (Curtis Committee). Cmd. 6922, X.

PP. 1974. Report of the Committee on One-Parent Families. Cmd. 5629–1, XVI.

Rathbone, E. 1924. *The Disinherited Family.* London: Arnold.

Riley, D. 1983. *War in the Nursery: theories of the child and the mother.* London: Virago.

Rimmer, L. 1981. *Families in Focus: marriage, divorce and family patterns.* London: Study Commission on the Family.

Roberts, E. 1978. The working class family in Barrow and Lancaster 1890–1930 (unpublished Ph.D. thesis, University of Lancaster).

Russell, B. 1932. *Marriage and Morals.* London: George Allen and Unwin.

Sainsbury, E. 1982. *Social Work in Focus: clients and social workers perceptions in long-term social work.* London: Routledge and Kegan Paul.

Savage, S. W. 1946. Intelligence and infant mortality in problem families. *British Medical Journal,* **1**, 86–7.

Sherrington, C. (1985). The NSPCC in Transition, 1884–1983. A Study in Organizational Survival (Unpublished Ph.D. thesis, University of London).

Smith, S. 1883. Social reform. *Nineteenth Century,* **13**, 901–12.

Spence, J. C. 1946. The Purpose of the Family (Convocation Lecture for the National Children's Home).

Stearns, P. 1973. Working class wives in Britain 1890–1914, in M. Vicinus (ed.), *Suffer and Be Still.* Bloomington: Indiana.

Stephens, T. (ed.) 1962. *Problem Families: an experiment in social rehabilitation.* London: Family Service Units.

Thane, P. 1978. Women and the Poor Law in Victorian and Edwardian England. *History Workshop Journal*, **6**, 29–51.

Thane, P. 1984. The working class and state 'welfare' in Britain, 1880–1914. *Historical Journal*, **27**, 877–900.

Titmuss, R. M. 1962. Foreword to A. F. Philp and N. Timms, *The Problem of the Problem Family*. London: Family Service Units.

Whitehead, A. 1976. Sexual antagonism in Herefordshire, in D. L. Barker, and S. Allan (eds), *Dependence and Exploitation in Work and Marriage*. London: Longman.

Wicks, M. 1983. Enter Right: The Family Patrol Group. *New Society*. 24 February.

Wilson, E. 1977. *Women and the Welfare State*. London: Tavistock Press.

Winnicott, D. 1957. *The Child and the Family: first relationships*. Edited by Janet Hardenberg. London: Tavistock Press.

Wofinden, R. C. 1950. *Problem Families in Bristol* (Occasional Papers in Eugenics, 6). London: The Eugenics Society and Cassell.

Women's Group on Public Welfare. 1948. *The Neglected Child and His Family*. Oxford: Oxford University Press.

Wootton, B. 1959. *Social Science and Social Pathology*. London: George Allen and Unwin.

Young, M. and Willmott, P. 1957. *Family and Kinship in East London*. London: Routledge and Kegan Paul.

Young, M. and Willmott, P. 1973. *The Symmetrical Family*. New York: Pantheon.

Yudkin, S. and Holme, A. 1963. *Working Mothers and Their Children*. London: Michael Joseph.

3

Judgements of Solomon: psychology and family law

Robert Dingwall and John Eekelaar

Then said the King, The one saith, This is my son that liveth, and thy son *is* the dead: and the other saith, Nay; but thy son *is* the dead, and my son *is* the living. And the King said, Bring me a sword. And they brought a sword before the King. And the King said, Divide the living child in two, and give half to the one and half to the other. Then spake the woman whose the living child *was* unto the King . . . and she said, O my lord give her the living child and in no way slay it . . .

1 Kings 4, 23–6

At its most basic, law is the set of procedures that a society has developed for the peaceful settlement of disputes between its members (Roberts, 1979). As soon as the simplest form of social organization is established, the possibility of conflict arises. But human society could hardly have survived long enough to commence evolving, let alone do so over several million years, if it were not the case that its members had established means for resolving most disputes most of the time without resorting to violence. Dispute resolution is like an iceberg: the greater part of it is socially invisible as disagreements are settled by everyday means. Where these devices are inadequate, however, the law exists as a second tier, a recognized procedure for managing otherwise insoluble conflicts (Atkinson and Drew, 1979). For the Israelites, the King's judgement was the legitimated way of imposing closure on disputes.

Family disputes, however, pose peculiarly intractable problems for the law. A comprehensive discussion of the relationship between kinship ties and other bases of social organization is beyond the scope of this chapter. In modern liberal states, however, a critical dilemma arises in the polarity between the family as a private sphere and the public consequences of events within it.[1] Liberalism simultaneously requires the autonomy of the family, as a check on the centralized power of the state, and the supervision of reproduction to ensure the transmission of the values on which its inner-directed normative order is constituted (Dingwall et al., 1983). Family law, then, exists in a state of tension between recognizing the family as a self-contained disputing arena, with its own procedures for resolution, and intervening to resolve disputes over the 'proper' means of social reproduction or to regulate the impact of disputes on non-participating parties. These two aspects correspond to child care law and divorce law.

Child care law is embodied in the statutory powers of public welfare agencies to survey and intervene in family life where children are thought to be subject to some form of mistreatment, and in the common law juris-diction of the courts to assume powers of wardship and to take over the guardianship of a child, where they consider this would be in the child's best interests. It is, at least in principle, a protective element of family law. Divorce law has become predominantly adjustive, providing a framework for managing the economic consequences of marriage breakdowns and the disputes which may arise from them, both between parties and between the parties and the state, with its interest in containing demands for material assistance. But with the growth of the acceptability of leaving such matters to 'private ordering' between the adults, the justification for intervention in divorce has increasingly had to rest upon a protective element in the regulation of the consequences of family breakdown for children. Indeed there are those who would argue that the inability of children to determine and prosecute their own interests in disputes which affect them is now the main justification for the special legal forms of family law (Eekelaar, 1984a). Nevertheless, these provisions exist within a legal framework which retains a third element, of support for the family by the restriction of intervention and the distribution of social benefits.

In the protective aspects of family law, there is clearly scope for the introduction of developmental psychology to assist the courts in their determination of a child's welfare. A number of psychologists have criti-cized the limited use which courts presently make of evidence from their discipline's work with children (e.g., Goldstein et al., 1980a, 1980b; Sutton and Moss, 1984; Richards, in press). Drawing mainly on English data, this chapter will begin by examining how judges reason when adjudicating on disputes relating to children by analysing a number of reported cases.[2] We shall then consider some of the criticisms from particular psychological perspectives. In our view, however, the comparative disregard shown by judges for psychology may actually reflect the intrinsically moral nature of their work. We shall conclude by discussing this suggestion and its impli-cations, that the incorporation of psychology into judicial practice is a problematic issue and that such a development may lead to further undesirable mystification.

A superintending power

On 18 May 1893, the Court of Appeal refused to order the return of a 15 year old girl whose mother had applied for a writ of *habeas corpus* against the woman in whose care the child was living. Giving judgement, Lord Esher, Master of the Rolls, declared:

> The Court is placed in a position by reason of the prerogative of the Crown to act as supreme parent of children, and must exercise that jurisdiction in the manner which a wise, affectionate and careful parent would act for the welfare of the child. The natural parent in the particular case may be affectionate, and may be intending to act for the child's good, but may be unwise and may not be doing what a wise, affectionate and careful parent would do. The Court may say in such a case that, although they find no misconduct on the part of the parent, they will not permit that to be done with the child which a wise, affectionate and careful parent would not do . . . The Court has to consider what is for the welfare of the child and for her happiness. (*R* v. *Gyngall* [1893] 2 QB 242–3)

The Court found that the child had a strong and stable relationship with her present caretaker and that this should not be disrupted by granting her mother's application.

The girl's mother had been deserted by her husband in Nice within a year of the birth. She had left her child there with another family for several years while she worked as a lady's maid in the USA. During that period her husband died and she remarried. The child, to her acknowledged distress, was reclaimed. After the family had lived variously in London and Paris, the stepfather died. The mother struggled to make a living as a dressmaker in London, while the daughter suffered extensive periods of ill-health. The combination of poverty and illness several times brought the child into the care of charitable individuals. During one of these episodes, in Weymouth, the girl had formed her present affiliation. It was to that household that she managed to return when she was effectively abandoned in London, when her mother took a maid's post in Paris.

This is a still familiar story, of a woman who must place her child in the care of others while she earns a living, only to find that the child develops a relationship with them that cannot be broken without the most visible distress. The Court, however, was not asked to deal directly with the economic disadvantages of single parenthood, although Lord Esher touches on these by specifically exonerating the mother from any allegation of misconduct in her behaviour. The importance, for family lawyers, of *R* v. *Gyngall* lies in the way in which the judges asserted the right of the state to act as a 'supreme parent' and declared their own duty to decide the case in line with what would now be called the 'welfare principle', that children's interests should be given priority over a narrow consideration of legal rights, even those of natural parents.

The judges' approach was not a novel one. Even given the present limitations on our knowledge of the history of English child care policy, we know that statutes were passed in the sixteenth century empowering civil parishes to regulate parental behaviour, subject to the check of local justices (Pinchbeck and Hewitt, 1969; Dingwall et al., 1984), that the Court of Chancery considerably extended the common law doctrine of *parens patriae* during the seventeenth century for the same purpose and that the welfare principle was clearly visible in reported court decisions from the early eighteenth century (Maidment, 1984). The interest of this case is the clarity of the judges' reasoning, especially in their formulation of the welfare principle which has since come to be the fundamental test which the courts have applied in adjudicating on disputes within or about a family.

The principle challenged

Mr Terrell, the barrister for the mother in *Gyngall*, argued that the Court had no jurisdiction to deny her the right of guardianship unless it was shown that she was guilty of misconduct or desertion:

> If the Court had a general jurisdiction to interfere with parental rights for the benefit of the child, it might deprive the parent of the child in any case where a person who had better means and a better position than the parent was willing to adopt it. (*R* v. *Gyngall* [1893] 2 QB 236)

The Court rejected this restrictive interpretation of its powers. We have already quoted Lord Esher's response. Lord Justice Kay, citing eighteenth-century judgements by Lord Thurlow, went even further:

> Lord Thurlow's opinion went upon this: that the law imposed a duty upon parents, and in general gives them a credit for ability and inclination to execute it. But that presumption, like all others, would fail in particular instances; and if an instance occurred in which the father [*sic*] was unable or unwilling to execute that duty, and, further was actively proceeding against it, of necessity the State must place somewhere a superintending power over those who cannot take care of themselves; and have not the benefit of that care, which is presumed to be generally effectual. (*R* v. *Gyngall* [1893] 2 QB 247)

As we have shown elsewhere (Dingwall et al., 1983; Dingwall and Eekelaar, 1984), this conflict of opinion remains endemic in debates on child care policy. Should our paramount concern be the rights of natural parents, as Mr Terrell would have it, or the welfare of children, as held by Lords Justice Esher, Kay and Smith? Do we emphasize the autonomy of families or the supervisory role of the state?

In the last five years or so, it seems that the balance has tipped in favour of Mr Terrell. An unlikely alliance of Left and Right libertarians have attacked the basis of state intervention in the family. On the Left, for example, Morris et al. (1980, 127), writing in a tradition which goes back to the counter-cultural currents of the 1960s, assert that:

> Parental autonomy in child-rearing must be respected. Diversity of views and lifestyles means that families raise children in a wide variety of living situations . . . Child-rearing practices also vary over time and in different classes, races and religious groups . . . intervention carries a substantial risk of 'saving' children from families who merely have different life-styles from dominant conceptions of appropriate child-rearing. But there is no 'proper' way to raise children.

From the radical Right, we find examples such as this, written by Ferdinand Mount, a former special adviser to a Conservative Prime Minister:

> The family's most dangerous enemies may not turn out to be those who have openly declared war . . . It is less easy to fight against the armies of those who are 'only here to help' . . . which declare that they are only acting out the principle that 'we are all members one of another' . . . What is always affronting is the simple fact of their *intrusion* into our private space . . . Domain-consciousness – the feeling that the State is intruding into private space more and more and ought to be stopped – is growing . . . an implied declaration of the moral independence and individuality of each family, of its right to adopt its own territory and its own values. (Mount, 1982, 173–5)

More recently, these doctrines have come under criticism with the exposition of an argument which has been influenced both by post-structuralism, especially as represented in the work of Donzelot (1980), and the restated liberalism of Rawls (1971). Writers such as Freeman (1983 a and b) and Eekelaar (1984a) have argued that it is unjust for children to be penalized for the irresponsibility, poor judgement or economic failure of their parents since they are not free entrants into a relationship with them. While there may be libertarian grounds for preferring to recognize the primary role of parents in determining the care of their children, their powers should be regulated or, in Lord Kay's words, 'superintended', to prevent the children from being deprived of 'that care, which is presumed to be generally effectual'.

Psychology in judicial reasoning

Psychology has played a central part in these disputes. The 'welfare principle' requires judges to employ a version of psychological reasoning in order to assess the current mental state of a child, to postulate a range of possible future environmental influences and to predict the child's response. In doing so, the judges effectively operate as experienced laymen rather than as experts. As a consequence, their decisions are vulnerable to criticism from the vantage point of specialized psychological knowledge. We propose, however, to treat the judges' activity as a 'commonsense psychology'. We use the word 'commonsense' to signify a form of knowledge, which is assumed, taken-for-granted and available to anybody, as opposed to 'scientific knowledge', which is derived from a particular set of investigative practices and restricted to socially licensed expert users. Our justification for describing the judges' reasoning as a 'psychology', and its limitations, will, we hope become apparent from our discussion, which begins with a further reading of *R* v. *Gyngall*.

Lord Esher set down the matters which the courts had to consider in custody disputes, 'the whole of the circumstances of the case, the position of the parent, the position of the child, the age of the child, the religion of the child as far as it can be said to have any religion, and the happiness of the child' (*R* v. *Gyngall* [1893] 2 QB 243). Looking at these factors, he observed that the child was 'not a mere infant' of six or seven and the court was not being asked to separate her from her mother but to force her to return. Nor was it exactly comparable with the case of a child who had been living with a substitute parent since infancy without contact with its natural parents, when no one would say that 'by force of mere instinct' the child would necessarily prefer to be with the latter. If the child were returned, however, she would be going to a parent whose economic circumstances had not made it possible to take continuous care of her and who was likely to have to place her with others again. The child had left her mother's Catholic faith and adopted the Protestantism of her benefactors. Lord Esher could find no evidence of improper pressure and considered that this was a matter on which the child had a capacity for taking a decision the Court should respect:

> If it were not a question of a choice of a religion, but of an occupation, and the child wished to follow some occupation such as that of a ballet-dancer, which the Court thought would not be for its welfare, the Court would disregard its wishes. But the Court ought to consider what the wishes of the child are in considering what will produce its happiness in a serious and important matter. So the child's views of religion are of importance in the present case. (p. 245)

The child was of above average intelligence, had the prospect of becoming self-supporting as a teacher and was almost of an age (16) when she would be able to act on her own preferences anyway. She was happy and well treated. If she were returned, she would go into the care of strangers of a different religion and lose her chance of a future career. The Court unanimously decided to dismiss the mother's application, although it ordered weekly access to the child.

Courts could, however, reason to a completely opposite conclusion. The outstanding example of this is *In re Thain* (1926). Margaret Thain's parents had married in 1911 when her father was Professor of Engineering at the Royal Agricultural College in Cirencester. He joined the Royal Air Force in 1915 and the couple lived in London until her mother, whose nerves and health had been affected by air raids, went to live with her married sister, Eliza Jones, in Newport, Mon. During August 1918 Mr Thain was posted to Cardiff and Margaret was born in April 1919. Her mother contracted puerperal fever and depression and was unfit to care for the child. She died in December 1919. Although Margaret's father had bought a house in Newport her mother had never been well enough for the family to live in it. At the time of her death, his continued employment in the RAF and its location was uncertain, as a result of post-war demobiliz-ation. Mr and Mrs Jones offered to bring Margaret up with their own children. Mr Thain contributed regularly to her maintenance and special expenses and visited whenever he had leave. Nevertheless, the arrangement with the Jones's was an open-ended one.

In 1922, Mr Thain remarried and established a home in Hampstead. There were no children to the marriage and, in February 1925, he asked for Margaret to be returned to him. Mr and Mrs Jones refused and this originated the case. In the first hearing, Mr Justice Eve took the view that the child would be as well cared for in one home as the other and that her father's claim should, therefore, prevail. Although he recognized that the child would be greatly distressed at being parted from the people she regarded as her parents, he went on, in a much-quoted passage, to observe that:

> At her tender age, one knows from experience how mercifully transient are the effects of partings and other sorrows, and how soon the novelty of fresh surroundings and new associations effaces the recollections of former days and kind friends, and I cannot attach much weight to this aspect of the case. (*In re Thain* [1926] Ch. 684)

Quoting an earlier judgement, *In re O'Hara* [1900], he declared himself 'bound to act on what is equally a law of nature and of society'.

The case was appealed on behalf of the child. Her counsel argued that the child's care should be shared until she went to boarding school. Given her father's professional commitments the effect of Mr Justice Eve's order was to deliver the girl from the care of one woman to another, from a familiar figure to a stranger. The judge had no grounds for thinking this would make her happier. The Court of Appeal rejected these arguments. Margaret's father had never intended permanently to relinquish his rights and was 'now in a position to offer his child a home where she can have a woman's care'. The child's true interests required that she be restored rather than perpetuating 'the peculiarity in a child always living with its aunt and uncle rather than with its father'.

A comparison of these cases enables us to see how the judges have utilized 'the law of nature and of society'. There are similarities. In both cases, the child, if returned to the natural parents, will go into the immediate care of others. But, whereas in *Gyngall* those others stand in no relationship to the child other than that of her mother's 'earnest and vehement' co-religionists, in *Thain* the caretaker will be a stepmother, living in a legally sanctioned relationship with the child's father. There are other contrasts. In *Gyngall*, the child's mother is a deserted single parent who is an itinerant foreign worker in irregular employment. In *Thain* the child's father has made a stable marriage following a tragic act of nature in the death of his first wife. He is securely employed in a professional capacity with the RAF. If the child in *Gyngall* remains where she is, she has the chance of becoming self-supporting in a 'respectable' career (as a teacher rather than a ballet dancer!), while Margaret Thain stands to inherit a significant amount of property under her mother's will, probably sufficient to support her, wherever she grows up.

Even on this limited analysis, one can see how a moral basis for the judgements might be elucidated. The court decisions amount to an endorsement of two-parent families in secure economic circumstances. In *Gyngall*, the mother's character was blemished by her foreign origins, the break-up of her marriage, her itinerant way of life and her economic insecurity. The court decision can be viewed as 'saving' her daughter for a more respectable life. The justifications used for these decisions, however, make no reference to such matters. The Court of Appeal in *Gyngall* invokes the natural concept of the 'wise parent'. This is not a real parent but a fictive character standing outside the immediate circumstances of a particular time, place or relationship and endeavouring to act in a way which will minimize distress and avoidable prejudice to the child in question. In *Thain*, however, the Court is clearly concerned to rectify a social anomaly. There is no discussion of what the proper actions of a wise parent might be. In so far as anybody's feelings are considered, they are those of Mr Thain:

> Grateful as he must always be to Mr and Mrs Jones for the affectionate care which they have bestowed upon his child, can it be a matter of surprise that he wishes without delay to put an end to a condition of things in which his only child regards and, as I gather, addresses another man as her father, and must, if matters continue as they are, be even more and more detached from him? (*In re Thain* [1926] Ch. 684)

Gyngall is justified by the judges' estimate of the child's happiness: *Thain* by their estimate of the father's.

Reviewing these and subsequent cases Michaels (1967) concluded that there was a 'tendency to minimise the effect of medical evidence and, wherever there are other significant factors in the case, to rely on these in preference or in addition to the medical evidence'. Three more recent cases show that judicial practices have changed little. The cases we have selected are *J* v. *C* (1969), *Re D. W. (a minor) (custody)* (1984) and *H* v. *H* (1984). *J* v. *C* concerned the custody of a boy born in England to Spanish parents in May 1958. His mother had been suffering from tuberculosis and he was taken into the home of foster parents at four days old. With the exception of a 17 month period in 1960–1, he had lived in the foster home in Surrey ever since and grown up alongside one of their six children, another boy of almost the same age. The child was thoroughly Anglicized in a relatively affluent middle-class family that proposed to sponsor him through private education together with their own son. His parents lived in a modern working-class housing estate in Madrid. Although there was a good state school, opportunities for education up to and beyond the age of 16 were limited. The courts refused to order the boy's return.

Mr Justice Ungoed-Thomas, in the first hearing of *J* v. *C*, introduced the psychiatric evidence with the statement:

> His prospects of education, and of a satisfying occupation in life afterwards would, in the circumstances appear to be substantially better if he were to stay in this country than if he were to return to Spain. This is important but it cannot in my view be decisive. If it were not for the dangers to the infant of adjustment to life in Spain, I, for my part, would have no difficulty in making the order for which the parents ask. Those dangers appear to go to the very core of his being. (*J* v. *C* [1969] 1 All ER 797).

The psychiatrist thought that the chances of the boy making a successful adjustment to life in Spain were very limited. The physical deterioration during the period he had spent there in 1960–1 was evidence of maladjustment rather than organic illness. The judge thought that the problems would be compounded by the father's rejection of the psychiatrist's concern. In the judge's words 'he is a good workman, but he is not the kind of person who could cope with or even understand the difficulties of adjustment of the infant, whom the Official Solicitor described as a "sensitive boy".'[3]

The parents' appeal to the House of Lords was unsuccessful. The judge had not failed to apply the appropriate principles of law and his downgrading of the view that the upset caused by a change of custody is 'transient' was upheld. 'Growing experience has shown,' remarked Lord MacDermott, in clear reference to more modern psychiatric opinion, 'that it is not always so.' Yet in *Re D. W.* the wheel turned again. A boy of ten,

who had been living with his step-mother happily for six years, was transferred to his natural mother when the marriage between his father and the
step-mother broke up. The 'risks' of living with a single parent who
combined child caregiving with an academic career outweighed the
perceived benefits of moving to a conventional family setting with his
mother, sister, step-brother and step-father. Even more strikingly, in *H* v.
H (child: custody) the Court of Appeal took the unusual course of
reversing the order of the trial judge and transferred a child who had lived
with his father since his mother had left the home just over a year earlier.
The father was unemployed and only intended to accept work if this could
be 'fitted in to his routine of looking after the child'. While such an
attitude would surely have been praised in a mother, Lord Justice Purchas
said: 'It would probably be in everyone's interest if the father postponed
no longer his return to work so that he can help to support this family and
to play a *proper part* in the upbringing of the child' (our emphasis). Later,
a differently constituted Court of Appeal said that the desirability that the
man should earn ought not to be considered *decisive*, but continued to be
a *relevant* factor in the decision (*B* v. *B* (1985)). Whatever status may be
afforded to psychiatric evidence about moving children, this is crucially
qualified by the context of each case. As Lord Upjohn said in *J* v. *C*,
unless the child was under medical treatment, such evidence could only be
'an element to support the general knowledge and experience of the judge.'

The appeal to commonsense psychological theories links court decisions
and social organization. The theories may best be viewed as a resource for
the production from the raw evidence of justifications for decisions
reflecting a preference for the maintenance of a particular mode of societal
organization. The law of nature has 'different connotations at different
times'. Expert witnesses may extend the courts' resources for the
elaboration of such linkages but they do not, at present, substitute for
judges, at least in the higher English courts. Our next task, however, is to
consider how the courts' critics emerge from a comparable analysis.

The biters bit?

The uses of psychology in the criticism of the legal regulation of child care
may be grouped into two broad categories. One might be termed a 'self-
determination' argument. The other is an 'uncertainty' argument.

Self-determination criticisms of family law are to be found in the ranks
of libertarian educationists (e.g., Holt, 1975; Farson, 1978; Hoyles 1979)
drawing on the same psychological sources as the child-centred pedagogy
which has strongly influenced English primary schooling since the 1960s.
Walkerdine (1984) has recently discussed the way in which this psychology,
particularly the work of Piaget, was incorporated into a reconstruction of

the relation between schooling, as an important medium of socialization, and society. Both the psychology and the politics were founded on a conception of the human subject as an inner-directed being whose development was the unfolding of an immanent nature. The psychologists began a search for the essential properties of the infant and the narrative of their emergence. The reformers sought to define a libertarian state against a succession of authoritarian models – Prussia, Nazi Germany, Soviet Russia. The imposition of a mental structure on children by teachers became a microcosm of these rejected political orders, a critique which was legitimated by the findings of a course of natural development by the psychologists. The teachers' task was re-defined as working with rather than on these processes.

In the same way the exponents of self-determination arguments attack the regulation of childhood by law. Like the school, the legal system interferes between children and their natures. It imposes an external structure and schedule on the child's development rather than allowing these to come from within. The psychology is used to emphasize the child's capacity to choose, to identify those experiences which are most appropriate to his or her present condition. Any regulation of these experiences – compulsory schooling, control of sexuality, impositions as to place of residence – risks warping the child's inherent potential for responsible adult life. In this extension the psychology used by the self-determination critics is tied into a programme of romantic anarchism which celebrates nature against society and takes the innocence of children as paradigmatic for adults.

While this programme is obviously open to various forms of criticism, not least for the potentially devastating impact of adult force, negligence or fraud on children (cf. Freeman, 1980, 1983b), how does its use of psychology stand up as a critique of present court practice? Walkerdine notes that this psychology is as much a social form as those it superseded:

> There is no psychology which exists outside the framework of a particular set of historical conditions . . . Neither the child nor the individual can be liberated by a radical stripping away of the layers of the social. Such a model assumes a psychological subject laid bare to be reformed in the new order . . . But if social practices are central to the very formation of subjectivity the laying-bare is an impossibility. In this analysis there is no pre-existent subject to liberate. (Walkerdine, 1984, 195)

Just as the judges invoke one psychology to legitimate a particular form of social organization, so their critics invoke another to discredit it. But the psychologies are not simple alternatives. They exist within specific cultural and social structures which generate their meaning. To opt for one against another is not merely to choose between one theory and another but to choose between different constructions of the human subject and the forms of organization predicated by them.

In their strongest forms, such arguments lead us to the total incommensurability of paradigms and a black hole of solipsism. We hope to proceed more cautiously. Our next step, however, is to consider the uncertainty critics in the same light.

Goldstein, Freud and Solnit (1980a, b) are undoubtedly the best-known and most influential exponents of the uncertainty arguments. At the heart of their case are the concepts of attachment and psychological parenthood. More important than the biological relationship between parent and child is the psychological bond between child and caretaker. 'Psychoanalytic theory . . . establishes, for example, as do developmental studies by students of other orientations, the need of every child for unbroken continuity of affectionate and stimulating relationships with an adult' (Goldstein et al., 1980a, 6). If this bond is disrupted, severe psychological consequences are likely to result. This firm predictive statement is then used to warrant proposals for substantial changes in law and practice which would effectively vest absolute power in a child's psychological parent, as identified to the court by psychiatric evidence. On the other hand, the reason why judges should not regulate this power is said to be the very uncertainty of prediction:

> No one – and psychoanalysis creates no exception – can forecast just what experiences, what events, what changes a child, or for that matter his adult custodian, will actually encounter. Nor can anyone predict in detail how the unfolding development of a child and his family will be reflected in the long run in the child's personality and character formation. (Goldstein et al., 1980a, 51)

The psychology that warrants confident predictions on one page is too uncertain for that purpose on another.

Quite apart from the logical inconsistencies, there are considerable problems in accepting this account. As Katkin et al. (1974) show, Goldstein et al.'s work is conspicuous for the insularity of its references, its lack of acknowledgement of the controversy which surrounds many of them and the absence of reasoned rejection of contrary findings. The emphasis on attachment, for instance, rests mainly on the writings of Bowlby (1951) and Spitz (1945, 1946; Spitz and Wolf, 1946) without reference to the critiques of Pinneau (1955), O'Connor (1956), Yarrow (1961) or Rutter (1972). The impact of the book, Katkin et al. argue, can only be understood by reference to the pre-existing status of the authors – two Yale professors (Goldstein and Solnit) and the daughter of a guru of contemporary US culture (Anna Freud) – and the way this has insulated them from conventional academic scepticism.

This seems unduly simplistic. Between them, distinguished professors of elite institutions publish a large number of books every year. Why do some get taken up and others not? The answer to this question is, surely, to be found in the way that they give scientific legitimation to significant cultural or political values. They function, by intention or not, as a pseudo-science, serving 'as a kind of wish-fulfilment, enabling people to discover what they would like to believe' (Blum, 1978, 156).

In place of the communitarian anarchism of the self-determination writers, Goldstein et al. embrace the authoritarian anarchism of the 1970s radical. In its 'right' manifestations, this is sometimes identified with Victorian liberalism but this misrepresents the extent to which classical liberal theory always recognized a special role for the state as the ultimate guardian of children's welfare. The demand for private ordering of family life is a new element in the liberal tradition of political thought. Goldstein et al. endorse the ideal of the night-watchman state, limited to the deterrence and punishment of violence, theft or fraud and to the enforcement of contracts. While it should act decisively to secure the physical integrity of children, it should not concern itself with their emotional or psychological welfare or their life chances in general. The latter is excluded because it substitutes the judgement of the state for that of parents who have the best information on their child, its capacities and prospects. To do otherwise would risk using the law to redistribute children from the poor to the rich, the spectre raised by Mr Terrell in *Gyngall*.

Where intervention is required, following the unique psychological damage said to be caused by acts of parental violence, it is to be swift, decisive and authoritative. This limited state can dispense with its armies of 'paediatricians, nurses, health visitors, social workers, probation officers, nursery school workers, school teachers and child therapists' – who presume to ignore the immutable natural laws of psychoanalytic psychology.

There is a sense in which such writings are immune from conventional academic criticism. While their material base persists, certain forms of social theorizing never become extinct. One can, for example, look at the successive transformations of the special relationship between mother and infant from the 'blood tie' to 'attachment' to 'bonding' and recognize a continuity of function behind changing modes of expression. The point of this discussion is to show that the judges' critics are performing exactly the same activity as the judges. Psychology is used selectively to legitimate an ideal of social organization so that moral or political choices are made to appear matters of natural law. The problem, however, is to find the Archimedean point from which such writings can be criticized. A scientific dissection may penetrate the ideological use of psychology as a legitimation but is itself a moral task. To the extent that the critical psychologist implies or proposes a particular solution to a human problem, he or she also endorses an alternative form of social organization whose features may properly be exposed for debate not merely in terms of their scientific justification but also in terms of their political or moral character.

Social organization and dispute resolution

How does this assist us in discussing the relationship between law and psychology? We believe that it points to the need to clarify what each involves as a form of social activity.

In our introduction, we discussed the basis of law in terms of the peaceful resolution of disputes. Anthropologists and sociologists of law have developed this approach in their attempt to establish a more or less culture-free means of comparing different societies' approaches to fundamental problems of human existence. It should be stressed, however, that this starting-point does not necessarily imply anything about the specific historical form of the social organization to whose maintenance a dispute resolution procedure, or body of law, contributes. Nor does it suggest how that procedure should necessarily be evaluated against abstract ideals of equity or justice. Radical critics, for instance, have frequently attacked aspects of contemporary English legal procedure as being systematically designed to intimidate, humiliate or otherwise oppress defendants (e.g., Carlen, 1976). As Atkinson and Drew (1979) point out, however, those features can also be analysed as solutions to the problem of organizing a complex, multi-party setting where important questions of truth and error are to be decided. Abolishing the criticized features may make it impossible for the court to function. The solutions to the problems may be historically contingent, but the problems themselves, are simply *there*.

This brings us to a similar position to that reached by Ingleby (1985 and Chapter 14) when he discusses the post-structuralist reaction to critical psychology. As he implies, the wheel has come full circle from the overly simplistic libertarian critique of all forms of social regulation. A society is, almost by definition, a way of structuring power. The question is to define criteria by which such power-structures can be evaluated other than the fact that they manifest power. Criticism can only begin from an understanding of the processes involved in their construction and maintenance and necessarily involves the explication of an alternative theory of value which recognizes both the historical contingency of specific forms and the fundamental issues of social organization which they manifest.

How does a scientific psychology contribute to this? There may be some lessons to be learnt here from the epistemological reappraisal which has taken place within sociology over the last 25 years or so and its increasing humility in relation to lay versions of the discipline. After all, humanity has evolved rather complex systems of social organization over several millenia without the benefit of academic social science. Given this, it may be presumptuous to suppose that we have nothing to learn from lay sociologies or psychologies. Indeed, there are those who would argue that the study of such theorizing and its work in assembling an order in social life is the proper topic for the scientist. There is no epistemological privilege, although he or she may be able to claim precedence over lay analysts by virtue of more extensive or detailed data or a more comprehensive theoretical account with greater predictive or pragmatic power.

To the extent that there are universal functional problems of human existence and social organization, the social scientist may contribute to an appreciation of the range of possible solutions and to the distinction between those problems which are truly generic and those which are specific to a given society. Reproduction is a central issue for any social group if it is to persist through time. Children must be born, must receive others' care during the period of their physical dependency and acquire the value system of the group. But the insitutional means by which all of these are accomplished can vary over quite a wide range between social groups. Indeed variation can occur within social groups and may be viewed as adaptive. In a time of famine a tribe with unbreakable dietary taboos might face extinction without its deviants. While psychology, then, could also hope to make comparative statements about the outcome matrix of particular styles of child-rearing in a given society, it must always be recognized that the evaluation takes place against a particular set of environmental conditions.

If this is so, can it confidently be said that there is or is not a 'proper' way to raise children? There are limits, which psychology and the other sciences may help to identify. Children fed on certain diets starve to the extent of death or serious malformation wherever they are brought up. More pertinently to the present case, children reared in certain ways experience avoidable prejudice to their life chances in the society in which they are born. The psychologist has a part to play in the elucidation of those processes. In a complex modern society, however, it is probably wrong to think of a single 'proper' way to raise children. A degree of diversity may well be part of that society's evolutionary dynamic. On the other hand, it is probably equally incorrect not to recognize a 'proper' range of variation, outside which children are unacceptably disadvantaged.

The question then becomes one of how that range is judged and its limits drawn. Is this a task for psychologists, taking over from Shelley's poets as 'the unacknowledged legislators of mankind'? We would suggest not. Our grounds for this derive from the point at which our work has departed from the orthodox post-structuralist account. Where Foucault and his followers have seen the insidious spread of regulation so that all human life is brought within the panoptic gaze, we identify the disunity among the regulators (Dingwall et al., 1983). It might be the image of the torus where frightening power is contained by the artful design of contradictory lines of magnetic force. Part of the answer to Ingleby's questions about the evaluation of power structures may well be the extent to which those structures are in a state of internal tension, where some part of the power is turned in against itself rather than radiating inexorably outwards.

To the extent that psychologists move into a prescriptive role, they begin to concentrate power, power which is mystified by the rhetoric of science. The professional adds to the licence to investigate and advise, the claim to a mandate to define 'not merely proper conduct but even modes of thinking and belief for everyone individually and for the body social and politic with respect to some broad area of life which they believe to be in their occupational domain' (Hughes, 1971, 287). As soon as psychologists begin to specify a form of child care practice, they imply a mode of social organization.

But the psychologist's aspiration is only one among many. The value which we attach to social reproduction by particular means must take its place among other values and interests. Take the case of surrogate motherhood. In *A* v. *C* (1984) the husband of an infertile wife agreed with another woman that, for payment, she should conceive his child by artificial means and deliver the baby to them for adoption. The mother reneged and the father, having failed to obtain custody, sought access to the child. The trial judge applied the orthodox view that it was in a child's interests to have contact with his biological father. The Court of Appeal reversed this decision stressing the deviant arrangement by which the child has been conceived ('a sordid commercial bargain').

It would be naïve to criticize judges for enforcing particular ideals of social reproduction, child care and family life. That is what they are there for. While social reproduction remains a matter for collective concern, it is unavoidably a focus for conflicts which are likely to involve the dispute resolution institutions of a society. Of course there is room for debate over the distribution of decisional power between these institutions, in particular, in our case, between the elected legislature and non-elected judges. We might argue for clearer direction by the legislature to the judges about the acceptable limits of variation in the social organization of family life, on the ground that such direction would be more visible and subject to democratic accountability (Eekelaar, 1984b). Another part of the answer to Ingelby's questions may be to do with the transparency of the exercise of power.

Few of the choices are black and white. Indeed this is reflected in our title. But the important thing about Solomon's judgement was not how he made it but that it had to be made. The relationship between parents, children and the state contains the possibilities of endemic dispute between competing conceptions of the good society and the character formation that will be constitutive of it. The tension between the professional psychology of the expert and the commonsense psychology of the court is part of what makes for a democratic resolution.

Notes

1 The term 'family' is used in a loose and commonsensical fashion in this paper. Its main focus is on children and the adults standing in a parental or quasi-parental relationship to them. A useful introductory discussion of the problems of defining 'the family' can be found in Morgan (1975). See also La Fontaine, chapter 1.
2 The biases introduced by the financial or emotional capacity of disappointed parties to pursue an appeal and by the selection of cases for reporting make such data unreliable for studies of the distribution of case outcomes. They are, however, more reliable as evidence of typical judicial reasoning, the more so since the correctness of the original judge's method of analysis is often a matter of considerable consequence in any appeal decision.
3 The Official Solicitor is a law officer whose duties, among others, include the representation of children in wardship proceedings.

Cases cited

A v. *C* (1984) 14 Family Law 241.
B v. *B* (1985) 15 Family Law 29.
H v. *H* (1984) 14 Family Law 112.
In re O'Hara [1900] 2 IR 232.
In re S (*infants*) [1967] 1 WLR 396.
In re Thain [1926] Ch. 676.
J v. *C* [1970] AC 668; [1969] 1 All ER 788.
R v. *Gyngall* [1893] 2 QB 232.
Re D. W. (*a minor*) (*custody*) (1984) 14 Family Law 17.

References

Arney, W. R. 1983. *Power and the Profession of Obstetrics*. Chicago: University of Chicago Press.
Atkinson, J. M. and Drew, P. 1979. *Order in Court*. London: Macmillan.
Blum, J. 1978. *Pseudoscience and Mental Ability: the origins and fallacies of the IQ controversy*. New York: Monthly Review Press.
Bowlby, J. 1951. *Maternal Care and Mental Health*. Geneva: World Health Organization.
Carlen, P. 1976. *Magistrates' Justice*. London: Martin Robertson.

Clarke, A. M. and Clarke, A. C. B. 1976. *Early Experience: myth and evidence*. London: Open Books.

Dingwall, R. and Eekelaar, J. M. 1984. Rethinking child protection, in M. D. A. Freeman (ed.), *State, Law and the Family*. London: Tavistock Press.

Dingwall, R., Eekelaar, J. M. and Murray, T. 1983. *The Protection of Children: state intervention and family life*. Oxford: Basil Blackwell.

Dingwall, R., Eekelaar, J. M. and Murray, T. 1984. Childhood as a social problem: a survey of the history of legal regulation. *Journal of Law and Society*, **11**, 207–32.

Donzelot, J. 1980. *The Policing of Families*. London: Hutchinson.

Eekelaar, J. M. 1984a. *Family Law and Social Policy*. London: Weidenfeld and Nicolson.

Eekelaar, J. M. 1984b. 'Trust the judges': how far should family law go? *Modern Law Review*, **47**, 593–5.

Farson, R. 1978. *Birthrights*. Harmondsworth: Penguin Books.

Freeman, M. D. A. 1980. The rights of children in the International Year of the Child. *Current Legal Problems*, **33**, 1–32.

Freeman, M. D. A. 1983a. Freedom and the welfare state: child rearing, parental autonomy and state intervention. *Journal of Social Welfare Law*, 70–91.

Freeman, M. D. A. 1983b. *The Rights and Wrongs of Children*. London: Frances Pinter.

Goldstein, J., Freud, A. and Solnit, A. 1980a. *Beyond the Best Interests of the Child* (1st edn, 1973). London: Burnett Books.

Goldstein, J., Freud, A. and Solnit, A. 1980b. *Before the Best Interests of the Child* (1st edn, 1979). London: Burnett Books.

Hayek, F. A. 1945. The Use of Knowledge in Society. *American Economic Review*, **35**, 519–30.

Hayek, F. A. 1960. *The Constitution of Liberty*. London: Routledge and Kegan Paul.

Henriques, U. R. Q. 1979. *Before the Welfare State: social administration in early industrial Britain*. London: Longman.

Holdsworth, Sir W. 1936. *A History of English Law*. London: Methuen/Sweet and Maxwell.

Holt, J. 1975. *Escape from Childhood*. London: Penguin Books.

Hoyles, M. (ed.) 1979. *Changing Childhood*. London: Writers and Readers.

Hughes, E. C. 1971. *The Sociological Eye*. Chicago: Aldine-Atherton.

Ingleby, D. 1985. Professionals as socialisers: the 'Psy Complex', in A. Scull and S. Spitzer (eds) *Research in Law, Deviance and Social Control, 7*. New York: JAI Press.

Katkin, D., Bullington, B., and Levine, M. 1974. Above and Beyond the Best Interests of the Child: an inquiry into the relationship between social science and social action. *Law and Society Review*, **8**, 669–87.

Maidment, S. 1984. *Child Custody and Divorce*. London: Croom Helm.

Michaels, N. 1967. The Dangers of a Change of Parentage in Custody and Adoption Cases. *Law Quarterly Review*, **83**, 547–68.

Morgan, D. H. J., 1975. *Social Theory and the Family*. London: Routledge and Kegan Paul.

Morris, A., Giller, H., Szwed, E. and Geach, H. 1980. *Justice for Children*. London: Macmillan.

Mount, F. 1982. *The Subversive Family*. London: Cape.

O'Connor, N. 1956. The evidence for the permanently disturbing effects of mother-child separation. *Acta Psychologica*, **12**, 174–91.

Pinchbeck, I. and Hewitt, M. 1969. *Children in English Society*. Vol. 1. *From Tudor Times to the Eighteenth Century*. London: Routledge and Kegan Paul.

Pinneau, S. R. 1955. The infantile disorders of hospitalism and anaclitic depression. *Psychological Bulletin*, **52**, 429–52.

Platt, A. 1969. *The Child Savers*. Chicago: University of Chicago Press.

Pollock, L. 1983. *Forgotten Children: parent-child relations from 1500 to 1900*. Cambridge: Cambridge University Press.

Rawls, J. 1971. *A Theory of Justice*. Cambridge, Mass.: Harvard University Press.

Richards, M. P. M. Developmental psychology and family law: a discussion paper. *British Journal of Developmental Psychology*, in press.

Roberts, S. 1979. *Order and Dispute*. Oxford: Martin Robertson.

Rutter, M. 1972. *Maternal Deprivation Reassessed*. London: Penguin Books.

Spitz, R. A. 1945. Hospitalism. *The Psychoanalytic Study of the Child*, **1** 53–74.

Spitz, R. A. 1946 Hospitalism: a follow-up report. *The Psychoanalytic Study of the Child*, **2**, 113–17.

Spitz, R. A. and Wolf, K. M. 1946. Anaclitic depression. *The Psychoanalytic Study of the Child*, **2**, 313–42.

Sutton, A. and Moss, G. 1984. Towards a forensic child psychology, in S. M. A. Lloyd-Bostock (ed.), *Children and the Law*. Oxford: Centre for Socio-Legal Studies.

Walkerdine, V. 1984. Developmental psychology and the child-centred pedagogy: the insertion of Piaget into early education, in J. Henriques, W. Hollway, C. Urwin, C. Vennar and V. Walkerdine (eds), *Changing The Subject*. London: Methuen.

Yarrow, L. J. 1961. Maternal deprivation: towards an empirical and conceptual re-evaluation. *Psychological Bulletin*, **58**, 459–90.

4

Feminism and motherhood[1]

Ann Oakley

> No social study that does not come back to the problems of biography, of
> history, and of the intersections within a society has completed its intellectual
> journey.
>
> C. Wrights Mills, 1959, *The Sociological Imagination*

> It is very difficult to define love.
>
> K. Horney, 1967, *Feminine Psychology*

The public revelation of motherhood as it is actually experienced by women
has constituted one of the greatest social changes of this century. Such a
revelation would not have been possible without the philosophy and political practice of the feminist movement; but feminism and motherhood have
often seemed to be fighting one another, pulling women in two different
directions, interposing a theme of divided loyalties instead of permitting
a political unity and sense of individual wholeness. It was the American
feminist writer Adrienne Rich (1980) who reflected that the experience of
motherhood in the modern capitalist-patriarchal world is itself, at the
same time, both radicalizing and conservatizing. This is one source of the
problem. The other lies with feminism, which like all political movements,
has developed an inclination to orthodoxy. The delineation of this or that
as the correct ideological line, the tight idealized fit between belief and the
exigential politics of living – these can be agents of an unsociable dilemma
for women, and thus for children, and thus for the wider community.

The twentieth-century revelation of motherhood-as-it-happens-to women
has conferred enormous benefits of various kinds, some of which I shall
discuss in this chapter. From that point of view my speculations on the
topic of feminism and motherhood arise from my role as an academic
social science researcher, yet from another point of view I cannot
comment on the theme of feminism and motherhood except as a person
whose life has been bound up with the articulation of these two conditions,
who 'knows' with that sharpness of 'real' experience what it is like to
engage in the dialectics of conflict, tessalation and reconciliation.

The illumination of personal experience

I have in front of me a series of photographs taken in Venice in early
January 1981. The light in them is of the translucence and iridescence for

which Venice is famous (Morris, 1960). One of the photographs was taken at the edge of St Mark's Square: the Doge's Palace is on the left, the Old Library is on the right and the camera is pointing out towards the sea. The whole central part of the picture is occupied by a golden mist, with two columns rising greyly through it. The clearest object in the foreground is of one of those wonderful street lamps, with four lights on arms like ballet dancer's. Around it the uneven stones of the square are lit with a glorious light – the sun fighting to make a point from the left. Perhaps a hundred figures are in the picture, but since the light is behind them you cannot see their faces. Right in the middle are three figures, myself and my two oldest children. There is something quite significant about the way we are standing. I am on one side, arms folded, looking a bit isolated. They stand not touching but overlapping in the photograph; she with the curl of her long hair turned to the sun, he with his legs majestically apart as appears to be the custom with adolescent males. There they are, the two of them, visibly entering puberty, and there am I with my arms folded, apparently resigned, in my stance maternal, in myself, who knows? By comparison the second photograph looks much less problematic. It is of my youngest daughter, then nearly four, on her own, amidst the pigeons in the centre of St Mark's Square. The birds have adopted various postures. The light is still extraordinary, but now it illuminates her infant face as it breaks into a self-conscious grin. There is, however, nothing self-conscious about her posture. Her little legs are planted firmly on the ground, her body is comfortably encased in a grey duffle coat (Marks and Spencer *c.*1971, it belonged to her sister), and from the arms of her coat hang two knitted gloves swaying on tatty white elastic. I like the picture. Only after it was developed did I notice that her boots are on the wrong feet, so that her toes turn outwards and upwards, like her smile. A 'good' mother would have made sure her boots were on the feet for which the manufacturer intended them; but I like them that way, and Laura herself, at the time, only minded being asked to do something she did not want to do. It is perhaps important to state that these photographs of myself and my children were taken by their father – very much a visible presence in their upbringing.

Photographs capture moments, so that these become the moments one remembers. But there are other moments in my head. The most poignant of these relate to times in my experience of motherhood, when, as a feminist I did not know what to do. For example:

1 Sometime in the early 1970s when I was heavily involved in the exhausting political work of consciousness-raising, my son, about five, wanted a gun. I gave him a speech about the inhumanity of guns and would not buy him one. He ran around the house sticking two fingers out horizontally to mimic a gun and persuaded a friend's mother to give him one as a birthday present. I then wondered if my daughter

should have a gun too. I bought her one. The ideological agony was terrible. She kept her gun behind the pillow in her doll's pram (yes, she had a doll's pram) and he kept his in an old handbag of mine (yes, he had an old handbag of mine).

2 Daughter no. 1 is at school: she is five. I am at home trying to write my Ph.D. The phone rings and an anonymous man in a call-box tells me he has her in his car and is going to rape her. Sometime later, when it turned out that the man was not speaking the truth, I did not know what to say to my daughter. Should I talk to her, aged five, about rape? Obviously I will need to talk to her about rape sometime. But when is the proper time to talk to one's daughter about rape? And should I keep my distress to myself or should I share it with her? What happens is that I sit her on my knee and cry into her hair with relief that she is still whole and tell her most of what might have transpired. Several years later, while doing a research project on motherhood, I meet a depressed young mother whose health visitor told her not to put the baby in another room when she felt most depressed but hold the baby tightly in her arms and share this dark, common, maternal secret with her. Then I see that patriarchy succeeds and feminism is needed in part because of the conspiracy of silence between women. Women, including mothers and daughters, habitually do not speak the truth to one another.

3 The same daughter, now aged 16, goes to a mysterious place the other side of London where many people of her age go and stay till the early hours of the morning. But on this occasion she does not come home. Nor does she phone and leave a message on my all-night answering-machine, as we had arranged. I do not know whether to worry or be angry, whether I should calmly accept or hysterically protest at the abrogation of this agreement between us.

A few days later I am asleep at 7am having a stirring dream. She wakes me from it, asking for money. Being rudely awoken from a dream provokes anger. I tell her she can't have it both ways – she can't have her adulthood and her childhood at the same time. She says why do *I* think I can treat her as a child sometimes and not at others? Who am *I* to decide? I slam the door and go back to bed. But I can't sleep and get up to throw my purse crossly downstairs after her.

4 Son, aged 17, keeps borrowing my car. This I don't mind, but why does he keep cleaning my car when he never cleans his room? Of course I know the answer – a shining car is more helpful to his peer-group status than a clean room (or about as helpful as a dirty room). I feel particularly insulted that whenever he uses my car he removes all traces of me from it. The classical music tapes, the magnifying glass (age affects map-seeing ability) and the Tampax get put in the boot.

He even has the temerity to ask whether he can take the anti-nuclear and peace tax campaign stickers off the back window (and at the same time being engagingly consistent, he applies to the Ministry of Defence and Rolls Royce for university sponsorship).

These incidents are of course symptomatic of motherhood in a certain privileged middle-class social location; material conditions profoundly affect which issues are experienced and articulated as problematic. But all such issues indicate a certain tension between the public politics of feminism and the private politics of motherhood. It may be right, as Rich (1980, 271) says, that 'The myth that motherhood is "private and personal" is the deadliest myth we have to destroy,' yet simultaneously the complexity of parenthood must be acknowledged. Some of what parents, and mothers, do has to do with the separation of generational, not gender, identities. Some of the anxiety and uncertainty, and anger and joy, that mothers feel is by virtue of the cultural nexus within which they mother: a culture that depends on experts to arbitrate the rights and wrongs of personal experience (and mothers are not experts), one in which the community is no longer a source of wisdom and support (although the golden age of community support was in some ways a dark age too), a place in which children and mothers are sanctified in ideology but abused in practice, a time in which the transition to parenthood is difficult enough, but the transition out of it (for parents and children) a *rite de passage* of unacknowledged proportions and difficulties.

Motherhood in theory: women's longest revolution

In the late 1960s and early 1970s a number of feminist thinkers produced competing theoretical accounts of women's oppression which variously described the place of motherhood in this oppression. These accounts were mostly produced as a response to established masculinist theories and most accept the same set of assumptions – that what is called for is a *causal* and moreover a *mono-causal* description of women's oppression. In *The Dialectic of Sex*, first published in 1970, Shulamith Firestone took the view that 'The heart of women's oppression is her childbearing and childrearing role' and said that the nature of the bond between women and children 'is no more than shared oppression': 'the mother who wants to kill her child for what she has had to sacrifice for it (a common desire) learns to love that same child only when she understands that it is as helpless, as oppressed as she is, and by the same oppressor: then her hatred is directed outwards, and "mother love" is born.' This was, of course, an electrifyingly different view from the prevailing psychological orthodoxy, which insisted that mothers loved their babies instinctually, and that any mother who did not wrap her own identity round that of her child's was not an accredited woman. Elsewhere in her book Firestone quoted Erich Fromm in *The Art of Loving*: 'Mother loves her newborn infant because it is her child . . . Mother is the home we come from, she is nature, soil, the ocean . . .' (p. 53). According to Fromm fathers specialize in *conditional* love which Fromm defined as *immature* love, so by this token at least women were granted a maturity in maternity they did not possess in femininity alone.

Firestone's approach, to see motherhood (*both* child-bearing and child-rearing) as the 'heart' of women's oppression, appears in a considerably more sophisticated version in Mitchell's 'Women: the longest revolution' (1966) and *Psychoanalysis and Feminism* (1974). Beginning with the puzzle of the 'area of silence' about women in contemporary socialist thought Mitchell spells out in 'Women: the longest revolution' the specific component structures of women's condition: production, reproduction, sexuality and child-socialization. Of reproduction, Mitchell said that it

is often a kind of sad mimicry of production. Work in a capitalist society is an alienation of labour in the making of a social product which is confiscated by capital. But it can still sometimes be a real act of creation, purposive and responsible. Maternity is often a caricature of this. The biological product – the child – is treated as if it were a solid product. Parenthood becomes a kind of substitute for work, an activity in which the child is seen as an object created by the mother.

The intrinsic possessiveness of mothers, thus identified by Mitchell, was not far from the 'shared oppression' of Firestone's mother love. Neither Mitchell nor Firestone saw much that might be pleasant in motherhood, nor any benefits or hazards that might possibly be generic to parenting; yet, on the other hand, it could be argued that this was not part of their theoretical enterprise which was, rather, to point a very large finger at motherhood as a structure which oppressed women and from which there was no escape except through revolution: 'It is not a question of changing (or ending) who has or how one has babies. It is a question of overthrowing patriarchy' (Mitchell, 1974, 416).

The same predominantly negative evaluation of motherhood is present in the works of other feminist social commentators, for instance Greer and Millett, though more by virtue of what is *not* said than what is, by implication rather than declaration. All these writers appear, indeed, much more concerned with sexuality and with general features of women's social construction as feminine, than they are with motherhood. This is in contrast to earlier feminists, for example, Wollstonecraft, who considers in some detail (and in a work published nearly two centuries before the present wave of feminist writing) how the qualities required for 'good' mothering are precisely the opposite of those bred in women through their effete psychological dependency on men. Wollstonecraft (1929) argues that only if women are allowed to run their own lives will they become satisfactory child-rearers. She was either uncritical of the potential of the institution of motherhood for oppressing women, or took an alternative view of motherhood as something which it might be good for women (and children) to be good at. Given her spirited attack on wet-nurses, boarding-schools etc., the latter seems the most probable interpretation. For motherhood needed to be socially redefined as a practical part of most women's condition, and it had to be experienced as in conflict with male-authenticated values before exposure of the effects of motherhood on women could sensibly enter into the enterprise of a second feminist movement.

One is tempted to speculate that some of this difference in emphasis between Wollstonecraft on the one hand, and Firestone, Greer and Mitchell and Millett on the other, who were impressed by its negative features, might have been due to their own experiences. Wollstonecraft was a mother and the other writers (at the time they wrote) were not. Wollstonecraft's daughter, at six months old, impressed her mother with her intelligence but less so with her early morning waking (see George, 1970). Getting on for two centuries later another feminist writer discovered the same sensuous passion in motherhood as Wollstonecraft knew, and understood that 'There is nothing like experience for making theories come alive' (Rowbotham, 1983, 80). The politics of child care are the smiles and howls of the night. It is of more than incidental interest that the main drift of this association between actual and theoretical motherhood is in the direction of experiencing motherhood under patriarchy promoting a perception of its benefits rather than its hazards. Since this is the case, we can draw a certain theoretical conclusion: that motherhood is most unequivocally one structure within which women's oppression is articulated and ensured, but at the same time it can be one in which women can experience autonomy and wholeness. Which is, of course, not to say that the experience of motherhood might not be improved were the social order transformed: this is obviously so, but the point remains that feminism and motherhood, even under patriarchy, are not necessarily incompatible conditions.

The subtitle of Adrienne Rich's book (1976) on motherhood, 'Motherhood as experience and institution', gave a name to this conceptual dilemma. Rich distinguished between 'two meanings of motherhood, one superimposed on the other: the *potential relationship* of any woman to her powers of reproduction and to children, and the *institution* which aims at ensuring that that potential – and all women – shall remain under male control, (p. 13). These two meanings surfaced because of Rich's own life as a mother, in which she had felt 'The most exquisite suffering – the

suffering of ambivalence: the murderous alternation between bitter resent-
ment and raw-edged nerves and blissful gratification and tenderness'
(p. 21).

This dexterous handling of the personal to produce political-theoretical
wisdom has been a motif in modern feminist philosophy, and there is
surely no better demonstration of its effectiveness than its application to
an understanding of motherhood. One of the problems encountered by
feminist theorists looking at motherhood has been how to disentangle
motherhood from another monolith, 'the family', given, especially, that
we have inherited two distinct theoretical approaches to the division of
labour betweeen human beings which do not so much compete with one
another as speak to entirely different questions. On the one hand, there is
the division of labour in production which is to be explained by the
differential allocation between social groups ('classes') of economic
resources and opportunities. On the other we are faced with pseudo-
biological theories of the division of labour between men and women in
reproduction. Within the family, within the position of women, both divisions of both types of labour apply, but it is not easy to say which is the
predominant one, probably because neither is. At the very least, theoretical understandings of the position of women require a vision of the social
which is not bifurcated into public and private, into work versus motherhood and housewifery (Stacey, 1982).

Over the last 15 years, research on motherhood has exposed the dangerous illusion that motherhood is a private labour of love (while other work
has revealed the underpinnings in the private of public life). Feminists
have challenged both Marxist and Freudian theory as the two generic
explanations of the private and public divisions of labour. Marx (and
Engels) did not allow for any dynamic of male domination that was not
based on property; they did not see the position of women, and the structure of gender relations, as central to any analysis of the contemporary
social system and its origins (Foreman, 1977). The elision in their thinking between women's interests and the interests of human beings in
the abolition of class society invalidated women's personal encounters
with the meanings of oppression. While Marx developed his theoretical
work, his daughters, Jenny and Laura, complained of the isolation
marking their lives as mothers, of the fragmentation of a mother's time
into moments too brief and unpredictable to be used authentically for
oneself; and these complaints were interpreted by the Marx clan as episodes
of personal misfortune to be borne with private fortitude. 'I do believe'
wrote Jenny, aged 38, to Laura, aged 49, in 1882, 'that even the dull
routine of factory work is not more killing than the endless duties of the
menage'. 'Those blessed babies, though really charming good-tempered
little fellows, put such a strain upon my nervous system by day and night,
that I often long for no matter what release from this ceaseless round of

nursing' (Meier, 1982, 137). Whatever Marx did not write about is there in the lives of his mother, wife and daughters. Four of his own children died in infancy and five out of nine of his daughters' children also died. Tussy, the youngest and paternal favourite among Marx's surviving children, remained childless, was notably short on self-esteem, developed anorexia when her mother was dying and finally killed herself with prussic acid at the age of 43. In the midst of death there is life – of a kind – and a classic theme in patriarchal control of motherhood was played out right at the heart of the Marx home as Helen Demuth, the family servant, gave birth to a son claimed by Engels but discovered by the surviving daughters after Marx's death, to be his.

Given the relative silence of Marxist theory on the topic of motherhood, the question is whether some kind of materialist feminism is possible that does not sweep gender under the carpet because to look at it makes everyone theoretically uncomfortable (Delphy, 1980). Much the same kind of question applies to the work of Freud as the other principal male theoretician on the division of labour. In the late 1960s and early 1970s feminists were quick to point out that in so far as post-war policies on motherhood were ideologically rooted in the 'maternal deprivation' theories of John Bowlby, their scientific standing was immensely dubious (Wandor, 1973). Generalizing about the intractable needs of children for mother love and mother care on the basis of the bad things that happened to children in bad institutions was 'a tissue of lies', (Cromer, 1974, 155) that only gained currency because it was politically convenient, then, to push women, not too gently, back into the home. If 'popularized Bowlby' did not bear much of a relationship with 'pure' psychoanalytic theory this did not matter to women. As Denise Riley (1983) more recently has observed, it is 'second-hand ideas' the transmogrification of academic precepts into media popularizations, that has an impact on the world.

Freud's contributions to human understanding in the shape of the 'discovery' of the unconscious and the reminder that even infants are 'sexual' beings are pieces of wisdom without which twentieth-century culture could not be the way it is; and feminist theorists such as Millett artfully dissected the sexism and subjectivity of Freudian theory at the same time as acknowledging its basic value. Feminists interested in motherhood have needed to take Freud seriously for the opposite reason from that which justifies the attention they have paid to Marxist writings: Marx said too little about mothers, Freud said too much. For Freud, motherhood as an ideal and actual state is an integral part of the psychology of women. Once a girl understands she lacks a penis, her only pseudo-salvation is motherhood (which places babies born without penises in a somewhat vulnerable position). But motherhood is not simply the only way out, it is also the demonstration and articulation *par excellence* of the essential qualities of femininity and masochism, narcissism and passivity. That this theory renders both motherhood and homosexuality as results of the same process (identification with, and desire for, the products of maleness), is an irony noted in Freud's own lifetime by Karen Horney (1967), his contemporary feminist critic. But however variable the actual sexual destinies of penis-enviers, the unalterable fact was that women's psychology determined their condition rather than the other way around. To be born female is the original disaster, repetitiously productive as it is of a secondary personality, and eternally redefining the inferiority of women's social role.

Freud's descriptions of motherhood are in part a documentation of some of its meanings within a male-dominated social order: this point is well made in Juliet Mitchell's *Psychoanalysis and Feminism* (1974), and in other writings of the feminist psychoanalytic movement. In that sense feminists may learn something about motherhood from the works of Freud (and in so far as society in the 1980s is becoming more, and not less, repressive of women's freedoms, they will learn more, not less). One unwieldy message which protrudes like a running sore from psychoanalytic accounts of motherhood is the responsibility women as a class shoulder for their own continuing oppression within this institution. Freud said that little girls blame their mothers for not having created them male. (If biology were taught in primary schools presumably little girls would soon appreciate the biological inability of women to control fetal sex, which is determined rather by the genetic material from men, and increased by the power of the medical profession in the form of new pre-natal and conceptional technologies (Arditti, Duelli-Klein and Minden, 1984)). But the role of women in rearing second-class citizens is certainly perplexing, since on the one hand it is clearly true that girls learn all the internal and external marks of minority group status from their mothers, while it is equally apparent that to call women their own original oppressors is to blame the victim in the best tradition of that particularly invidious 'social problem' response.

This conundrum is explored by Nancy Chodorow (1978) in her *The Reproduction of Mothering*. Chodorow, like Freud, begins from the unquestionable social truth that most child-rearing is done by women (both inside and outside families), that most women want to have children, and that most of them get some satisfaction from it. The success with which women mother may be indicated by a recent British finding that, when asked to describe the kind of mothers that they themselves would like to resemble, many were unable to do so. One interpretation of this finding is that women through their inferiorized status, tend not to hold one another in high esteem (Hacker, 1969). Another is that there is no such person as an ideal mother. Unlike Freud, Chodorow incorporates a sociology of gender into her psychoanalytic account in order to build up a picture of a cyclical reproduction of motherhood and gender divisions from one generation to another. The picture goes as follows: women as mothers produce daughters whose desire to become mothers themselves is a consequence of the mother-daughter relationship. Women as mothers, and men as non-mothers, produce sons who repress their nurturant capacities in the interests of 'primary' participation in the impersonal extra-familial world of work and family life (Chodorow, 1978). Thus mothers and fathers generate a division of psychological capacities in daughters and sons which makes a reproduction of the *same* division of labour in the next generation more likely than not.

Chodorow's use of both sociological and psychoanalytic perspectives to explain the phenomenon of motherhood achieves insights which neither on its own is able to do. For example, the key point – that processes of identity development are *relational* (the infant's identity develops in relation to the mother's), is often missed in mechanistic role-learning expositions of gender-role socialization. At the same time Chodorow's account suffers from the very determinism of conventionality of which Freud is reasonably accused – not all children are brought up by their mothers in intact nuclear families; indeed, only a minority now have the fortune or misfortune to be thus reared. How do such theories apply to them? The fact, that exceptions to the rule are many, answers another objection which can be put against Chodorow's view that mothers are blighted to rear sexist children – the objection that social change does occur (from time to time) and that therefore the system must be flexible enough to admit it somehow, even if over-systematized analyses seem to allow little space for it.

Researching motherhood: feminism and the 'bitter, bedrock truth of the way things are'[2]

Motherhood is one of those topics on which many expert dicta have been lavished, and every expert has been absolutely sure he (usually he) has been right (Ehrenreich and English, 1979). Perhaps motherhood is not only a good example of such sanctimonious professional jurisdiction, but actually the subject which is likely to arouse the greatest need for certainty and control – in everyone – precisely because of its tremendous personal and social importance, and because the people who mother are women who in any event represent a threat to the social order (Douglas, 1970).

Given this, it is quite impressive that feminist evaluations have had a considerable impact on social-scientific research on motherhood. This impact has occurred in three main ways:

a Feminist researchers have documented the experiences of mothers with the institution of motherhood.
b There has been a feminist reappraisal of the medicalization of biological aspects of reproduction and its prevention.

c Attention has been drawn to the institution of fatherhood, which is
not exactly a parallel institution to that of motherhood. (But nor is it
quite the same thing, fortunately, as patriarchy.)

a   What is it like to be a mother?

Between literary accounts of motherhood and social scientists' use of
mothers to construct theoretical portraits of marriage and family life,
there existed until the late 1960s an uncomfortable hiatus. Works such as
Mirra Komarovsky's (1967) *Blue Collar Marriage*, or Elizabeth Bott's
(1957) *Family and Social Network* acquired information from mothers.
But only by default did they respect the inherent validity and power of
mothers' accounts of their situations, a principle now built into the new
genre of marriage and family studies both in Europe (Brannen and Collard,
1982) and North America (Rubin, 1976). One very important theme which
has a high degree of visibility in the new literature on motherhood is the
collision within the politics of mothers' experiences between one's actual
existence as a mother, on the one hand, and idealized expectations about
motherhood, on the other. To some extent the same is true of marriage;
but ideas of modern marriage comprise some notion of the mutual meeting
of individualized needs and this does not apply to motherhood – which is
precisely one of the problems.

The discrepancy between the social norm that motherhood is good and
the personal experience of motherhood as bad is a matter of personal discovery for many mothers. It is actually not so much that motherhood is
bad but that social arrangements do not make it easy to enjoy it:

> Society's attitude to small children is hypocritical in the extreme . . . children
> are not welcome anywhere. Like dogs, they are only tolerated if they're on a
> lead . . . there is no similar large scale male experience to the depths of des-
> peration which every mother sinks to, having dragged, pushed and carried an
> alternatively boisterous and recalcitrant small child up and down escalators,
> on and off buses, in and out of shops and whose only recognition is . . . a sea
> of disapproval, condemnatory and hostile glances. (Cromer, 1974, 77)

My own study, *Becoming a Mother* (Oakley, 1979), made a similar point
and gave prominence to the overall disappointments women tended to feel
in achieving motherhood, which was, in most cases, not the bed of roses
they had expected. The study was based on interviews with 66 women
having their first babies in 1975–6. Reviews criticized it for presenting a
'bleak' picture of motherhood; though some welcomed it for flushing out
the suspected truth, and I had thought I had been very careful in the book
(which was mostly constructed directly from transcribed interview
material, thus also methodologically offending sociological convention) to

present the critical mix of benefits and hazards conveyed in the interviews. As Mary Boulton (1983), in another study of mothers' experiences, has written:

> What do we know already about women's experience as mothers? In a sense we already know too much. On the one hand, 'everyone knows' that it is 'depressing' to stay at home with young children. On the other hand 'everyone knows' that children are 'naturally rewarding' to their mothers. It is hardly surprising, then, that the nature of women's experience as mothers is the subject of vociferous debate. (p. 2)

Boulton distinguished in her study between women's immediate responses to looking after their children and the sense of meaning and purpose derived from the role. Around two-thirds of her sample of 50 women found motherhood meaningful in this way, but at the same time about half found child care a predominantly frustrating and irritating experience. The fact that these two attitudes may coexist is symptomatic of the in-built cultural clash between ideal and actualized motherhood; the cultural ambivalence which appears as a theoretical product in academic work translates into the moment in the kitchen when the children are dreadful but the opportunity to be a mother remains somehow stubbornly miraculous.

'Proper' mothers are supposed to find child care enjoyable and, conversely, to view paid work as a responsibility reluctantly to be undertaken to add to the family income when money is tight. The literature on 'working mothers' is too vast and emotionally untidy to be described in detail here, except to note that just as research on mothers' experiences of children has needed to inflate the negative note, so research on mothers' employment has confronted the opposite task: working at a paid job is a lot nicer than it is often made out to be (Sharpe, 1984). In these not-so-mysterious ways, feminist research and writing on motherhood has been carried out dialectically with the predominant paradigm.

While feminism has inspired a cool, clear look at how mothers feel it has also promoted explorations into the ideational world of motherhood. Religious ideas of motherhood are not without their importance even in the modern world, and the myth of the Virgin Mother Mary expresses a deep patriarchal duality between biological and social motherhood: 'Mary establishes the child as the destiny of woman, but escapes the sexual intercourse necessary . . . to fulfil this destiny. Thus the very purpose of women established by the myth with one hand is slighted with the other' (Warner, 1976, 336). Mary does not copulate and she gives birth in a moment, without the ordinary pangs of childbirth. As Marina Warner observes in her book the only biological functions allowed Mary are lactating and weeping. While the early icons could hardly show her holding a bottle, as the Renaissance advanced the nursing Virgin waned in popularity and other high status ladies were portrayed with intact nubile bosoms and obese wet-nurses in the background. Given the profound denial of bodily functions in Catholicism, and given the modern evidence about the lack of parallelism between femininity and biological femaleness, one wonders whether a woman such as Mary really would have breast-fed, her lack of sex being balanced by an abundance of gender in the shape of selfless and passively sacrificial femininity. In Knock, the most popular shrine of the Virgin in Ireland today, one of the best-selling pictures testifies to the continuing relevance of this cult of femininity. The picture harnesses Virginal selflessness to the culture of housewifery in poverty; its legend runs thus:

> Lord of all pots and pans and things
> Since I've not time to be a saint
> By doing lovely things
> Or watching late with Thee
> Or dreaming in the dawn light
> Or storming heaven's gates
> Make me a saint by getting
> Meals and washing up the plates.
>   (Cited in Warner, 1976)

In many different ways feminist scrutiny of myths about motherhood has made visible the complexity and basic structural importance of motherhood as an institution. Simone de Beauvoir (1970) in her unsurpassed *The Second Sex* began her commentary on motherhood with a seven-page attack on the illegality of abortion. Others have asked why women want children, which is simultaneously to query whether they do, to examine the experiential bases on which women's choices about child-bearing are made, and to insist on the simple principle that women can be women and people without being mothers (Macintyre, 1976; Dowrich and Grundberg, 1980). One important area of work has concerned the totality of what mothers in families do, and medical sociologists have fed in new insights on the activities of women as lay health-carers (an aspect of motherhood that significantly passes unmentioned in the theoretical niceties of both materialist feminism and psychoanalytic feminist debates). Indeed, it is possible to conceptualize women's functions in the family in terms of their role as health-carers which also means that the family can be seen as a health care institution (Graham, 1984). If these new research initiatives plunge us again and again into the divide between experience and ideals, the question arises as to how and why the two are constantly held in an attitude of opposition. Little girls 'know' that motherhood is an inspirational state and a socially deprived condition (Steedman, 1982). Adolescents, as the work of Shirley Prendergast and Alan Prout (1980) has made plain, are very well aware of the bad moments in the kitchen and possess an 'illegitimate' knowledge about motherhood which cannot be reconciled with the sentimental model. Thus the experiential crisis of first-time motherhood may in part be a crisis of resurgence of that knowledge, which surfaces when the privatized and romantic routes to personal happiness selected as 'ways out' by teenage girls have been tried and found to fall short of the promise they offer. On a different level of analysis one might say that keeping women in ignorance, or at least in a state of uncertainty about motherhood, serves the interests of both capitalism and patriarchy, the greatest of these interests being that women should not find in motherhood a sense of their own active power to change the world.

b Medicalized reproduction and its alternatives

Between the fading of the suffragette movement and the reawakening of feminist politics half a century later, the prevention, promotion and management of child-bearing became increasingly the property of the medical profession. This 'medicalization' and its consequences for women have provided the impetus for a substantial amount of research. Much of the early attention was focused on contraception and abortion as areas over which women as a collectivity require control as a precondition both for successful non-motherhood and for successful motherhood. Furthermore, it was essential to point out that the medical doctrine of female irresponsibility distorted the rational choices real women make about the forms of contraception they use – or choose not to (Luker, 1975). Pregnancy and birth, which entered the arena of public debate via the 'consumer' movement in the early 1960s, have constituted more of a problematic in feminist thinking. Issues such as 'should women undergo pain in childbirth?' have met with conflicting responses, as the unhelpful burden of feminine masochism has been shelved on the one hand, while intimations of 'mastery' being an aid to successful child-bearing have not been very successfully argued on the other (Seiden, 1978).

Within this research domain the primary task was, naturally, to give the subjective experiences of child-bearing women the status of valid data. Whatever medical and other professionals said ought to happen to women sometimes did not, and the hidden hiatus might have indicated a rampant desire to control women, or it might not, but at least it added up to a problem requiring attention and co-operation rather than inattention and confrontation. Barbara Katz Rothman's (1982) *In Labor* opened with the claim that 'Jimmy Carter was the first president of the United States to be born in hospital', since there had to be some way of making the politics of maternity care connect with conventional political notions of what is, and is not important. Rothman's book discusses home versus hospital birth, midwives versus obstetricians, some of the peculiarly extreme reactions of

American obstetric and alternative-obstetric culture to the ectopic role of birth as a natural process located in an unnatural society. But the principal character in this drama is power: the power of professionalized experts; the power of male-dominated obstetrics and paediatrics to force a wedge between mother and baby by turning the image on the ultrasound scanner away from the face of the mother and insisting that mother-baby bonding is an invention of paediatric science; and the power of the state either to collude in, or oppose, this dangerous erosion of women's expertise as mothers.

Feminist research on reproduction has also challenged the basic precept behind its medicalization, which is the existence of a value-free scientific mode within which medical practice is systematically evaluated. Until the 1970s feminism was something that occurred outside science, and would not engage with science, caricaturing it instead as a monolithic enemy. In the 1970s biological determinism sought to 'renaturalize' women (and motherhood, defined in a certain way, has always been central to any such renaturalization strategy). First, the point was made that all scientific work is a social product. From this it followed that discriminatory social ideologies of women were likely to be part-and-parcel of most scientific enterprises, including supposedly scientific definitions of procreation. The next step was to dissect the modern obstetrical drama into its component scenes, work out where each had come from, and whether each was justified according to commonsense scripts of effectiveness, safety and satisfaction. This re-evaluation has been accompanied by (has helped to create?) a spirit of self-criticism within medicine. The most potent critics of modern medicine are, however, not feminists, just as some of the 'scientific' work that has provided a greater understanding of what happens to mothers has been done by male-led research teams who have studied women because of practical convenience rather than political urgency (e.g., Brown and Harris, 1978).

The example of 'postnatal depression' provides a good illustration of the different understandings arrived at by medically oriented professionals and those who have queried the standing of postnatal depression as a scientific concept. Like all such technical vocabularies, there was a time when postnatal depression (or unhappiness), did not exist. It was born in its modern form in the second half of the nineteenth century, when postnatal breakdown first came to be socially recognized as a potentially serious disorder (Day, 1981).

Since then the area of maternal experience to which the concept refers has been partitioned off as an area of psychiatric and biochemical expertise. What this means is that considerable effort has gone into (1) searching for a physical-mechanical cause of mother's unhappiness following childbirth; and (2) theorizing about the similarities or differences between postnatal depressions and other types of 'mental illness'. My own research into first-time motherhood pointed an accusing finger at other kinds of factors, including lack of previous acquaintance with the work of child care, living in poor housing, not having any kind of paid work and childbirths characterized by a high level of medical intervention (Oakley, 1980). Other research work has confirmed these findings, for example, Hilary Graham and Lorna McKee (1978), in a survey of mothers in York found a strong predictive value for postnatal depression attached to housing conditions. Parallel with these research activities has been the setting up of self-help health groups, and the promotion of popular work on the subject (Welburn, 1980). Emotional distress following birth and during the whole period of active motherhood is possibly the greatest health problem faced by women in industrialized societies today. But so critical to the social fabric is the myth of the contented mother (the benign smiles of the Virgin Mary contain no hint of her depression) that maternal unhappiness is deemed normal, temporary and solvable by means of such well-worn feminine remedies as pills, new dresses, and marital trips to the cinema.

Within the last few years, the advent of new reproductive technologies, particularly those concerned with *in vitro* fertilization and pre-natal sex diagnosis and selection, have raised ethical and political questions about the medical control of reproduction as literally a life-and-death matter for mothers and for women. It is common to see reproductive technologies as about choice (though we need to know whose choice they are about). But they can also be seen another way, as closing down options and preventing choice. But basically, women as mothers have never been consulted about the multitude of policy-decisions that have been made and which have aided and abetted the growth of a reproductive technology industry. 'Woman adapts to a self and a world she never created' (Raymond, 1984).

c Inventing fatherhood

Women have written in scathing and often funny 'fictional' terms of fathers' marginality to family life. Characters such as Tina in Sue Kaufman's (1971) *Diary of a Mad Housewife* or Jane in Diane Harpwood's (1981) *Tea and Tranquilisers* (subtitled *The Diary of a Happy Housewife*) fight their way through housing problems, children's illnesses, and the loss of self-esteem that seems to accompany women's withdrawal into the home to a drugged acceptance of the unilateral job child-rearing normally turns out to be. 'This evening I bathed the children' remarks Jane in *Tea and Tranquilisers*, 'I brought them down to say goodnight to Daddy. I always do that to make sure they remember his name.'

Structural social change – rising unemployment rates, shorter employment work hours, the increasing number of single-parent families, and so forth – have had an impact on the position of fathers. The advent of the contemporary women's movement and its academic presence have also undoubtedly led researchers to think about fathers in the context of family life and child-rearing where they would not have done so before. This has meant, among other things, that feminists do themselves a disservice if they ignore fatherhood; indeed, it means that a feminist discussion of motherhood which omits fatherhood is liable to be interpreted as appealing to the media stereotype of anti-men motherhood unless a different position is stated.

Thus we now have available to us interview studies concerning men's experiences of fatherhood, their experiences in the labour ward and their adjustment to the 'crisis' of first childbirth (Fein, 1974, Brown, 1982, Wandersman, 1980); we have, too, a mountain of observational data on what fathers and babies actually do with one another. Since the observational studies (e.g., Rebelsky and Hanks, 1971) seem to outweigh the interview ones, it is perhaps not entirely out of order to remark that people studying fatherhood may find it somewhat easier to watch and record 'hard' observed facts than collect and cope with subjective information about feelings.

As with the traditional neglect of women in academic disciplines, it is scarcely adequate merely to 'add men in' to the study of motherhood. Much of the new work on fatherhood is disappointingly additive, as Martin Richards (1982) has observed. A classic instance is Rodholm's (1981) research on father-infant contact following caesarean birth. This transplanted bonding research from mothers to fathers, and asked whether leaving fathers alone with their naked infant for ten minutes after birth influences the quality of the father-infant relationship three months later (as compared with seeing the infant in an incubator and being forbidden to touch it). The answer was yes. But it is either simply a preliminary observation to note that fathers can behave like mothers, or it is information about human capacities we already possess. Men's potential to be active and involved fathers is not in question; what is in question is why so few of them assume this commitment, how their present and possible roles as fathers interact with the cultural support for a more public ethic of masculinity, and what such a revised pattern of fatherhood might do for men, women, children and society as a whole. The generic difficulty in studying fathers is twofold: first, our inherited model of parenting cannot easily be separated from cultural constraints of femininity; and secondly, to analyse the activities and capabilities of men as the biological fathers of children is to isolate for study one tiny brick in an enormous edifice – that of patriarchy. In so far as feminists concern themselves with the study of fatherhood, they are liable to say that fathers can only be seen as the carriers of a far weightier culture than that bequeathed by the revisionist impact of the women's movement on the patriarchal world view.

What kind of mothers do feminists make?

This is a question at once impertinent and essential. It is impertinent because the vitality and importance of feminist perspectives on motherhood stand irrespective of their personal praxis. It is essential because personal experience is the stuff of which intellectual visions are made, and because if child-rearing is to be done in a feminist fashion, it is at least relevant to ask what difference the difference will make.

The question may be asked: but cannot be answered. Some work has been done on mothers and fathers who attempt an endeavour called 'non-sexist child-rearing'. (This is what I was trying to do when I bought my daughter a gun in 1971.) Even here there are few studies, and no large-scale national data. In America a survey carried out in 1976–7 of over 1,000 families with children under 13, classified 57 per cent as traditionalists on the subject of gender, while 43 per cent could be said to believe that boys and girls should be reared alike (General Mills, 1976). Beliefs and practice may not, of course, coincide – and most commonly do not in the particular area of gender. In the UK, June Statham's research, which has involved interviewing parents of one to 12 year olds, suggests that the major drift of non-sexist child-rearing is in the direction of opening up options via the provision of equal informal and formal educational opportunities and resources to boys and girls. At the same time there is a concern to ensure and maintain a 'secure gender identity' especially for boys: lack of masculinity is seen as a more blatant handicap for a boy than its possession is for a girl (Statham, no date given).

There is in quite a lot of writing on parenting and child socialization a significant elision between 'identity' and 'gender identity'. Is one's identity as female or male separable from one's identity as an individual? Should it be? To what extent are the chronologically ordered tasks (for children and parents) of identification and separation elements in the fusion and fission of gender; is gender-identity development primary or not? More pragmatically, it is quite obviously not enough to give boys dolls and girls train sets and school them together so boys can bake cakes and girls can bake atom bombs. More and more evidence is pointing to the need for an authentic and consistent sense of self-worth in both females and males. The challenge therefore would seem to lie in revamping both the experience and the institution of motherhood to provide this essential basis of self-worth for children of both sexes; and at the same time to pursue the social policy question as to how the self-authenticating aspects of mothers' own experiences may themselves be strengthened and confirmed.

Notes

1 The author would like to thank Sandra Stone, for help with the preparation of her typescript.
2 Rich, 1980, 270.

92   *Children of social worlds*

References

Arditti, R., Duelli-Klein, R. and Minden, S. (eds) 1984. *Test-Tube Women*. London: Pandora Press.

de Beauvoir, S. 1970. *The Second Sex*. London: Four Square Books.

Bott, E. 1957. *Family and Social Network*. London: Tavistock Press.

Boulton, M. G. 1983. *On Being a Mother*. London: Tavistock Press.

Brannen, J. and Collard, J. 1982. *Marriages in Trouble*. London: Tavistock Press.

Brown, A. 1982. Fathers in the labour ward: medical and lay accounts, in L. McKee and M. O'Brien (eds), *The Father Figure*. London: Tavistock Press.

Brown, G. W. and Harris, T. 1978. *Social Origins of Depression*. London: Tavistock Press.

Chodorow, N. 1978. *The Reproduction of Mothering*. Berkeley: University of California Press.

Cromer, L. 1974. *Wedlocked Women*. London: Feminist Books.

Day, S. 1981. Towards a social history of postnatal depression (unpublished paper, Child Care and Development Group, University of Cambridge).

Delphy, C. 1980. A materialist feminism is possible. *Feminist Review*, **4**, 79–105.

Douglas, M. 1970. *Purity and Danger: an analysis of concepts of pollution and taboo*. London: Penguin Books.

Dowrich, S. and Grundberg, S. 1980. *Why Children?* London: The Women's Press.

Ehrenreich, B. and English, D. 1979. *For Her Own Good: 150 years of the experts' advice to women*. London: Pluto Press.

Fein, R. A. 1974. Men and young children, in J. H. Pleck and J. Sawyer (eds), *Men and Masculinity*. New Jersey: Prentice Hall.

Firestone, S. 1972. *The Dialectic of Sex*. London: Paladin.

Foreman, A. 1977. *Femininity as Alienation: women and the family in Marxism and psychoanalysis*. London: Pluto Press.

General Mills American Family Report. 1976. *Raising Children in a Changing Society*.

George, M. 1970. *One Woman's Situation: a study of Mary Wollstonecraft*. Chicago: University of Illinios Press.

Graham, H. 1984. *Women, Health and the Family*. London: Wheatsheaf Books.

Graham, H. and McKee, L. 1978. The first months of motherhood (unpublished report, Health Education Council).

Hacker, H. 1969. Women as a minority group, in B. Roszak and T. Roszak (eds), *Masculinity/Femininity: readings in sexual mythology and the liberation of women*. New York: Harper and Row.

Harpwood, D. 1981. *Tea and Tranquillisers*. London: Virago.

Horney, K. 1967. *Feminine Psychology*. London: Routledge and Kegan Paul.

Katz Rothman, B. 1982. *In Labor: women and power in the birthplace*. New York: W. W. Norton.

Kaufman, S. 1971. *Diary of a Mad Housewife*. London: Penguin Books.

Komarovsky, M. 1967. *Blue Collar Marriage*. New York: Vintage Books.

Luker, K. 1975. *Taking Chances*. Berkeley: University of California Press.

Macintyre, S. 1976. Who wants babies? The social construction of 'instincts', in D. L. Barker and S. Allen (eds), *Sexual Divisions and Society: process and change*. London: Tavistock Press.

Meier, O. (ed.) 1982. *The Daughters of Karl Marx.* New York: Harcourt Brace Jovanovich.

Mitchell, J. 1966. 'Women: the longest revolution. *New Left Review*, **40**, 00–0.

Mitchell, J. 1974. *Psychoanalysis and Feminism.* London: Allen Lane.

Morris, J. 1960. *Venice.* London: Faber and Faber.

Moss, P. Transition to parenthood study. (unpublished research, London: Thomas Coram Research Unit).

Oakley, A. 1979. *Becoming a Mother.* Oxford: Martin Robertson. (Also published as *From Here to Maternity.* 1981. London: Penguin Books.)

Oakley, A. 1980. *Women Confined.* Oxford: Martin Robertson.

Oakley, A. 1981. Normal motherhood: an exercise in self-control, in B. Hutter and G. Williams *Controlling Women.* London: Croom Helm.

Prendergast, S. and Prout, A. 1980. What will I do . . .? Teenage girls and the construction of motherhood. *The Sociological Review*, **28**, 517–35.

Raymond, J. 1984. Feminist ethics, ecology and vision, in R. Arditti, R. Duelli-Klein and S. Minden (eds), *Test-tube Women.* London: Pandora Press.

Rebelsky, F. and Hanks, C. 1971. Fathers' verbal interaction with infants in the first 3 months after birth. *Child Development*, **42**, 63–8.

Rich, A. 1980. Motherhood: the contemporary emergency and the quantum leap, in *On Lies, Secrets, Silence.* London: Virago.

Rich, A. 1976. *Of Woman Born.* London: Virago.

Rich, A. 1980. *On Lies, Secrets, Silence.* London: Virago.

Richards, M. P. M. 1982. How should we approach the study of fathers?, in L. McKee and M. O'Brien (eds), *The Father Figure.* London: Tavistock Press.

Riley, D. 1983. *War in the Nursery.* London: Virago.

Rödholm, M. 1981. Effects of father-infant postpartum contact on their interaction 3 months after birth. *Early Human Development*, **5**, 79–85.

Rowbotham, S. 1983. *Dreams and Dilemmas.* London: Virago.

Rubin, L. B. 1976. *Worlds of Pain.* New York: Basic Books.

Seiden, A. M. 1978. The sense of mastery in the childbirth experience, in M. T. Notman and C. C. Nadelson (eds), *The Woman Patient.* Vol. 1. New York: Plenum Press.

Sharpe, S. 1984. *Double Identity: the lives of working women.* London: Penguin Books.

Stacey, M. 1982. The division of labour revisited, or overcoming the two Adams, in P. Abrams, R. Keen, J. Finch and P. Rock (eds), *Practice and Progress: British Sociology 1950–1980.* London: George Allen and Unwin.

Stanley, L. and Wise, S. 1983. *Breaking out: feminist consciousness and feminist research.* London: Routledge and Kegan Paul.

Statham, J. Growing up equal: childrearing without sex roles (unpublished paper, Open University). Undated.

Steedman, C. 1982. *The Tidy House.* London: Virago.

Wandor, M. (ed.) 1973. *The Body Politic: writings from the women's liberation movement in Britain 1969–72.* London: Stage 1.

Wandersman, L. P. 1980. The adjustment of fathers to their first baby: the roles of parenting groups and marital relationship. *Birth and the family journal*, **7** 155–61.

Warner, M. 1976. *Alone Of All Her Sex: the myth and cult of the Virgin Mary.* London: Weidenfeld and Nicholson.

Welburn, V. 1980. *Postnatal Depression*. London: Fontana.

Wollstonecraft, M. 1929. *Vindication of the Rights of Women*. (first published 1792) London: Everyman.

Wright Mills, C. 1959. *The Sociological Imagination*. New York: Oxford University Press.

Part 2

Social development in context

Introduction

In one way or another, the family continues to have a central role in the chapters in part 2, though the emphasis here is more directly on the development of the child. Students of child development have in recent years become increasingly concerned with the identification of elements in children's social environment which might play a key role in shaping their development. As Judy Dunn shows, the almost exclusive concern with the emotional attachment of mother and child, which marked psychological research in the 1960s, has given way to a much broader set of concerns which extend to many aspects of family life.

Michael Wadsworth's chapter draws on the long-term longitudinal studies which have been such an important feature of work on parents and children in Britain to document the importance of social-contextual factors in child development. Examining a variety of processes of transmission of long-term effects, he points out that social factors may operate by affecting individuals' life circumstances and/or by influencing their attitudes and self-concepts. Relevant social factors include public and professional attitudes as well as such things as place of residence and experience of education. Some, such as parental attitudes to education, produce effects which can be sustained across generations.

Possible influences of the ways parents talk to and relate to their children are considered both by Dunn and by Chris Henshall and Jaqueline McGuire. Dunn points out that in the last decade there has been a great deal of research on the social development of children and on the parent-child relationship, but rather little on the dynamic features of relationships within the family and the different experiences of children within the same family. She points out the advantages of combining long-term longitudinal research such as that described by Wadsworth with fine-grained observation of the processes within the family which may mediate or modify the effects of particular environmental circumstances or stressful events.

Henshall and McGuire are concerned with parental influences in the context of children's gender development. They see much of the available research, for example, on father absence, as based on inadequate and oversimplified conceptions of the variables involved. Echoing an emphasis in Oakley's chapter, they stress the *meaning for the participants* of particular behaviour patterns and situations. Children, from an early age, are sensitive not only to what people do, but to why they do it. Likewise, Dunn argues compellingly for a high level of social sensitivity in very young children, and gives a key role to the emotions in the development of such sensitivity.

Where Dunn draws attention to the misleading Piagetian conception of the pre-schooler as a social incompetent, Henshall and McGuire point to the failure of Piagetian inspired attempts to explain gender development in terms of pre-school cognitive deficiencies. Such dissatisfactions with the long dominant Piagetian approach to understanding child development will surface more explicitly in part 3.

5

Growing up in a family world: issues in the study of social development in young children

Judy Dunn

Perspectives on the study of social and emotional development in young children have broadened greatly in the last decade from a focus on the implications of the attachment between mother and child for children's emotional security to a much wider set of concerns. One of the most striking changes is a growing interest in examining children's development within the *family* (loosely defined here as the familiar members of a household, and visiting kin), rather than in the context of the mother-child relationship. Most children grow up in families – families that frequently undergo marked changes even within the first years of children's lives. It is within the family that they develop not only a sense of emotional security but powers of communication and language, a sense of self, and a growing understanding of the intentions, feelings and perceptions of others, and of the shared world of cultural rules and roles. Although by three or four years old many children's social worlds include people *outside* the family, for the first two or three years it is within a relatively closed world of a particular household and a few familiar visitors or relatives that babies make the transition from infancy to childhood. The importance of understanding the impact of this complex social world of the family – a network of different and changing relationships – upon children's understanding and personality is a theme that has become increasingly evident in the work of psychologists interested in the development of social relationships.

A second change is an increasing concern with developments in the social understanding involved in the child's relationships during the preschool years. Already in 1974 several of the contributors to *The Integration of the Child into a Social World* argued that we must consider the significance of the relation between child and mother for the development of language and human communicative capabilities, as well as for children's emotional and physical security. This concern with the development of communication between mother and child remains, of course, an urgent one. But other issues in the study of early social relationships are also pressing: the links between early social relations and the development of social understanding, the mutual influence of different relationships within the family and their impact on the growing child, the developmental implications of changes within the family such as parental divorce or death, the relations between children's behaviour and experiences within the family and their social behaviour outside the family in the world of peers and school. And as an overarching issue, it is evident that we need to understand more clearly the relations between affect and cognitive development in the early years.

These are large and in some cases extremely intractable questions; on most of them we have made as yet little progress towards answers in which we can have much confidence. But in the very recognition of the significance of these questions we *have* made progress, and in this chapter I hope to show why their delineation reflects an exciting change in the framework within which we attempt to understand early human development. The argument will be that by studying children's relationships with other family members in the context of family life we gain not only some understanding of the importance of these different family relationships for the development of individual differences in personality, and of the impact of environmental changes on individual development, but also a new perspective on the nature of the child, and on the part that emotional experiences play in developmental change. These issues will be considered in relation to two general developmental topics: the development of children's understanding of their family world, and the development of individual differences. First, a brief comment on the complexity of the interrelations between different family members is needed in explanation for the focus on family rather than mother-child relationships.

It is increasingly evident that to understand fully the development of any one dyadic relationship in the family we should take account of the influence of other family relationships. In the last decade it has been shown, for instance, that the quality of the marital relationship is importantly linked to the course of pregnancy, childbirth, and the mother-child relationship in infancy. The birth of a child in turn affects the relationship between husband and wife, and the *kind* of baby born to a family – in terms of temperament – affects the marital relationship (see Maccoby & Martin, 1983 for review). The importance of these 'second-order' effects, stressed so clearly by Bronfenbrenner in 1974 (and see Bronfenbrenner, 1979) have been emphasized particularly in relation to fathers. Parke (1979), for example, has delineated both the direct and indirect (second-order) ways in which fathers may influence their children's development. Several studies of the mother-father-child triad have now been conducted – the results showing, for instance, that fathers' presence increases mothers' effectiveness in controlling two year olds (Lytton, 1979), that some behaviour patterns such as smiling to the baby increase in the presence of the spouse (Parke and O'Leary, 1976), others decrease in frequency (e.g. see Belsky, 1979; Clarke-Stewart, 1978). More interesting than these 'frequency count' comparisons of the different combinations of mother-child, father-child, and mother-father-child are studies such as that by Pedersen, Yarrow, Anderson and Cain (1979), that suggest the emergence in children as young as five months of some complex behaviour co-ordinated with the behaviour of the parents towards one another. More recently, such direct and indirect effects have also been described for grandparents and for siblings. And the broadening of perspective has included a new awareness of the importance of including in studies of second-order effects parental perceptions and attitudes as well as their observed behaviour (Parke, 1979).

The patterns of mutual influence of these family relationships are extremely complex, even within small families, as the studies of siblings and their mothers illustrate. One study showed that individual differences in the relationship between mothers and their firstborn at the time of the birth of the secondborn, for instance, were systematically linked to the quality of the relationship between the siblings one year later (Dunn and Kendrick, 1982). In those families in which the relationship between mother and firstborn daughter was close and intense, the siblings one year later were relatively hostile. The children's relationship with their father was also systematically associated with differences in the sibling relationship. And if the firstborn child had a very affectionate relationship with the father, the escalation of conflict and confrontation between mother and firstborn that commonly accompanied the arrival of the second was less marked. When the mother's developing relationship with the second child was also taken into account the patterns of influence became even more complicated. This mother-secondborn relationship was systematically linked to the quality of the sibling relationship later in time. In families in which the mother played a great deal with the second child when he or she was aged eight months, both children six months later were particularly hostile to one another. There were links too between the quality of the sibling relationship at one time point, and the later relationship between each child and mother. The frequency of sibling quarrels at one time point, for example, was linked to individual differences in the mother's behaviour to each individual child six months later.

In a subsequent study of slightly older siblings and their mothers we have found equally complex triadic patterns. For instance, differences in mother's behaviour towards the older child during sibling quarrels is systematically linked to differences in the younger child's behaviour to both sibling and mother at a later time point (Dunn & Munn, 1985a).

These correlations between sets of individual differences in family relationships over time do not, of course, permit us to draw causal inferences about the direction of influence within the family. But they make clear how misleading it is to consider any one of these dyadic relationships in isolation from the others. If we consider the mother-child relationship as an important influence on children's development then we must take seriously the impact of father, siblings, and grandparents upon that relationship.

Analysis of family triadic interactions raises a further important point. It is striking how closely children, even as infants, monitor the interaction and relationships between other family members. They rarely ignore interchanges between their parents and siblings, for instance – and the developmental changes in their response to the interaction between others within the family presents us with an important opportunity to study their growing understanding of the feelings and intentions of others – the first topic of this chapter.

The development of understanding others' feelings

The nature of a child's relationship with another person will be profoundly affected by the extent to which he or she understands the feelings and intentions of the other. It has been widely assumed that children have, as Piaget argued, major difficulties during the pre-school years in understanding that other people have perceptions and feelings that differ from their own. However, this view is now being increasingly questioned. One important source of this change of orientation is the research that has employed naturalistic observation of children in the emotional context of family life. This gives us a very different picture from the accepted view of children in their second and third years as unable to recognize the feelings and perceptions of others.

One of the first and most revealing studies was one carried out by Zahn-Waxler, Yarrow and King (1979), who trained mothers to record their children's responses to displays of distress and anger by others, from the end of the first year through the second and third year of life. The results were striking:

> Very young children were often finely discriminative and responsive to others' need states. Children in the youngest cohorts showed distress to parental arguments and anger with each other. Responses were sometimes marked: crying, holding hands over ears, comforting a distraught parent, or (punitively) hitting the parent perceived as the guilty one. Parental affection toward each other was equally arousing: Children of 1 to 2 and a half years showed consistently different responses depending on whether mother or father initiated the affectionate hug or kiss. (Yarrow and Waxler, 1975, 78)

> By two years of age, children bring objects to the person who is suffering, make suggestions about what to do, verbalise sympathy, bring someone else to help, aggressively protect the victim and attempt to evoke a change in

affect in the distressed person. Such means-ends behavior implies that children can keep in mind the other's distress as a problem to be solved. (Radke-Yarrow, Zahn-Waxler and Chapman, 1983)

Direct observation of children at home tells a very similar story. In a study of secondborn children followed through their second and third year, we traced the increasing sophistication of the children's ability to 'read' the emotions and intentions of other family members (Dunn and Munn, 1985a). Some grasp of what would annoy or upset the sibling was evident remarkably early: teasing the sibling was for instance recorded from 14 months on, and became increasingly frequent and elaborate in nature during the second year. By 24 months, for example, one child teased her older sibling by pretending to be the sister's imaginary friend – an extremely sophisticated piece of behaviour, involving transformation of identity *and* an understanding of what would annoy this other person. The children teased their mothers, too, but it was towards the sibling that this behaviour was shown most frequently. Accurate anticipation of their mothers' behaviour was revealed in a variety of ways – for instance in the children's appeals to their mothers during conflict with the sibling. The children appealed to their mothers frequently after their sibling had been physically aggressive, had teased or taken a favourite possession. When they themselves had acted in this way, however, they were extremely unlikely to appeal to their mothers. For instance, in one study, while 65 out of 99 sibling 'hostile acts' of this sort were followed by the child appealing to the mother, only four out of 125 child 'hostile acts' were followed by an appeal. Evidence of some understanding of when their mothers' help was likely to be forthcoming, and when it was not, was already evident in the first half of the second year.

The children's powers of understanding how to annoy and comfort were also evident in their responses to disputes between others. We have stressed that children monitor closely the exchanges between other family members. Between 18 and 24 months 'supporting' actions were often shown to one or other of two family antagonists engaged in a dispute that did not initially involve the child. The supportive actions were not simply imitations of actions carried out by others, but were 'innovative' acts that reflected some grasp of what the other person wanted or needed.

In their family relationships, then, children during their second year demonstrate much greater powers of understanding others' emotions and intentions than those that have been attributed to them on the basis of experimental studies and Piagetian theory. It is presumably both the *familiarity* of these other family members and the intense emotions involved in these relationships – rivalry with a sibling, or conflict with the parents over new-found independence – that contribute to the development of this relatively sophisticated behaviour. Looking at the children in the context of family relationships that are of real emotional significance gives us an illuminating perspective on their capabilities, and some glimpse of why it is so important that they should develop such powers. It is clearly extremely adaptive to be able to 'read' and anticipate the feelings and actions of the people who share your family world – especially those with whom you compete for parental love and affection.

This emphasis on the emotion involved in such family interactions is crucially important. It is a feature that has for several years been stressed in fine-grain studies of the early mother-infant relationship (e.g. Stern, 1977), perhaps because those studying the relationship of very young infants and their mothers have often come from a psychoanalytic background. Yet in studies of the relationships of children from the second year onwards, little systematic attempt has been made by psychologists to relate developments in emotion, in social behaviour or in cognition. The work on the changes in social understanding in the second year, however, suggests that there are strikingly close connections between developments in emotional behaviour and in understanding, and that the nature of these connections deserves our close attention and rigorous thought. Paralleling the changes in social understanding are dramatic increases in the anger and distress that children show: the very exchanges in which children begin to demonstrate strikingly early the ability to 'read' the emotions and intentions of others are often those which include tantrums, self-abuse and deliberate destruction of objects (Dunn and Munn, 1985a). Changes in emotional behaviour have usually been interpreted as reflecting new stages of cognitive development: the changes in response to separation from the mother during the first year and the appearance of 'fear of strangers' are seen as reflecting developments in memory and in cognitive capacity, for instance. Yet it is highly likely that the connection between affective experience and cognitive change is more complex than this. It is quite possible, for instance, that during particular emotional states a child's attention is heightened, and his memory processes influenced – that *because* of the emotional urgency of a particular situation he is particularly likely to attend to and learn from those around him (see Zajonc, 1980). The data on changes in understanding in the second year serve to highlight the general developmental question at issue here, and provide an example where systematic research could certainly be carried out.

Children's interest in the emotional state of other family members, and their grasp of what those emotional states might be, can be illustrated in two further examples from the work on young siblings and their mothers. The first concerns children's monitoring of conflict interactions between their siblings and their mothers, during the second year. Their behaviour during such conflicts ranged from laughter, imitation, sober watching, to prohibition, punishment, comfort or support. *How* the children responded to any particular exchange depended in large measure upon the emotion expressed by the participants. Support was offered to siblings in extreme distress or anger; laughter was the most frequent response to conflicts in which the sibling had laughed. The second illustration comes from analyses of family conversations about emotions. Discussion of feeling states was relatively common between mothers and their 18–24 month old children (Dunn, Bretherton and Munn, 1985); however, individual differences between families in the frequency of such discussion were marked. In families in which mothers commented frequently on feeling states to their 18 month old children, the children six months later were themselves making more frequent explicit references to feeling states than the rest of the sample. And in families in which mothers discussed feelings and social rules in the context of family disputes, the children were, six months later, more likely to make conciliatory moves in quarrels with their siblings than children whose mothers had not discussed feelings in this way (Dunn and Munn, 1985b). That the interest young children show in the emotional state of others is reflected in their early language has been documented by Bretherton and her colleagues (Bretherton, McNew and Beeghly-Smith, 1981), and by the study of Hood and Bloom (1979) that examined the early causal statements of children. The results showed that it is *psychological* causality that is of particular salience to young children. Their first enquiries into why and how concern the behaviour of people, rather than the behaviour of the physical world.

This is evidence that supports and extends the arguments of some of those concerned with early cognitive development that many of the discrepancies and inconsistencies in the studies of very young children – involving for instance their perspective-taking abilities, or their understanding of conservation – can be explained by the extent to which the test situations employed make 'human sense' to the children. If such cognitive tasks are presented to the children in terms that have real emotional meaning for the children, they reveal capabilities not apparent in tasks that are set in more abstract terms (e.g., Donaldson, 1978 and see chapter 8, this volume). The results from the sibling studies suggest, further, that differences in the interest that mothers show in engaging their children in conversations in which feelings and intentions are discussed may well contribute to differences both in the children's verbal discussion of inner states, and in their observed behaviour.

Family relations and family rules

Studying children's developing relationships with other family members and their behaviour in the emotional context of family life gives us then a new view of their capacity to respond to the emotions and intentions of

others, and highlights the importance of taking seriously the possible role
of emotional experiences in these developments. It also shows us a
different aspect of their growing understanding of the social world in
which they grow up: the beginnings of their understanding of the shared
sanctions, practices and social rules of the family. We know very little
about the early stages of this understanding in young children. Recent
work on non-human primates has demonstrated just how important it is
for a social animal to recognize features of the relationships between other
members of the social group, and to understand the 'rules' of the group.
Recent work by Cheney and Seyfarth (1982) and by Datta (1981) shows
that non-human primates categorize others within their group not only on
the basis of kinship and dominance but also on the previous history of
alliances and support offered between particular individuals within the
group.

When do children first begin to be interested in and to understand the
'rules' of their family world? Kagan's work suggests that children during
the second year become increasingly aware of the 'standards' of the adults
in their world, and increasingly concerned if they fail to achieve these
standards (Kagan, 1981). Studies of children in school settings show that
even three and four year olds respond differently to different kinds of
rule-breaking or transgression (Pool, Schweder and Much, 1983). Schools
do, of course, involve a rather special set of 'institutional' rules, and it is
interesting but perhaps not surprising that by three or four years children
are clearly differentiating between the 'conventional' rules of the institution, and the 'moral' rules that concern hurting the feelings of others,
and so on. It is presumably within the family that the initial stages of
children's understanding of cultural rules begins, and within the emotional
context of particular family relationships that individual differences in
children's perceptions of and response to such rules begins. The evidence
for this argument is developed elsewhere (Dunn, 1985). Here I want simply
to emphasize three points from our studies of children at home. The first is
the salience for children of transgression of social rules – especially breaches
of rules of possession, rudeness, wild boisterous behaviour. Such
transgressions are a source of curiosity, shared humour and delight as well
as sometimes of distress. Children make jokes about rule violations from
18 months onwards, jokes to share with others. They appear to recognize
that the rule is shared and that its breach will be a source of interest and
often humour to others within the family.

The second point concerns the role of others in the development of this
understanding. In the English families that we studied, reference to social
rules by both mothers and siblings was frequent, and increased in frequency
as the children grew up. By 24 months the children themselves communicated explicitly about social rules. And as with the discussion of feelings,
there were systematic links between the nature of the mothers' discussion

of social rules, and individual differences in the children's behaviour six
months later.

The third point is that there appears to be a close connection between
the growth of this understanding of social rules and the quality of particular
family relationships (Dunn, 1985). Both in terms of the general pattern of
development for all children, and in terms of individual differences it is
important to consider this close connection. It appears likely that it is the
emotional urgency and significance of these family relationships that leads
children to attend to, explore and play with social rules at such an early
age, and to use their understanding of social rules as a source of pleasure
and power in their family relationships even as two year olds. We are still
very far from being able to describe with precision how emotional development and cognitive changes are linked. But it is clear where we should pay
attention if we are to make progress towards understanding the developmental processes involved in either the cognitive changes or the developments in children's relationships with their parents, siblings or peers.

Implications for studies of attachment

If children so young can take such an involved part in family life, can
reflect upon and communicate about the shared rules, practices and jokes
of their family world, then the quality of their relationships with these
other family members cannot be described simply in terms of 'attachment'
(*A*, *B* or *C*). This categorization, the classification of children's attachment to their parents derived from their behaviour in a series of separation
and reunion experiences in the laboratory, as 'avoidant', 'secure' or
'resistant', is still by far the most widely used method of assessing
children's relationships. Although, as I have noted, perspectives on socio-
emotional development have greatly broadened, it is still the case that the
great majority of studies of children's emotional relationships in the early
childhood years focus on attachment and the 'security' aspects of the
relationship between child and parent. Differences between children in the
nature of their attachments are described in almost all the work on children
between the ages of one and three in terms of the three-way classification
of their behaviour in laboratory separations.

These security aspects are without question of major importance in
children's development. The recent research on attachment has demonstrated important links between quality of mother-child attachment and
children's relations with their peers, their mastery motivation, attention
patterns in play, approach to problem-solving, and self-esteem (see
Bretherton and Waters, 1985). But it is striking that among those writing
within the attachment paradigm some have begun to stress the importance
of understanding the relation between quality of attachment and the

developments in social understanding that we have focused upon here. Bretherton (1985) has pointed out that in order to illuminate the development of the child's 'internal working model' of self and of caregiver – a crucial feature of Bowlby's attachment model – integration of attachment theory with new ideas about children's socio-cognitive development is essential. It was Bowlby's (1973) original idea that an individual's internal working models of self and caregiver developed in the context of the first attachment, and that this came to determine how adult relationships were established. But if we are to progress from using this general and rather vague metaphor towards some more precise understanding of what these 'internal working models' might be, we need research that takes a broader look at the nature of children's understanding of self and others. As Bretherton comments 'It is self-evident that the massive new findings in the area of social cognition must be taken into account in studying the development of internal working models' (Bretherton, 1985).

Individual differences and family relationships

In the remaining section of the chapter I want to consider briefly at a more general level two aspects of recent work on the developmental significance of family relationships that share this focus on the network of family relationships within which the child grows up. The first concerns a shift of emphasis on the role of parenting in the development of individual differences. In the last decade there has been a great wealth of research on the socialization of children, on the parent-child relationship, on historical, cultural and economic influences on parents and their families, on the impact of stressful events, and on continuities and discontinuities in patterns of individual development. This research is comprehensively reviewed in Hetherington's volume of the recent Mussen Handbook (Hetherington, 1983). All I shall attempt here is to highlight certain directions in this body of work that are particularly exciting, provocative or important – topics that link with the earlier emphasis on the importance of studying children's development within a network of family relationships.

How important is parental influence?

The view of most psychologists on what constitutes 'competent' or 'sensitive' parenting is, according to Maccoby and Martin (1983), beginning to be clear, and to be supported by some consistent themes in the results of the large number of studies of parents and children (admittedly within a very narrow range of cultures). However, a striking note of caution about the significance of such findings has been sounded by behaviour geneticists (Rowe and Plomin, 1981; Scarr and Grajek,

1982). They point out that studies of siblings, children who share 50 per cent of their segregating genes, and who are brought up within the same family, show that they differ on measures of personality almost as much as unrelated children brought up within quite different families. And adopted siblings, biologically unrelated children who are brought up together are quite unalike. Why should this be? It is a finding that suggests that many of the features of parental behaviour that we have assumed to be important, which are shared by the siblings, are relatively unimportant in accounting for differences in the children's personalities. What the results of the studies of twins, siblings and adopted children indicate is that 'micro-environments' *within* the family create differences rather than similarities between the children and may be one of the most important sources of environmental variation in behavioural development (Rowe and Plomin, 1981). (Clearly different experiences outside the family may also contribute to differences between siblings.)

How can growing up within the same family entail such powerfully different experiences for different children? A number of different possibilities are now being explored. The first and most obvious is that the same parents differ markedly in their behaviour towards the different children within the same family on those dimensions that matter most. Another is that other sources of influence within the family – such as the direct influence of the siblings themselves – contribute to the development of personality. One particular theory – that of sibling 'de-identification' (Schachter, Gilutz, Shore, and Adler, 1978) – holds that the very presence of a sibling drives a child to develop contrasting characteristics from those of the sibling. A third possibility is that influences outside the family that are not shared by the siblings, such as particular groups of peers, are of major importance in personality development, and a fourth is that 'accidental' events that affect one sibling but not the other, such as illnesses, do have long-term importance.

These different possibilities are spelled out in the discussion by Rowe and Plomin (1981). And from a very different perspective, Maccoby and Martin (1983), at the end of their long review of research into parental influence, emphasize how little of the variance in children's development is accounted for by studies of parent behaviour. Again the stress is upon the importance of looking at different experiences *within* the same family for different children and at the nature and influence of experiences *outside* the family for siblings. It is a point that is being noted with increasing frequency. Scarr and Grajek (1982), for instance, emphasize that what we need in order to evaluate the contributions of mother, father, siblings and peers to children's development is longitudinal study of families with more than one child. At present we have little information on the contribution of these various sources of differential influence – even on the issues of how far parents treat their different children similarly, let alone information on whether differences in parental behaviour contribute to developmental differences in the children. Research is beginning on these issues (see, for instance, Bryant and Crockenberg, 1980; Dunn, Plomin and Nettles, 1985; Dunn, Plomin and Daniels, 1985). So far the findings indicate that mothers are very consistent in their behaviour towards their successive children when they are very young – at least in the circumstances in which they have been studied – but that differential maternal treatment becomes more evident as children grow up. Bryant and Crockenberg also report that, in their study, the relative differences in certain features of the mothers' behaviour towards their daughters were systematically linked to differences in the children's behaviour. No cause-effect inferences can be drawn from this cross-sectional study, but its implications are important.

It is interesting that two large-scale studies of adolescent siblings showed that siblings perceived their parents to treat them quite similarly (Daniels and Plomin, 1985; Daniels, Dunn, Furstenberg and Plomin, 1985). In contrast, the siblings were much more likely to report large differences in their treatment of each other, and direct observations of young siblings confirms that children within the same family can and do treat each other very differently (Bühler, 1939). The interview studies of adolescent siblings also show that siblings report that their peer groups and friends are often very different from those of their siblings. It appears, therefore, that sibling and peer relationships may be likely sources of the differences between siblings. In contrast, birth order and spacing of siblings, the family structure variables that have received most attention up till now, appear to be relatively unimportant sources of sibling differences. How far stressful changes or experiences such as illness also contribute to differences in children within the same family we do not yet know; however, this issue of the effects of illness or accident on the development of individual differences is just one aspect of a much larger topic that is gaining increasing attention because of its obvious social importance. This is the impact of environmental change and stress upon individual family members and upon the family as a whole.

The impact of stress and environmental change

All children experience potentially stressful events – in our society an alarmingly high proportion have to cope before they are five years old with changes in family structure, separation or discord between parents, the acquisition of step-parents, experiences in hospital, changing child care arrangements, moving house, and so on. It is not my brief to discuss this large and important field, which is excellently reviewed in a recent book edited by Garmezy and Rutter (1983) (see also chapter 6). I want to consider just one aspect of the recent research that relates to the issues discussed earlier: the part played by family interaction in mediating the effects of stressful events. Individual differences in children's responses to stress are striking in all studies. It is clearly very important that we should understand why this should be. There is some evidence that family interaction patterns before and in response to stressful events may play an important role in the processes linking the stressful events and differences in individual outcome. Rutter (1983) reviews studies of a number of different kinds of stressful event, such as divorce, admission to hospital, birth of a sibling, and so on, and shows that family interaction patterns may well be significant in accounting for how children respond to the event. Hospital admission studies, for instance, suggest that the procedures that help children may in fact be effective through decreasing parental anxiety. Rutter also argues that the explanation for the long-lasting effects of two hospital admissions in childhood may lie in the nature of the child's experiences within the family after reunion. Persisting disturbance is more likely, for instance, if the child comes from a deprived family or if the previous parent-child relationship was poor. Studies of the effects of the birth of a sibling show that disturbance in firstborn children increases following the sibling birth, but that this disturbance is paralleled and probably contributed to by a marked increase in confrontation and difficulty between mother and firstborn, and a decrease in sensitive maternal attention to the firstborn (Dunn and Kendrick, 1982).

Clearly, changes in parent-child interaction are not the only variables of importance here. In both hospital admission and sibling birth studies the findings showed that temperamental differences between the children before the crisis event were systematically linked to the way in which individual children responded. Temperamental differences in themselves, however, are associated with differences in parent-child relationships (Stevenson-Hinde and Hinde, 1985) and there is a powerful case for taking seriously the argument that changes in family interaction patterns may play a significant part in determining which children suffer most from stressful change.

Rutter makes an important point here. He argues that the particular effects on family interaction and relationships are not necessarily the same in different situations. The question that we need to ask, he urges, is how far different kinds of events – hospital admission, birth of a sibling, death of a parent – lead to different kinds of family interaction and lead to different outcomes. Some children do appear to cope very well with particular kinds of stressful change – indeed they seem to be in some respects protected by the experience against the effects of further stressful change. Not all the consequences of stress are deleterious. After the arrival of a sibling, half the firstborn children in our Cambridge study made rapid developmental advances – and similar advances have been reported by other studies of the arrival of a sibling.

Here the studies of stressful events raise a series of important developmental questions. How does the experience of the event contribute to developmental *advance*? How far is the emotion that is experienced linked to the developmental change? It seems likely that temperamental factors are again important in accounting for individual differences – but how are family interaction patterns involved? Can particular kinds of family relationships protect children against certain kinds of stress? In adulthood, individuals are apparently protected from the effects of stressful events by close intimate relationships and by the existence of a close social network (Brown and Harris, 1978). We know little of how far this might also be true in childhood, though we do know that children in discordant homes who had one good relationship were much less likely to develop conduct disorders than those who lacked such a good relationship (Rutter, 1983).

The work on depression in adults raises another issue that may well be important in relation to children's response to stressful change: the importance of the cognitive appraisal made by an individual of a particular event. Both the interpretation that Brown and Harris (1978) offered for the link between vulnerability factors and the incidence of depression in adults, and the 'learned helplessness' model of Seligman and his colleagues suggest that the individual's own conceptualization of the cause and implications of the event, and the relation of this appraisal to the individual's sense of self-worth are crucially important. Seligman's group has proposed that the attributional style with which an individual interprets events – both good and bad – is closely linked to the probability that crises will lead to depression. Indeed some evidence has been put forward suggesting that maternal attributional style is correlated with children's attributional style, and that both are linked to the incidence of later depression in children (Seligman, Abramson, Semmel and Von Balyer, 1979; Seligman and Peterson, 1982). The processes involved here are not at all clear, and much more systematic work is needed, work that includes study of the nature of family conversations between mothers and their young children. But such work would surely be worthwhile. In the first half of the chapter we discussed how early children appear to be interested in and to reflect upon psychological causality and family interaction over conflict. It is a very big jump from these findings on the nature of the interest two year olds show in psychological causality to speculation about cognitive appraisal and response to stressful events. But given the clinical and social importance of the topic we should be imaginative in our approaches to elucidating why some children are so much more vulnerable to stress and change than others. It will be important to investigate possible links between maternal attributional style, children's reflections and sense of self-worth on the one hand, and these individual differences in response to stress.

The topic of stressful experience and family interaction cannot be left without mention of one of the most fruitful directions of current research – namely epidemiological work that is truly intergenerational. Two examples from very different backgrounds that illustrate how powerful a strategy this can be are Elder's work on the impact of the Great Depression on children (Elder and Liker, 1982, 1983), and the intergenerational study of women raised in institutions recently completed by Rutter and his colleagues (Quinton, Rutter and Liddell, 1984). Elder emphasizes the importance of processes *within* the family as the medium through which the children were affected by economic hardship, and by which the pattern of their later development was influenced. Marital discord, and irritable behaviour of father, mother or children all increased the probability of poor long-term consequences of unemployment. Rutter and his colleagues studied mothers of two year olds, who themselves had been studied as children in institutions. The results demonstrated not only the long-term effects of that early experience in the institution on the women's own parenting behaviour, but also the protective effects of an intimate relationship with a spouse, and the significance of certain kinds of adolescent experience. Their study included both a broad-based epidemiological sweep of two generations and fine-grain observations of family interaction – a combination that is particularly powerful and should surely be emulated. Intergenerational influences are further discussed in chapter 6.

Conclusions

Seeing the child as an individual developing within a family world – an emotionally charged, changing world – gives us a perspective on his or her growing social relationships that both provides new insights and highlights particularly intractable problems. The new insights are there, for instance, in the picture that we gain of the powers and capabilities that even two year olds possess: powers to anticipate the feelings and intentions of other family members, powers to recognize and transgress social rules and to understand that jokes about such transgressions can be shared with other people.

To study the child as a family member, even during infancy, adds to the picture of social development that we have gained from attachment research in several ways. It shows the child to be a social sophisticate at an age he or she was presumed to be a social incompetent: it may illuminate the nature of his or her 'internal working models', and most importantly it shows us why it is so urgent for children to understand their social world. It shows us just how adaptive it is that children by the time they are two should know how to use their understanding of their relatives and their shared family world as a resource for pleasure and power as well as for comfort and the expression of their affection and concern. It offers us insights, too, into the urgent questions of why some children appear to be so much more vulnerable than others to stressful change. And it is an essential part of the research strategy that we need to understand within-family variation and the origins of individual differences in personality.

Perhaps the most difficult challenge that this perspective presents us with concerns the connections between affective and cognitive development – a connection that cannot be ignored when you study children in their family world. The claim that emotional experiences and affective development are importantly related to developments in understanding is certainly not new; to repeat it leaves us facing the challenge of specifying the nature of that relationship. It is hardly an easy challenge to meet. However, to recognize what it means to say that children are from infancy members of a family world is at least to take a first step towards facing the challenge.

References

Belsky, J. 1979. Mother-infant interaction: a naturalistic observational study. *Developmental Psychology*, **15**, 601–7.

Bowlby, J. 1973. *Attachment and Loss Vol. 2. Separation, anxiety and anger.* New York: Basic Books.

Bronfenbrenner, U. 1974. Developmental research, public policy, and the ecology of childhood. *Child Development*, **45**, 1–5.

Bronfenbrenner, U. 1979. *The Ecology of Human Development.* Cambridge, Mass.: Harvard University Press.

Bretherton, I. 1985. Attachment theory: retrospect and prospect, in I. Bretherton and E. Waters (eds), *Growing Points in Attachment Theory and Research* Monographs of the Society in Child Development, serial No. 209.

Bretherton, I., McNew, S. and Beeghly-Smith, M. 1981. Early person knowledge as expressed in gestural and verbal communication: when do infants acquire a 'theory of mind'?, in M. E. Lamb and L. R. Sherrod (eds), *Infant Social Cognition.* Hillsdale, NJ: Erlbaum.

Brown, G. and Harris, T. 1978. *Social Origins of Depression.* London: Tavistock Press.

Bryant, B. K. and Crockenburg, S. B. 1980. Correlates and dimensions of pro-social behaviour: a study of female siblings with their mother. *Child Development*, **51**, 29–544.

Bühler, C. 1939. *The Child and His Family.* London: Harper.

Cheney, D. and Seyfarth, R. 1982. Recognition of individuals within and between free ranging groups of vervet monkeys. *American Zoologist*, **22**, 519–29.

Clarke-Stewart, K. A. 1978. And daddy makes three: the father's impact on mother and young child. *Child Development*, **49**, 466–78.

Daniels, D. and Plomin, R. 1985. Differential experience of siblings in the same family. *Developmental Psychology*, **21**, 747–760.

114   *Children of social worlds*

Daniels, D., Dunn, J., Furstenberg, F. and Plomin, R. 1985. Environmental differences within the family and adjustment differences within pairs of adolescent siblings. *Child Development*, 56, 764–774.
Datta, S. 1981. Dynamics of dominance among free-ranging rhesus females (unpublished Ph.D. dissertation, University of Cambridge).
Donaldson, M. 1978. *Children's Minds*. London: Fontana.
Dunn, J. 1985. The beginnings of moral understanding. *The Emergence of Morality*. Chicago: University of Chicago Press, in press.
Dunn, J. and Kendrick, C. 1982. *Siblings: love, envy and understanding*. Cambridge, Mass.: Harvard University Press.
Dunn, J. Bretherton, I. and Munn, P. 1985. Conversations about feeling states between mothers and their young children. Submitted for publication. *Developmental Psychology*.
Dunn, J. and Munn, P. 1985a. Becoming a family member: family conflict and the development of social understanding in the second year. *Child Development*, 56, 480–492.
Dunn, J. and Munn, P. 1985b. Sibling quarrels and maternal responses: individual differences in aggression. *Journal of Child Psychology and Psychiatry*, in press.
Dunn, J., Plomin, R. and Daniels, D. 1985. Consistency and change in mother's behavior toward two year old siblings. *Child Development*, in press.
Dunn, J., Plomin, R. and Nettles, M. 1985. Consistency of maternal behaviour toward infant siblings. *Developmental Psychology*, 21, No. 6, 1188–1195.
Elder, G. H. and Liker, J. K. 1982. Hard times in women's lives: historical influences across forty years. *American Journal of Sociology*, 88, 241–69.
Elder, G. H. and Liker, J. K. 1983. Parent-child behavior in hard times: some life-course implications (Unpublished paper, Cornell University).
Garmezy, N. and Rutter, M. 1983. *Stress, Coping and Development in Children*. New York: McGraw Hill.
Hetherington, E. M. (ed.) 1983. *Socialisation, Personality and Social Development*, Volume 4 of *Mussen's Handbook of Child Psychology*. New York: Wiley.
Hood, L. and Bloom, L. 1979. What, when and how about why: a longitudinal study of early expressions of causality. *Monographs of the Society for the Study of Child Development*, 44, no. 6.
Kagan, J. 1981. *The Second Year*. Cambridge, Mass.: Harvard University Press.
Lytton, H. 1979. Disciplinary encounters between young boys and their mothers: is there a contingency system? *Developmental Psychology*, 15, 256–68.
Maccoby, E. E. and Martin, J. A. 1983. Socialisation in the context of the family: parent-child interaction, in E. M. Hetherington (ed.), *Socialisation, Personality and Social Development*, Volume 4 of *Mussen's Handbook of Child Psychology*, New York: Wiley.
Parke, R. D. 1979. Perspectives on father-infant interaction, in J. D. Osofsky (ed.), *Handbook of Infant Development*. New York: Wiley.
Parke, R. D. and O'Leary, S. 1976. Father-mother-infant interaction in the newborn period, in K. A. Riegal and J. Heacham (eds), *The developing individual in a changing world*. Vol. 2. *Social and Environmental Issues*. The Hague: Mouton.
Pedersen, F. A., Yarrow, L. J., Anderson, B. J. and Cain, R. L. 1979. Conceptualisation of father influence in the infancy period, in M. Lewis and L. A. Rosenblum (eds), *The Child and its Family*. New York: Plenum.

Pool, D. L., Schweder, R. A. and Much, N. C. 1983. Culture as a cognitive system: differentiated rule understanding in children and other savages, in E. T. Higgins, D. N. Ruble and W. W. Hartup (eds), *Social Cognition and Social Development*. London: Cambridge University Press.

Quinton, D., Rutter, M. and Liddell, C. 1984. Institutional rearing, parental difficulties and marital support. *Psychological Medicine*, **14**, 107–24.

Radke-Yarrow, M., Zahn-Waxler, C. and Chapman, M. 1983. Children's prosocial dispositions and behavior, in E. M. Hetherington (ed.), *Socialisation, Personality and Social Development*. Volume 4 of *Mussen's Handbook of Child Psychology*. New York: Wiley.

Rowe, D. C. and Plomin, R. 1981. The importance of non-shared (El) environmental influence in behavioural development. *Developmental Psychology*, **17**, 517–31.

Rutter, M. 1983. Stress, coping and development: some issues and some questions, in N. Garmezy and M. Rutter (eds), *Stress, Coping and Development in Children*. New York: McGraw Hill.

Scarr, S. and Grajek, S. 1982. Similarities and differences among siblings, in M. E. Lamb and B. Sutton-Smith (eds), *Sibling Relationships*. Hillsdale, NJ: Erlbaum.

Schachter, F. F., Gilutz, G., Shore, E. and Adler, M. 1978. Sibling deidentification judged by mothers. *Child Development*, **49**, 543–6.

Seligman, M. E. P., Abramson, L. Y., Semmel, A. and von Balyer, C. 1979. Depressive attributional style. *Journal of Abnormal Psychology*, **88**, 242–7.

Seligman, M. E. P. and Peterson, C. 1982. A learned helplessness perspective on childhood depression: theory and research (paper presented at the Social Science Research Council conference on 'Depressive disorders: developmental perspectives', Philadelphia, 1982).

Stern, D. 1977. *The First Relationship: Infant and Mother*. Cambridge, Mass.: Harvard University Press.

Stevenson-Hinde, J. and Hinde, R. A. 1985. Changes in associations between characteristics and interactions. In R. Plomin and J. Dunn (eds), *The Study of Temperament: changes, continuities and challenges*. New York: Erlbaum, in press.

Yarrow, M. and Waxler, C. Z. 1975. The emergence and functions of prosocial behavior in young children (paper presented at the SRCD Meeting, Denver, 1975).

Zahn-Waxler, C., Radke-Yarrow, M. and King, R. A. 1979. Child rearing and children's prosocial initiations towards victims of distress. *Child Development*, **50**, 319–30.

Zajonc, R. B. 1980. Feeling and thinking: preferences need no inferences. *American Psychologist*, **35**, 151–75.

6

Evidence from three birth cohort studies for long-term and cross-generational effects on the development of children

Michael Wadsworth

Introduction

Ideas about the vital importance of childhood as an irrevocable preparation for many aspects of later life are remarkably consistent in their general view that infancy and childhood uniquely constitute a time of great receptivity, during which foundations are laid for the child's future health, intelligence, behaviour and chances in the social world. Throughout this century British parents have regarded education, for example, as a very important part of preparation for life, seeing it as an almost indispensable stepping-stone to upward social mobility and to 'getting on in the world'. Floud et al. (1956) noted that 'The 1920s saw a tremendous public demand for secondary education. This was based on a realistic appreciation of its advantage in the struggle for better jobs and social advancement.' Later, Jackson and Marsden (1962) found in their study of education that for the manual socio-economic class parent 'perhaps the commonest feeling was that education promised a kind of classless adulthood in which you could mix freely and talk with every kind of man and woman'. Not surprisingly, therefore, there has also been a very considerable post-war growth in demand for pre-school educational facilities of all kinds (Osborn, 1980), and parents say that they want their children to have the experience of nursery school or kindergarten in order to increase social experience and to prepare the child for later full-time school (Wadsworth, 1981). Parents also want their children to begin the process of education early in life because of the prevailing views that learning is easiest in childhood, and that good habits of learning inculcated then will be lasting. Expert advice in a widely available book, now in its thirteenth edition, offers a similar notion: 'It is true that the pre-school years are vitally important in influencing the intellectual growth and curiosity of a child, and that by the age of five the measure of his intelligence gives a rough estimate of his future performance' (Jolly, 1977).

Philosophers of education, too, have hoped for much, seeing it as a way of improving society: Russell, for example, wrote:

> The nursery school, if it became universal, could, in one generation, remove the profound differences in education which at present divide the classes, could produce a population all enjoying the mental and physical development which is now confined to the most fortunate and could remove the terrible deadweight of disease and stupidity and malevolence which now makes progress so difficult. (Russell, 1926)

And whilst politicians may not always have had such purely philanthropic ideas about social improvement, they too have certainly seen the education of children as a powerful means of long-term social change. From the discovery that 31 per cent of British army recruits at the turn of the century were unfit for service (Mackenzie and Matthew, 1904), and from the later German example of the need for investment in individual care for the future good of the nation (Marshall, 1965), the functions of welfare and education services have been seen not only as appropriate caring and compassionate activities for society, but also as investments in the future, and in the case of education as investments that may be manipulated, in order to change aspects of society in later years.

Thus, there is a close association between social concerns and child health and development, through parents' concern for the best possible future for their children, and through the hopes of philosophers and those who work in education, as well as politicians, to improve and to change society by effecting change in child-rearing. In this volume Jane Lewis reviews examples of such desire for social improvements and change. As a result, there is a reflection of contemporary personal and social values in notions about what is best in child-rearing, and of the relevance of childhood to later life. Hardyment's (1984) historical review of advice on child-rearing, for example, shows how early nineteenth-century ideas 'of rooting up evil, before good could be introduced; of breaking the natural will, crossing the natural inclination, and subduing pride by constant mortification' reflected the religious, social and even political climate of the time: and she observes that by the 1950s 'there were psychological justifications for fun morality – but society needed to be in the right mood to take it up. Reaction from austerity, military discipline and sudden death made parents peculiarly inclined to indulge the new generation.'

Reflections of contemporary values in current ideas about the importance of childhood that are shown by comparison across time can also be seen in cross-cultural comparisons, as well as in studies that compare parenting methods and values within a culture through the study of these in different socio-economic groups. Cross-cultural work has demonstrated the importance of the parent-child relationship as a vital channel for the interpretation and imprinting of cultural values (Erikson, 1950). And studies that compare socio-economic differences in parent-child relationships within a culture reveal the subtle means by which class identity and values are transmitted (Bernstein, 1971), as well as the ways in which class values and aspirations shape parenting practices at any one time (Miller and Swanson, 1958; Kohn, 1959), and in the way they change with the changing demands of the times (Elder, 1974).

If, however, we try to gain greater understanding of these processes by asking about the origins of a society's changes of values, we are immediately up against the difficulty that pressures for change come from very many sources, ranging from changes in the material circumstances of life to what seem to be the normal desires for intergenerational difference that may result in change (Wadsworth and Freeman, 1983). But although such complexity may be daunting, the fact that change occurs gives investigators of child development the opportunity to use the elements of change in a para-experimental form, in what has had to become a traditional fashion in such studies, since real experimentation is impossible. Animal studies have been used, for example, to investigate the long-term effects of the separation of infant from mother under various environmental circumstances (Harlow, 1961; Hinde and Spencer-Booth, 1970): twin studies are the chief source of information on genetic and environmental influences in humans. But apart from anthropological research and its use of cross-cultural comparisons, studies of social factors have to use time as the control element, and this is achieved in two ways. First, time may be used as time passing for the individual, in other words human individual development. Secondly, child development under different social circumstances can be compared by cross-generation investigations, that is by comparison of different social times; the magnitude of change experienced in most Western urban societies in recent decades gives very good opportunities for such research, particularly in Britain and the USA where many aspects of changes in child-rearing and family life have been well documented for a long time (Newson and Newson, 1973; Hareven, 1978; Walvin, 1982; Hardyment, 1984).

This chapter is concerned with both of these uses of time in the study of social factors and their association with child development, and draws its information from three British long-term follow-up studies of cohorts of children, that between them span a quarter of a century of very great social change. During this time the British population experienced great improvements in the material circumstances of life, the majority of people acquired greater purchasing power (*Social Trends*, 1984), two fundamental changes were made in the education system, and the National Health Service and many other aspects of the welfare state began. Also during this time the number of divorces in England, Wales and Scotland, for example, rose from 30,193 in 1951 to 116,000 in 1971, and to 180,000 in 1981 (*Social*

Trends, 1970; *Social Trends*, 1984). There is also evidence on a national scale of increased alcohol consumption in the widowed, separated and divorced members of the population compared with others (*Social Trends*, 1984). More recently, rates of smoking have decreased considerably, and large population sample studies show that whereas 52 per cent of men and 41 per cent of women were smokers in 1972, by 1982 the rates had fallen to 38 per cent of men and 33 per cent of women (*Social Trends*, 1984). As well as such changes as these, which are well charted, there were equally great, but much less well-recorded changes in attitudes to certain aspects of childhood such as illegitimacy, and various forms of handicap and disability (Gorer, 1955; Calder and Sheridan, 1984) although efforts to remedy this omission have begun to take place (Jowell and Airie, 1984). In fact, such a great amount of change has occurred that in the three studies described here it proves to be very hard, and sometimes impossible, to identify a specific kind of change as being solely associated with a particular generation difference. The general rise in prevalence rates of reported childhood eczema may, for example, be partially and hypothetically attributed to a number of changes, ranging from the use of agricultural chemicals to changes in public levels of knowledge about this disorder. These cohort studies, nevertheless, provide evidence of generation difference, which in turn may be investigated or acted upon as appropriate in research directed wholly towards the topic concerned.

The first of these follow-up studies began in 1946: after an initial investigation of clinical, social and economic circumstances of birth of all children born in England, Wales or Scotland in the week 3–9 March (Joint Committee, 1948), a sample was taken for follow-up. Multiple and illegitimate births were not included in the population from which the follow-up cohort was sampled, and the cohort comprises all single, legitimate births to wives of non-manual and agricultural workers, and one in four of single, legitimate births to wives of manual workers, giving a population of 5,362 children. A statistical weighting procedure is used to compensate for the effect of sampling one in four of children from manual social class homes, but no allowance can be made for the initial exclusion of illegitimate and multiple births. However, comparison of medical findings in the cohort children with those in children born in the same week, but not sampled, reveals no major differences. Comparisons have been made with census data from other months, and with other studies, in order to check prevalence rates of, for example, crime and illness. When statistical weighting is applied to 1946 cohort findings they are found to be representative of the population of their age (Atkins et al., 1981). Losses through death and emigration have occurred at an age-appropriate rate.

Contact was made with this cohort of 5,362 children at intervals of two years or less in infancy, childhood and adolescence, and at intervals of approximately five years in adult life. In childhood and in the school years data were collected by health visitors (community nurses), school nurses and teachers, and in adult life by health visitors, by self-reporting and by a team of interviewers and nurses trained by the survey staff.

The study continues still (Atkins et al., 1981) and includes a follow-up of firstborn children of the birth cohort (Wadsworth, 1981).

The second study began in 1958, and it too is a national follow-up investigation, but comprises a larger cohort of 17,000 children born during the week 3–9 March of that year. Contact was made at birth and then at ages seven, 11, 16 and 23 years; the study population at the first three contacts comprised all children who could be identified as having been born in the original study week, and thus includes subsequent immigrants. Data were obtained at each contact from four main sources, namely the children themselves, parents, schools and local authority medical staff, and thus a wide range of subject matter was ensured. This study is also still continuing and details of its methods and validity and reliability tests may be found in Fogelman (1983).

The third study began in 1970, and it follows a national population of 13,000 children born 5–11 April of that year. This study collected data when the index children were born and at ages five and ten years; like the 1958 cohort, it has followed up all children with birthdays in the study week, and therefore also includes subsequent immigrants. Data have been collected through schools and local authority medical facilities, as well as from children and parents themselves. Again, a wide range of data, including medical, social, psychological and developmental information has been collected, and full details of this information and of methods used to check the validity and reliability of the data may be found in Osborn et al. (1984): this study also continues.

It is particularly appropriate to use these three national prospective studies to look at long-term effects in their social context, since not only do they cover a very long time-span in terms both of individual development and, between them, of social time, but they have also each collected a very wide range of data, including medical, psychological, social and educational information on true population samples. They have been concerned both with the exploration of whether early life circumstances are associated with later illness and behaviour, and also with the natural history of certain illnesses and behaviour. Findings from these sources are now reviewed to give evidence of possible long-term effects, using medical, educational and psychological examples: the following three sets of examples have been chosen to represent different ways in which the transmission of effect of early life experience has been investigated in these three studies. In some instances genetic predisposition may play a part in transmission of effect, but these studies have no appropriate data to contribute to this aspect of the discussion.

a Long-term medical effects

The first medical example provides evidence of a straightforward physical effect that persists for more than 20 years. Respiratory complaints amongst children in the 1946 cohort were examined, and at age 20 years the rates of chest illness amongst those who had had serious chest illness in the first two years of life were significantly higher when compared with those who had not had this early life experience (Douglas and Waller, 1966; Colley et al., 1973; Kiernan et al., 1976).

In this instance the question of how the association of an early life event with a later adult life experience was maintained, was easily answered by examining the possible methods of transmission of effect from early to later life. It was argued that children's initial vulnerability to early life respiratory tract illness was brought about by exposure to high levels of atmospheric pollution and a combination of other factors represented by social class, and that as a result of this early life illness some degree of irrevocable damage was inflicted on children's lungs. It was concluded that scarring would have resulted, and made these individuals more vulnerable in the face of later life experience, such as smoking, that tended to increase the risk of lower respiratory illness in adult life and to exacerbate its effects. Since levels of the particular atmospheric pollutant thought to be largely responsible for this long-term effect have been greatly reduced by legislation enacted in 1956 then comparison of the three cohort studies in due course will show the importance of this factor.

A second medical example, of a quite different kind, is concerned with the early life experience of serious illness and the apparent long-term effect it had on achievement in education, occupation and on socio-economic position; this is, as Starfield and Pless (1980) observe, a relatively unexplored area. This investigation (Wadsworth, 1986), which was carried out on the 1946 cohort, found that the 821 children (15.3 per cent) who had been seriously ill whilst aged less than ten years grew up with significantly reduced chances of achievement at school, and those from low socio-economic class homes were significantly shorter than their healthy class peers. And in adult life, those who had been seriously ill as children were more likely than others to experience downward social mobility, particularly if their families of origin had been of lower socio-economic class. The extent of this long-term association was surprising, especially in the light of improvements in the medical and education services. It may he expected that such long-term damage will be less in future cohorts, partly because illness in childhood is generally nowadays less serious and disrupting than before; but if serious illness has a depressing effect on self-image and self-perception of capabilities and life chances, as some evidence from this first cohort study suggests (Douglas et al., 1968; Britten et al., 1984; Britten et al., 1986), then the long-term effect may continue to be strong for those individuals who were seriously or chronically ill in childhood. Some similar processes are suggested by Essen and Wedge (1982) in a study of continuities of social disadvantage in the 1958 cohort. Here again comparison with later cohorts born in a different social time will help to unravel the various strands of transmission of effect postulated here.

Other medical examples of long-term effects are concerned with the long-term effects of low birthweight in the 1946 study (Douglas and Gear, 1976), of smoking in pregnancy in the 1958 and 1970 studies (Butler and Goldstein, 1973; Fogelman, 1980; Rush and Callahan, 1984), of breast-feeding on later ability and attainment in the 1946 cohort (Rodgers, 1978) and in the 1970 cohort (Taylor and Wadsworth, 1984), of breast-feeding on plasma cholesterol and weight in subsequent adult life in the 1946 cohort (Marmot et al., 1980) and of obesity in childhood in the first two cohorts (Peckham et al., 1983; Braddon et al., forthcoming). This last example shows the advantage of comparison of the cohorts. Children of the 1946 cohort were born at the time of food rationing, and for some foods this continued throughout their infancy and early childhood; also at this time, as compared with the 1970s, plumpness in childhood was not generally thought to be a problem. When the 1958 cohort were children, however, considerable dietary change had occurred, and children in this second cohort are, like the children of the 1970 cohort, strikingly more prone to be overweight in comparison with the children born in 1946.

b Long-term educational effects

Educational examples provide evidence for another kind of long-term effect. This information is about parental interest in children's education, which in the first two cohorts has been found to be powerfully associated with achievement at later ages. As Douglas (1964) wrote of the 1946 cohort

> Within each social class . . . the parents who give their children the most encouragement in their school work also give them the best care in infancy. The children who are encouraged in their studies by their parents do better in each type of test, in picture intelligence as well as in those of reading, vocabulary and arithmetic.

A score of parental interest and encouragement was made in the 1946 study from data given by teachers when children were aged five years, nine years and 11 years, and on the records of the number of times each parent had visited the school to discuss their child's progress with the head teacher or the class teachers. Parental interest and encouragement, even when taken to be that assessed at the earliest age, was strongly associated with children's achievement up to school-leaving age (Douglas et al., 1968), and has been found to be equally strongly associated with reading attainment at age 26 years (Rodgers, personal communication). Similarly in the 1958 cohort study parental interest and encouragement was associated with educational success and failure at age 16 years (Essen et al., 1978; Hutchinson et al., 1979).

These data raise the notion of another kind of transmission of effect over time. This kind of effect may to a large extent be maintained by reinforcement, in that children who are especially encouraged in schoolwork by their parents achieve better results, which together with the approval and encouragement of teachers that such success brings, helps to reinforce the child's self-image and subsequent performance, and thus to raise the child's sights and ambitions in educational terms. This effect carries over substantially into the next generation; 1946 cohort members who received high parental encouragement and interest in their education were subsequently the group most likely to send their own firstborn child to some kind of pre-school kindergarten (Wadsworth, 1981), and in due course this experience enhanced their chances of getting high scores on verbal attainment tests taken at the age of eight years, that is four years after the experience of kindergarten (Wadsworth, 1981; Wadsworth, forthcoming). This generation carry over illustrates the conclusion of Douglas et al. (1968) and the reports of others referred to in the introduction that:

> Education widens the horizon for each generation and this in turn affects the level of attainment of the children, shaping their ambitions for the future. Parents who have themselves enjoyed a high standard of education see the necessity of education for the future employment of their children while others, who have failed to get the education they aimed at for themselves, try to ensure that the chances they missed would be taken up by their children.

Comparison of the British cohorts on this subject will be especially interesting, since it is arguable that parents now have a wider spectrum of views about appropriate ambitions for their children.

c Long-term effects of early life emotional disruption

This example from the 1946 cohort is concerned with evidence for long-term effects as a result of the experience of parental divorce or separation whilst the child was aged under five years, and in particular the association of the experience of a family break by this age with delinquency by age 21 years. By age 21 years a significantly higher percentage of boys convicted of an offence had experienced parental divorce or separation before they were aged five years, and this was particularly significant for those convicted of sexual and violent crimes. The very large literature on this subject suggests that, in particular, two kinds of mechanisms of trans-mission of effect from early life experience of parental separation to early adult life crime should be investigated, namely stress and stigma (Gerhardt and Wadsworth, 1984): this is in addition to subsequent economic and educational difficulties that children from divorced homes experienced in comparison with others (Wadsworth and Maclean, forthcoming), as well as possible loss of self-esteem. Stress is postulated because of the possibility that the years before five may be a time of particular vulnerability to gross emotional disturbance, and therefore a time when failure in such a dependent relationship as that with a parent would be particularly likely to have a long-term effect. Stigma, on the other hand, might also play a part, since the years when the 1946 cohort members were under five years old and in their first schools (1946/56) were also the years when books of advice for both professional child carers and for parents tended to con-clude that loss of a parent from the family home, however caused, was likely to be 'utterly destructive to the moral fibre of the child who falls its victim' (Watson, 1950; World Health Organisation, 1951). Some of the origins of such notions may be seen in chapter 2 by Jane Lewis.

Certainly the boys in families broken by divorce or separation before they were five years old were in some ways distinguishable from others in the time between the family break and their later teenage years. Closest in time to the experience of parental divorce there was evidence of a signifi-cantly greater prevalence of enuresis in these boys, not only at the ages closest to the experience itself, but also going on into the teenage years up to age 15 (Douglas, 1973). Also in these earlier years health visitors (com-munity nurses) significantly more often rated mothers of boys from divorced homes as less competent than other mothers, regardless of social class (Wadsworth, 1979). Similarly teachers significantly more often rated parents from divorced families as less interested than others in their sons' school progress, and boys from families broken in this way were signifi-cantly more often rated as poor or lazy workers at the age of eight years (Wadsworth, 1979). By the age of 11 years there is another kind of evidence of difference amongst these boys, namely a difference in auto-nomic function. There has been a considerable amount of investigation of the relationship between autonomic functioning and unsocialized behavi-our, or psychopathology. Tong and Murphy (1960) observed that 'faulty fear responsiveness to stress is at the basis of continual psychopathic instability': other studies of psychopathy and antecedent family history have noted that early emotional deprivation or disruption is a very common feature of later psychopathic behaviour (McCord and McCord, 1964). Since early emotional disruption is also known to be a feature of those who are later delinquent, and since it is known that criminal behavi-our in males can be associated with abnormal autonomic functioning (Schalling et al., 1973) it was worth investigating the data on autonomic functioning available in this study. Therefore, information on pulse rates of boys in the 1946 cohort was used to see whether the pulse rates of those with childhood experience of parental divorce were, as the previously published work would lead one to expect, lower than those of others: this was found to be so, regardless of physical fitness, and low pulse rates were associated in due course with a significantly greater likelihood of violent offending (Wadsworth, 1976). Further evidence comes from medical examinations carried out on the cohort at age 15 years. These data show that the boys who were soon to become delinquent, particularly those who were to commit sexual or violent crimes, were significantly more likely to have been given low physical maturity scores (Wadsworth, 1979). This difference may well be showing some evidence of the effects of emotional or nutritional deprivation, perhaps here expressed as failure to thrive by this group of boys in earlier years.

Even though these different sources of evidence show that delinquent boys were significantly more likely to have experienced parental divorce during their pre-school years, and that those who were most likely to be delinquent were significantly different from others in the years between this early life experience and delinquency, nevertheless there is no reason why this particular childhood experience should have such a specific outcome as delinquency in early adult life. In fact there is data from the 1946 cohort to show a range of other kinds of problems in early adult life that were associated, both for men and women, with early life experience of a family break of this kind. Prevalence rates of a number of behavioural, psychosomatic and social problems experienced in the late teenage years and up to age 26 years were found to be significantly higher. These problems include not only officially reported delinquency, but also illegitimate births to women, own divorce and separation, and admission to hospital for treatment for stomach ulcers and adult colitis in men, and for emotional disturbance in men and women (Wadsworth, 1979; Wadsworth, 1984) and reduced chances of gaining university qualifications (Wadsworth and Maclean, forthcoming). Even after allowing for the effects of home circumstances and socio-economic factors which might have mitigated or exacerbated these associations, it was clear that rates of these behaviour problems and illnesses were still significantly higher amongst those who had experienced this kind of broken home in childhood.

The argument for a long-term effect of early experience of parental divorce or separation, in the 1946 cohort, is strengthened by this range of significantly associated possible outcomes, which in itself illustrates a particularly important strength of such prospective longitudinal studies. The evidence of physical and psychological differences of this group after the experience and in the interim years, also argues for a long-term effect.

These data do not give a clear answer about transmission of effect over time. Although the differences in health visitors' and teachers' ratings could be interpreted as stigma, their effect might have been made by way of stress, by emphasizing, in a way unwelcome to a boy, his difference in home background compared with others. It is also possible that there was a chain effect, such that divorce or separation of parents in turn led to a drop in income, which was further associated with a change in opportunities, and a subsequent change in outlook, and that all of these things had the effect of changing both others' and the boy's own expectations of his chances in the world. A similar chain of events may take place within the family, and lead to a change in others' as well as self-expectations. Evidence that such chains of problems occur after childhood disadvantage, is provided from the 1958 cohort study by Essen and Wedge (1982). They examined the health, school attainment and behaviour of cohort children in one-parent families, those in particularly large families, of children in poor home circumstances and those receiving state help because of poverty. Essen and Wedge (1982) found that a constellation of adversities tended to cluster round children who had suffered such disadvantages both at ages 11 and 16 years. These children significantly more often did less well in educational attainment, had more behaviour problems, and even tended to be shorter on average than other children. These authors conclude that:

> It is not solely the low attainment levels of the disadvantaged on entering secondary school which are associated with their limited progress . . . It is their disadvantaged status itself which seems to be associated with their poor progress . . . as shown by our comparison of children born in 1946 and 1958, gradual improvement in social conditions, such as housing, results in fewer children falling into our socially disadvantaged group.

Further and more detailed comparison of the cohorts will help to show the relevance of the postulated stigmatizing action of teachers' and community nurses' attitudes, since the prevailing views of the effects of parental divorce and separation on children have changed so much during the time that these three cohort studies have taken place.

Evidence for transmission of another kind comes from the biological and psychophysiological data of the 1946 cohort, as reviewed above. They show that a high percentage of children continued to experience physical signs of emotional disturbance long after their pre-school experience of parental divorce or separation; since these signs were not significantly more common amongst children who experienced parental divorce or separation at later ages, it was reasonable to speculate that, in the pre-school years, experience of this kind of family disruption may well have a long-term effect on the child, in the sense that the risk of some kinds of late adolescent and early adult life behaviour and illness problems was considerably raised amongst children from such disrupted circumstances.

Not everyone was affected, perhaps because, as Clarke and Clarke (1984) note:

> Increasing age is associated with some stabilisation of characteristics and probably attenuates the potential for change, especially in normal circumstances. There may be several reasons for this (eg factors intrinsic to the ageing process, social pressure, forced or chosen life paths, external or self-labelling, or all in combination). But such attenuation does not necessarily imply an end to responsiveness, even at relatively late ages, especially among the disadvantaged.

Continuing work on the 1946 cohort, at age 36 years, on blood pressure, on experience of disturbing life events and on emotional illness, will show whether this group of apparently especially vulnerable children continue to experience higher rates of problems.

Discussion

This chapter on evidence for long-term effects has necessarily considered social factors and the likelihood of their considerable change over the time periods concerned. It is therefore necessary to examine now three sets of arguments or stances, often put forward in discussions about long-term effects that seem to originate in childhood; first, arguments about problems of adducing evidence for long-term effects of early life experience, secondly, arguments about the reversibility of apparent early life effects, and thirdly, arguments about constancy and change of early life effects.

Apparent long-term associations that seem to have childhood origins have, in general, been a source of controversy, not only because of problems of interpretation and reliability and validity of data, but also because they raise the question of whether childhood really can be said to constitute a particularly vulnerable time. Those who are inclined to feel that children are not especially vulnerable or susceptible argue that long-term effects are readily assumed simply because of the length of time that can elapse between early life and later circumstances, or because childhood precedes everything else. It might also be said that since the child's social world is so much simpler than it becomes in later life, then understanding possible sources of prediction is relatively easier at this early stage; which is simply to say that long-term effects may well begin at later times in life, but our chances of detecting them are made much more difficult as the child becomes adult and selects and adds experiences to those of childhood (Scarr and Weinberg, 1983). Since in these three British longitudinal studies possible long-term associations have been investigated prospectively, and findings have in some important examples provided not only strong statistical associations of experience at a particular time with supposed outcome at a later time, but in addition evidence of seeming vulnerabililty during the intervening time, this provides quite strong evidence of long-term effect. As Clarke and Clarke (1984) summarize: 'It may be concluded that the quality of the social relationships experienced during the major rearing period . . . are likely to have a critical bearing upon outcome in later life.' But this is, of course, in no way to be interpreted as evidence that long-term effects can *only* begin in childhood.

The second argument concerns the question of especial vulnerability of childhood, which is often confused with claims that childhood experience is likely to be irreversible in effect. There is evident social pressure for this argument since, as outlined in the introduction, philosophers and planners of education, teachers, politicians, physicians and parents have been inclined for a long time to think of childhood in terms said to have been used by a Jesuit teacher, as a time in which adult views, behaviour patterns and even character are moulded: these notions are exemplified in the well-known sayings 'give me the child and I will show you the man' and 'the child is father of the man'. There is, however, evidence that even very drastic childhood experiences can be reversed in effect (Clarke and Clarke, 1976), although the evidence is of the effect of intervention to achieve reversal, rather than of a reversal that may be said to have occurred spontaneously. Data from the longitudinal studies discussed here could not truly be used to demonstrate naturally occurring reversibility, because even though, for example, relatively high percentages of children from families broken by parental death, divorce or separation in early childhood did not disproportionately suffer such ill effects as stomach ulceration and admission to psychiatric hospital by their early twenties (63.5 per cent of males and 76.7 per cent of females), nevertheless we do not know enough about the first experience itself to assess relative degrees of later vulnerability in the study population. But if we believe that socialization through experience can occur throughout life then it seems logical to suggest that socialization through experience might well have the effect of reversing potential long-term damage through the reduction of vulnerability.

The third set of arguments about long-term effects has been concerned with constancy. Brim and Kagan (1980) summarize this as the traditional view 'that the experiences of the early years, which have a demonstrated contemporaneous effect, necessarily constrain the characteristics of adolescence and adulthood'. Unfortunately the greater part of the discussion of this topic has been about IQ and about personality, and has included little reference to the social context of these two measures. However, the various authors in Brim and Kagan's volume cast their intestests and concerns very widely, and the editors conclude that 'The view that emerges from this work is that humans have a capacity for change across the entire life span.' But the British birth cohort studies, as prospective long-term investigations, have not considered long-term effect solely in terms of constancy or change, but, as exemplified above, have found it more profitable to ask whether certain times in childhood constitute periods of particular vulnerability to damage which may apparently have a long-term effect, to investigate what constitutes the source of damage, whether damage happens to all children or only to some children, what forms of outcome damage may take, and when and under what circumstances the apparent long-term effect of damage may be seen. These three studies are also concerned with the question of stability or relative lack of change of behaviour in beliefs and attitudes across generations, as discussed above. For some kinds of behaviour and beliefs the time-scale of observation needs to be particularly long, in order to differentiate true generation difference or change, from the effect of early adult life assertions of difference which may be a movement away from the beliefs and attitudes of families of origin that is relatively short lived (Wadsworth and Freeman, 1983).

Each of the processes of transmission of long-term effect suggested by the data reviewed in this chapter involves social factors that operate either by affecting the individual's life circumstances and opportunities or by influencing behaviour and self-concepts. These social factors include public and professional attitudes towards divorce and separation and towards the importance of education, as well as socio-economic position of family of origin, sex, place of residence, experience of education and educational achievement. Although such variables are still sometimes referred to as 'social background indicators' it nevertheless seems evident from the work of these three studies that, both for the individuals studied and for their effects on later population characteristics, such social variables are an important and integral part of the processes that transmit and determine long-term effects.

Social factors are also associated with the determination of the type and timing of individuals' experience of some kinds of long-term effects. Brown and Harris (1978) described how an already established, but in effect currently dormant vulnerability may be triggered into a stressful outcome by the experience of a particularly disturbing event. To some extent peak ages of risk for such events may be found at certain times in the life cycle: for example, during the years of adult identity formation in late adolescence and at the time of first employment, at the average age of marriage and child-bearing, at the average times of divorce and separation and parental death, and at the times of retirement. The effect of such experiences on the individual may be determined by a very wide range of factors, including genetic predisposition and earlier life experience: those who are considered to be vulnerable, for whatever reason, may at these times experience some form of life crisis, and the form or outcome of the crisis may also be, in part, determined by social and cultural factors. Morris's (1984) argument for cultural determinants of different kinds of criminal behaviour through learned response styles is a likely explanation for the fact that the apparent long-term effect that took the form of crime in the 1946 study was predominant amongst lower socio-economic group individuals. Illness outcomes, on the other hand, are probably a combination of genetic predisposition, personality and personal experience. But even illness outcomes are bound by cultural and life cycle factors. Thus, we would anticipate that if apparent long-term vulnerability continues amongst those who in childhood experienced parental divorce or separation, the form of effect will be age, sex and social class appropriate. For example, we might expect that in women, but not so much in men, depression would be an important long-term effect whilst in the late thirties and early forties, and that in men, but probably very little in women, a higher than normal blood pressure might be found in the vulnerable at these ages. Similarly, problems with alcohol and higher than average rates of divorce and separation would also be expected amongst the vulnerable at these ages. Work is currently in hand in the 1946 study to examine these propositions.

Elsewhere, research is being carried out on the question of the processes by which social factors, such as those considered here, come to be associated with apparent physical outcomes and with illness, originally investigated in children by Meyer and Haggerty (1962). They found that children in families currently experiencing greatest psychological stress were those most likely to succumb to acute streptococcal infections. Since that time a great amount of work has been carried out on this subject amongst adults (see for example McQueen and Siegrist, 1982), and it is likely to be a valuable source of greater understanding of how social factors are associated with the development of illness.

Thus, it seems evident from the work reported in this chapter that both for the individuals studied and for their effect on later life population characteristics, social factors are an important and integral part of the processes that seem to determine and to transmit long-term effects, even across generations.

References

Atkins, E., Cherry, N. M., Douglas, J. W. B., Kiernan, K. E. and Wadsworth, M. E. J. 1981. The 1946 British birth cohort: an account of the origins, progress and results of the National Survey of Health and Development, in S. A. Mednick and A. E. Baert (eds), *Prospective Longitudinal Research: an empirical basis for the primary prevention of psychosocial disorders.* Oxford: Oxford University Press.

Bernstein, B. 1971. *Class, Codes and Control.* London: Routledge and Kegan Paul.

Braddon, F. E. M., Wadsworth, M. E. J., Colley, J. R. T. and Davies, J. M. C. Forthcoming. The natural history of obesity in a birth cohort.

Brim, O. G. and Kagan, J. 1980. *Constancy and Change in Human Development.* Cambridge, Mass.: Harvard University Press.

Britten, N., Wadsworth, M. E. J. and Fenwick, P. B. C. 1984. Stigma and early epilepsy in a national longitudinal study. *J. Epidemiology and Community Health*, **38**, 291–5.

Britten, N., Wadsworth, M. E. J. and Fenwick, P. B. C. 1986. Sources of stigma following early life epilepsy: evidence from a national birth cohort study, in S. Whitman and B. P. Hermann (eds), *The Social Dimensions of Psychopathology in Epilepsy.* Oxford: Oxford University Press.

Brown, G. W. and Harris, T. O. 1978. *Social Origins of Depression: a study of psychiatric disorder in women.* London: Tavistock Press.

Butler, N. R. and Goldstein, H. 1973. Smoking in pregnancy and subsequent child development. *British Medical Journal*, **iv**, 573–5.

Calder, A. and Sheridan, D. 1984. *Speak for Yourself: a mass observation anthology 1939–1949.* London: Cape.

Clarke, A. D. B. and Clarke, A. M. 1984. Constancy and change in the growth of human characteristics. *J. Child Psychology and Psychiatry*, **25**, 191–210.

Clarke, A. M. and Clarke, A. D. B. 1976. *Early Experience: myth and evidence.* London: Open Books.

Colley, J. R. T., Douglas, J. W. B. and Reid, D. D. 1973. Respiratory disease in young adults: influence of early childhood lower respiratory tract illness, social class, air pollution and smoking. *British Medical Journal*, **ii**, 195–8.

Douglas, J. W. B. 1964. *The Home and the School.* London: MacGibbon and Kee.

Douglas, J. W. B. 1973. Early disturbing events and later enuresis, in I. Kolvin, R. C. MacKeith and S. R. Meadow (eds), *Bladder Control and Enuresis.* London: Spastics International Medical Publishers.

Douglas, J. W. B. and Gear, R. 1976. Children of low birthweight in the 1946 national cohort. *Archives of Disease in Childhood*, **51**, 820–7.

Douglas, J. W. B., Ross, J. M. and Simpson, H. R. 1968. *All Our Future.* London: Peter Davies.

Douglas, J. W. B. and Waller, R. E. 1966. Air pollution and respiratory infection in children. *British J. Preventive and Social Medicine*, **20**, 1–8.

Elder, G. H. 1974. *Children of the Great Depression.* Chicago: University of Chicago Press.

Erikson, E. H. 1950. *Childhood and Society.* New York: W. W. Norton.

Essen, J., Fogelman, K. and Ghodsian, M. 1978. Long-term changes in the school attainment of a national sample of children. *Educational Research*, **20**, 143–51.

Essen, J. and Wedge, P. 1982. *Continuities in Childhood Disadvantage.* London: Heinemann Educational Books.

Floud, J. E., Halsey, A. H. and Martin, F. M. 1956. *Social Class and Educational Opportunity.* London: Heinemann.

Fogelman, K. 1980. Smoking in pregnancy and subsequent development of the child. *Child Care Health Development*, **6**, 233–51.

Fogelman, K. (ed.) 1983. *Growing Up in Great Britain.* London: Macmillan.

Gerhardt, U. E. and Wadsworth, M. E. J. (eds) 1984. *Stress and Stigma: explanation and the use of evidence in the sociology of crime and illness*. London: Macmillan; New York: St Martin's Press.

Gorer, G. 1955. *Exploring English Character*. London: The Cresset Press.

Hardyment, C. 1984. *Dream Babies: child care from Locke to Spock*. Oxford: Oxford University Press.

Hareven, T. K. (ed.) 1978. *Transitions: the family and the life course in historical perspective*. New York: Academic Press.

Harlow, H. F. 1961. The development of affectional patterns in infant monkeys, in B. M. Foss (ed.), *Determinants of Infant Behaviour*. Vol. 1. London: Methuen.

Hinde, R. A. and Spencer-Booth, Y. 1970. Individual differences in the responses of rhesus monkeys to a period of separation from their mothers. *J. Child Psychology and Psychiatry*, **II**, 159–76.

Hutchinson, D., Prosser, H. and Wedge, P. 1979. The prediction of educational failure. *Educational Studies*, **5**, 73–82.

Jackson, B. and Marsden, D. 1962. *Education and the Working Class*. London: Routledge and Kegan Paul.

Joint Committee. 1948. *Maternity in Great Britain*. Oxford: Oxford University Press.

Jolly, H. 1977. *Book of Child Care*. London: Sphere Books.

Jowell, R. and Airie, C. (eds) 1984. *British Social Attitudes*. Aldershot: SCPR and Gower.

Kiernan, K. E., Colley, J. R. T., Douglas, J. W. B. and Reid, D. D. 1976. Chronic cough in young adults in relation to smoking habits, childhood environment and chest illness. *Respiration*, **33**, 236–44.

Kohn, M. 1959. Social class and parental values. *American Journal of Sociology*, **64**, 337–51.

Mackenzie, W. L. and Matthew, E. 1904. *The Medical Inspection of School Children*. Edinburgh and Glasgow: William Hodge.

Marmot, M. G., Page, C. M., Atkins, E. and Douglas, J. W. B. 1980. Effect of breast-feeding on plasma cholesterol and weight in young adults. *J. Epidemiology and Community Health*, **34**, 164–7.

Marshall, T. H. 1965. *Social Policy*. London: Hutchinson University Library.

McCord, W. and McCord, J. 1964. *The Psychopath*. Princeton: Van Nostrand.

McQueen, D. V. and Siegrist, J. 1982. Social factors in the etiology of chronic disease: an overview. *Social Science and Medicine*, **16**, 353–67.

Meyer, R. J. and Haggerty, R. J. 1962. Streptococcal infections in families: factors altering individual susceptibility. *Pediatrics*, **29**, 539–42.

Miller, D. and Swanson, G. E. 1958. *The Changing American Parent*. New York: John Wiley.

Morris, T. P. 1984. Social causes of deviant behaviour, in U. Gerhardt and M. E. J. Wadsworth (eds), *Stress and Stigma: explanation and the use of evidence in the sociology of crime and illness*. London: Macmillan; New York: St Martin's Press.

Newson, J. and Newson, E. 1973. Cultural aspects of childrearing in the English-speaking world, in M. P. M. Richards (ed.), *The Integration of a Child into a Social World*. Cambridge: Cambridge University Press.

Osborn, A. F. 1980. Under fives in school in England and Wales 1971–9. *Educational Research*, **23**, 96–103.

Osborn, A. F., Butler, N. R. and Morris, T. C. 1984. *The Social Life of Britain's Five Year Olds*. London: Routledge and Kegan Paul.

Peckham, C. S., Stark, O., Simonite, V. and Wolff, O. H. 1983. Prevalence of obesity in British children born in 1946 and 1958. *British Medical Journal*, **286**, 1237–42.

Rodgers, B. 1978. Feeding in infancy and later ability and attainment. *Developmental Medicine and Child Neurology*, **20**, 421–6.

Rush, D. and Callahan, K. R. 1984. Maternal smoking and subsequent child development, in N. R. Butler and B. D. Corner (eds), *Stress and Disability in Childhood: the longterm problems*. Bristol: John Wright.

Russell, B. 1926. *On Education, Especially in Early Childhood*. London: George Allen and Unwin.

Scarr, S. and Weinberg, R. A. 1983. The Minnesota adoption studies: genetic differences and malleability. *Child Development*, **54**, 260–7.

Schalling, D., Lidberg, L., Levander, S. E. and Dahlin, Y. 1973. Spontaneous autonomic activity as related to psychopathy. *Biological Psychology*, **1**, 83–97.

Social Trends. 1970. No. 1. London: HMSO.

Social Trends. 1984. No. 14. London: HMSO.

Starfield, B. and Pless, I. B. 1980. in O. G. Brim and J. Kagan (eds), *Constancy and Change in Human Development*. Cambridge, Mass.: Harvard University Press.

Taylor, B. and Wadsworth, J. 1984. Breast feeding and child development at five years. *Developmental Medicine and Child Neurology*, **26**, 73–80.

Taylor, B., Wadsworth, J., Wadsworth, M. E. J. and Peckham, C. 1984. Changes in the reported prevalence of childhood eczema since the 1939–45 War. *Lancet*, **ii**, 1255–7.

Tong, J. E. and Murphy, I. C. 1960. A review of stress reactivity research in relation to psychopathology and psychopathic behaviour disorders. *J. Mental Science*, **106**, 1273–95.

Wadsworth, M. E. J. 1976. Delinquency, pulse rates and early emotional deprivation. *British Journal of Criminology*, **16**, 254–6.

Wadsworth, M. E. J. 1979. *Roots of Delinquency: infancy, adolescence and crime*. Oxford: Martin Robertson; New York: Barnes and Noble.

Wadsworth, M. E. J. 1981. Social class and generation differences in pre-school education. *British Journal of Sociology*, **32**, 560–82.

Wadsworth, M. E. J. 1984. Early stress and associations with adult health, behaviour and parenting, in N. R. Butler and B. D. Corner (eds), *Stress and Disability in Childhood*. Bristol: John Wright.

Wadsworth, M. E. J. 1986. Serious illness in childhood and its associations with later life achievements, in R. Wilkinson (ed.) *Generating Inequalities*. London: Tavistock.

Wadsworth, M. E. J. Forthcoming. Effects of parenting style and preschool experience on children's verbal attainment. *Early Childhood Research Quarterly*.

Wadsworth, M. E. J. and Freeman, S. R. 1983. Generation differences in beliefs: a study of stability and change in religious beliefs. *British Journal of Sociology*, **34**, 416–37.

Wadsworth, M. E. J. and Maclean, M. Forthcoming. Parents divorce and children's life chances. *Children and Youth Services Review.*

Walvin, J. 1982. *A Child's World: a social history of English childhood 1800–1914.* London: Penguin Books.

Watson, J. D. 1950. *The Child and the Magistrate.* London: Cape.

World Health Organisation. 1951. *Expert Committee on Mental Health: report on the Second Session.* Geneva: WHO.

7

Gender development

Chris Henshall and Jacqueline McGuire

So much has been written about gender development in recent years that it is difficult to know what to include in this chapter. What follows is certainly not a comprehensive review. Rather, we have attempted to identify and discuss what appear to us to be some of the main themes in all this work.

We shall start with a discussion of gender-differences in behaviour. Here we shall identify some of the assumptions that underly the conceptualization and study of gender-differences and the problems which arise from them. We shall then discuss work on the role of cognitive factors. There appears to be no doubt that children are learning about gender very early in life, but the nature of this knowledge and the relationship between their knowledge and behaviour remain uncertain. We shall conclude the chapter with a discussion of research on the importance of parents for children's gender development.

We have tended to concentrate throughout upon the pre-school and early school years, partly because this is where our own research interests lie and partly because this is where the majority of research has been undertaken. Whether or not these years are more influential than others in the development of gender is difficult to say; other periods have received relatively little attention, and there have been few longitudinal studies. We do not, therefore, wish to imply that the early years are necessarily the most important.

Before we begin, it is important to define what we mean by gender since the terms used in this area are often taken to be indicative of a particular theoretical orientation. We shall use the term sex to refer to the biological distinctions between males and females and the term gender to refer to all aspects of being male and female that are not *directly* related to this biological division. Thus, cognitive and behavioural differences between males and females will be referred to as gender-differences. This is not meant to imply anything about the extent to which such differences can be attributed to biological or environmental factors, but simply that they do not arise directly from biological differences.

Gender is clearly related to sex, but sex does not determine gender. Transexuality shows that it is possible for an individual of one sex to live as one of the other gender. Moreover, differences between cultures in the definitions of the male and female gender show that there is more associated with being male or female in a particular culture than is determined directly by biological sex (Oakley, 1972).

Males and females tend to dress and behave differently, to do different work, to have different status and to take different responsibilities within the family. The term gender-role is generally used to refer to the constellation of behaviour and attitudes that is typical of a particular gender in a particular culture. Gender-role stereotypes refer to the beliefs that people in a particular culture hold about the behaviour and attitudes typical of, and appropriate for, males and females. As Maccoby and Jacklin (1975) have shown, these beliefs do not always correspond to the gender-differences that may actually exist, so it is important to distinguish between them.

Since gender varies between cultures, it is important to emphasize that in the discussion which follows we are considering only development in North American and Western European cultures. What happens elsewhere may well be different. Indeed, what happens within even this limited group of cultures may vary considerably; for example, one suspects that gender differs considerably between Italy and California. An examination of variations within Western cultures might provide valuable information about the cultural specificity of our conceptions of gender development, but little research appears to have been attempted in this area.

Gender-differences in behaviour

Gender-differences have been studied extensively in the behaviour of both adults and children. Frequently, however, psychologists interested in gender-differences are also interested in *why* there might be such differences and for this reason there has been particular interest in the behaviour of newborn and young infants. The assumption underlying much of this research, and many discussions of it, is that if gender-differences in behaviour were to be demonstrated in the early months of life this would indicate that they were the result of biological factors and this would in turn indicate that biological factors were mainly responsible for gender-differences in subsequent behaviour.

It is not difficult to see that this assumption involves at least three fallacies. First, if, as recent research suggests, adults behave differently towards males and females from birth onwards, gender-differences in any but the literally newborn cannot be assumed to be innate. Secondly, differences even in neonatal behaviour cannot simply be ascribed to 'biological' factors; environmental factors, albeit mediated by biological mechanisms, play a part from before birth. Thirdly, as various writers on this topic have argued (Archer 1980; Birns 1976; Maccoby and Jacklin 1975), even if there were gender-differences in infancy, such differences would not in themselves necessarily account for subsequent differences. Dunn (1979) has shown that continuity in behavioural characteristics even within infancy is far from established. Indeed, a consideration of the nature of neonatal and early infant behaviour suggests that simple, direct continuities cannot be expected. With the exception of a few characteristics such as the level of gross motor activity, most child and adult behaviour does not have clear and direct antecedents in early infancy. In which newborn behaviour, for example, should we seek a gender-difference in order to 'explain' a gender-difference in adults' levels of aggressive behaviour?

These problems with the study of infancy have forced those wishing to argue the importance of biological factors in gender-differences to rely heavily on studies of slightly older children whose behaviour can be more directly related to adult behaviour. Despite the obvious possibility that the environment may have played a considerable part in the development of the behaviour of children of pre-school age, it frequently seems to be assumed that children of this age are *relatively* unaffected by their social environment and that, if consistent gender-differences are found, then this is evidence of the importance of biological factors. We shall argue at the end of this section that this position is, in fact, untenable both in the light of research on the general social functioning of pre-school children and in the light of the research on gender-differences themselves. First, however, we shall make some more general points about the study of gender-differences in behaviour. Many of these points have been made elsewhere but they bear repeating.

Most psychological research includes males and females and many studies look for a gender-difference in what they have studied simply because it is another variable to investigate and not because they wish to test any specific hypothesis about why there might be a difference. Indeed, some psychological journals even make an analysis of gender-differences a condition of acceptance of a paper. In addition, psychologists often tend to regard statistically significant effects as interesting results worth reporting and non-significant effects as 'non-results' not worth reporting. The result may well be that gender-differences appear to be more pervasive and consistent than the results of the relevant research would actually show were it available.

There is also a tendency amongst researchers, reviewers and readers alike to confuse statistical significance with relevance or importance. That a difference is statistically significant does not, in itself, tell us the extent of the difference, nor its significance for our understanding of human behaviour. Many statistically significant gender-differences in fact represent only small differences between males' and females' behaviour. The distribution of males' and females' behaviour may overlap considerably, and most males and females may fall within a common range.

The results of those studies which do report the presence or absence of a significant gender-difference are frequently contradictory. This makes it possible for reviewers to reach almost any conclusions they may wish to about the extent and origins of gender-differences by selective use of the available evidence. Hutt's (1972) widely read book has been strongly criticized on these grounds, as has the work of Garai and Scheinfeld (1968) and Bardwick (1971) by Birns (1976).

Clearly, any serious review must attempt to include all the relevant studies available. This, however, presents the problems of how to deal with discrepant results. The solution adopted by many reviewers, unfortunately including Maccoby and Jacklin (1975) who have attempted by far the most ambitious and widespread review to date, is a sort of 'league table' approach whereby the number of studies finding a difference is compared with the number not finding a difference to decide whether there 'really' is a difference in a particular behaviour.

As Block (1976) has argued, some consideration of the quality of the evidence being compared is essential. Some studies employ more relevant measures than others of the behaviour concerned. Some studies use larger samples than others and are thus more able to decide whether a difference of a certain extent is or is not likely to be due to random variations. Moreover, there is also the very real possibility of bias within studies. Psychologists who study gender-differences frequently do so because they have strong views about their extent and origins in much the same way as psychologists who study IQ frequently have strong views about the origins of differences in IQ. In the case of IQ Kamin (1974) and others have shown how, by careful choice of what to study, of how to study it, of which results to report and which to omit, and of how to analyse and interpret these results, psychologists are generally able to conclude what they would like to conclude about differences in IQ. It seems likely that similar factors are involved in studies of gender-differences. Moreover, many studies of gender-differences in behaviour involve the use of human observers which introduces another source of bias since it is difficult to make observers blind to the sex of the subjects.

The work of Kamin has demonstrated what 'radical' psychologists have argued for some time, namely that the conclusions of psychological studies cannot be taken as neutral, scientific 'facts' existing in some kind of vacuum within the social and political world in which we live. Indeed, it is highly questionable whether even the raw data produced by psychologists represent neutral 'facts'. Kamin has also shown, however, that careful examination of the raw data and of the way in which it was collected, and comparison of the data from different studies can give us useful insights into topics addressed by those studies as well as an indication of the integrity and scientific rigour of the investigators. Unfortunately, it is this careful examination of the data that is missing in the 'league table' approach to reviewing gender-differences. The conclusions of studies are taken at face value, little attention is paid to the actual data reported and little attempt is made to understand *why* the findings of studies may differ.

We would like to argue that attention to variations between studies can lead to some very interesting discoveries about the nature, extent and even the origins of gender-differences in behaviour. Most reviews of gender-differences, however, ignore this because they set out to determine whether there 'really' is a gender-difference in a particular behaviour. This approach is misleading for two reasons. First, as we have seen, it tends to focus attention away from the question of the extent and importance of the gender-difference. Secondly, it presupposes that the behaviour can be isolated from the context in which it is observed or measured, or that contextual effects are relatively unimportant. We shall illustrate how misleading it can be to ignore the effect of context and the question of the extent of differences by looking at studies of gender-differences in pre-school children's aggressive behaviour and their use of toys.

Almost all observational studies of pre-school children's use of toys during free-play report gender-differences and all reviewers appear to agree that this is an aspect of behaviour in which gender-differences have been clearly established. This apparent consensus, however, masks three important features of children's use of toys.

First, while all these studies report gender-differences in toy use, a detailed examination of these reports reveals that gender-differences in toy use vary between these studies. It is not, of course, surprising that the nature of the group of children observed and the environment in which they are observed may affect the pattern of toy use observed, but it is interesting to note that these factors affect the pattern of *gender-differences* observed as well as the groups' overall use of particular toys.

The second important feature of children's use of toys is that many toys are used equally by boys and girls. This is not usually apparent in the literature, however, because some studies observe children's use of only a few toys chosen in advance as those most likely to show a gender-difference, and of those studies that do observe children's use of all the available toys, many report data only for the toys in which there was a significant gender-difference in use. In a large American study, however, Fagot (1977) found that play with toys used more by their own gender accounted for less than half the time that children spent playing with toys in general (although it takes some detective work to arrive at this figure from the data reported). In an earlier British study, Clark et al. (1969) found that play with such toys accounted for less than a fifth of the time children spent playing with toys. Thus, whilst gender-differences in toy use are reported in all studies, children actually spend most of their time playing with toys which are not gender-differentiated.

The third important feature of children's toy use is that gender-*differences* are not necessarily gender-*preferences*, although many reports state or imply that they are. This point is illustrated nicely by Clark et al.'s (1969) data which show that, whilst boys used building blocks significantly more than girls and girls used dolls significantly more than boys, girls used blocks more than three times as much as dolls.

A detailed examination of aggressive behaviour also reveals that important information may at first sight be obscured by the general conclusion that there is a gender-difference in pre-school children's levels of aggressive behaviour. Whilst most observational studies report a significant gender difference, two carefully conducted studies (Blurton Jones 1972; Smith and Connolly 1972) do not, and the ratio between boys' and girls' mean rates of aggressive behaviour varies from 1.4:1 to 6:1 between the remaining studies. These variations are presumably the result of variations in the measures used, the groups of children observed and the environments in which they are observed.

As far as measures of aggressive behaviour are concerned, there are many variations between studies in the observational methods and sampling techniques employed, each of which may produce different distortions. A more obvious source of variation, however, is the differences between the definitions of aggressive behaviour. Some include only direct physical aggression, whilst others include verbal insults, assertive or dominant behaviour. Grabbing toys without physical injury may or may not be included, and it is possible that rough-and-tumble play may be included as aggression in studies in which these are not carefully distinguished.

There is also the problem of the relationship between aggression and the behaviour from which it is deduced. Blurton Jones and Konner (1973) found that boys showed significantly more 'agonistic' behaviour than girls, but that boys also interacted with other children more than girls so that there was no significant difference in the *proportion* of children's interactions which was 'agonistic'. These considerations highlight the problems of defining exactly what we mean by aggression. Until we have some agreement about what is meant by aggression it is clearly not very easy, or for that matter meaningful, to try to decide whether boys are more aggressive than girls.

Variations in measures of aggression make comparison between the behaviour of children observed in different groups very difficult. Some studies, however, have included more than one group of children and can therefore provide some indication of the extent to which aggressive behaviour may vary between different groups of children in different environments. Gribbin (1979) found a twenty-fold variation in the incidence of aggressive behaviour between the two groups she studied and Smith and Green (1975) found a ten-fold variation between the 15 day nurseries, nursery schools and play groups which they observed. These differences between groups are considerably greater than those typically found between boys and girls within groups.

The extent to which these variations are due to the characteristics of the groups of children involved, and the extent to which they are due to the nature of the environment in which they were observed is difficult to determine since these factors are confounded in these naturalistic studies. Experimental studies suggest that the amount of space and play equipment available is likely to have only small effects, if any, upon the levels of aggressive behaviour observed. There are strong indications, however, from a variety of studies (Gribbin 1979; Reuter and Yunik 1973; Patterson et al., 1967; Smith and Connolly 1980) that variations in the attitudes and behaviour of the adults in charge of the group are related to the levels of aggressive behaviour observed. The extent of group differences in aggressive behaviour independent of differences in the observational environment is still more difficult to assess. Such differences appear quite plausible, however, since different types of pre-school institutions tend to draw their children from different backgrounds and to use different intake criteria.

Another interesting source of variation between groups of children may be the presence or absence of unusually aggressive children in each group. Such children may affect mean levels of aggressive behaviour in a group in two ways. First, their aggressive behaviour may elicit such behaviour in other children. And secondly, whether or not such children affect the behaviour of other children in the group, their behaviour will itself inflate the mean level of aggressive behaviour for the group. If such children are generally boys, then it is possible that their behaviour may be largely responsible for differences in boys' and girls' mean rates of aggressive behaviour, and variations in gender-differences between studies may be the result of variations in the number of such boys in the groups observed.

Several indications from existing studies support this idea. Blurton Jones and Konner (1973) found a bi-modal distribution in their measure of aggression for boys in their London sample. This sample was relatively small, but Blurton Jones (1972) found a similar effect in another, slightly larger sample, and he refers to a similar effect in a third study. DiPietro (1981) reports a similar effect in the distribution of rates of 'rough-and-tumble' play; six boys showed rates well beyond the range of scores of the remaining 46 boys and girls in the sample.

If group gender-differences in aggression and perhaps other kinds of behaviour are indeed the result of the behaviour of a minority of children, then it is clearly misleading to generalize from group gender-differences to the behaviour of 'typical' boys and girls; it may well not be true that boys typically show higher levels of aggressive behaviour than girls. And when we attempt to *explain* gender-differences, it may well be that we should be attempting to explain what leads a *minority* of children of one gender to behave in a way atypical of most children of both genders, rather than trying to explain what may lead most boys to behave differently from most girls.

We have discussed studies of pre-school children's aggressive behaviour and toy use at some length because we feel that there are important lessons to be learned from these studies, not only about children's use of toys and aggressive behaviour but also about the ways gender-differences are conceived, studied and discussed. Careful examination of the available data reveals that, even in areas where gender-differences in behaviour are considered by many to be clearly and unambiguously demonstrated, the actual differences between boys' and girls' behaviour are often relatively small and seem to depend upon the characteristics of the group observed and the environment in which they are observed. We are thus unlikely to be in a position to understand the origins and importance of a gender-difference until we understand the origins of the behaviour itself and the reasons why levels vary between groups and environments.

Unfortunately, most studies and discussions of gender-differences do not concern themselves with such matters; the problem addressed is simply whether there is or is not a gender-difference in a particular behaviour. This provides an interesting insight into the implicit model of development and socialization that informs this work, a model in which the environment is seen as an essentially one-dimensional phenomenon varying only in the degree of normalizing pressure it may exert, and in which socialization is seen as the progression from a neutral, asocial starting-point in infancy to the finished product of the adult successfully fulfilling his or her pre-ordained role in the social structure. As Martin Richards argued in *The Integration of the Child into the Social World* (Richards, 1974), this concept of socialization ignores the major part of what that term would normally imply, namely the process of becoming a social being, concerning itself rather with the issue of why people become social beings of one particular sort or another, be they delinquents or honest citizens, male role-players or female role-players, etc. To argue that the concept of socialization needs to be broadened to include all those processes involved in becoming a social being of whatever sort, is not to argue that the process by which individuals or groups of individuals become different sorts of beings is unimportant. It is to argue, however, that the latter processes can only really be understood in the context of the former, and that until this is accepted, studies of gender-differences undertaken and discussed in isolation from more general work on social development are unlikely to make a useful contribution to our understanding of gender development.

Work such as that discussed by Judy Dunn and by Paul Light in this volume shows that pre-school children have a more sophisticated awareness of, and sensitivity to, their social environment than many developmental psychologists would have dreamed of twenty or even ten years ago. It is clear that children's behaviour is dependent upon their interpretations of the intentions and expectations of those around them from a very early age and certainly from before the time when they are observed by psychologists in nursery schools and play groups. We mentioned at the beginning of this section that many studies of gender-differences in behaviour appear to have focused on pre-school children because of an underlying assumption that children of this age are relatively unaffected by the processes of socialization (in the narrow sense). It is now clear, however, that even at this age children are highly socialized in so far as they are able to function with considerable sophistication within their social environment and show considerable sensitivity to its demands. It is thus no longer possible to assume that their behaviour reflects some sort of 'natural' or 'biological' basis of human behaviour. Even young children's behaviour reflects their perception of the social environment in which they are operating, and until we try to understand what these perceptions are, how they develop and how they interact with the behavioural repetoire which children develop we are unlikely to make much sense of the gender-differences we may observe in children's behaviour.

Cognitive factors

The first attempt to consider the importance of children's perception of their environment in gender development was made by Kohlberg (1966). His paper has been very influential, generating a considerable body of empirical work but surprisingly little theoretical discussion. Kohlberg's position is probably best understood as part of the American 'discovery' of Piaget; it is an explicit attempt to break away from social learning theory and psychoanalytic theory that had dominated work on gender development until then.

Social learning theory relies upon the concepts of identification and modelling to 'explain' the development of gender-stereotyped attitudes and behaviour. Kohlberg argues, however, that children's identification with and modelling of adults and children of the same gender requires that they understand that the social world is divided into two genders and that they belong to one of them. Kohlberg proposes that this understanding is the result of children themselves structuring and making sense of their own experience.

This aspect of Kohlberg's theory has stimulated a large number of studies that have shown that children as young as two years of age can sort pictures of people into boys and girls or mummies and daddies, and can correctly identify themselves as a boy or a girl. It has also been shown that children of this age are aware of differences in the behaviour of adults and children of each gender. Moreover, boys and girls seem to be equally aware of the behaviour typical of each gender, and this strongly suggests that such knowledge is indeed based upon children's observations of the social world rather than deriving from their awareness of the behaviour which they are modelling from same-sex children and adults.

Whilst work on children's awareness of gender and gender-roles has tended to emphasize the sophistication of pre-school children's understanding, other aspects of Kohlberg's theory and the work which they have generated have tended to emphasize the pre-schooler's incompetence. This is largely a result of the emphasis upon pre-operational thought processes which Kohlberg puts forward both as an alternative explanation to psychoanalytic explanations of children's apparently bizarre beliefs about sex and gender and as an explanation for young children's adoption of the gender-stereotyped attitudes and behaviour which they are able to observe around them.

Psychoanalytic theory proposes that children become aware of genital sex-differences very early in life but that this discovery leads boys to believe that they may lose their penis or be castrated and leads girls to believe that they may be given a penis or that they were castrated in infancy. These beliefs and anxieties are thought to affect children's subsequent relationships with their parents and to lead boys to adopt the behaviour and attitudes of their father in particular and males in general and girls to adopt feminine behaviour. Kohlberg argues, however, that children's apparent beliefs that genital form may change and that boys might grow up into women or girls into men result from the inability of the pre-operational child to understand the constancy of underlying concepts such as sex and gender rather than from anxiety or wish-fulfilment. Pre-operational children's inability to understand sex and gender is likened to their supposed inability to understand the underlying constancy of concepts such as number or length as demonstrated in Piaget's conservation tasks. Not until the concrete operational stage is reached are children thought to understand that gender is constant and thus understand the significance of genital form in the definition of gender.

Following Kohlberg's paper, there have been many studies of children's ability to understand the constancy of gender. Many of these studies have used a technique developed by De Vries (1969) in which a child or a picture of a child is physically transformed in front of the child being tested, for example by superimposing the image of a dress over a figure in shorts. The child is then asked whether the figure is a girl or still a boy.

De Vries deliberately attempted to make her tests as similar as possible to Piaget's conservation tasks. As Paul Light's chapter (chapter 8) in this volume shows, however, it is extremely difficult to decide what children's reponses in tests of this kind can tell us about what they think. Indeed, it is highly debatable whether what children 'really' think can ever be isolated from the social context in which it is being assessed. The investigation of gender constancy highlights these problems.

Most studies of gender constancy use pictures. The gender of a figure in a picture, however, can be determined by no means other than its physical appearance and children may well assume that it is this relationship between image and referent which is being addressed in the tests. Other studies have investigated children's understanding of gender constancy by asking them direct questions without accompanying visual material. These studies typically find that children of four or five years of age tend to give 'correct' answers to such questions whereas they typically 'fail' Piagetian-style tests. It would be naïve, however, to assume that purely verbal tests provide any truer assessment than Piagetian tests of children's understanding. As Paul Light (chapter 8) argues, children's responses will reflect their interpretation of what it is the experimenter is asking and this depends upon much more than what is actually said. The importance of verbal context is illustrated by a review of these studies by one of the present authors (Henshall, 1983a, 1983c) which notes that children's responses appear to be related to the wording of the questions employed.

The biggest problem with all this work on gender constancy, however, is the failure of those devising the tests to think clearly about the nature of gender and the meaning of gender constancy. The relationship between anatomical sex, outward appearance and gender is actually very complex as a moment's thought about transexuality will show. A transexual may live and be accepted in society as someone of the gender opposite to their anatomical sex by consistent adoption of the behaviour and appearance of that gender. Whilst pre-school children may not be aware of transexuality, they may well be sufficiently aware of the subtleties involved in the definition of gender to want to know whether the change of appearance being referred to in a test is temporary or permanent and to want to know whether the judgement being sought is that which would be made by someone familiar or someone unfamiliar with the person whose appearance has been transformed. If a stranger were to come across a small boy in a dress they would be very likely to take him for a girl, and if a boy consistently wore dresses and showed typically feminine behaviour his gender might well come into question if only by the psychologists to whom he would probably be referred.

Compared with children's understanding of gender constancy, their understanding of genital differences might appear to be relatively simple to investigate. Kohlberg, as we have seen, proposes not only that children under about six years of age do not understand that genital form is consistently related to gender and can generally be used to determine a person's gender, but also that they are *unable* to understand this. This proposal will probably seem absurd to anyone who has given their children the opportunity to learn about genital sex-differences. It has received little criticism from developmental psychologists, however, even though, as one of the present authors has argued (Henshall, 1983a, 1983b, 1983c; in preparation), there is really no evidence to support it.

Studies of children's understanding of genital differences present two basic problems to anyone attempting to discover from them what children of a particular age are *able* to understand. The first concerns the validity of the methods used to assess children's understanding and the second concerns the process of deducing what children *can* understand from what they *do* understand.

As far as validity is concerned, some tests which have been used introduce apparently bizarre confusions. For example, Thompson and Bentler (1971) showed children a series of dolls embodying all possible combinations (that is mathematically possible, not biologically possible) of gender-typical hair styles, sex-differences in genital form and sex-differences in breast formation and body-build. Children's choices of clothes for these dolls were then assumed to indicate their judgements of gender. It is far from clear what this indirect measure of children's perceptions of these bizarre dolls can tell us about their understanding of the relationship between gender and genital form in normal people. Nevertheless, this study is often quoted to show that small children do not understand genital differences.

Even when simple tests are used, there is always the possibility that children may deliberately conceal from the examiner what they know about this sensitive topic. Conn and Kanner (1947), in an early study, report that many children were extremely reluctant to reveal what they knew and it is difficult to believe that this was not also an important factor in a study by Levin et al. (1972) in which 48 per cent of seven year olds apparently made two or more errors in identifying the gender of figures in pictures from the form of their genitalia. It is probably significant that children in this study were tested by medical students whilst attending a hospital out-patients' clinic; this situation is hardly likely to have put children at ease.

When it comes to deducing what children are *capable* of understanding it is clearly essential to know what opportunities they have had to learn. Most studies of children's understanding of genital differences have not actually addressed this, but Conn and Kanner, whose study is one of those cited by Kohlberg, found that those children of four and five years of age in their sample who had had the opportunity to learn about genital differences generally appeared to understand them.

A more recent study by one of the present authors of a group of predominantly upper-middle-class children, many of whom had had frequent opportunities to observe genital differences, found that 80 per cent of four year olds could reliably decide gender by genital form and understood that boys could not have the female form and vice versa (Henshall, 1983a,

1983c; in preparation). In this study the experimenter spent several weeks at the nursery with the children to allow them to become familiar with him and this potentially sensitive topic was only tested after the children had become accustomed to the test situation in the course of a series of other tests and 'games'. Even in these conditions, however, only 30 per cent of the children aged between two-and-a-half and four years could reliably decide gender by genital form. Whilst the exact degree of opportunity that these children had had to learn about genital differences at home was not investigated, boys and girls shared the same open-plan toilets in the nursery in which they were tested. This suggests that children of two or three years of age may not be sure about the systematic nature of genital differences even when they do have the opportunity to observe them, and a more detailed investigation of very young children's understanding in relation to the exact nature of their experience would clearly be interesting. It would appear, however, that most four and five year olds are well able to understand genital differences and their relation to gender.

As we mentioned earlier, Kohlberg's proposal that four and five year olds cannot understand genital differences or the constancy of gender plays an important part in his account of the development of gender-stereotyped attitudes and behaviour. He proposes that children adopt stereotyped attitudes and behaviour at this age for two reasons. First, the egocentric view of the world that Piaget claims to be characteristic of children of this age leads them to prefer indiscriminately all those things that they have learned to be associated with the self. In this way, the construct of egocentrism is used to 'explain' why children adopt the behaviour and attitudes which they have observed to be typical of their gender. Secondly, Kohlberg proposes that children's uncertainty about the constancy of gender and its genital basis leads them to adopt rigidly all gender-stereotyped attitudes and behaviour in an attempt to maintain a stable self-identity.

The concept of egocentrism has recently been extensively criticized. As far as Kohlberg's specific proposal about egocentrism is concerned, clear evidence against it can be found in work with children on both race and gender. Studies of children's racial awareness and attitudes have shown that children under six or seven years of age from black minority groups in Western societies frequently devalue themselves, their colour and their race in favour of the white majority (Milner, 1975). As far as gender is concerned, there are indications from various studies that young boys tend to value and to adhere more rigidly to their gender-role than do girls. It would thus appear that the extent to which children prefer the role associated with their own social group depends upon the values and pressures in the society in which they are developing and does not arise in some automatic way from their learning about social divisions and roles. Indeed, to suggest that it does could well be seen as an attempt to divert attention from the aspects of social organization that are responsible for the development of these attitudes.

Conformity to gender-typical behaviour does not necessarily follow from learning about that behaviour. Henshall (1983a; in preparation) found that children could be well aware of the pattern of toy use typical of their own gender in their nursery but not actually conform to this pattern themselves. The supposed importance of conformity for young children is also questioned by a study by Eisenberg et al. (1982). Whilst three and four year olds in this study tended to refer to gender-stereotypes to explain their choices of the toys which they considered appropriate for boys and girls to play with, they seldom referred to gender-stereotypes when asked why they had chosen the toys that they were using during free-play.

Kohlberg's proposal, that children's inability to understand the nature of genital differences and the constancy of gender leads them to identify rigidly with their gender-role, is also not supported by the evidence. The proposal is based, on the one hand, on his observation that children's attitudes towards gender-roles become increasingly stereotyped up to about seven years of age and subsequently become more moderate, and, on the other hand, on his proposal that gender constancy and genital understanding are not achieved until around this age. Ullian (1976) also reports that children become less prescriptive in their attitudes towards gender-roles and adopt a more descriptive view of gender-differences between the ages of six and eight years. Like Kohlberg, she attributes this to the development of an understanding of gender constancy during this period, but she provides no direct evidence that this is indeed the case.

Given our preceding discussion of children's understanding of gender constancy and of genital differences, these explanations are hardly convincing. If children of four years or younger are able to understand the relationship between gender and genital form and there is no good reason to believe that they really believe that their own gender may not be constant, it is clearly unreasonable to 'explain' increases in gender-stereotyped attitudes and behaviour in the late pre-school and early school years in terms of these supposed cognitive deficiences. Furthermore, the available evidence suggests that any confusion that children may entertain over these topics is not related to their behaviour or attitudes. Henshall (1983a, 1983c; in preparation) found no relationship between the extent to which children's use of toys during free-play in a nursery conformed to the pattern typical of their gender and their apparent understanding of either genital-differences or gender constancy, and Marcus and Overton (1978) found no relationship between understanding of gender constancy and various measures of children's preference for their own gender-role.

How, then, are we to explain why most children do develop gender-stereotyped attitudes and behaviour at this age? One approach is to replace one set of supposed cognitive factors with another. Martin and

Halverson (1981), for example, have suggested that there is a general tendency for young children to dichotomize continua and to emphasize differences, and that this tendency is responsible for the exaggerated nature of children's gender-role attitudes and behaviour in the early school years.

Like Kohlberg's interpretation, this explanation fails to acknowledge the true nature of the social context in which children are developing and neatly diverts psychologists' attention from the possible effects of this context by locating the aspects of the situation worthy of attention firmly inside the child's head. It is possible, however, to maintain a cognitive approach without ignoring the true complexity of the social environment about which children are learning. Children are developing in an environment in which behaviour has meaning and intention, and they are learning not only *what* people do, but also *why* they do it. Moreover, as the chapters by Paul Light and Judy Dunn in this volume show, children are coming to grips with these concerns much earlier than has previously been supposed.

We have already noted that many studies have shown that children as young as two years of age are aware of gender-differences in behaviour. But children are probably learning much more than that males and females behave differently; they are probably also learning about *why* males and females behave differently, and this 'hidden curriculum' of the behaviour which they observe may provide the key to understanding why children may adopt the attitudes and behaviour that they have learned to be typical of their own gender.

In broad terms, if children perceive that the behaviour of those around them is constrained by social norms then they are likely to come to perceive gender-roles as a set of *prescriptions* for their own and others' behaviour. On the other hand, if children perceive that those around them are free to behave as they as individuals wish then they are likely to perceive gender-roles as *descriptions* of typical patterns of behaviour which individuals are free to adopt or reject as they please. The distinction being drawn here is similar to that proposed by Bernstein (1971) between personal and positional family styles, and it seems likely that the attitudes that children encounter to social roles in general, and not simply to gender-roles, may be important determinants of their perception of gender-roles.

In this context, Kohlberg's and Ullian's reports that children take an increasingly prescriptive approach towards gender-roles between the ages of about four to eight years may take on a new significance. This is, of course, the age when children in America are making the transition to primary schooling and the shift to prescriptiveness may well result from children's move into this environment rather than from changes in inherent and isolated features of children's cognitive processes over this period. The school system itself may encourage a positional approach to social relationships and parents may also encourage a similar change in their children's approach to social relationships at this age so that they are able to fit in with what the parents perceive as the demands of the social relations into which the child will have to enter with both peers and teachers at school.

These ideas are speculative at present. Nevertheless, research in other areas does make it clear that young children are learning a great deal not only about the ways in which people around them behave, but also about the reasons for that behaviour. Clearly, cognitive research on gender development is going to have to match the sophistication of children's ability to perceive and draw inferences about the social world if it is going to further our understanding of the role of children's cognition in gender development.

Parental influences

The way in which parental influences on gender development are conceived and studied varies with theoretical position. Social learning theory has tended to dominate research in this area and to focus interest upon two main themes. One is the idea of the parent as role-model. Here research has concentrated upon the relationship between children's conformity to gender-role stereotypes and their parents' conformity, and upon the relationship between children's conformity and the presence or absence of the same-sex parent in the family. The other theme is that of the parent as contingent reinforcer of gender-appropriate behaviour. Here research has attempted to establish the extent to which parents' behaviour towards their children is dependent on the child's sex.

Psychoanalytic theory also emphasizes the importance of differences in parental behaviour towards boys and girls but, whereas social learning theory concentrates upon parental approval for gender-appropriate behaviour and disapproval for gender-inappropriate behaviour, psychoanalytic theory tends to concern itself with more subtle aspects and implications of parent-child relationships.

As we have seen in the previous section, cognitive theory views parents as one of a variety of sources of information available to the child about gender-differences in behaviour and about gender-stereotypes. Within this framework research concentrates upon the relationship between parents' behaviour and their children's concepts of gender and gender-roles.

Research on parental influences on gender development in fact includes all these different and sometimes overlapping perspectives. Some historical shifts can be identified which reflect an increasing methodological sophistication as well as shifts in theoretical perspectives. Thus, much research in the 1950s and 1960s concentrated upon the effects of father-absence, particularly on boys. This research was conceived within both the social learning theory and the psychoanalytic traditions; the father was seen both as a role-model for boys and as a figure with whom boys and girls needed to relate. In general, however, little attention was paid to the actual circumstances in which children growing up without a father might live. The reason for the father's absence and the possible importance and availability of other adult male figures for such children was frequently ignored (see chapter 6).

Research on two-parent families at this time tended to concentrate upon differences in parents' treatment of boys and girls, it generally being taken for granted that mothers and fathers all provided 'appropriate' role-models for their children. The question of whether or not boys and girls received different discipline and the relationship between any such differences and gender-differences in aggressive behaviour was an important theme at this time. In general, however, data on parents' behaviour were collected by interviewing the parents themselves and the validity of such data is clearly dubious.

More recently there has been a shift towards collecting data on parents' behaviour from observations in the home. The validity of this method is also open to question; parents may well behave differently when observers are present. Observational studies, however, have generally pointed to more differences in parents' behaviour than interviews have suggested. Maccoby and Jacklin, in a review of studies mostly using parental interviews, concluded that there was 'a surprising degree of similarity in the rearing of boys and girls' (1975, 362). More recent studies, however, have emphasized differences and it now appears to be generally accepted that some differences do exist in parental treatment of boys and girls (e.g., Hoffman, 1977; Kagan, 1979; Maccoby and Jacklin, 1980a, 1980b).

Whilst the recent interest in observing what parents do in addition to asking them what they do is certainly a step forward, research still has a long way to go to capture the true complexities and nuances of parental behaviour and the effects that these may have upon the child. As we argued in the previous section, children are probably highly sensitive to the meanings implicit in what is done. Consider the question of discipline, for example. The number of times that children are smacked by each parent may not be particularly salient; children may be smacked more by their mothers than by their fathers but still perceive fathers as the primary agent of physical discipline if particularly severe misdemeanours are referred to them. Or consider fathers' involvement in child care and domestic work. Even if a father spent more time in child care and domestic activities than his wife their children would probably still perceive these activities as their mother's work if their father had to refer to his wife continually for help and guidance in such matters.

It is these aspects of behaviour that future research will have to find ways of capturing. To achieve this researchers will, as adult members of a culture, have to reflect upon the significance of the behaviour they are observing for other members of that culture, something which most experimental psychologists have been reluctant to do for many years. The psychoanalytic tradition, on the other hand, has long concerned itself with the meanings underlying behaviour and it is perhaps significant that it is to this tradition that two thoughtful and interesting theses on parents and gender development have turned. Both Dinnerstein (1978) and Chodorow (1978) focus upon the fact that the vast majority of boys and girls in Western societies are brought up by women. They consider the implications of this basic fact for children's relationships with, and perceptions of, each parent and they consider the implications of these relationships and perceptions for the child's personality development and subsequent adult behaviour.

Despite the interest shown in these issues in some quarters there remains a gap between these theoretical discussions and most empirical research; the research generally ignores the subtleties addressed in the theory. It is to be hoped that the current interest in psychoanalytic ideas shown by some developmental psychologists might lead to an increased sophistication in some empirical research. It is probably over-optimistic, however, to expect much change when so many in the psychological world appear to be satisfied with the scope of the present empirical research.

Methodological differences apart, there has certainly been a growth in interest in recent years in the possible importance of parental influences on gender development. This seems to result from two factors. First, there is a growing awareness that many children are now spending a substantial part of their childhood with only one parent and this has led to an interest in the possible effects of these experiences. Secondly, there appears to be a widespread belief that parents in two-parent families are becoming less gender-role stereotyped; it is often supposed that fathers are becoming more involved in child care and domestic work and that both men's and women's attitudes to gender and gender-roles are becoming more flexible. We shall examine whether or not such changes really are taking place later in this section. Whatever the basis of these beliefs, however, they have led to a renewed interest in parental influences, the common and perhaps naïve theme being that today's less gender-stereotyped parents are producing a less gender-stereotyped generation of children and that this process of change will gather momentum as time passes.

In addition to this renewed interest in parents there has been a recent surge of interest in fathers amongst developmental psychologists. These two themes in fact complement each other well since much of the recent research on parental influences has concentrated upon supposed changes in father's behaviour or presence in the home. For the remainder of our discussion of parental influences we shall therefore concentrate upon

research on father-absence and upon research on various aspects of
fathers' behaviour in two-parent families.

Father-absence

As we suggested earlier, a frequent problem with research on father-
absence is the failure to consider why the father is absent, who is actually
present in the child's home, and the social and economic realities of the
home situation. These factors may be vital for an understanding both of
children's actual experiences and of the meaning of those experiences for
the child, and they may help us to understand some of the apparently
contradictory findings of research in this area.

Research on father-absence has been reviewed by Biller (1976, 1981).
Boys in father-absent homes have often been found to have less stereotypically male interests and to show lower achievement motivation. In
some cases, however, father-absence has been associated with impulsive,
antisocial or delinquent behaviour. Girls from father-absent homes have
often been found to have difficulty in interacting with men, either because
of excessive flirtatiousness or because of anxious withdrawal and avoidance of men. Hetherington (1972) has related these two patterns of
behaviour to the reason for the father's absence, the former being related
to the loss of father by divorce and the latter to the loss of father by
death.

As we have already noted, early work on father-absence tended to focus
upon the effects on boys and was strongly influenced by social learning
theory, the emphasis being upon the father as a role-model for boys. The
fact that father-absence may also affect girls and that the reason for the
father's absence can make a difference strongly suggests that a more
sophisticated theoretical framework is appropriate. It would appear that
the importance of fathers lies not simply in their presence and supposed
example of stereotypically male behaviour but in the opportunity they
provide for boys and girls to learn to relate to a male as well as a female
parent. Clearly the extent, nature and meaning of these opportunities, or
lack of them, will vary considerably, both within two-parent families and
within supposedly father-absent families.

Recent research has attempted to come to terms with some of these
complexities. Golombok, Spencer and Rutter (1983), for example, studied
two groups of children growing up without a father, but in somewhat
different social circumstances. One group lived with their heterosexual
single-parent mothers and the other group lived with their lesbian
mothers. It was expected that the latter group might show more gender-
atypical behaviour and more problems in relationships with the opposite
sex. However, no evidence of disturbed gender-identity, of atypical

activity preferences or, for the older children, of atypical choice of sexual object was found in either group.

It is tempting to conclude from this that children's family circumstances are relatively unimportant for their gender development, at least as measured by activity preferences in childhood and later sexual object choice. Several factors, however, make this research difficult to interpret. Some, but not all, of the lesbian mothers lived with their female partner. Children living with lesbian mothers had significantly more contact with their fathers than children in the other group, and most children had spent the early years of their life with their fathers present. There may, of course, be other factors involved as well. Mothers bringing up children without fathers are subjected to many financial, social and psychological pressures which may vary according to the mother's sexual orientation and various aspects of her actual circumstances. These pressures may well have both direct and indirect effects upon the child.

It is clear, then, that research still has some way to go to come to terms with the actual situations of children growing up without fathers. It is doubtful, however, whether this line of research will ever tell us a great deal about the importance of fathers for their children's gender development. On the one hand, father-absence is almost inevitably confounded with other factors and, on the other hand, an understanding of the effects of father-absence will not necessarily help us to understand the importance of what fathers do when they are present.

This is not to say that research on father-absence is unimportant. Many children are growing up without fathers and it is clearly important to know what effects this and its associated conditions may have. But if we want to understand the role that the father plays in gender development we should study families where fathers are present. It is to research in this area that we will now turn.

Two-parent families

We referred earlier to the belief that fathers are becoming more involved in child care and domestic activities and that fathers and mothers now have more flexible attitudes towards gender-roles. As Lewis (1984) has shown, this belief appears to be widespread amongst psychologists as well as non-psychologists. It is highly debatable, however, whether there have been any substantive changes in recent years, either in parents' behaviour or in their attitudes. McGuire (1984) found that a group of British parents with young children had very similar ideas to American parents interviewed in earlier decades (Sears, Maccoby and Levine, 1957; Kagan, 1971) about the behavioural characteristics typical of, and appropriate for, boys and girls.

There are several indications that there has been little change in recent years in parents' behaviour. Sweden has had laws for some years which permit fathers to take leave to care for young children. However, an examination of parents' activities when apart from their young child revealed that men and women were still very traditional. Home repairs, car maintenance, work on boats and motor cycles were all mentioned exclusively by men whilst women did much more shopping (Sandqvist, 1985). An Australian study also suggests that recent changes may have been exaggerated. Russell (1982) identified families in which the parents agreed that the father was highly participant in child care. One might think that such a sample would be atypically egalitarian. However, when both parents were at home together mothers did substantially more child care than fathers and the 'highly participant' fathers did less child care overall than the mothers and much less than 'traditional' mothers. Interestingly, despite these differences in child care, the 'highly participant' fathers spent about the same amount of time alone with their children as their wives. Lewis (1984) also suggests that British fathers are no more involved in child care than they were 30 years ago. Fathers of one year old children in his sample did not report any more child care activities than were reported by the wives of a similar sample of men in the 1950s (Newson and Newson, 1963).

As we have already noted, this research focuses upon *what* parents do. Even if fathers spend no more time in child care activities than fathers did 30 years ago, it is possible that today's fathers perform such activities more competently or more independently or are more prepared to be seen doing them in public than their predecessors were. Such relatively subtle changes in behaviour and attitudes would not be detected in the research which we have discussed but might, nevertheless, make an important difference to children's perception of gender-appropriate behaviour.

Radin (1981) and Radin and Sagi (1982) attempted to investigate the effect that fathers' participation in child care might have upon their children. They studied families in America and Israel in which fathers described themselves as highly involved in child care. Children were aged between three and six years at the time of the study and their 'sex-role orientation' was assessed with the 'It scale'. No relationship was found between the extent of paternal caretaking and children's 'It' scores for the American boys and girls or the Israeli boys. Israeli girls with the most highly participant fathers were more 'masculine' in their responses, though they were still very different from boys in their preferred toys and activities.

Unfortunately, it is difficult to see what research of this kind can tell us about the effects of fathers' involvement in child care. The main problem with this particular study is the use of the much criticized 'It scale' which provides an indirect indication of some mixture of children's awareness of gender-differences in children's behaviour and their preference for gender-typical activities. This is too crude a tool to use for research in this area. What we need to know is whether children's perceptions of the behaviour typical of, and appropriate for, males and females is related to their fathers' behaviour in the home. We also need to know whether there are any relationships between fathers' and children's behaviour.

A more general problem with this research is the rather simplistic conception of father involvement. Fathers may be involved in child care out of necessity or out of desire, and they may do it in addition to, or to the exclusion of, activities outside the home. It is interesting to note that the 'highly participant' American fathers in Radin's study were not functionally equivalent to a traditional, home-based mother; all but one of them had other major activities, such as being a student or working away from home in some capacity.

At a time when many fathers are spending more time at home and perhaps also more time in child care as a result of unemployment it is obviously very relevant to ask whether this will have any effect on children's concepts of gender. But as we have already argued, it is the meaning implicit in what parents do, not simply what they *do*, that we must consider if we want to understand the ways in which parents' behaviour may affect their children's perception of, and attitudes towards, gender-roles. This will require a considerably more sophisticated analysis of parents' behaviour than has been attempted in most research to date, particularly when dealing with the emotive topic of unemployment and its effects upon men's roles and self-esteem. It is possible, for example, that a man may behave in ways that will exaggerate his masculinity if he is forced to spend a lot of time doing traditionally female work against his wishes.

Our discussion of the behaviour of fathers in two-parent families has so far concentrated upon their involvement in child care. There are many other aspects of what fathers do and think, however, which may have as much, if not more, influence upon their children.

Beail (1983) and Dukes (1978) both concluded that the extent of fathers' child care activities as assessed by interviews was not related to the sex of their three or eight month old infants. Other research, however, suggests that fathers are initially more interested in boys, nearly always preferring their first child to be a boy (McGuire, 1982; Moss et al., 1980; Williamson, 1976) and showing more interest in newborn sons than daughters (Parke and O'Leary, 1976; Woollett et al., 1982). Whilst the time spent subsequently in child care may not show any general relationship to the infant's sex, Rendina and Dickerscheid (1976) found an interaction between infant temperament, sex and father involvement, with fathers of difficult girls being slightly less likely to be involved in caretaking. It seems likely that fathers' greater interest in boys may help them to cope with difficult male infants, and it is also possible that this interest may affect fathers' behaviour in other subtle ways.

There are some suggestions that fathers play more with sons than with daughters, though this may only be so in laboratory situations. Two studies of American fathers showed that they played more with sons at three months (Field, 1978) and 18 months (Weinraub and Frankel, 1977). Observations in the home, however, have generally not found differences in the amount of time that fathers spend playing with boys and girls (McGuire, 1983). There do appear to be differences, however, in the way in which they play with boys and girls.

Young boys have been found to be more physically active than girls in several studies (Feldman et al., 1980; Melson, 1977; Smith and Connolly, 1972) and older boys show more interest than girls in sport and team games (Lever, 1976; Newson and Newson, 1976; Rosenberg and Sutton-Smith, 1960). Clinical studies also show that many more boys than girls are identified as abnormally active (Campbell et al., 1977; Goggin, 1975; Silver, 1981; Thorley, 1984).

Recent studies of fathers point to their influence being particularly relevant to the development of gender-differences in activity and preferences for sport. Fathers tend to play in a more physical manner than mothers (Clarke-Stewart, 1978; Yogman, 1980; McGuire, 1983). With older children they are more likely to participate with sons than with daughters in shared sporting activities (Lewis, Newson and Newson, 1982) and even at two years it has been seen that they criticize girls more than boys when they are active (Fagot, 1978) whilst sharing more active games with sons (McGuire, 1983). McGuire (1982) asked fathers of two year olds if there were any activities or games which they shared with their child and their wife did not. Even at this age sports, and particularly football, were specified by nearly three-quarters of the boys' fathers whilst the father of only one girl named a sport and that was swimming. In fact, fewer fathers of girls than of boys said they had any activities or games that were exclusive to them but, amongst those who did, general active games such as jumping on the bed and giving rides were mentioned more than any other kind of play.

These differences in fathers' behaviour may, of course, be partly a response to children's interests. The differentiation of fathers' behaviour, however, is much more extreme than the extent of gender-differences reported in levels of physical activity for pre-school children. It is clear, therefore, that the fathers' behaviour tells us something about what they consider appropriate for boys and girls. It is also clear that both for boys and girls fathers see physical games as more appropriate for themselves than for the child's mother and this may well influence the children's general perceptions of the appropriateness of physical activity for males and females.

These factors may also help us to understand children's preferences for fathers and mothers as playmates. Lynn and Cross (1974) presented two, three and four year olds with a forced choice of mother or father for play-mate. Boys expressed a preference for their father at all ages. Girls preferred fathers at age two, showed no consistent preference at three years and preferred mothers at age four. This change in girls' preference might reflect their growing awareness both of their shared identity with their mothers and of the inappropriateness for someone of their gender of the physical activities preferred by their fathers. It might also indicate that fathers are less interested in, or less able to relate to, girls by this age.

Another interesting aspect of the behaviour of fathers emerges from studies of parents and children working at games or tasks. Work on adults' teaching strategies is discussed in detail by David Wood in this volume, but we would like to discuss some gender-differences in this behaviour here. Bellinger and Gleason (1982) studied the directives given to five year olds engaged in a construction task. They did not find more directive statements to either boys or girls but they did find that fathers were more directive than mothers. In a similar study in which parents completed a jigsaw and taught their child to perform a memory task, parents were more directive and strategy oriented with sons whilst they gave daughters more concrete instructions with specific feedback (Frankel and Rollins, 1983). McGuire (1983) also reports that fathers were particularly reluctant to help boys.

These few findings suggest that parents, and particularly fathers, appear to adopt different strategies when trying to instruct or direct sons and daughters. The pattern of boys being encouraged to be more independent and strategy oriented and girls being encouraged to be more concrete and dependent on guidance bears a striking resemblance to the differences discussed by Walkerdine (1985; forthcoming) in the cognitive styles expected of, and encouraged in, boys and girls by teachers in the primary school. It may be that gender-differences in cognitive style with their possible implications for success within the educational system and for career opportunities are being established by parents even before children enter the formal educational system. This is clearly an interesting and important area for future research.

Another important theme which emerges from much of the work on fathers and gender development is the greater concern fathers appear to have about their children's conformity to gender-role stereotypes and the greater pressure on boys to conform to gender-stereotypes. McGuire (1982) found that fathers identified more toys than mothers as appropriate for only boys or girls. This was particularly so for fathers of boys, and in general fathers were much more likely than mothers to think that toys related to housework (e.g., an iron or a cooker) were unsuitable for boys. Goodenough (1957) and Newson and Newson (1968) also found that fathers were often strongly opposed to boys dressing up and using make-up whereas mothers did not appear to be so concerned and sometimes even encouraged it. More recently Langlois and Downs (1980) noted stronger reactions from fathers than from mothers to children's play with gender-inappropriate toys.

The pressure upon boys, particularly from their fathers, to avoid stereotypically female behaviour may be related to parents' and society's attitudes towards homosexuality. Western societies appear to be both more aware and more intolerant of male than female homosexuality. It is also frequently, and falsely, assumed that an interest in activities typical of the other gender is indicative of homosexual object choice. Such attitudes, of course, can tell us much about the sociology of gender. Whatever their origins and significance, however, parents may well pressurize boys to conform to gender-role stereotypes to protect them from the stigma of supposed deviance.

The fact that there is more emphasis for boys than for girls upon what behaviour is inappropriate may also reflect an important difference in the nature of the development of boys and girls. Chodorow (1978) in her reanalysis of object-relations theory has suggested that while girls develop a gender identity by identifying closely with their mothers, males have to develop a gender identity by negating the mother and becoming what she is not. It may be parents' conscious or unconscious appreciation of this aspect of boys' development that leads them to emphasize what boys should not do. Dinnerstein (1978) has suggested that this pattern of development also leads males to devalue the position and role of women in society whilst at the same time viewing them as mysterious and potentially dangerous. This may help us to understand why fathers are more concerned than mothers about boys not behaving in stereotypically female ways.

Much attention has quite rightly been paid to the disadvantages facing girls and women as a result of the low expectations which teachers and parents may have of them. The pressure upon boys to be masculine, however, may produce other problems peculiar to them. It may be partly responsible for boys' higher incidence of problems at all ages and for the fact that their problems are frequently outwardly directed conduct disorders such as aggression and destruction (Rutter et al., 1970). During the pre-school period, in particular, boys have been found to show more tantrums and defiance than girls (Beller and Neubauer, 1963), to cope less well with a variety of stressful situations such as failure (Zunich, 1964), starting school (Hughes et al., 1979) or experiencing family discord (Hetherington, 1979; Whitehead, 1979). Moreover, boys reported by their parents to be difficult at three years of age are more likely than similarly difficult girls to be described as having problems five years later (Richman et al., 1982).

Pressure on boys to be independent, brave and to show emotional control may also be important. May (1980) has proposed that the archetypal male myth concerns reckless bravery, as illustrated by Paethon, son of Phoebus, whose brave but foolish attempts to emulate his father ended in disaster but nevertheless earned him the respect of other males. Two studies of parenting have concluded that boys receive more encouragement than girls to be independent, self-reliant and to assume personal responsibility (Block, 1979; Barry et al., 1957), and McGuire (1983) found that two year old boys were allowed on more dangerous outdoor play equipment than girls and received much less comfort when they experienced minor injuries at home. Accident rates are higher for boys than for girls at all ages both inside and outside the home. Most child accidents outside the home are on the road and it appears that boys get more freedom than girls to go out without an adult (Newson and Newson, 1976) and are given more chores which take them out of the house (Duncan and Duncan, 1978).

Finally, the fact that fathers may be more concerned than mothers about their sons' masculinity may put additional pressures on boys. McGuire (forthcoming) found more disagreements between parents of boys than between parents of girls about discipline and about the existence of behaviour problems in their child. In another study, a relationship was found for boys but not for girls between parental agreement over child-rearing practices and the development of their pre-school children's impulse control and resilience (Block et al., 1981). Unfortunately, parental agreement in this study was related to parents' educational qualifications and to children's IQ for boys in the sample but not for girls, so that it is not possible to draw any conclusions about the effects of parental agreement *per se*.

Research of this kind, however, in which children's behaviour is studied in the context of the patterns of relationships between family members represents a considerably more sophisticated attempt to come to terms with the complexity of parental influences on gender development than more traditional studies of parents' differential treatment of boys and girls. An interesting example comes from a recent study by Simpson and Stevenson-Hinde (1985) who found that shyness in boys was associated with negative family interactions while the reverse was true for girls. Gender-differences such as this in patterns of family interaction and in relationships between these interactions and children's development may well provide more important information about the role that parents and siblings may play in a child's gender development than information about how each behaves with the child alone.

We concluded our section on father-absence by suggesting that we should study families in which fathers are present if we wish to understand the role that the father plays in a child's gender development. We would like to conclude this section on two-parent families by suggesting that we should study the behaviour and interactions of all those present in the family if we wish to understand the role that each may play in gender development. As Judy Dunn's chapter in this volume shows, some recent research appears to be moving in this direction, but studying the influence of family members on a child's development in this way is a highly complex task. It is probably too early yet to say whether this line of research will prove to be as fruitful as it now promises.

Conclusions

As we said at the beginning of this chapter, there has been no shortage of research on gender development in recent years. It is disappointing, therefore, that there have been so few real advances for us to point to. One reason for this, as we have argued throughout this chapter, is that much of this research fails to come to grips with the complexity of children's behaviour and environments and with the extent of children's ability to understand their social world. It is to be hoped that the sophisticated research perspectives currently being developed in the study of children's cognition and social understanding and in the study of family interactions will filter through to work on gender development during the next decade.

Whether or not this is likely to happen is difficult to say. The increasing sophistication shown over the last two decades in work on parental influences on gender development is encouraging. In contrast, the stream of fragmentary and seemingly pointless studies of gender-differences in this or that behaviour continues unabated, and much of the recent work on children's understanding of gender pays no attention whatsoever to the issues which have been discussed for over a decade now in other work on cognitive development. Part of the explanation for this probably lies in the nature of academic career structures and in the policies of journals which have grown up around them (both of which are discussed in more detail in the introduction to this volume); there can be few easier ways to produce a publication than to study gender-differences in some behaviour or other, and when the pressure is on, who is going to spend time attempting to assimilate new theoretical ideas if they can get work published which simply ignores them? All the signs are that the pressure on academics to publish will increase during the next decade. We must hope that this will not stop some researchers addressing the issues which we have attempted to identify in this chapter.

References

Archer, J. 1980. Sex differences and models of development (paper presented to the Annual Conference of the British Psychological Society, Aberdeen, March 1980).

Bardwick, J. M. 1971. *The Psychology of Women*. New York: Harper and Row.

Barry, H., Bacon, M. and Child, I. 1957. A cross cultural survey of some sex differences in socialization. *Journal of Abnormal and Social Psychology*, 55, 327–32.

Beail, N. 1983. Father involvement in pregnancy, birth and early parenthood (Ph.D. dissertation, University of London).

Beller, E. K. and Neubauer, P. B. 1963. Sex differences and symptom patterns in early childhood. *Journal of Child Psychiatry*, 2, 417–33.

Bellinger, D. C. and Gleason, J. B. 1982. Sex differences in parental directives to young children. *Sex Roles*, 8, 1123–39.

Bernstein, B. 1971. *Class, Codes and Control.* London: Routledge and Kegan Paul.

Biller, H. B. 1976. The father and personality development: paternal deprivation and sex role development, in M. E. Lamb (ed.), *The Role of the Father in Child Development.* New York: John Wiley.

Biller, H. B. 1981. The father and sex role development, in M. E. Lamb (ed.), *The Role of the Father in Child Development* (2nd edn). New York: John Wiley.

Birns, B. 1976. The emergence and socialization of sex differences in the earliest years. *Merrill-Palmer Quarterly*, 22, 229–54.

Block, J. H. 1976. Issues, problems and pitfalls in assessing sex differences: a critical review of *The Psychology of Sex Differences. Merrill-Palmer Quarterly*, 22, 283–308.

Block, J. H. 1979. Another look at sex differentiation in the socialization behaviors of mothers and fathers, in J. Sherman and F. L. Denmark (eds), *The Psychology of Women: future direction of research.* New York: Psychological Dimensions.

Block, J. H., Block, J. and Morrison, A. 1981. Parental agreement and disagreement on child-rearing questions and gender-related personality correlates in children. *Child Development*, 52, 965–74.

Blurton Jones, N. 1972. Categories of child-child interaction, in N. Blurton Jones (ed.), *Ethological Studies of Child Behaviour.* Cambridge: Cambridge University Press.

Blurton Jones, N. and Konner, M. J. 1973. Sex differences in behaviour of London and Bushmen children, in R. P. Michael and J. H. Crook (eds), *Comparative Ecology and Behaviour of Primates.* London: Academic Press.

Campbell, S. B., Endman, M. W. and Bernfield, G. 1977. A three year follow-up of hyperactive preschoolers into elementary school. *Journal of Child Psychology and Psychiatry*, 18, 239–49.

Chodorow, N. 1978. *The Reproduction of Mothering.* Berkeley: University of California Press.

Clark, A. H., Wyon, S. M. and Richards, M. P. M. 1969. Free-play in nursery school children. *Journal of Child Psychology and Psychiatry*, 10, 205–16.

Clarke-Stewart, K. A. 1978. And daddy makes three: the father's impact on mother and young child. *Child Development*, 49, 466–78.

Conn, J. H. and Kanner, L. 1947. Children's awareness of sex differences. *Journal of Child Psychiatry*, 1, 3–57.

De Vries, R. 1969. Constancy of generic identity in the years three to six. *Monographs of the Society for Research in Child Development*, 34, no. 3.

Dinnerstein, D. 1978. *The Rocking of the Cradle, and the Ruling of the World.* London: Souvenir Press.

DiPietro, J. A. 1981. Rough and tumble play: a function of gender. *Developmental Psychology,* **17,** 50–8.

Dukes, P. J. C. 1978. The relationship between paternal interaction style and infant behavior as a function of socio-economic status and sex of infant. *Dissertation Abstracts International,* **39,** 2959–60.

Duncan, B. and Duncan, O. D. 1978. *Sex Typing and Social Roles: a research report.* New York: Academic Press.

Dunn, J. 1979. The first year of life: continuities in individual differences, in D. Shaffer and J. Dunn (eds), *The First Year of Life: Psychological and Medical Implications of Early Experience.* Chichester: John Wiley.

Eisenberg, N., Murray, E. and Hite, T. 1982. Children's reasoning regarding sex-typed toy choices. *Child Development,* **53,** 81–6.

Fagot, B. I. 1977. Consequences of moderate cross-gender behavior in preschool children. *Child Development,* **48,** 902–7.

Fagot, B. I. 1978. The influence of sex of child on parental reactions to toddler children. *Child Development,* **49,** 459–65.

Feldman, J. F., Brody, N. and Miller, S. A. 1980. Sex differences in non elicited neonatal behavior. *Merrill-Palmer Quarterly,* **26,** 63–73.

Field, T. 1978. Interaction behaviors of primary versus secondary caretaker fathers. *Developmental Psychology,* **14,** 183–4.

Frankel, M. T. and Rollins, H. A. 1983. Does mother know best? Mothers and fathers interacting with preschool sons and daughters. *Developmental Psychology,* **19,** 694–702.

Garai, J. E. and Scheinfeld, A. 1968. Sex differences in mental and behavioral traits. *Genetic Psychology Monographs,* **77,** 169–299.

Goggin, J. E. 1975. Sex differences in the activity level of preschool children as a possible precursor of hyperactivity. *Journal of Genetic Psychology,* **127,** 75–81.

Golombok, S., Spencer, A. and Rutter, M. 1983. Children in lesbian and single-parent households: psychosexual and psychiatric appraisal. *Journal of Child Psychology and Psychiatry,* **24,** 551–72.

Goodenough, E. W. 1957. Interest in persons as an aspect of sex differences in the early years. *Genetic Psychology Monographs,* **55,** 287–323.

Gribbin, M. 1979. Granny knows best. *New Scientist,* **84,** 350–1.

Henshall, C. H. 1983a. Gender, behaviour and cognition in pre-school children (Ph.D. dissertation, University of Cambridge).

Henshall, C. H. 1983b. Cognitive theories of gender development: an examination of children's concepts of gender and of psychologists' concepts of gender development (paper presented to the Seventh Biannual Meeting of the International Society for the Study of Behavioural Development, Munich, August 1983).

Henshall, C. H. 1983c. Investigating young children's concepts of gender (paper presented to the Third Margaret Lowenfeld Day Conference, Cambridge, 1 September 1983).

Henshall, C. H. In preparation. An empirical investigation of some aspects of the cognitive-developmental theory of children's understanding of gender and of the relationship between this understanding and behaviour.

Hetherington, E. M. 1972. Effects of father absence on personality development in adolescent daughters. *Developmental Psychology,* **7,** 313–26.

Hetherington, E. M. 1979. Divorce: a child's perspective. *American Psychologist*, **34**, 851-8.

Hoffman, L. W. 1977. Changes in family roles, socialization and sex differences. *American Psychologist*, **32**, 644-57.

Hughes, M., Pinkerton, G. and Plewis, J. 1979. Children's difficulties on starting infant school. *Journal of Child Psychology and Psychiatry*, **20**, 187-96.

Hutt, C. 1972. *Males and Females*. London: Penguin Books.

Kagan, J. 1971. *Change and Continuity in Infancy*. New York: John Wiley.

Kagan, J. 1979. *The Growth of the Child*. Brighton: Harvester.

Kamin, L. 1974. *The Science and Politics of I.Q.* London: Penguin Books.

Kohlberg, L. 1966. A cognitive-developmental analysis of children's sex-role concepts and attitudes, in E. E. Maccoby (ed.), *The Development of Sex Differences*. London: Tavistock Press.

Langlois, J. H. and Downs, A. C. 1980. Mothers, fathers and peers as socialization agents of sex-typed behaviors in young children. *Child Development*, **51**, 1217-47.

Lever, J. 1976. Sex differences in the games children play. *Social Problems*, **23**, 478-87.

Levin, S.M., Balistrieri, J. and Schukit, M. 1972. The development of sexual discrimination in children. *Journal of Child Psychology and Psychiatry*, **13**, 47-53.

Lewis, C. 1984. Men's involvement in fatherhood: variation across the lifespan suggests that impressions of historical change are over-inflated (paper presented to the Annual Conference of the Developmental Section of the British Psychological Society, Lancaster, September 1984).

Lewis, C., Newson, E. and Newson, J. 1982. Father participation through childhood and its relation to career aspirations and delinquency, in N. Beail and J. McGuire (eds), *Fathers: psychological perspectives*. London: Junction Books.

Lynn, D. B. and Cross, A. 1974. Parent preference of preschool children. *Journal of Marriage and the Family*, **36**, 555-9.

Maccoby, E. E. and Jacklin, C. N. 1975. *The Psychology of Sex Differences*. London: Oxford University Press.

Maccoby, E. E. and Jacklin, C. N. 1980a. Psychological sex differences, in M. Rutter (ed.), *Scientific Foundations of Developmental Psychiatry*. London: Heinemann.

Maccoby, E. E. and Jacklin, C. N. 1980b. Sex differences in aggression: a rejoinder and reprise. *Child Development*, **51**, 964-80.

McGuire, J. 1982. Gender specific differences in early childhood: the impact of the father, in N. Beail and J. McGuire (eds), *Fathers: psychological perspectives*. London: Junction Books.

McGuire, J. 1983. The effect of a child's gender on the nature of parent-child interactions in the home during the third year of life (Ph.D. dissertation, University of London Institute of Education).

McGuire, J. 1984. Parents of the future: what are they learning about the roles of men and women in society? (paper presented to the Annual Conference of the Developmental Section of the British Psychological Society, Lancaster, September 1984).

McGuire, J. Forthcoming. Differences in the parental control of two year-old girls and boys.

Marcus, D. E. and Overton, W. F. 1978. The development of cognitive gender constancy and sex role preferences. *Child Development*, **49**, 434–44.

Martin, C. L. and Halverson, C. F. Jr. 1981. A schematic processing model of sex typing and stereotyping in children. *Child Development*, **52**, 1119–34.

May, R. 1980. *Sex and Fantasy: patterns of male and female development*. London: W. W. Norton.

Melson, G. 1977. Sex differences in the use of indoor space by preschool children. *Perceptual and Motor Skills*, **44**, 207–13.

Milner, D. 1975. *Children and Race*. London: Penguin Books.

Moss, P., Bolland, G. and Foxman, R. 1980. Transition to parenthood (unpublished report, Thomas Coram Research Unit, University of London Institute of Education).

Newson, J. and Newson, E. 1963. *Patterns of Infant Care in an Urban Community*. London: Penguin Books.

Newson, J. and Newson, E. 1968. *Four Years Old in an Urban Community*. London: Penguin Books.

Newson, J. and Newson, E. 1976. *Seven Years Old in the Home Environment*. London: George Allen and Unwin.

Oakley, A. 1972. *Sex, Gender and Soceity*. London: Temple Smith.

Parke, R. D. and O'Leary, S. E. 1976. Family interaction in the newborn period: some observations and some unresolved issues, in K. F. Reigel and J. Meacham (eds), *The Developing Individual in a Changing World*. The Hague: Mouton.

Patterson, G. R., Littman, R. A. and Bricker, W. 1967. Assertive behaviour in children: a step toward a theory of aggression. *Monographs of the Society for Research in Child Development*, **32**, no. 113.

Radin, N. 1981. Childrearing fathers in intact families, I: some antecedent and consequences. *Merrill-Palmer Quarterly,* **27**, 489–513.

Radin, N. and Sagi, A. 1982. Childrearing fathers in intact families, II: Israel and the USA. *Merrill-Palmer Quarterly*, **28**, 111–36.

Rendina, I. and Dickerscheid, J. D. 1976. Father involvement with firstborn infants. *Family Coordinator*, **25**, 373–8.

Reuter, J. and Yunik, G. 1973. Social interaction in nursery schools. *Developmental Psychology,* **9**, 319–25.

Richards, M. P. M. 1974 (ed.) *The Intergration of a Child into a Social World*. Cambridge: Cambridge University Press.

Richman, N., Stevenson, J. and Graham, P. 1982. *Preschool to School: a behavioural study*. London: Academic Press.

Rosenberg, B. G. and Sutton-Smith, B. 1960. A revised conception of masculine-feminine differences in play activities. *Journal of Genetic Psychology*, **96**, 165–70.

Russell, G. 1982. Highly participant Australian fathers: some preliminary findings. *Merrill-Palmer Quarterly*, **28**, 137–56.

Rutter, M., Tizard, J. and Whitmore, K. (eds) 1970. *Education, Health and Behaviour*. London: Longmans.

Sandqvist, K. 1985. Fatherhood in Sweden (paper presented to the Fatherhood Research Group, Reading, January 1985).

Sears, R. R., Maccoby, E. E. and Levin, H. 1957. *Patterns of Childrearing*. New York: Peterson and Row.

Silver, L. B. 1981. The relationship between learning disabilities, hyperactivity, distractability and behavioral problems. *Journal of the American Academy of Child Psychiatry*, **20**, 385–97.

Simpson, A. E. and Stevenson-Hinde, J. 1985. Temperamental characteristics of three- to four-year-old boys and girls and child-family interactions. *Journal of Child Psychology and Psychiatry*, **26**, 43–53.

Smith, P. K. and Connolly, K. J. 1972. Patterns of play and social interaction in pre-school children, in N. Blurton Jones (ed.), *Ethological Studies of Child Behaviour*. Cambridge: Cambridge University Press.

Smith, P. K. and Connolly, K. J. 1980. *The Ecology of Preschool Behaviour*. Cambridge: Cambridge University Press.

Smith, P. K. and Green, M. 1975. Aggressive behavior in English nurseries and play groups: sex differences and response of adults. *Child Development*, **46**, 211–14.

Thompson, S. K. and Bentler, P. M. 1971. The priority of cues in sex discrimination by children and adults. *Developmental Psychology*, **5**, 181–5.

Thorley, G. 1984. Hyperkinetic syndrome of childhood: clinical characteristics. *British Journal of Psychiatry*, **144**, 16–24.

Ullian, D. Z. 1976. The development of conceptions of masculinity and femininity, in B. Lloyd and J. Archer (eds), *Exploring Sex Differences*. London: Academic Press.

Walkerdine, V. 1985. Science and the female mind: the burden of proof. *Psych Critique*, **1**, 1–20.

Walkerdine, V. Forthcoming. *The Mastery of Reason*. London: Methuen.

Weinraub, M. and Frankel, J. 1977. Sex differences in parent-infant interaction during free play, departure and separation. *Child Development*, **48**, 1240–9.

Whitehead, L. 1979. Sex differences in children's responses to family stress: a re-evaluation. *Journal of Child Psychology and Psychiatry*, **20**, 247–54.

Williamson, N. E. 1976. *Sons or Daughters? A cross-cultural survey of parental preferences*. London: Sage Publications.

Woollett, A., White, D. and Lyon, L. 1982. Observations of fathers at birth, in N. Beail and J. McGuire (eds), *Fathers: psychological perspectives*. London: Junction Books.

Yogman, M. W. 1980. Development of the father-infant relationship, in H. Fitzgerald, B. Lester and M. W. Yogman (eds), *Theory and Research in Behavioral Pediatrics*. Vol. 1. New York: Plenum Press.

Zunich, M. 1964. Children's reactions to failure. *Journal of Genetic Psychology*, **104**, 19–24.

Part 3

Developing minds: learning and communication

Introduction

The chapters in part 2 were concerned with 'context' in the wider sense of the child's long-standing social relationships, and were focused mainly on social-emotional aspects of development. Part 3 is also concerned with 'context', but in a narrower and more specific sense, and in relation to the child's intellectual and communicative development.

In the opening chapter, Paul Light critically addresses the Piagetian conception of intellectual development as a matter of acquiring new logical competences through a stage-like progression. The principal focus of the chapter is on what Piaget would term 'concrete operational thinking', and on conservation as an index of such thinking. An examination of context effects in conservation testing brings out the key role played by conversational conventions. Light argues that the embedding of quantity terms within socially intelligible contexts may play an important part not only in testing for conservation but also in its acquisition. If conservation concepts are conceived of as having a history and a relation to specific social practices, then the child's developmental task is to gain access to these culturally elaborated abstractions. The support given by contextual ones may significantly facilitate such access.

Such a view offers a role not only for contextual support of the child's understanding in 'spontaneous' discourse, but also for more deliberate or contrived *teaching*. David Wood, in the second chapter of part 3, argues that to a large extent the processes involved in teaching remain obscure. The teaching of groups of children in classroom settings is a relatively new and poorly understood activity. Wood shares with Light an emphasis on the tacit ground rules of adult-child interchanges, highlighting the special forms of discourse in the classroom that make certain things relevant, others irrelevant. Apparent similarities between the competences demanded in different situations may be misleading, he argues, if the implicit ground rules which constrain those situations are different. In contradistinction to Piaget's view, the child is seen as developing not mental operations derived from his actions but concepts jointly constructed through interaction with others. The activities of teacher and learner are conceptualized as joint problem-solving.

If young children are in some respects highly sensitive to the nuances of communicative intent, they may by the same token be relatively insensitive to precisely what is *said*. Peter Robinson's chapter illustrates young children's frequent failure to distinguish what is said from what is meant. Robinson sees this as symptomatic of a tendency for the child to treat his or her interpretations as if they were direct, unmediated apprehensions of reality. Young children rarely stop to ask for clarification or guidance, even when they have been given insufficient information on which to act. They have yet to appreciate what they *don't know*. Robinson suggests that for the child to appreciate that 'I don't know' (in other words 'I know that I don't know') presupposes a critical achievement of reflective self-awareness. His argument is that it may be only through the behaviour of other people, and perhaps crucially in the context of ambiguities in communication, that such self-awareness is achieved.

8

Context, conservation and conversation

Paul Light

Introduction

Our view of cognitive development in early childhood has been subject to two quite clear shifts in the last ten years or so. One of these has to do with precocity: much recent work seems to show that young children, especially three to six year olds, are much more intellectually capable than we had previously supposed. The other pronounced shift has been in our aware-ness of the significance of the social context of children's cognitive functioning. The two issues are of course closely related; exploration of the effects of varying the social context in which cognitive tasks are presented has been a major source of evidence for high levels of cognitive competence in the pre-school child. As I shall argue, however, it is unclear whether the role of social context can be properly understood simply in terms of 'masking' or 'revealing' the child's true levels of cognitive com-petence. An alternative conception seems to be emerging in which 'the social context' moves to centre stage, as a fundamental and constitutive element in cognitive development.

In the English-speaking world the study of cognitive development has for the last quarter of a century been dominated by Piaget, so much so that the label 'cognitive developmental' is synonymous with Piagetian or neo-Piagetian approaches. Earlier theoretical positions which attempted to ground an account of cognitive development in the child's social experiences (e.g., Mead, 1934; Vygotsky, 1962) were almost totally eclipsed by Piaget's essentially individualistic account of cognitive develop-ment. Even with the more recent rise of 'social cognition' as a research topic, the dependence of social development upon cognitive development has been stressed while the role of social experience in cognitive develop-ment has received scant attention (Light, 1983).

Nevertheless, the hegemony of the cognitive over the social has been challenged, and is increasingly being challenged in contemporary work. In this chapter I shall examine just one aspect of such work, that concerning Piagetian tests of operational thinking. Detailed evaluation will be restricted to one key element in the Piagetian scheme, namely conservation. I hope, however, that even within such a narrow compass it will be possible to illustrate some of the arguments for a radically social recon-struction of the still prevailing Piagetian account.

The tests which Piaget and his co-workers devised to distinguish the pre-operational from the operational thinker (Piaget, 1952, 1955; Piaget and Inhelder, 1956, 1969) achieved very wide currency in the 1960s and 1970s, and Piaget's findings were broadly replicated in countless studies. But increasingly in the last decade other studies with different methodologies have generated conflicting data, indicative of a whole range of seemingly precocious logical abilities. As well as in conservation, this can be seen for classification, number concepts, arithmetic and measurement (Donaldson, Grieve and Pratt, 1983). In all these areas it is claimed that 'pre-operational' children's abilities have been underestimated in previous (Piagetian) research.

Should this issue be seen as merely a matter of methodology, with im-proved methods offering more sensitive indices of the young child's abilities? Or is there more to be learned from these disparities? I shall argue the latter case, and suggest that a more fundamentally *social* approach both illuminates the sources of the apparent disparities in per-formance and hints at the need for a very different account of the process and nature of cognitive development itself. At the outset, however, a rather more detailed sketch of some aspects of the Piagetian account of the development of operational thinking will be necessary.

Piaget: structures and stages

At the heart of Piaget's theory is the idea of structure. Cognitive develop-ment, and in particular the emergence of operational thought, is charac-terized in terms of the emergence of new logical or logicomathematical structures. While Piaget's theory has a functional aspect, concerned with intelligence as adaptation, with assimilation, accommodation and equil-ibration, his main contribution and influence lay in his structural account of cognition.

Logic was used extensively to model cognitive structures – to the extent that the two were sometimes identified one with the other. Thus, for example, Inhelder and Piaget claimed that 'reasoning is nothing more than the propositional calculus itself' (1958, 305). Further, the structures were posited as real, 'actually present' (1958, 307). They were not merely heuristic devices whereby psychologists could better conceptualize some aspect of the child's behaviour – the structures directly reflected 'actual psychological activities' (Piaget, 1957, 7) going on in the child's head.

The role of specific types of experience in the elaboration of cognitive structures was left largely unexplored by Piaget. His starting-point was very much the individual thinking subject. Moreover, he placed heavy emphasis on the individual's structuring of his or her own experience. The focus on the isolated individual, and on assimilation as a condition for experience, means that experience is in large measure an individual construct. Ultimately, this conception makes genuine interaction with the environment impossible, and stages reduce to the unfolding of a pre-ordained programme (Broughton, 1981; Moore, 1985). Certainly, the stages outlined by Piaget in respect of the achievement of operational thought would seem to have more to do with the constraints of endogenous organization than with the exigencies of the external environment.

Children's thought was to be interpreted in terms of their 'possession of' or 'lack of' certain operational competences. The local, historical, particular aspects of a child's situation and behaviour were treated by Piaget as merely obscuring the emerging competence, defined in terms of logicomathematical structures. The image was of a clear-cut underlying 'form' beneath the untidy surface of actual day to day behaviour (Light, 1983; Russell, 1978). Since everyday behaviour offered only occasional and unreliable glimpses of this underlying order, relatively formal investigatory procedures were needed, and Piaget and his co-workers consequently devised a wide range of procedures designed to demonstrate the presence or absence of particular hypothesized logical competences.

During the 1960s and 1970s Piaget's tests of operational competences became very much part of the 'stock in trade' of developmental psychologists and educators. Perhaps the best known and most widely used of these 'litmus tests' of cognitive development were the various conservation tests, their popularity probably owing as much to their apparent elegance and simplicity as to the central significance which Piaget (e.g., 1952) attached to conservation in the development of logical thought. It is to these conservation tests that we now turn.

Conservation

Perhaps the best known of Piaget's procedures for assessing conservation is the equivalence test for liquid quantities, so that this provides a suitable vehicle for outlining the basic three-stage procedure. First, the equality of two quantities is established. In this case, for example, juice might be poured into two identical beakers to the same level. The child is asked to judge the equality of amount. Next, one of the two entities is transformed – in this case the juice from one beaker might be poured into another beaker of a different shape. Finally the child is asked whether the equality of amount still obtains.

Piaget observed that children below about seven years of age typically have no difficulty correctly judging the *initial* equality of the two quantities, but erroneously suppose that the post-transformation quantities are no longer equal. They may judge that the juice in the 'new' beaker is more, or less, basing their answers on single salient perceptual dimensions ('it's taller', or 'it's fatter', etc.) rather than on any logical inferences. Older children correctly judge that the quantities remain the same after the transformation, and can support their answers using 'logical' justifications, linking the pre and post-transformation states (e.g., reversibility) or linking the several dimensions of difference in the post-transformation array (compensation).

These judgements and justifications are evidence, according to Piaget, of the emergence of a new logical competence in the child, marked by a 'decentred' consideration of the interplay of multiple co-varying elements within a logical grouping. Up until this stage the pre-operational, egocentric, child is the creature of his own perceptions. Appearance and reality are not distinguished; the child does not recognize that changes in shape are reversible, or that changes in different dimensions can compensate for one another.

Just as young children fail to recognize that liquid quantity is unchanged by pouring, so they fail to recognize that weight is unchanged by alterations of shape, or that number is unchanged by spatial rearrangement of the elements. All of these quantitative concepts, so important in an educational context, depend crucially upon mastery of conservation.

Mastery of conservation is thus a critical element in the emergence of operational thought – Piaget sometimes refers to it as *the* psychological criterion of operational structures (e.g., Piaget, 1968, 121). Any experimental findings which point to the need for a radical reappraisal of the development of conservation may thus offer a significant challenge to the Piagetian account of cognitive development. In fact there have been a number of such findings over a considerable period (e.g., Braine, 1959; Mehler and Bever, 1967), but the resulting skirmishes have been more or less inconclusive. Recently, however, a distinctive strand of research focusing on the social context of cognitive testing has begun to offer an important new dimension to this debate.

'Naughty teddy' and after

A landmark in the study of contextual factors in conservation testing was the publication of a paper entitled 'Conservation Accidents' (McGarrigle and Donaldson, 1975). Four and five year old children's judgements on number and length conservation problems were studied under two conditions, which differed only in how the transformation of the materials was handled. In the standard condition, following Piaget, the rearrangement of the materials after the child's judgement of equality was made quite deliberately and openly by the experimenter. In the modified condition the same rearrangement was achieved, but this time by agency of a 'naughty' teddy bear. The toy bear (manipulated by the experimenter) 'escaped' from his box and rushed about causing mayhem until 'captured'. The rearrangement of materials was thus represented as accidental. Only 16 per cent of the children gave consistently conserving judgements after the standard transformation, whereas 63 per cent did so after the modified, 'naughty teddy' transformation.

In a partial replication, Light, Buckingham and Robbins (1979) conducted conservation of length tests with five year olds, comparing standard Piagetian and 'naughty teddy' transformation conditions. The overall frequencies of conserving judgements were lower than McGarrigle and Donaldson had found in both conditions, but their finding of a significantly higher success rate in the accidental condition was confirmed. Other studies using similar procedures have found similar results, though the differences have not always been statistically reliable (e.g., Hargreaves, Molloy and Pratt, 1982; Miller, 1982; Neilson, Dockrell & McKechnie, 1983a).

McGarrigle and Donaldson's interpretation of their results is essentially that young children's failure to conserve in Piaget's tests arises, at least in part, from misleading features of the procedure. The experimenter, in drawing the child's attention to his own actions in rearranging the materials, is giving implicit cues to the child as to what to expect next. Thus if the experimenter lengthens or shortens one row of counters relative to another the child may interpret the ensuing question as having to do with length, whereas in fact it has only to do with the number of counters. The experimenter's actions seem to refer to one dimension while his words refer to another, and the child's incorrect response may simply reflect a confusion between these two. The child's non-conserving responses thus reflect not so much a misunderstanding of the effects of the transformation as a misunderstanding of the experimenter's intentions. Having the transformation effected by an errant teddy bear goes a long way towards removing the confusion.

McGarrigle and Donaldson conclude that their results 'give clear indications that traditional procedures for assessing conservation seriously underestimate the child's knowledge' (1975, 347). They regard their modified procedure as giving a truer, more sensitive indication of the young child's logical competence. The competence in question is at least implicitly accepted as that described by Piaget; as Hughes puts it: 'It seems that some children may fail on the standard conservation task yet still have a good understanding of . . . conservation' (1983, 207).

McGarrigle and Donaldson do not address themselves to the origins of this precocious logical competence, though others (e.g., Gelman, 1982) have suggested that it may be innate. Gelman describes the pre-school child's competence as fragile, visible only in restricted settings, revealed only under 'appropriate circumstances' (1982, 218). Donaldson, in her influential book *Children's Mind's* (1978) has offered a broader characterization of such 'appropriate circumstances' with her concept of *human sense.*

The child's true cognitive abilities will only be revealed, Donaldson argues, in situations which make human sense to the child, i.e, when the cognitive task is set within a context which is fully intelligible to the child as a social interchange. To take a well-known example from another domain of cognitive development, Hughes and Donaldson (1979) have shown that perspective-taking tasks involving a boy doll hiding from one or more toy policemen are much easier for pre-schoolers than Piaget and Inhelder's (1956) classic 'three mountains' task. Why are the new tasks easier? 'We believe it is because the policemen tasks make human sense in a way that the mountains task does not. The motives and intention of the characters are entirely comprehensible' (Hughes and Donaldson, 1983, 253). In much the same way McGarrigle and Donaldson's modifications to the conservation task can be seen as reshaping a socially unintelligible or even paradoxical procedure so as to give the sequence of events some degree of human sense.

In the case of the modified perspective-taking tasks, it could be argued that the relatively familiar nature of the materials and events is an important aspect of their intelligibility. But in fact with conservation it appears that using natural and familiar transformations, such as boats floating apart or children moving around, does *not* produce precocious successes (Miller, 1982). The vital ingredient of 'human sense' would seem to lie in the intelligibility of the social exchange between the experimenter and the child, rather than in the familiarity of the materials or events *per se.* Setting the transformation within a socially intelligible action sequence makes it possible for the child to express his latent grasp of the invariance of quantity, number, or whatever.

Using the perspective-taking example again, however, it is arguable that a more important difference between the modified procedure and Piaget and Inhelder's original lies in the relatively elementary level of the inferences required for success (Light, in press). In a similar vein it has been held that success on the 'naughty teddy' task may actually be achieved on the basis of less than 'operational' abilities. Indeed it has been suggested by some that apparent success on this task may be no more than an artefact, having little or nothing to do with an understanding of conservation.

One source of doubt about the status of young children's judgements on the 'naughty teddy' task has come from the examination of the justifications they offer for their judgements. McGarrigle and Donaldson did not seek justifications from the children, but examination of justifications has led authors of some subsequent studies to view the precociously correct judgements as only partially 'operational' (Parrat-Dayan and

Bovet, 1982) or even as essentially spurious (Neilson, Dockrell and McKechnie, 1983b).

Neilson, Dockrell and McKechnie replicated the 'naughty teddy' study successfully, with more than twice as many four to six year olds offering conserving judgements in the 'naughty teddy' as in the standard condition. However, when it came to offering justifications for their conserving judgements only about a quarter of those asked in either condition were able to offer any 'logical' justification. On the basis of a detailed appraisal of the justifications given in the modified condition, the authors concluded that many of the children saw the teddy bear as simply having made a mess of things. This being so, they ignored the post-transformation array altogether and responded to the conservation question in terms of how things were before they were messed up. The apparent successes, therefore, have little to do with genuine conservation.

Neilson, Dockrell and McKechnie's quantitative analysis of their data on justifications is ambiguous, however, as Donaldson (1983) has pointed out. What they do show clearly is that most children in *both* conditions are unable to provide logical justifications for their judgements. But, as Donaldson (1983) also notes, the status of justifications as criteria for the genuineness of conservation, or any other logical operation is itself questionable (Brainerd, 1973; Brown and Desforges, 1979). Children may not be able to articulate, or may not even be aware of, the factors which influence their responding.

Thus the issue of the 'operational status' of young children's successful judgements on the 'naughty teddy' task remains unresolved at this point. In order to provide a broader base from which to discuss the issue further, I want for the moment, to leave the argument about the 'naughty teddy' effect and to turn to a group of studies which have explored other ways of manipulating the context of the conservation task.

Incidental transformations

While the children in the 'naughty teddy' studies were clearly willing to play along with the experimenter in attributing agency to the teddy bear, they clearly also knew that the experimenter was responsible for both introducing and manipulating it. We have expressed the matter thus: 'The extent to which the child holds separate the intentions of the tester and those of the teddy must remain in doubt. As any parent knows, children at this age have an unnerving tendency to 'step outside' role-playing situations of this kind just when the adult has been drawn in most deeply' (Light et al., 1979, 307).

In an attempt to create a less ambiguous situation, we designed a conservation test in which the transformation of materials would appear to be merely *incidental* to some other activity. Five and six year olds were tested in pairs. In the standard condition children watched as two identical beakers were filled to the same level with pasta shells. When the children had both judged the quantities equal, the experimenter introduced a further, larger container, into which he tipped the contents of one of the beakers. The children were then asked (in turn) to judge whether or not the amounts of shells were still the same.

In the 'incidental' condition the pairs of children were first shown grids into which the pasta shells could be inserted, one per cell, and it was explained to them that they would be playing a game in which the first child to get all his or her shells into the grid would be the winner. So when, in this condition, the shells were initially put into the two identical beakers, the children understood this to be preparatory to the competitive game. When the children had judged that the two beakers contained the same amount (i.e., that the game was fair) one of the beakers was given to one of the children. But just as the other was about to be handed over to the other child, the experimenter 'noticed' that the rim was chipped to a razor sharp edge. With suitable non-verbal accompaniments (signifying surprise and alarm, followed by perplexed pause, followed by 'ah') the experimenter 'found' another container and tipped the shells from the chipped beaker into it. The usual conservation question followed.

Since social influence within the pairs might amplify any differences, we looked at just the first child questioned in each pair. We found 5 per cent of children offered conserving judgements in the standard condition, while 70 per cent offered conserving judgements in the 'incidental' condition. The effect of the change on conditions was thus a fairly massive one.

Miller (1982) has replicated this 'chipped beaker' study, as have Bovet, Parrat-Dayan and Deshusses-Addor (1981), though in this case without a standard comparison condition. In both studies the level of conserving judgements obtained from five year olds in the incidental condition was around 80 per cent. Miller (1982) also showed significant facilitation of conservation judgements in a quantity conservation task in which the experimenter 'accidentally' knocked over one of the beakers. In yet another version Miller (1982) got the child at the end of a session to help him to spread out two rows of counters equally. He then 'remembered' that only one of the rows was supposed to be spread out for the next child, and so changed it. Here again the idea was to render the transformation incidental to the main course of events, and in this case over 90 per cent of the five year olds asserted that the two rows still contained the same number of counters.

Rates of conserving judgements approaching 90 per cent have also been obtained from five year olds by Hargreaves, Molloy and Pratt (1982). In their procedure two equal rows of counters in 1:1 correspondence were set up and initial judgements of equality obtained. Then a second adult, ostensibly testing other children in the next room, came in to 'borrow' some of the counters, taking them from the table. The experimenter protested that the counters were needed, and they were returned. Naturally, in the course of this they became disarranged. Here again the transformation has been successfully embedded within a socially intelligible sequence of actions and events. And here again children who fail on a 'standard' version of the conservation tests, involving the same rearrangement of materials, offer what appear to be conserving judgements.

The authors of these 'incidental transformation' studies have for the most part been fairly equivocal as to the status of the correct conservation judgements obtained. The Genevan view is that they simply reflect distraction of the child's attention from the task in hand (Bovet et al., 1981). But before entering into the issue of interpretation in any detail, I want to draw upon one further group of empirical studies.

Conservation and conversation

We have thus far been considering the effects of changing the way in which the transformation of materials is handled within the conservation task. As far back as 1974, Rose and Blank published a paper concerned with the effects of changing quite a different aspect of the procedure. The conservation procedure basically consists of two questions, separated by a transformation. The two questions are the same (e.g., 'are there more smarties in this row, or more in this row, or do the two rows have the same number of smarties?'). Normally, almost all children will answer the question correctly at the first time of asking, since the materials are arranged so as to make the equality obvious. When the question is put again, after the transformation, young children characteristically (and erroneously) change their answer. Rose and Blank speculated that the repetition of the question itself may have a significant role in generating this error. Repetition of the question by the adult may lead the child to suppose that his first answer was wrong. Alternatively, repetition of the question after the transformation may lead the child to suppose that the transformation *must* be relevant to the question, whereas, of course, it is not.

Rose and Blank (1974) tested this idea in a study of number conservation carried out with six year olds. They compared the standard, two-question procedure with a modification in which the initial question was simply left out. They found significantly higher levels of correct post-transformation judgement in the modified, one-question condition. While attempts to replicate this study have not always succeeded (Miller, 1977) it has been successfully replicated not only for number, but for several other quantity conservation tasks (Samuel and Bryant, 1984). The one-question task has been found to be easier compared not only to the standard task but also to a control condition in which the child only saw the post-transformation array.

Perner, Leekam and Wimmer (1984) have recently extended this work in a slightly different direction. They have sought to alter the impact of question repetition not by omitting one of the questions but by having the two questions asked by different people. In the context of a task involving a horse and a cow who were to be given equal drinks, the children (four to six year olds) had to fill two identical buckets to equal levels. They were asked at this point whether the two amounts were equal. They then poured the 'drinks' into the animals' drinking troughs, which were of different shapes. For some of the children the experimenter then once again asked for a judgement as to the equality of the two amounts. For others, though, the experimenter suddenly said that he had to leave, and asked another adult from the next room to take over. In this condition, therefore, the post-transformation question was asked by someone who had not asked a similar question previously, and who had not seen the pre-transformation array. Substantially more children offered correct conserving judgements in this condition.

There is a problem with this study, in that the post-transformation question actually used was 'did you give them the same?' This might well have been taken to refer to the pre rather than to the post-transformation array, and such a 'retrospective' question would seem especially natural in the modified condition. While this consideration perhaps weakens the force of their evidence, the authors' analysis of their own and others' studies is of interest.

Answering a question 'correctly', they suggest, involves the respondent in discerning why the question was asked in the first place. Taken as a straightforward request for information the crucial question in the conservation test is anomalous, since the respondent has no privileged information inaccessible to the questioner. If the child knows the answer, so too must the adult. Why then is he asking the question? The reality is, of course, that this question is what Searle (1969) termed an 'examination question', rather than a straightforward request for information. If the child does not realize this, he or she will be in difficulty.

Perner, Leekam and Wimmer suggest that young children may be unable to grasp such second-order questions (not 'I want to know X', but 'I want to know whether *you* know X'). Failing to comprehend this second-order intention the child falls back upon an interpretation of the question simply as a request for comment on what is happening – in this case perhaps a comment on whether the amounts now look the same, which typically they do not.

Extending this analysis to the case of Rose and Blank's one-question task, described earlier in this section, they suggest that asking the first question establishes mutual appreciation of equal quantity beyond dispute, while omitting it leaves open the possibility that the experimenter might not have noticed or remembered the equality. This possibility allows the child to treat the post-transformation question as a sincere request for information about amount, and thus to answer it correctly.

Similarly, the 'accidental' and 'incidental' transformation studies described in earlier sections could be interpreted not so much in terms of the distraction of the child (cf. Bovet et al., 1981), as in terms of the putative distraction of the experimenter. The apparently unforeseen events (interruptions, etc.) associated with the transformations allow of the possibility that the experimenter is unsure about the actual state of affairs when the critical question is asked, so once again the question can be understood by the child as being 'in good faith'.

Such an interpretation clearly rests on the assumption that young children do in fact have an understanding of conservation. In effect the source of difficulty in the conservation task is relocated from conservation *per se* to the complexities of second-order questions. The difficulties are still conceived in terms of the individual child's cognitive capacities and limitations, and the modified formats are seen as giving a better indication of the child's underlying competence. In my own work I have adopted a more sceptical view, but one which, I shall argue, points toward a more radical revision of the Piagetian account.

Acquiescence and acquisition

At this point I want to return to the question of the interpretation of the accidental and incidental transformation studies, and in particular to our own interpretation of the 'chipped beaker' study (Light et al., 1979). Although the context manipulation used in this study produced a very large effect, we were doubtful about the kind of interpretation which had been offered by McGarrigle and Donaldson (1975) for such effects. As indicated earlier, they saw their 'naughty teddy' manipulation as a way of circumventing an artefact in the standard assessment procedure, and thus as offering a better estimate of the child's true logical ability. We suggested a rather different interpretation of the success of the accidental or incidental transformation conditions in promoting correct conservation judgements.

We agreed with McGarrigle and Donaldson that in the case of the standard Piagetian procedure, failures may arise as a consequence of the implicit message 'take note of this transformation – it is relevant', contained in the experimenter's actions. However, by extension of the same argument we further suggested that in the 'incidental' conditions of testing successes may arise from the converse message: 'this transformation makes no difference – ignore it', implicit in the experimenter's actions.

For example, in our own 'chipped beaker' condition the experimenter was apparently faced with an unexpected problem – a hitch that threatened to interfere with the flow of the game. The experimenter 'solved' this problem by pouring the contents from the chipped beaker into another, larger beaker. In asking the children afterwards whether the amounts were equal (i.e., whether it was still fair), the experimenter could be seen as simply asking the children to endorse his 'solution'. Seen in this light, their apparently conserving judgements represent little more than acquiecence.

Thus, the same kinds of social-interactional processes which militate against conserving judgements in the standard condition of testing may militate in favour of them in the modified condition. Indeed, once this Pandora's box is opened, it becomes hard to see how any testing situation could ever be neutral. The very human sense or social intelligibility deemed so necessary for a valid test of the child's ability will surely almost inevitably introduce such subtle social cues and biases. Our conclusion was that 'we seem to be further from, rather than nearer, an unbiased assessment of the child's logical abilities' (Light et al., 1979, 310).

This scepticism about the claim that the modified conservation tasks revealed a true logical grasp of conservation led us to a further study (Light and Gilmour, 1983). Here we sought to demonstrate that the same factors which lead children to 'success' on a conservation task can lead children into error in a situation where the properties in question are not in fact conserved. In all the studies we have examined this far, the precocious conserving judgements elicited by the modified formats have been correct, the difficulty being to know whether the children are right for the right reasons. In this study we sought to establish whether conserving judgements could be facilitated by the modified formats even when they were *in*correct.

The task chosen involved transformations of area within a fixed perimeter. Two square fields, each made up of eight 10 cm fence sections (i.e., 20×20 cm fields), were assembled on a large green board, and the children selected animals to put in these fields. The children (five and six year olds) were then asked whether the animals in the two fields had the same amount of grass to eat. All agree that they did. In the standard condition the experimenter then rearranged one of the fields by pulling it out from a 20×20 cm square to a 30×10 cm rectangle, without disconnecting the fence sections from one another. The children were then once again asked whether the animals in the two fields had the same amount to eat. Only about 20 per cent of the children judged that they had.

In the modified condition the only difference was in the provision of a plausible reason for transforming one of the fields into a rectangle. After the initial equality of the fields had been established, the experimenter produced a model farmhouse and went as if to put this on the board next to the fields. The farmhouse was the wrong shape for the space. After a suitable 'pause for thought' the experimenter put the farmhouse down beside the board while transforming the field as if to make a suitable space for it. The question about the equality of 'amounts to eat' was then asked, before the farmhouse was positioned. In this condition some 60 per cent of the children judged the fields still to be equal.

Since the areas of the fields were in fact substantially different after transformation, the modified format could hardly be said in this case to be revealing a latent grasp of conservation. Rather it seemed to us that the children were simply tending to comply with what they saw as the experimenter's request for support and confirmation. The implicit request may be glossed as: 'Oh dear, the farmhouse doesn't fit, so I've got a problem. Ah, but I can solve it just by rearranging this field. There, that's OK isn't it?' The implication being that the transformation does not prejudice the fairness of the situation – in this case the equality of the amounts of grass. The child is in effect being given a strong hint that the transformation is irrelevant, or at least that the experimenter wishes to regard it as such.

The issue of the *relevance* of the transformation is the central one, as Donaldson (1982) has acknowledged. What distinguishes the task we have used here from bona fide conservation tasks is not that the transformation lacks reversibility, nor that it lacks co-variation of different dimensions – the rectangular field is after all longer but thinner than the square one. It is simply that this kind of fixed perimeter transformation does, as a matter of fact, lead to changes in area.

Shultz, Dover and Amsel have an important point when they argue that the real mystery about conservation acquisition is how children come to distinguish those transformations which alter a quantity from those which do not (1979, 120). Shultz and colleagues suggest that the child comes to appreciate what transformations are relevant to what as much through a process of empirical discovery as through deduction from some internal logical structure. There is no suggestion, however, of a social dimension to this process of 'discovery'.

What the context-manipulation studies may be showing us is that the child does not have to sort these things out on his or her own. The embedding of quantity terms within socially intelligible contexts of transformation, and the overdetermination of the child's correct responses by cues in the intra and extra-linguistic context, may play an important part in the process of acquisition.

Light and Gilmour focused on a quirky instance of non-conservation where even adults make mistakes. Older children and adults who wrongly suppose that area is conserved in such cases justify their judgements in just the same terms that they use to justify a 'genuine' conservation judgement (Gold, nd, Russell, 1976), which perhaps casts further doubt upon the 'logical' status of such justifications. One factor responsible for this over-generalization of conservation may have to do with ecological validity. Problems concerning area will most frequently be encountered, both by adults and by children, in the context of fixed surfaces of land, for example, or of paper, or of fabric. In these practical, everyday contexts fixed perimeter transformations just do not arise. Transformations typically take the form of rearrangements – cutting up, sticking together, and so on. Area is an abstract concept catching precisely at what *is* conserved across such rearrangements.

Likewise, the other quantity terms which are involved in conservation tasks can be seen as *embodying* conservation. What earthly use would a concept of number be for example if it did not refer to a property of a group of objects which was independent of their spatial arrangement? The irrelevance of certain transformations is part of what we mean when we talk about number or amount, volume, etc., and it is implicit in the way we talk about them. Moreover, at least outside the testing situation, we can reasonably assume that when adults talk to children they intend the children to understand what they mean. The adult's apparent intentions are therefore a good guide to what his or her words actually mean. The child can typically rely on contextual guidance to support an appropriate interpretation of what it is that he or she is being asked or told.

To the extent that this is true, children's contextual sensitivity does not simply leave them exposed to arbitrary and extraneous influences. On the contrary, it offers an access to meanings and may often enable children to make correct judgements in respect of concepts they apprehend only dimly. While such judgements may for some purposes be regarded simply as 'false positives', the contextual support which produces them may have an important part to play in securing proper reference for terms such as amount and number, in which conservation across certain kinds of trans-formation is intended to be implicit.

It may be, therefore, that we should concern ourselves rather less with the issue of whether the child's precocious but context-specific judgements are 'genuine' or not, and rather more with the part played by contextual sensitivity in the acquisition of understanding. This issue will be taken up within the broader discussion which follows, which relates not only to conservation, but to 'operational thought' in general. Much the same story told here for conservation could be repeated with respect to class inclusion (e.g., McGarrigle, Grieve and Hughes, 1978) and other 'oper-ational competences'. A number of theorists have begun to use this body of evidence to argue the need for a radical revision of the Piagetian approach to the study of children's thinking.

Context and competence

Donaldson (1978) has graphically portrayed the young child's logical competence as context bound, dependent for its expression upon suitable 'embedding' in familiar, intelligible social contexts. The pre-school child's problem, as Gelman and Gallistel (1978) put it, is typically not in any lack of competence but in the failure of performance. It is not that the child lacks the reasoning principles required, but rather that he or she may fail to *use* them appropriately in many contexts.

It can be seen that while context is important in such a view, a distinction between competence and performance is maintained, and competences continue to be treated, in Piagetian fashion, as substantive entities of some kind, 'possessed' by the child. For the young child, as Donaldson sees it, context limits the expression of competence, whereas in the older child, thinking has become relatively 'disembedded' or context free.

This approach, and especially the treatment within it of the notion of competence, has come under increasing criticism. Stone and Day (1980) have argued cogently against granting a competence model psychological reality. They use as one analogy the case of web-spinning spiders, where, fairly clearly, formal descriptions of the patterns of the webs need to be sharply distinguished from the operation of the functional systems that are responsible for web construction. They argue that the attempt to treat psychological (or logical) competence models as 'properties' of the child generates theoretical confusion, 'and in the case of students of cognitive development, has led to a form of "negative rationalism" rampant in current attempts to explain the cognitive activity of children' (1980, 337).

Rommetveit (1974, 1978), who himself coined the term 'negative rationalism' to characterize attempts to account for the child's cognitive stage in terms of deviations from some idealized logical structure, has attempted to refocus attention firmly at the level of shared social understandings. He is dubious about the search for context free and formally defined structures of thought even for adults, and argues that progress in understanding the development of thinking is most likely to be made by studying how people achieve intersubjective reference. Words, statements, questions, all are largely uninterpretable except within the context of the intersubjectively established 'here and now' of acts of speech. The process of learning is an inherently social process in which 'what is initially unknown to the listener is made known to him in terms of a progressive expansion and modification of an actual or intersubjectively presupposed shared social world' (1974, 95).

We see here the beginnings of a shift in which the social context moves from having the status of a performance variable, simply limiting the expression of the child's competence, towards a more central and constitutive role. In the UK, Walkerdine has done much to develop this standpoint, criticizing Donaldson's work as an attempt to 'weld context onto the Piagetian edifice' (1982, 129). The problem, as she puts it, is that cognition remains 'inside', influenced by a context which is 'outside'.

This inside/outside distinction finds an echo in the simple primacy given in the Piagetian account to the signified over the signifier – to the concept over the word, or to knowledge over language. Walkerdine argues that this relationship is in fact a complex and dynamic one, in which meanings are created and negotiated. Social contexts, social practices and discourses are, within this account, granted a key role in the elaboration of the child's conceptual knowledge.

Moreover, the role of context is not a passing phenomenon, overtaken with development by a progressive decontextualization of thought. Even explicitly formal or logical reasoning is a practice, supported and maintained as an activity between people (Walkerdine, 1982). Rommetveit makes the same point. Piaget treats logic as the very stuff of intellectual development, while treating language simply as a conventional system of signs. Rommetveit (1978) observes that a formal logical system is also a ready-made system of signs and moreover one which was developed for particular purposes and with carefully considered gains and costs. Formal, logical or abstract forms of thought may be considered to be just as closely linked to particular 'contexts of appropriateness' as any other. New contexts, and perhaps particularly the forms of discourse associated with schooling and literacy (Olson and Torrance, 1983; Walkerdine, 1982), educe new forms of thought. Intellectual development, viewed from this standpoint, is more a matter of recontextualization than of decontextualization.

The focus of attention is thus shifted away from the abstract 'epistemic subject' of Piaget's structuralist approach, towards the real child's experience in specific social contexts. Paradoxically, the achievement of abstract thought is seen as context dependent, and context driven. The classroom is clearly an important setting, and the tacit ground rules of the teacher-child interchange are increasingly coming to be seen as critical features of the effective context (Mercer and Edwards, 1981).

The examination of these ground rules promises to generate an intriguing social psychology of cognitive development. As we have seen in relation to the conservation task, the role of questioning by an adult is of particular interest. The prominent place such questioning has in teacher-child discourse, has often been noted, and is discussed by Wood in the following chapter. The typical 'teacher's question' is one to which the teacher already knows the answer. Moreover 'even when the form of the question is one which seems to invite a variety of answers, there is often only *one* that is really acceptable to the teacher' (Wells, 1983, 140).

All such questions are second-order questions in the sense discussed earlier in this chapter, and Perner, Leekam and Wimmer have suggested that as such they may be too cognitively complex for pre-school children to grasp. However, these questions are by no means the exclusive pre-rogative of the school, and at least in some circumstances they would seem to be both familiar and well understood by pre-schoolers (Elbers, 1984; Wood, chapter 9). For the most part, whether at home or at school, such questions are asked in the context of providing help and support for the child working on some task. However, Elbers (1984) distinguishes between the assumptions and presuppositions involved in this 'instructional meta-contract' and those which are involved in the 'metacontract of testing'. Here the relationship of question and context is very different, and questioning is being used not in a supportive and constructive way but rather as a means of examination. It is this form of questioning which character-izes the cognitive testing situation and it is this, Elbers suggests, which will be unfamiliar to children lacking much experience of formal educational practices.

The attempt to refine such distinctions and to characterize what is taken for granted in particular contexts of discourse is clearly a contemporary growth point. Recent studies of children's responses to bizarre and nonsensical questions (Finn, 1982; Hughes and Grieve, 1983) provides an interesting sidelight on this, while Walkerdine's (1982, 1984) detailed observational work on classroom teaching of number concepts more directly illuminates some of the presuppositions and expectations character-istic of particular discourses. I want to return, however, to take a final look at conservation in the light of the theoretical concerns expressed above. If conservation is not to be thought of as a fundamental logical competence signalling the beginning of the operational period, how is it to be thought of?

Cowan (1981) has pointed out that most of the conservations with which we are concerned are in fact rather more matters of rough approximations than of exact truth. In the liquids conservation task described at the outset of this chapter, for example, we conveniently forget differential evaporation, and the residue left in the first container. Cowan observes that 'if the psychologist was a physics student the physical scientist might regard him as being in need of remedial teaching' (1981, 7). Conservation in this case is not exact, but it is nonetheless good enough for most practical purposes.

The practical purposes which the conservations serve seem, however, to have been given little attention. A pragmatic approach to understanding and problem-solving conceived in terms of 'tricks of the trade' (Goodnow, 1972) or 'rules of thumb' which allow us to work on the world predictably (Simon and Newell cited in Goodnow, 1972) may actually have as much to offer in this area as the universalistic cognitive-developmental account.

The child is apprenticed to a language and a culture which are grounded in practical human purposes. The concepts of amount and number, of area, volume, weight and so on, embodying as they do the various conservations, are a part of that language and culture. Their historical origins can again be assumed to be rooted in particular practical contexts of action. While direct evidence will necessarily be difficult to come by in this area, it may not be wholly inaccessible. The work of Damerow (1984) on the number concepts of early Mesopotamian civilizations offers one example of an attempt to trace such origins and to relate the evolution of concepts to the demands of changing social practices. More work of this kind could be immensely valuable.

Our argument, then, is that conservation concepts can and should be thought of not as transcendent logical entities but as the historically determined products of specific human purposes and practices (cf. Russell, 1978). The child's task, seen in this light, is to gain access to these culturally elaborated abstractions. This is no easy task, given that amount, number, etc. are not pointable-at properties of the materials concerned. However, the child's sensitivity to the subleties of discourse, of which we have seen much evidence in this chapter, may have a vital part to play in successfully achieving shared reference with these concepts.

Such a formulation is undoubtedly partial and oversimplified. Our ignorance of the processes involved is pitiful, but at least the space within which useful work could be done is becoming clearer. Vygotsky, writing in the 1930s referred to the then current views of intellectual development as 'one sided and erroneous primarily because they are unable to see facts as facts of historical development, [they] regard them as *natural* processes and formations . . . fail to differentiate the organic from the cultural, the natural from the historical, the biological from the social . . . in a word, these views of the nature of the phenomena in question are fundamentally incorrect' (Vygotsky, 1966, 12). Nothing is new then, but if ever the time was ripe for building on these criticisms and working constructively towards a new understanding of cognitive development, it is surely now.

References

Bovet, M., Parrat-Dayan, S. and Deshusses-Addor, D. 1981. Peut-on parler de précocité et de régression dans la conservation? I Précocité. *Archives de Psychologie*, **49**, 289–303.

Braine, M. 1959. The ontogeny of certain logical operations: Piaget's formulations examined by non-verbal methods. *Psychological Monographs*, **73**, no. 5.

Brainerd, C. 1973. Judgements and explanations as criteria for cognitive structures. *Psychological Bulletin*, **79**, 172–9.

Broughton, J. 1981. Piaget's structural developmental psychology III. Function and the problem of knowledge. *Human Development*, **24**, 257–85.

Brown, G. and Desforges, C. 1979. *Piaget's Theory: a psychological critique.* London: Routledge and Kegan Paul.

Cowan, R. 1981. On what must be – more than just associations? (paper presented at 11th Annual Interdisciplinary Conference on 'Piaget and the Helping Professions', Los Angeles, February 1981).

Damerow, M. 1984. Individual development and cultural evolution in arithmetical thinking (paper presented at second Tel-Aviv Workshop on Human Development, 'Ontogeny and Historical Development', Tel-Aviv University, October 1984).

Donaldson, M. 1978. *Children's Minds.* London: Fontana.

Donaldson, M. 1982. Conservation: what is the question? *British Journal of Psychology*, **73**, 199–207.

Donaldson, M. 1983. Justifying conservation: comment on Neilson et al. *Cognition*, **15**, 293–5.

Donaldson, M., Grieve, R. and Pratt, C. 1983. *Early Childhood Development and Education.* Oxford: Basil Blackwell.

Elbers, E. 1984. The social psychology of the conservation task (paper presented at BPS Developmental Section Conference, 'Future Trends in Developmental Psychology', Lancaster, September 1984).

Finn, G. 1982. Children's experimental episodes, or 'Ask a silly question but get a serious answer' (unpublished paper, Department of Psychology, Jordanhill College of Education).

Gelman, R. 1982. Accessing one-to-one correspondence. *British Journal of Psychology,* **73**, 209–20.

Gelman, R. and Gallistel, C. 1978. *The Child's Understanding of Number.* Cambridge, Mass.: Harvard University Press.

Gold, R. nd. Inappropriate conservation judgements in the concrete operations period (unpublished paper, Department of Psychology, University of Melbourne).

Goodnow, J. 1972. Rules and repetoires, rituals and tricks of the trade, in S. Farnham-Diggory (ed.), *Information Processing in Children*. New York and London: Academic Press.

Hargreaves, D., Molloy, C. and Pratt, A. 1982. Social factors in conservation. *British Journal of Psychology*, **73**, 231–4.

Hughes, M. 1983. What is difficult about learning arithmetic? in M. Donaldson, R. Grieve and C. Pratt (eds) *Early Childhood Development and Education.* Oxford: Basil Blackwell.

Hughes, M. and Donaldson, M. 1979. The use of hiding games for studying the coordination of viewpoints. *Educational Review*, **31**, 133–40.

Hughes, M. and Donaldson, M. 1983. The use of hiding games for studying coordination of viewpoints, in M. Donaldson, R. Grieve and C. Pratt (eds), *Early Childhood Development and Education*, Oxford: Basil Blackwell.

Hughes, M. and Grieve, R. 1983. On asking children bizarre questions, in M. Donaldson, R. Grieve and C. Pratt (eds), *Early Childhood Development and Education*. Oxford: Basil Blackwell.

Inhelder, B. and Piaget, J. 1958. *The Growth of Logical Thinking from Childhood to Adolescence*. London: Routledge and Kegan Paul.

Light, P. 1983. Social interaction and cognitive development: a review of post-Piagetian research, in S. Meadows (ed.), *Developing Thinking*. London: Methuen.

Light, P. In press. Taking roles, in H. Weinreich-Haste and J. Bruner (eds), *Making Sense: the child's construction of the world*. London: Methuen.

Light, P., Buckingham, N. and Robbins, A. H. 1979. The conservation task as an interactional setting. *British Journal of Educational Psychology*, **49**, 304–10.

Light, P. and Gilmour, A. 1983. Conservation or Conversation? Contextual facilitation of inappropriate conservation judgements. *Journal of Experimental Child Psychology*, **36**, 356–63.

McGarrigle, J. and Donaldson, M. 1975. Conservation accidents. *Cognition*, **3**, 341–50.

McGarrigle, J., Grieve, R. and Hughes, M. 1978. Interpreting inclusion: a contribution to the study of the child's cognitive and linguistic development. *Journal of Experimental Child Psychology*, **26**, 528–50.

Mead, G. H. 1934. *Mind, Self and Society*. Chicago: University of Chicago Press.

Mehler, J. and Bever, T. 1967. Cognitive capacity of very young children. *Science*, **158**, 140–2.

Mercer, N. and Edwards, D. 1981. Ground-rules for mutual understanding, in N. Mercer (ed.), *Language in School and Community*, London: Edward Arnold.

Miller, S. 1977. A disconfirmation of the quantitative identity–quantitative equivalence sequence. *Journal of Experimental Child Psychology*, **24**, 180–9.

Miller, S. 1982. On the generalisability of conservation. *British Journal of Psychology*, **73**, 221–30.

Moore, C. 1985. The effect of context on the child's understanding of number and quantity (unpublished Ph.D. thesis, University of Cambridge).

Neilson, I. Dockrell, J. and McKechnie, J. 1983a. Does repetition of the question influence children's performance in conservation tasks? *British Journal of Developmental Psychology*, **1**, 163–74.

Neilson, I., Dockrell, J. and McKechnie, J. 1983b. Justifying conservation: a reply to McGarrigle and Donaldson. *Cognition*, **15**, 277–91.

Olson, D. and Torrance, N. 1983. Literacy and cognitive development, in S. Meadows (ed.), *Developing Thinking*. London: Methuen.

Parrat-Dayan, S. and Bovet, M. 1982. Peut on parler de précocité et de régression dans la conservation? II. *Archives de Psychologie*, **50**, 237–49.

Perner, J., Leekam, S. and Wimmer, H., 1984. The insincerity of conservation questions (paper presented to BPS Developmental Section Conference 'Future Trends in Developmental Psychology', Lancaster, September 1984).

Piaget, J. 1952. *The Child's Conception of Number*. London: Routledge and Kegan Paul.

Piaget, J. 1955. *The Construction of Reality in the Child*. London: Routledge and Kegan Paul.

Piaget, J. 1957. *Logic and Psychology*. New York: Basic Books.

Piaget, J. 1968. *Six Psychological Studies*. London: University of London Press.

Piaget, J. and Inhelder, B. 1956. *The Child's Conception of Space*, London: Routledge and Kegan Paul.

Piaget, J. and Inhelder, B. 1969. *The Psychology of the Child*. London: Routledge and Kegan Paul.
Rommetveit, R. 1974. *On Message Structure*. London: John Wiley.
Rommetveit, R. 1978. On Piagetian cognitive operations, semantic competence, and message structure in adult-child communication, in I. Markova (ed.), *The Social Context of Language*, Chichester: John Wiley.
Rose, S. and Blank, M. 1974. The potency of context in children's cognition. *Child Development* **45**, 499–502.
Russell, J. 1976. Nonconservation of area: do children succeed where adults fail? *Developmental Psychology*, **12**, 367–8.
Russell, J. 1978. *The Acquisition of Knowledge*. London: Macmillan.
Samuel, J. and Bryant, P. 1984. Asking only one question in the conservation experiment. *Journal of Child Psychology and Psychiatry*, **25**, 315–18.
Searle, J. 1969. *Speech Acts*. Cambridge: Cambridge University Press.
Shultz, T., Dover, A. and Amsel, E. 1979. The logical and empirical bases of conservation judgements. *Cognition*, **7**, 99–123.
Stone, C. and Day, M., 1980. Competence and performance models and the characterisation of formal operational skills. *Human Development*. **23**, 323–53.
Walkerdine, V. 1982. From context to text: a psychosemiotic approach to abstract thought, in M. Beveridge (ed.), *Children Thinking Through Language*. London: Edward Arnold.
Walkerdine, V. 1984. Developmental psychology and the child centred pedagogy, in J. Henriques, W. Holloway, C. Urwin, C. Venn and V. Walkerdine (eds), *Changing the Subject*, London: Methuen.
Wells, G. 1983. Talking with children: the complementary roles of parents and teachers, in M. Donaldson, R. Grieve and C. Pratt (eds), *Early Childhood Development and Education*. Oxford: Basil Blackwell.
Vygotsky, L. 1962. *Thought and Language*. Cambridge, Mass.: MIT Press.
Vygotsky, L. 1966. Development of the higher mental functions, in A. Leontyev, A. Luria and A. Smirnov (eds), *Psychological Research in the USSR*, Vol. 1. Moscow: Progress Publishers.

9

Aspects of teaching and learning

David Wood

Introduction:
Images of the learner and reflections on the teacher

Teaching is a complex, difficult and often subtle activity. Although I will be arguing that a great deal of teaching is spontaneous, 'natural' and effective, deliberate teaching of groups of children in formally contrived contexts is an intellectually demanding occupation. It is also a relatively new one. Compulsory, formal education for all has a short history and the technologies and consequences it has spawned, both material and mental, are still poorly understood and the subject of political and academic debate.

Some years ago, Greenfield and Bruner (1969) argued that the invention and widespread availability of schooling has had dramatic effects on the nature of human knowledge; not simply creating wider dissemination of facts but fundamental changes in the nature of thinking itself. Although ensuing studies of the impact of schooling on the human intellect have shown that the effects are somewhat less general than this hypothesis suggested (e.g., Cole and Scribner, 1974) they have shown that schooling, in company with other technologies (notably literacy), has marked effects on various intellectual 'skills'. Donaldson (1978), in a critical examination of Piagetian theory, argues that schooling does help to create certain varieties of human reasoning, particularly a capacity to deploy powers of reasoning to solve problems that involve abstract, hypothetical entities. In such contexts, thinking out problems and understanding what is implied by them demands attention to the formal structure of the problem and cannot be achieved by appeals to common sense or plausible inferences. Thus, Donaldson concludes that schooling is the source of special ways of thinking about and operating upon the world.

One implication of this view is that teachers (broadly rather than narrowly conceived) are responsible for inculcating certain ways of thinking in children. Not only do they pass on facts and information about things but also ways of conceptualizing and reasoning. Where they succeed, teachers recreate their own ways of thinking in their pupils; where they fail they may inhibit or prevent a child's access to power within his own society.

Our knowledge of the 'psychology of teaching' is derived from several sources. The first and most obvious is from theories and studies of learning and development. Theorists of human development, notably Bruner, Vygotsky and Piaget, offer not only radically different views of what children are like, what *knowledge* is and how it develops; they sketch out radically different images of the teacher. In this chapter we will examine some of the major features of these theories in relation to the issue of what teaching *is*.

A second source of information about teaching stems from the now numerous attempts to describe and analyse teaching as it occurs in class-rooms. Unfortunately, many such studies are largely atheoretical and even idiosyncratic, so it is seldom possible to utilize the data they provide to inform our arguments about theories of what teaching is. One possible reason for this is that teachers do not actually do what any of the theories dictate they should do, either because teachers are ignorant of theories or theorists are ignorant of teaching. One view is that theories developed out of psychological research cannot be used to develop categories to describe what goes on in classrooms because their relevance is limited to what happens in laboratories. There has been a good deal of debate in recent years about the status and relevance of theories about children based largely on experimental, psychological research. For example, Cole and his colleagues (1979) observed children in home-like contexts and reported that they seldom found evidence of the sorts of demands, tasks and inter-actions that cognitive psychologists use in the laboratory to explore learning and development. Thus, psychologists *qua* psychologists are likely to be working with very different raw material in fashioning their theories of children's thinking to that which informs the views of parents and others. Herein, perhaps, lie some reasons for different conceptualiz-ations of the nature of children by psychologists and non-psychologists. Psychologists may be accused of having created 'straw children' and imaginary learners who haunt the psychological laboratory but not the 'real' world.

I shall be arguing, however, that the differences between children's behaviour in different contexts (e.g., laboratory versus home) are of more interest and importance than this interpretation suggests. More specific-ally, I will be exploring the idea that interactions between adults and children in 'spontaneous' and 'contrived' encounters are different in nature. By contrived, I mean teaching/learning/testing encounters that are deliberately brought about by those with power (e.g., teachers or psychologists) as opposed to those which 'arise' spontaneously out of adult-child contacts. I shall also work on the assumption (not totally without evidence) that most interactions at home are spontaneous and child initiated, and those in schools or psychological laboratories are usually contrived and adult controlled. I also suggest that when adults and children in the two different contexts appear to be working on the 'same' tasks or doing superficially similar things, the processes involved are dissimilar. The interactions follow different 'ground rules' and create different demands of both the adult and the child and this explains why children often appear to display varying levels of intellectual or linguistic competence in different situations. We will consider, for example, why children who are inquisitive and loquacious at home may show little initiative in school.

But what are 'ground rules'? Mercer and Edwards (1981) have provided some examples in a consideration of classroom interactions, drawing attention to differences between the constraints which operate in classroom and everyday discourse. For example, being able to answer questions such as 'It takes three men six hours to dig a certain sized hole. How long would it take two men to dig the same hole?' demands more than a knowledge of how to apply and execute the sums involved. One must also appreciate what constitute appropriate and inappropriate answers. Problems demanding similar decisions in everyday life (e.g., working out how long a certain job will take) might legitimately concern issues such as when the ground was last dug over; what tools are to be used; how experienced the men are and so forth. In mathematics lessons, however, such considerations are 'irrelevant'. To know what is relevant, a child has to discover or infer the rules underlying what is a very special form of discourse. Arguments, for example, about making mathematics 'relevant' are likely to founder if they simply choose 'everyday' situations and ignore the fact that the ground rules for solving everyday, practical numerical problems and abstract, formal mathematical problems are different.

If one accepts that activities occurring across contexts may be governed by different, implicit social practices and rules, then what may seem like the 'same' task in different contexts may, to children who have yet to acquire all the rules, appear very different. Several researchers (e.g., Donaldson, 1978) have shown that young children often appear able to do things in some contexts but not others. They possess competence that does not always emerge in their performances. One may seek to understand such discrepancies in the fact that some contexts are more threatening, unfamiliar or less motivating to children. But it is also likely that the apparent similarities between the competence demanded in such situations are misleading. Thus, identifying the reasons why observations of teaching and learning in home, school and laboratory often yield different views of the processes involved is no simple matter. What might seem to be essentially similar tasks and activities in various contexts may well be located in quite different 'rules' of conduct and interpretation.

Another line of evidence relating to the question of what effective teaching is would seem, on first sight, to offer the most direct and compelling way of adjudicating between competing theories. A number of educational programmes have been set up, particularly in the USA, to help provide young children from economically poor homes with a 'Headstart' in their educational life by providing pre-school educational experiences (see Woodhead, 1985, for an overview). There have been some successful intervention programmes. But these were inspired by a range of *different* theories of learning and development. No one theory held the day. Weikart (1973), commenting upon the success of his own, neo-Piagetian programme and those of others who had based their interventions on other theories, concludes that the important common element in success was not the curriculum *per se* nor the material it employed but the commitment and competence of its teachers! The *nature* of such competence remains obscure.

We will examine just a few aspects of what teaching competence might involve. I do not claim, however, to be more than scratching the surface of what is undoubtedly an extremely complex issue.

Learning and Development

I will in this part of the chapter be discussing in some detail a series of studies of the teaching-learning process that have employed a common task. The children being taught range from three to five years of age. Left to their own devices, the children would not be able to do the task at hand. Nor do they learn how to do the task if they are taught ineffectively. Given effective instruction, however, they can be taught how to do most or all of it alone (Wood and Middleton, 1975).

Although the task we shall be considering is a specific and concrete one I shall argue that some aspects of the teaching-learning process it identifies are general ones which are relevant to and implicated in many naturalistic encounters between adults and children. I shall also try, however, to identify some important differences between the nature of interactions observed in such contrived teaching-learning encounters and those found in more spontaneous encounters between adults and children in homes and schools.

The conceptual framework adopted in this chapter is derived from the theorizing of Vygotsky (1978) and Bruner (1968). Vygotsky, for example, contributed the concept of a 'zone of proximal development'. This expression refers to the gap that exists for a given child at a particular time between his level of performance on a given task or activity and his potential level of ability following instruction. Vygotsky offers a conceptualization of intelligence that is radically different from that promoted either by conventional, psychometric intelligence tests or Piagetian theory. Vygotsky's theory of intelligence takes the capacity to learn through instruction as central. The intelligence of a species is deter-mined not only by a capacity to learn but also to teach. Furthermore, two children who behave similarly in a given task situation, suggesting similar levels of competence, may in fact be quite different, in that one may prove able to benefit far more from instruction in that task than another.

Underlying this view of the role of instruction in learning are radically different conceptions of the nature of knowledge, development and maturity from those embodied in Piagetian theory. Piaget's child is an epistemologist; a natural seeker after, and architect of, his own under-standing. He learns largely through his own activity in the world. He constructs progressively more powerful, abstract and integrated systems of knowing by discovering how his actions affect reality. All a teacher can do is to facilitate that understanding by providing appropriate materials and contexts for the child's actions and by helping the child to discover inconsistencies in his own views. The primary motivator of developmental change for Piaget is 'disequilibration'; a state of conflict between what the child expects as a result of his interactions with the world and what actually transpires. Knowing the stages of development and materials and activities that are likely to be relevant to the activities dictated by each stage, a teacher can facilitate developmental change by helping the child to discover implicit contradictions in his own thinking. But any contradic-tions must be *latent* in the child's structure of knowledge. They can be activated but not induced. There is no point and may even be harm in confronting the child with hypotheses, demonstrations or explanations that are not 'natural' to his stage of development.

Whilst there is evidence favouring the view that one basis for develop-mental change or learning is cognitive conflict and contradiction (e.g., Glachan and Light, 1982) I will be arguing that far more is invovled in effective teaching than simply providing material for the child to 'digest' or activating competing ideas that are already implicit in his thinking. We will explore the view that adult and child, working together, can construct new schemes through shared interaction. The potential effects of teaching will prove to be far greater than Piagetian theory allows. What the child develops, in this alternative conceptualization, are not mental operations derived from his actions on the world but 'concepts' that are jointly constructed through interaction with those who already embody them, together with ways of doing and thinking that are cultural practices, recreated with children through processes of formal and informal teaching.

The nature of effective instruction: contingent control of learning

We are confronted with two individuals who are in asymmetrical states of knowledge about a problem facing them. The more knowledgeable, the teacher, is attempting to communicate a more informed understanding to the less knowledgeable, the learner. How are practical skills and ideas transferred from one body to the other?

Our task here is to discover an analysis of teaching and learning inter-actions that will enable us to relate instructional activity to the learning process. If we are successful in identifying the crucial features of effective teaching, then it should be possible to examine a range of different teaching styles or strategies and make testable predictions about their relative effectiveness.

Some years ago we attempted to meet these goals in an analysis of mother-child interactions in an experimental situation (Wood and Middleton, 1975). The children involved were four years old and the task the mothers were asked to teach them was a specially designed construction toy. When a child first encountered the task, he or she saw 21 wooden blocks of varying size and shape. The mother had already been shown how these could be assembled to create a pyramid, but the child had no knowledge of the solution to the problem. The mother was asked to teach the child how to put the blocks together in any way she saw fit. She was also told that when the pyramid had been put together, it would be taken apart and the child asked to assemble it alone.

Each block in the toy is unique and will only fit into one position in the final construction, but the task was designed to incorporate a number of repeated rules of assembly. The pyramid (more accurately, a ziggurat) comprises five, square levels, each a different size. The bottom level is approximately nine inches square and is constructed out of four, equally sized, square pieces. Two of these assemble by fitting a peg in one into an equally sized hole in the second. When this pair is assembled in the correct orientation, two half pegs, one on each block, are brought together. Similarly, two other blocks assemble by a hole and peg arrangement but to bring two half-holes together. When the two pairs are constructed, the peg and hole formed can be fitted together to produce a level of the pyramid. This rule of assembly is repeated with sets of blocks of diminishing size to construct four more levels. The assembly of each set of four also creates connectives to enable them to be piled on top of each other. On the 'top' of each block is a quarter section of a round peg. When each level is assembled correctly, these come together to form a peg which fits into a circular depression in the base of the level above, which is similarly created from four quarter depressions in each block. Thus, the levels can be piled to form a rigid structure. The assembly is completed by placing a single block with a depression in its base on the top level.

The blocks were designed so that any peg would fit into any hole and any level could fit onto any other. Thus, the task presents many possibilities for 'incorrect' assembly. Left to their own devices, four year olds cannot do the task but given effective instruction they can. But what does effective instruction look like? How are we to describe the maternal attempts to teach children?

Imagine we are watching a mother and child in a teaching-learning encounter with these blocks. The mother has just given an instruction. First, we determine how much *control* the instruction implicitly exerts over what happens next. Five categories are listed in table 1 which, we have found in a number of studies, can accommodate any instruction a teacher might make in this situation. These vary in terms of degree of control.

Table 1   Levels of control

Level	Example
1 General verbal prompts	'Now you make something'
2 Specific verbal instructions	'Get four big blocks'
3 Indicates materials	Points to block(s) needed
4 Prepares for assembly	Orients pairs so hole faces peg
5 Demonstrates	Assembles two pairs

The first category, general verbal prompts, includes instructions that demand activity but do not specify how the child should proceed to meet such demands. Specific verbal instructions give the child information about features of the task that need to be borne in mind as he or she makes the next move. If the teacher not only tells the child what to attend to in making his or her next move but also shows him or her what is referred to by pointing at or picking out relevant material, then the instruction is classified as Level 3. If the teacher not only identifies material but goes on to prepare it for assembly then the child is simply left with the problem of how to complete the operation in question. Finally, if the teacher demonstrates, he or she takes full control of the next step in the construction whilst the child, hopefully, looks on and learns.

As we come down the list, then, the instructions become more controlling, with the teacher implicitly taking more, and offering the child correspondingly less, scope for initiative.

Mothers vary enormously in the way they attempt to teach their young children how to do this task, and children also vary widely in their ability to do the task alone after instruction. Does the style of teaching affect what is learned? It does. Mothers whose children do well after instruction are those who are most likely to act in accordance with two 'rules' of teaching. The first dictates that any failure by a child to bring off an action after a given level of help should be met by an immediate increase in help or control. Thus, if the teacher, say, had provided the child with a specific verbal instruction and then found that the child did not succeed in complying with it, the appropriate response is to give more help either by

indicating the material implicated in the previous instruction or by prepar-
ing it for assembly.

The second rule concerns what should happen when a child succeeds in
complying with an instruction. This dictates that any subsequent instruction should offer less help than that which pre-dated success. In other
words, after success the teacher should give the child more space for
success (and error).

The pattern of responses by the teacher to a child's momentary successes and failures *judged in relation to the instructions which pre-dated
them* is the basis for our evaluation. Every time a teacher acts in accordance with the rules she is deemed to have made a *contingent* response.
Every time she does something different (i.e., fails to provide an instruction
immediately after a child fails or gives one at an inappropriate level) the
instruction is non-contingent. What we find is that the more frequently
contingent a teacher is the more the child can do alone after instruction.

Stated simply and boldly, the rules of contingent teaching sound easy.
However, even in our experimental situation involving a practical task
with a single solution, it is difficult to teach all children contingently all the
time. Indeed, when we trained an experimenter to teach children according
to different rules we found that she was only able to follow the
contingency rules about 85 per cent of the time (Wood, et al., 1978).
Monitoring children's activity, remembering what one had said or done to
prompt that activity and responding quickly to their efforts at an
appropriate level is a demanding intellectual feat. Effective teaching is as
difficult, if not more so, as the learning it seeks to promote.

Scaffolding the learning process

We have defined the *process* of effective instruction as the contingent
control of learning. Elsewhere, using the metaphor of 'scaffolding', we
have identified some of the *functions* that instruction may fulfil for the
learner (Wood, Bruner and Ross, 1976). Since this notion has been
extended beyond laboratory studies to help describe more naturalistic
teaching-learning processes, it is necessary to explore the characteristics of
scaffolding and its relationship to control and contingency before moving
on to consider more general aspects of teaching and learning.

One of the most influential approaches to the study of human intelligence stems from a view of a human being as a 'limited information
processor'. Individuals can only take in so much information about their
situation at any moment in time, so they must organize their activities over
time (develop a plan) in order to assimilate and operate within that
situation. The development of knowledge and skill involves the discovery
of what is best paid attention to, borne in mind and acted upon in an
appropriate (goal-achieving) sequence.

At the heart of this conception of human abilities is the notion of 'uncertainty'. When we find ourselves needing to act in a very unfamiliar situation, uncertainty is high and our capacity to attend to and remember objects, features and events within the situation is limited. Observation, practice, trial and error, the growing appreciation of regularities and learning, involve the progressive reduction of that uncertainty. Accompanying its reduction are increased accuracy of perception and powers of memory. Thus, experts in a task are able to observe, take in and remember more of what they experience (within the task situation) than novices.

Children, being novices of life in general, are potentially confronted with more uncertainty than the more mature and, hence, their abilities to select, remember and plan are limited in proportion. Without help in organizing their attention and activity, children may be overwhelmed by uncertainty. The more knowledgeable can assist them in organizing their activities, by reducing uncertainty; breaking down a complex task into more manageable steps or stages. As the children learn, their uncertainty is reduced and they are able to pay attention to and learn about more of the task at hand.

But such assisted learning presupposes that the children are actively involved in trying to achieve task relevant goals. Clearly, what individuals attend to and remember in a given context is dictated by their purposes and goals; relevance is relative to the purpose in mind. Children may perceive a situation differently from an adult because they face greater uncertainty and/or because they may be entertaining different ideas about the opportunities for activity offered by the task situation.

Where a child is already involved in the pursuit of a goal or the fulfilment of an intention, then provided that the would-be teacher is able to discover or infer what that goal is, the child may be helped to bring it off. In formal or contrived situations, where the teacher decides what purpose the child must pursue, *task induction* becomes a primary scaffolding function and a *sine qua non* for effective learning. Children also face additional problems in contrived encounters because, given that they are compliant, they have to discover what their intentions are supposed to be.

How does one invoke intentions or a sense of goal directedness in the young child? More specifically, can demonstrations or verbal instructions be used effectively to invoke relevant activity? Clearly, showing children things or asking them to perform activities that they are currently unable to do will only be successful if the child understands enough of what was said or shown to lead to relevant, if not fully successful, task activity. Instruction must, to use Vygotsky's term, operate within the learner's 'zone of proximal development'. For such a concept to be useful, perception must, in some way, help to lead or constrain action and understanding.

I suggest that young children often think they understand and are capable of doing what an adult shows or tells them when, in fact, they do not. Young children, in short, often overestimate their own abilities. However, children's beliefs about their own competence lead to intentional activity and trap them in problem-solving; into trying to do what they think they can do. Provided that effective help is forthcoming, the child may be led to construct new skills. These, in turn, accompany modified perceptions of what is seen and heard. The learner comes closer to mature understanding. Put another way, both demonstrations and verbal instructions can be used to define problem spaces within which adult and child can work co-operatively and contingently to promote learning. Perhaps a few examples will illustrate this argument.

In the experimental situation already outlined we found that three year old children showed signs of *recognizing* what was an appropriate task goal before they were able to *achieve* that goal. For instance, they appreciated the fact that four dissimilar blocks could be put together to create a single and more parsimonious *Gestalt*. They would usually attempt to reproduce such a configuration after a demonstration. When their attempted constructions did not look similar to that demonstrated, they would usually take them apart and try again. However, they almost never took apart a construction that did look like the model; evidence both that they possessed some sense of what was task relevant and that their activities were goal directed.

Although, purely verbal instruction proved an ineffective teaching strategy, every child so taught did begin by attempting to do what was requested. We suggest that the young child possesses sufficient linguistic competence to derive plans from verbal instructions which are partially but not fully understood. Thus, when told to 'Put the four biggest ones together' they never selected the smallest blocks and usually attempted to fit pegs into holes. Although they did not realize, early in the instructional session, all the constraints that were implicated in such general verbal instructions, they understood enough of what they implied to lead them into task relevant activity.

Even when children do not fully understand what we show them or ask of them, they may believe that they understand and understand enough to lead them into task relevant, if initially unsuccessful, action. We suggest, then, that a learner's *incomplete* understanding of what he or she is shown and told (what is perceived) is a vital basis for learning through instruction. Perhaps incomplete but relevant understanding of what children see adults doing and hear them saying is at the heart of what Vygotsky termed the 'zone of proximal development'.

Once the learner is involved in task relevant activity other scaffolding functions become operative. I have already said that young children, like all of us, are limited in how much they can attend to and remember in problematic situations. There is also evidence that, left to their own devices, they are unlikely to realize whether or not they have actually examined a situation 'fully' (Vurpillot, 1976). Pre-school children do not search exhaustively or systematically for evidence that might be relevant to what they are trying to do; tending to make up their minds on the basis of a limited inspection of the situation at hand (in contrived problem situations, at least).

There is also evidence, again from contrived situations, that young children are unlikely to 'rehearse' what they are trying to remember. Thus, their powers of memory may be limited not only by an uncertain world but also because they have yet to learn (or to be taught) how best to remember what they seek to retain.

Given children's propensity to attend to a limited range of features of problematic situations and, perhaps, their immature strategies for deliberate memorization, a teacher will often have to scaffold their immediate actions. They may, for example, *highlight* crucial features of the task situation that have been ignored or forgotten. In so doing, they also help the child to *analyse* the task. They may act as an external source of memory and planning for the child, either by prompting recall of a previous activity or, more subtly, by holding constant the fruits of past activities whilst the child concentrates his or her limited resources on another domain. For example, children in our task situation would often put together two pieces and then try to add a third one. The blocks are so designed that it is extremely difficult to put together four pieces without first constructing the two pairs. By directing the child's attention away from the first-assembled pair or by keeping hold of it whilst the child attempted to assemble the second pair, the instructor helped the child by breaking down a goal into a series of less complex sub-goals.

Scaffolding functions effectively support and augment learners' limited cognitive resources, enabling them to concentrate upon and master manageable aspects of the task. With experience, such elements of the task become familiar and the child is able to consider further related task elements. Contingent control helps to ensure that the demands placed on the child are likely neither to be too complex, producing defeat, nor too simple, generating boredom or distraction.

Teaching: natural and contrived

So far, we have been exploring the concepts of scaffolding, control and contingency in contrived encounters between adults and children in laboratory settings. We have also been dealing with very specific, short-term learning outcomes in a well-structured, concrete task with a specific 'right' answer. Are such concepts useful in more naturalistic situations?

Are the effects of contingent teaching task specific or does it engender more general effects?

In this section, I will explore some attempts to extend the concepts of scaffolding and contingency to adult-child interactions in studies of language acquisition to see how far their use in this, more naturalistic research, involves more than a metaphorical relationship with their use in more formal, specific contexts.

Bruner's (1983) account of the development of the pre-verbal foundations of language acquisition extends the concept of scaffolding to the analysis of mother-child interactions. He argues that the development of early linguistic competence in the child depends upon the (informal) teaching roles played by the adult. The development of the infant's communication abilities takes place within frequently recurring 'formats' of interaction. Initially, such formats (families of interactions such as simple games, feeding sessions, nappy changing etc., which take on a predictable pattern), are largely regulated by the adult and are the basis of what Bruner terms 'Language Acquisition Support Systems'. The frequent repetition of formats provides infants with opportunities to discover and exploit regularities in their experiences. But adults play the major role in initiating and structuring the early interactional formats. Bruner writes:

> If the 'teacher' in such a 'system' were to have a motto, it would surely be 'where before there was a spectator, let there now be a participant'. One sets the game, provides a scaffold to assure that the child's ineptitudes can be rescued by appropriate intervention, and then removes the scaffold part by part as the reciprocal structure can stand on its own. (1983, 60)

Whilst he sees adults taking the leading role in the construction of such systems of support, it seems that what is involved is not so much a process of *directing* the child but one more akin to 'leading by following'. Once the child's involvement has been gained and he is inducted into activity that can be orchestrated into an emerging system of interaction, adults tend to make what they do contingent upon their interpretation of what is likely to be the current focus of interest or relevance to the child. Thus, 'it becomes feasible for the adult partner to highlight those features of the world that are already salient to the child and that have a basic or simple grammatical form.' To the extent that adults make where they look and what they do and say contingent upon their interpretation of the child's current interest, what they are likely to be putting into words is relevant to what is in the child's mind. Thus, adults help to bring the infant's experience of the world and linguistic communication about that world into contact.

Bruner's use of the concepts of scaffolding and contingency shares formal similarities with the processes described in the analysis of contrived teaching. The task of inducting the infant into what is to become a predictable format of interaction; supplementing and orchestrating the child's role in the interaction by actions designed to highlight critical features of the joint task or activity; reducing degrees of freedom for action (buffering from distraction) to encourage the infant to focus on critical aspects of the situation; trying to hand over increasing responsibility for the execution of actions that have been constructed with the child; attempts to perform such functions in a manner that is contingent upon the child's activities, are important features of the teaching process, whether natural or contrived. Whilst I would argue, however, that the scaffolding functions are common to both types of activity with children of very different ages, the means whereby such functions are achieved change with the developing competence of the infant. Induction, for example, changes from a process that we might term 'capture' to one of 'recruitment'. This change occurs in response to the (co-ordinated) development of planning and self-consciousness in the child.

For example, in the early encounters described by Bruner and others, what might initially be a 'chance' or unintentional act by the child may be highlighted and responded to by the adult 'as if' it were an intended component of an envisaged performance. Such highlighting can be achieved by the adult performing a marked, exaggerated action or *display* that is contingent upon and follows closely in time behind the infant's activity. To the extent that this display captures the infant's attention and interest, it may evoke a repetition of the child's initial activity. Initially spontaneous, unpremeditated movements by the baby may thus form the basis for the emergence of intentional acts of communication.

A number of studies have highlighted the degree of 'fit' between both the content and timing of events that are likely to grasp the infant's attention and the 'natural' or spontaneous displays of adults (or even very young children) *en face* with the infant (e.g., Brazelton, 1982). The adult achieves induction of the infant by *capturing* his attention.

With older children, induction is easier in some contexts and more difficult in others. Once attention and interest can be solicited by verbal invitations or demonstrations, the teacher may evoke intentional action towards a goal from the child. As early as nine to 18 months, young children also display some knowledge of the fact that the adult can be *recruited* to help them in an activity that they are unable to bring off alone (Geppert and Kuster, 1983). By 30 months, teaching-learning encounters may be solicited by either party. But, around the same age, infants also show evidence of wishing, at some times, to maintain the independence of their own actions; of wanting to 'do it myself'.

Although, as we have seen, it is possible to induce the pre-schooler into joint problem solving, evidence from naturalistic observations in the home indicates that most encounters between young children and their parents are of the children's own choosing. In short, they tend to solicit rather than be inducted into most exchanges with parents.

The evidence comes from Wells (1979) who found, from audio-taped recordings of exchanges between parents and their three year olds at home, that 70 per cent of interactions were initiated by the child. Thus, what adult and child are likely to be working on, attending to and talking about is still largely determined by the *child's* interests.

Wells's analyses also indicate that parents who respond contingently to the child's utterances by elaborating, developing and negotiating about what they mean are more likely to engender conditions for establishing mutual understanding and the development of linguistic competence in the child. Although his analyses do not make explicit use of concepts such as scaffolding and control he does employ the term contingency in a similar way. I suggest that his findings are consistent with the view that effective scaffolding and control are factors that influence the development of linguistic competence in children. To extend this argument, however, I need to make reference to other research in which the notions of control and contingency have been exploited to study the effects of different styles of talking to children on the child's performances in school contexts.

Asking and telling: who is contingent upon whom?

We are studying two complex systems that know things: teacher and child. We believe that these two systems are in asymmetrical states, in that the teacher knows more than the child and has responsibility for transferring that knowledge. But the asymmetry is not entirely one-sided. The child also knows things about the world and himself that the teacher does not know. The desire to make teaching 'relevant', 'learner centred', to 'start where the learner is at' or to be contingent upon their attempts to learn is implicated in most theories of learning and development (Wood, 1980b). Thus, teachers must also seek to understand what the child knows if they are to help develop, extend, clarify and integrate that knowledge.

Wells's studies, in company with research by Tizard and her colleagues (Tizard and Hughes, 1984) suggests that pre-school children tend to initiate interactions, ask questions and seek information more readily at home than school. Much of their 'epistemic' activity is directed towards achieving explanations about facts of everyday life and is occasioned by happenings in the local culture. The parent tends to be in a privileged position in relation to these requests and demands, being a *part* of that culture. Their practices and talk are embedded in what it is that the child seeks to know. Further, their privileged access to the child's history provides a basis for intersubjectivity. Their implicit hypotheses about what is likely to have motivated an epistemic act from the child; what the child is already likely to have experienced in relation to it, to know, think and feel about it, are more likely than those of strangers to prove workable or enactable.

Thus, the conditions that promote the quest for knowledge from the child are often present in the home and the needs of the child are most likely to be interpretable to those who know them. Conditions for the generation of a contingent learning environment are more likely to be endemic to the home or local culture in a way that they are not to school. Thus, the pre-school child at nursery or school is less likely to be prompted to wonder about the 'why's' and 'wherefore's' of what is going on, which is perhaps why their discourse often centres on the happenings of the moment and thus seems 'context dependent'. Where children *do* talk about things outside the classroom, not surprisingly, it tends to be to mention significant others in their daily life (relatives), or the events, happenings, promises and surprises that occur at home (Wood, McMahon and Cranstoun, 1980).

Children, then, 'present' themselves differently at home and at school. Even when teachers set out to work with individual children, they face considerable difficulties in establishing a contingent interaction because children generally give them relatively few epistemic offerings to be contingent upon. Thus, task induction becomes a more demanding activity for the teacher than the parent (and, by the same token, for a psychologist in a laboratory setting, Wood, 1983). Other factors also operate against the establishment of child-initiated, adult-contingent encounters. One is group size. At home, the presence of a third person, particularly a younger sibling, is likely to promote talk between parent and child about the actions, needs and morality of another (Dunn and Kendrick, 1982). Children, in their second year of life, begin to wonder about the nature of other people. At school, however, surrounded by numbers of relative strangers, observations by children about the 'psychology' of other people around are relatively rare (Wood et al., 1980). Faced with groups of children, the teacher encounters purely numerical difficulties in any effort to promote and sustain productive encounters with individuals. Management of self, time and resources becomes an important feature of the teaching role. Any attempts to instruct or inform are thus embedded within a wider set of roles and objectives.

The common teacher response to these difficulties is to initiate and sustain interactions not by showing or telling but by demanding and asking. Both demands and questions are exercises in *control*. In a number of different studies several classroom observers have noted the very high frequency of teacher questions. Such studies range from pre-schoolers to children about to leave school (Wood and Wood, 1985). Furthermore, teacher questions tend to display a number of 'special' characteristics. They are often specific, demanding a narrow range of possible 'right' answers (e.g., MacLure and French, 1981; Tizard et al., 1976; Wood et al., 1980). Teachers often know the answers to the questions they ask, and children, by four years of age, possess the ability to recognize this fact, in some contexts at least (Wood and Cooper, 1980). Furthermore, the readiness of children to talk about what they know is likely to be inhibited by such questions.

Several reasons have been given for the frequency and nature of teacher questions. Questioning groups is one strategy whereby (at best) the minds of all involved can be focused on the same idea or topic. Questions are one tactic for the achievement of 'group intersubjectivity'. When a child is not forthcoming with numerous, spontaneous epistemic acts, then questions will usually achieve a response and, therefore, may be used as tactics for initiating and, perhaps, modelling epistemic inquiry. Speculating further, it might be the case that the use of questioning represents a historical reaction to 'talk and chalk' or 'didactic' methods of education. Questioning may be seen as a tactic designed to engage the child actively in the teaching-learning process. Rather than 'passively' sitting and listening to the teacher's declarations the child should be enjoined, through questions, to wonder and think about the topic at hand.

Whatever the rationale or 'cause' of frequent questioning by teachers, I would argue that the strategy is counter-productive.

If we accept the fact that, particularly with young children, what we seek to show them and tell them demands a knowledge of what they can already do and what and how they think about the task at hand, how are we to encourge them to display their knowledge? Focusing for the moment on mainly verbal exchanges, I suggest the following 'operationalized' definition of knowledge display. Children will ask questions about the topic, revealing their uncertainty and what they seek to know. They will take up openings to contribute to and comment upon the topic at hand. They may go beyond a direct answer to the teacher's questions to add additional information, ideas or observations that they consider supplement or qualify their answers. Further, if, as Wells argues, adult and child need to negotiate their perspectives on and objectives in a given domain, we may find that a child responds to the teacher's questions with requests for clarification or to negotiate the conditions under which they are prepared to answer.

These aspects of children's discourse define a set of conditions in which the teacher can gain access to the *child's* thoughts and uncertainties about, opinions and attitudes towards the topic at hand.

These conditions are inhibited to the extent that teachers manage the interaction through questions. The more they question the less children say. Children's contributions (even when an opportunity is given) become rarer and more terse the more questions are asked (e.g., Wood and Wood, 1983). Children are only likely to go beyond the force of teachers' questions to give additional ideas and explanations if questions are relatively infrequent. In some contexts at least, they are less likely to seek information through questions themselves when the teacher is asking a lot of questions.

Pupils tend to take single 'moves' in dialogue with the teacher. Whereas teachers display a number of offerings in their turns (e.g., accepting what a child has said, offering a contribution to the discourse and immediately asking a question) pupils are most likely to make a single type of move. Thus, if the teacher terminates his or her utterance with a contribution (i.e., statement, opinion, speculation) children are likely to respond with a contribution of their own; more so if the teacher's contributions are frequent. Similarly, if a teacher accepts or acknowledges what a child says but offers no further question or observation, the child is likely to continue with the topic at hand. There are also a number of second-order effects of teaching style. The less a teacher interrogates children, the more likely they are to listen to, make contributions about and ask questions of what the other children say (Griffiths, 1983; Wood and Wood, 1983). Such findings occur both as correlations between teaching style and pupil responses in natural classroom discourse and can be brought about in experimentally contrived encounters in which teachers vary their style of responding to groups of children (Wood and Wood, 1983, 1984).

The extent to which a child reveals his or her own ideas and seeks information is thus inversely proportional to the frequency of teacher questions – and this finding embraces studies of pre-school children through to 16 year olds, deaf children and children acquiring English as a second language.

Some of the teachers who have participated in experimentally contrived classroom sessions in which they have modified their style of talking to children by asking fewer questions, becoming less controlling and giving more of their own views and opinions have commented that they found out things about the children's experiences, views and ideas that they did not know and would not have thought to ask questions about (Lees, 1981). Questions may solicit the information demanded by the teacher and serve as specific probes and checks for retention of information or of a child's capacity to draw inferences. As tools for finding out things that a child thinks or knows that are not already anticipated or known by the teacher they are ineffective, at least when used in excess. If it is a teacher's goal to discover 'where the child is at' in order to respond contingently to their ideas and thoughts, the established 'register' of the classroom is generally ineffective in achieving this goal. Teachers can, however, engender sessions in which children show more initiative, if they are prepared to ask fewer questions and say more about their own ideas and views. Just as effective teaching of practical skills demands a contingent combination of showing and telling, so the extension of children's understanding through discourse demands an integration of the declarative and interrogative voice.

There is now an extensive and growing literature on the 'effective use of questioning' (e.g., Blank et al., 1978; Sigel et al., in press). Although the issue of what constitutes a 'good' and timely question is not resolved and the literature on the effects and effectiveness of questions has produced somewhat equivocal results, a few general points and reasonable speculations are emerging from the literature. First, as we saw above, several researchers have concluded that too many teacher questions are 'closed' and lead children to search for specific right answers rather than into processes of reasoning and weighing evidence. Secondly, teachers tend to leave relatively short pauses after their questions before taking back control of the interaction. When they are helped to extend these pauses (from one to three seconds) the frequency and level of student response increase (Rowe, 1974; Swift and Goodling, 1983). It seems that pupils usually need more time to think about their answers to teacher questions than teachers normally allow. Questions to which the teacher already knows the answer are also common. Thus, the implicit theory of learning involved is one in which the teacher knows all the answers and the child's task is simply to find them. Sigel and his colleagues (Sigel et al., in press) analysing discourse between parents and children, have shown, for example, that more open-ended, demanding parental questions (which, in Sigel's terms 'distance' the child from and encourage him to reflect upon his immediate experiences and concerns) are positively correlated with various measures of the child's intellectual development, whereas more closed questions are not. Similarly, Redfield and Rousseau (1981), in a review of questioning, concluded that the use of questions high in 'cognitive demand' by teachers has a positive effect on student achievement.

Unfortunately, however, studies in this area usually concentrate on comparisons of different types of questions and fail to explore any effects of different levels of teacher contributions or statements. In a small-scale study (Wood and Wood, 1983) we found that where a teacher offers contributions that are high in level of presentation (e.g., speculations, opinions, reasoning, etc.) children are likely to respond in kind. Questions high in cognitive demand (similar to the definitions of Blank et al., 1978) also solicit high cognitive responses from children but at the cost of inhibiting follow-through, elaboration or spontaneous comments from them. Where teachers, in one sense, answer their own putative questions to provide possible answers, opinions and so on, children as young as four years of age reciprocate by adopting a similar cognitive-linguistic stance and remain relatively active and forthcoming at the same time.

High control of interactions by teachers in natural or contrived encounters, in laboratory, home or school, are likely to inhibit overt epistemic activity from children. Furthermore, the fact that children are not contributing ideas, asking questions or elaborating on their answers to the teacher's questions, but spending the vast majority of their time in complying or answering questions means that their thinking (unless they 'drop out' of the interaction) is almost entirely contingent upon the demands of the teacher. If teachers are not gaining knowledge from the children, then they have few opportunities for making any questions, comments or ideas that they have contingent upon the children's own thoughts, for these are simply not revealed or displayed.

The role played by children in teaching-learning encounters is fundamentally constrained by the way in which teachers manipulate control. If a child is not active, forthcoming and curious about the task at hand, the main cause of this inactivity may lie not in some 'inner resource' lacked by the child, but in the level of control and ensuing lack of opportunity for contingent instruction determined by the manner in which the teacher orchestrates the interaction.

Teaching as epistemic inquiry

Teaching is usually defined as the *transmission* of knowledge and the inculcation of skills and understanding. Such definitions seem reasonable but are inadequate and even misleading. Teaching also involves learning; it provides opportunities for the acquisition of knowledge. It is epistemic activity. Furthermore, the knowledge obtained from acts of teaching informs the process of effective teaching.

Piaget has characterized the child as a 'natural' epistemologist. We have not rejected this basic stance but argued that the epistemological activity of the child is, and often must be, enveloped within that of a teacher. Piaget has also demonstrated how the study of the systematic and 'universal' errors that children make can be exploited to investigate the nature and development of knowledge. Similarly, I have suggested that the study of 'errors after instructions' is a primary basis for learning about the learner, learning, what is being learned and teaching. An instruction from a teacher is, potentially, an epistemic probe as well as an attempt to prompt epistemic activity in the child. If it is treated as a hypothesis about the child's 'zone of proximal development', for example, then a failure to comply by the child suggests that the hypothesis may be invalid and that he or she needs more help. Conversely, success serves as a signal to the teacher to update her hypothesis about where the child is 'at' and, hence, to revise future instruction; in Bruner's economic metaphor to 'up the ante'. Teachers may utilize the fate of their own instructions as a basis for learning and revising their 'theory' of the child and what he or she is learning. The tremendous difficulties in doing this in school environments, however, often preclude such contingent instruction, and demand, essentially, that it is the child who must make his or her thinking contingent upon that of the teacher. If children are able and willing to be contingent upon the thought processes and actions of another, then learning may proceed. If they are not, then it seems unlikely that learning will follow.

Although we have been stressing the importance of teaching and exploring the complex questions of what effective instruction involves, this does not imply that effective teaching is a sufficient or always a necessary condition for learning. We have not been advocating a return to classical learning theory nor rejecting the now extensive evidence which shows that young children form hypotheses, infer and generalize rules to make creative and productive use of their experiences. But I have tried to identify some factors in natural and contrived encounters that serve to facilitate or inhibit such epistemic activities by the young child. Such a view leads us, for example, to attribute failure or lack of progress by a learner not simply to factors located 'in' the child but to constraints that arise as an emergent property of teacher-learner interactions. These, in turn, are tightly constrained by the nature of the institutions that we have invented to bring teachers and learners together. If we find ourselves dissatisfied with the interactions that take place in such institutions, measured against what we take to be the optimum contexts for learning, then we must question not simply the teacher's 'skills' but the form of the institution within which we expect these to be deployed.

References

Blank, M., Rose, S. A. and Berlin, L. J. 1978. *The Language of Learning: the Preschool Years.* New York: Grune and Stratton.

Brazelton, T. B. 1982. Joint regulation of neonate-parent behavior, in E. Z. Tronick (ed.), *Social Interchange in Infancy: affect, cognition and communication.* Baltimore, Mld: University Park Press.

Bruner, J. S. 1968. *Toward a Theory of Instruction.* New York: Norton.

Bruner, J. S. 1973. The organisation of early skilled action. *Child Development*, **44**, 1–11.

Bruner, J. S. 1983. *Child's Talk: learning to use language.* Oxford: Oxford University Press.

Cole, M. and Scribner, S. 1974. *Culture and Thought: a psychological introduction.* New York: Wiley.

Cole, M., Hood, L. and McDermott, R. 1979. *Ecological Niche Picking.* New York: Rockefeller University Monographs.

Donaldson, M. 1978. *Children's Minds.* London: Fontana.

Dunn, J. and Kendrick, C. 1982. *Siblings: love, envy and understanding.* London: Grant McIntyre.

Geppert, U. and Kuster, U. 1983. The emergence of 'wanting to do it oneself': a precursor of achievement motivation. *International Journal of Behavioral Development*, **6**, 355–70.

Greenfield, P. M. and Bruner, J. S. 1969. Culture and cognitive growth, in D. A. Goslin (ed.), *Handbook of Socialisation Theory and Research*. New York: Rand McNally.

Glachan, M. and Light, P. 1982. Peer interaction and learning: can two wrongs make a right? in G. Butterworth and P. Light (eds), *Social Cognition: studies of the development of understanding*. Brighton: Harvester.

Griffiths, A. J. 1983. The linguistic competence of deaf primary school children (Ph.D. thesis, University of Nottingham).

Lees, J. M. 1981. Conversational strategies with deaf children (M.Phil. thesis, University of Nottingham).

MacLure, M. and French, P. 1981. A comparison of talk at home and school, in G. Wells, *Learning Through Interaction: the study of language development*. London: Cambridge University Press.

Mercer, N. and Edwards, D. 1981. Ground rules for mutual understanding, in N. Mercer (ed.) *Language in School and Community*. London: Edward Arnold.

Murphy, C. M. and Wood, D. J. 1981. Learning from pictures: the use of pictorial information by young children. *Journal of Experimental Child Psychology*, **32**, 279–97.

Piaget, J. and Inhelder, B. 1969. *The Psychology of the Child*. London: Routledge and Kegan Paul.

Redfield, D. L. and Rousseau, E. W. 1981. A meta-analysis of experimental research on teacher questioning behavior. *Review of Educational Research*, **51**, 237–45.

Rowe, M. B. 1974. Wait-time and rewards as instructional variables, their influence on language, logic and fate control. I. Wait time. *Journal of Research in Science Teaching*, **11**, 81–94.

Sigel, I. E. and McGillicuddy-Delisi, I. In press. Parents as teachers to their children, in A. D. Pellegrini and T. D. Yawkey (eds), *The Development of Oral and Written Language: readings in developmental and applied linguistics*. Norwood, NJ: Ablex.

Swift, J. N. and Gooding, C. T. 1983. Interaction of wait time, feedback and questioning instruction on middle school science teaching. *Journal of Research in Science Teaching*, **20**, 721–30.

Tizard, B. and Hughes, M. 1984. *Young Children Learning: talking and thinking at home and school*. London: Fontana.

Tizard, B., Philps, J. and Plewis, I. 1976. Staff behaviour in pre-school centres. *Journal of Child Psychology and Psychiatry*. **17**, 251–64.

Vurpillot, E. 1976. *The Visual World of the Child*. London: George Allen and Unwin.

Vygotsky, L. S. 1978. *Mind in Society: the development of higher psychological processes*. Cambridge, Mass.: Harvard University Press.

Walkerdine, V. 1982. From context to text: a psychosemiotic approach to abstract thought, in M. Beveridge (ed.), *Children Thinking Through Language*. London: Arnold.

Weikart, D. P. 1973. Cited in Brainerd, C. J. 1983. Modifiability of cognitive development, in S. Meadows (ed.), *Developing Thinking: approaches to children's cognitive development*. London and New York: Methuen.

Wells, G. 1979. Variation in child language, in P. Fletcher and M. Garman (eds), *Language Acquisition*. Cambridge: Cambridge University Press.

Wood, D. J. 1980a. Teaching the young child: some relationships between social interaction, language and thought, in D. Olsen (ed.), *Social Foundations of Language and Cognition: essays in honor of J. S. Bruner*. New York: Norton.

Wood, D. J. 1980b. Models of childhood, in A. J. Chapman and D. M. Jones (eds), *Models of Man*. London: The British Psychological Society.

Wood, D. J. 1983. Teaching: natural and contrived. *Child Development Society Newsletter*, no. 32. London, Institute of Education.

Wood, D. J., Bruner, J. S. and Ross, G. 1976. The role of tutoring in problem solving. *Journal of Child Psychology and Psychiatry*, **17**, 89–100.

Wood, D. J. and Cooper, P. J. 1980. Maternal facilitation of 4–5 year old children's memory for recent events. *Proceedings of the XXIIn'd International Congress of Psychology*. Leipzig, East Germany: International Union of Psychological Science.

Wood, D. J. and Middleton, D. J. 1975. A study of assisted problem solving. *British Journal of Psychology*, **66**, 181–91.

Wood, D. J., McMahon, L. and Cranstoun, Y. 1980. *Working with under-fives*. London: Grant McIntyre.

Wood, D. J., Wood, H. A. and Middleton, D. J. 1978. An experimental evaluation of four face-to-face teaching strategies. *International Journal of Behavioral Development*. **1**, 131–47.

Wood, D. J., Wood, H. A., Griffiths, A. J., Howarth, P. and Howarth, C. I. 1982. The structure of conversations with 6- to 10-year-old deaf children. *Journal of Child Psychology and Psychiatry*, **23**, 295–308.

Wood, D. J. and Wood, H. A. 1985. Teacher questions and pupil initiative (paper to the American Educational Research Association, Chicago, USA).

Wood, H. A. and Wood, D. J. 1983. Questioning the preschool child. *Educational Review*. **35**, Special Issue (15), 149–62.

Wood, H. A. and Wood, D. J. 1984. An experimental evaluation of five styles of teacher conversations on the language of hearing-impaired children. *Journal of Child Psychology and Psychiatry*, **25**, 45–62.

Woodhead, M. 1985. Pre-school education has long effects: but can they be generalized? *Oxford Review of Education*, **11**, 133–55.

10

Children's understanding of the distinction between messages and meanings: emergence and implications

W. Peter Robinson

Introduction

In studying child development the particular and concrete ought to be seen as examples of the general and abstract, just as the general and abstract need to be instantiated in everyday activities. Had I known ten years ago, however, that the mundane and small communication issue we decided to explore would eventually require me to resume my previously unsuccessful struggle to understand Kant's concept of the transcendental 'I', then my 'I' would possibly have exerted its free will in the direction of some more tractable matters. From beginnings in asking how young children come to understand that their speech has to meet the needs of their listeners, we have found ourselves wrestling with the complicated and profound problem of the emergent awareness of self as a partially self-organizing agent.

Whilst I can describe the steps up this path historically, I will not claim that all can now be explained. The experimental studies of verbal communication to be discussed in this chapter do reveal that younger children's failure to understand that speech can be ambiguous is closely related to a failure to distinguish between what is said and what is meant. What is true for verbally communicated information appears to be equally true for visually communicated information. Children who do not understand that speech can be ambiguous are also likely to believe that visual perception is direct rather than mediated by interpretation. I shall argue that for children to come to understand about these matters will require them to develop new ideas about the status of perceived information and to develop and apply new strategies of interaction; they will need to know when they have insufficient information to act and how to set about obtaining that information. We have demonstrated that the necessary understanding *can* be promoted by others treating them *as if* they already have that understanding. Finally, I try to mount an argument relating these developments to a more profound change in the child: the child who can say that a message is ambiguous because the speaker has not made the meaning explicit enough for a listener to act correctly has also to be able to say, 'I know that I do not know.' The first 'I' in this statement has a significantly different status from the second 'I' (cf. Harré, chapter 13); it marks the self as being able to experience itself as both subject and object. The argument lacks coherence, and is presented more as an important problem that we need to address than as an elegant solution to a long-standing issue. But, to begin at the beginning . . .[1]

Flavell et al. (1968) listed requirements that speakers have to meet if they are to be deliberately effective communicators of factual information unknown to a listener. They have to know that a problem of *perspective* exists; that what recipients of a message can see, hear, feel, or otherwise detect may not coincide with what the speaker can perceive. They have to know whether or not there is a *need in the present situation* to take differential perspectives into account. If they decide there is such a need, they have to *analyse* the implications of the differences in perspective, and, taking into account the presumed characteristics of the listener, they have to *encode* appropriate messages.

Our initial explorations were intended to probe children's understanding of the first two of these requirements – perspective and need – in circumstances where the last two factors were controlled to be within the child's intellectual and verbal competence. We exploited the kind of situation used by Krauss and Glucksberg (1969) in which each of two participants is seated at either end of a table with identical arrays of items in front of them, separated by an opaque screen. The speaker has to select an item and tell the listener about it, so that the listener can pick up the corresponding item. The listener makes a choice. Each person then shows his or her choice to the other. The items may be sets of objects or cards with distinguishable characteristics.

Initially using cards with stickmen in this context, we added an interrogatory sequence through which the child was asked whether the speaker had told the listener enough to choose the correct item, and whose fault it was if there was a mismatch and why. The materials and procedures were designed to yield failures in communication. Almost all errors arose because the message referred to more than one item in the listener's array; for example, the speaker would say, 'A man holding a flower', when there were two such cards, one with a red flower and one with a blue. This constituted our operational definition of ambiguity.

The great majority of children participating have been between five and eight years old. Most of the older children in this age range would state that a mismatch had occurred because the speaker had not said enough about the item. They blamed the speaker for this and could supply the disambiguating information, originally omitted. These judgements were independent of the role actually being played by the child. Whilst more complex accounts of the mismatch could be offered by adults, these children at least saw that the ambiguity of the message was a crucial factor in communication failure. In contrast many of the younger children claimed that the speaker *had* said enough and that the listener was at fault. Typically these children said the reason for the mismatch was that the listener had picked up the wrong item. The message and its characteristics were not mentioned as a reason for the listener's error.

This pattern has withstood many attempts to eliminate it. These have included variations in role (speaker versus listener, participant versus observer), variations in materials (stickmen, playpeople, ink-blots, real-life cartoon strips, model-building) and in procedure (varied instructions, counter-suggestions, questions about success rather than failure). Comparable and consistent results have been obtained in a succession of studies by a variety of investigators (e.g., Flavell, Speer, Green and August, 1981; Lefebvre-Pinard, Charbonneau and Feider, 1982; Patterson and Kister, 1981; Sonnenschein and Whitehurst, 1984). It is not the case, how-ever, that these younger children will blame the listener if the message is actually incompatible with the item displayed by the speaker (Roberts and Patterson, 1983; Robinson and Robinson, 1977a). If the message is 'A man with a red flower', but the item subsequently displayed by the speaker is a red flag, then these younger children will blame the speaker. Hence they can judge messages to be inadequate. Even in this case, however, they are likely to say the mismatch occurred because the speaker picked up the wrong item.

What are we to say about these younger children? Negatively we might say that they do not show any evidence of knowing that spoken messages can be ambiguous. More positively we can say they appear to be operating with a double rule which might be expressed as: 'If the message fits the item, then it is all right; if it does not fit, it is inadequate.' Is this really so, or is this inference based on results which are artefacts of the situations and procedures used? Artificiality and unfamiliarity of settings have been invoked to question the status of reported findings in child development. Children's interpretations of the task are not necessarily those defined by the experimenter (see Light, chapter 8). Children's notions of the social order may provoke them into behaviour that may be erroneously inter-preted.

Experiments can be viewed as artificial by definition, and we have not been unaware of their disadvantages. They can show what might happen, but cannot show what commonly does happen. Hence we have used uncontrolled observations of the natural world of children when possible, both to probe and complement results from experiments and to serve as a resource for hypotheses to test. Fear or anxiety arising from unfamiliarity of setting or task have not been apparent. The investigations have been conducted by amiable adults who converse happily with the children while sitting themselves on small chairs. An overwhelming majority of children 'tested' have positively enjoyed the 'games' we have played with them. It is true, however, that by and large these children have come from Caucasian families with fathers in white-collar or skilled manual occupations who accept that leaving their classrooms to play games with friendly adults is an unproblematic and pleasant part of life in school.

With respect to the tasks themselves, the behaviour of the children who refer to the ambiguity of messages as reasons for communication failure does not stand in need of special explanation. Some of them occasionally give ambiguous messages with a knowing smile and present the experimenter with a problem of choice. They are masters of the task and the context of situation. On the other hand, those who do not refer to the message and blame the listener for a wrong choice appear to believe that their explanation is correct. It must be conceded, however, that the procedure does involve an element of compliance. Sometimes such children spot that the adult's message refers to more than one card. Nevertheless they make a choice. Here they do seem to be following a social rule. The adult has stopped speaking. It is now their turn to act, and they do so. They do not, however, refer back to that problem of choice during the interrogatory sequence, but why should they if they (and the experimenter) are satisfied with their explanations?

Whilst we would defend the reasonableness of our methodology, we are not happy with the linguistic abbreviations we have used for the phenomena described. Generally we have referred to 'listener-blaming' and 'speaker-blaming' children. This labelling has a double disadvantage. It refers to the children rather than to the rules of thinking guiding their conduct. It draws attention to blaming rather than to conceptions of how language works. Reference to 'younger' and 'older' children could be seen as focusing on maturity as a potential explanation which it is not. Elsewhere I have used 'Fitok–following' for the earlier phase when children appear to be following the rule, 'If the message FITs, it is OK.' Those children who can refer to the ambiguity of a message as a reason for communication failure and can cite the speaker as responsible for the message have been referred to as 'Nurok-following' – 'Message Needs Unique Reference to be OK, otherwise it is inadequate.' Unfortunately these awkward abbreviations have not been well received by colleagues (neither do I like them), and here I shall defer to those objections and risk misunderstanding arising from the use of 'younger' and 'older'.

Saying and meaning

Olson and E. J. Robinson (Robinson, Goelman and Olson, 1983) drew an appropriate but seemingly unlikely inference from the generalizations which summarize the rules children appear to be following. If younger children have just chosen a card and said, 'A man with a flag', and the experimenter replies with, 'A man with a red flag. Is *that* what you said?' then such children should agree with this if the flag was in fact red. This description fits the card. To realize that messages can be ambiguous, it is necessary to distinguish between the actual message on the one hand and the speaker's intended meaning on the other. It will only be after the child is able to treat the message as a clue to the speaker's intended meaning and to evaluate it as adequate or not to that intention that he or she will be able to understand about ambiquity. Younger children should not be able to distinguish between saying and meaning in respect of ambiguity; saying and meaning should be equivalent. Memories of what was said should relate to the correctness of the card rather than to the verbal description of it. Experiments were designed to test this hypothesis (Robinson, Goelman and Olson, 1983; Robinson and Robinson, 1982b).

In one study five to six year old children participated in a communication evaluation game and were thence classified as understanding or not understanding about ambiguity. In the other part of the game, whenever a listener's error was caused by an ambiguous message, the child was asked to accept or reject a suggestion about what the message had been: on one-third of the occasions the experimenter gave an *exact repetition* of the ambiguous message and then asked the child, 'Is that what you/I said?' On one-third of the occasions, she suggested an *inappropriate* version, which did not refer to either the speaker's or the listener's chosen drawing. On one-third of the occasions, the experimenter gave a *disambiguated* version. All the children correctly accepted the exact repetitions as having been said, and correctly rejected the inappropriate versions. Of the 17 children who incorrectly accepted the disambiguated versions as having been said, 11 were those who, in the other part of the game, had incorrectly judged the ambiguous messages to be adequate: just one child of the 22 who rejected the disambiguated message did not understand about ambiguity. The relationship between judgements in the two parts of the game was highly significant. Children who judged that the disambiguated version had actually been said, accepted that the speaker's intended meaning was conveyed by the message. In this respect, they confused what the speaker meant with what was actually said. These same children were likely to judge ambiguous messages as adequate. Failure to realize that messages can be ambiguous *may*, then, be a symptom of a more general failure to make a distinction between a speaker's intended meaning and the message.

The result encouraged us to analyse the problem further. In so far as the investigation just mentioned can be argued to include two components of *speech per se* on the one hand and *communication* on the other, were the results particularly associated with one rather than the other? Is the child's problem peculiar to interpretation of verbal messages or is the issue something to do with communication as such? We designed two further tasks the first of which would eliminate speech as the medium of the message and the second would eliminate the communicative nature of the task.

Verbally versus visually based communication

For the experiment eliminating speech as the medium of message communication (Robinson and Robinson, 1982b) we used cards from our normal referential communication task, but exploited additional pieces of white cardboard to obscure parts of the cards chosen by the experimenter speaker. The formulae for deciding which parts of the card to obscure included covering the values of irrelevant as well as relevant variables. By holding up such cards and asking the child-listener to select the corresponding card from his or her set, we thought we would be making it rather obvious to the child that the message might be inadequate. To cover part of a picture appears to be a reduction in information more explicit than the omission of certain words from a message.

The results from 52 children who had correctly judged that they had been told/shown enough when messages were indeed adequate (unambiguous) were clear cut: when confronted with ambiguous verbal and visual messages, 37 said they had enough information for both visual and verbal, five said they had insufficient information in both cases. This gave 42 children who were consistent across modes of presentation. Ten children gave different responses for visual and verbal: six made more correct judgements about verbal messages, four about visual messages.

We drew three conclusions:

a failure to make a distinction between what is said and what is intended is not just specific to verbal communication tasks;
b children are generally consistent across the visual and verbal modes of presentation of communication tasks;
c there are no grounds for believing the visual is easier than the verbal (or vice versa).

It does seem moreover that younger children may not yet have a concept of *part-information*, but we wished first to eliminate the other person as communicator from the situation to see whether the communicative component was a critical feature.

Contact with the world: direct or mediated?

For the third study we (Robinson and Robinson, 1982b) selected 60 children aged from 5.4 to 6.7 who correctly identified unambiguous verbal and visual information as such in a pre-test. Each child played two games (1) the normal verbal communication evaluation game, (2) a pointer game. The stimulus cards were the same in each and the order of presentation varied systematically. The cards bore drawings of men holding balloons varying on two attributes with two or three values each (large/small; red/green/blue). The pointer game was based on two separate discs with windows. After the pointer was spun, it stopped facing a segment in which one of the cards was located. Only a part of the card could be seen through a rectangular slit. Although slits were the same size on the two versions, they were oriented differently, so that in one version the size of the balloon could not be seen. Hence the child could see both colour and size on one disc, but only colour on the other. The experimenter and child had a set of the six corresponding cards laid out in front of them. The child spun the pointer, and when it stopped the child was asked 'Does it show you enough for you to pick the right one?' If the child said 'No' he or she was asked 'What would you have to see?'

In comparing the results from this visual task with those from the verbal communication evaluation task we found 43 children giving consistent judgements across both and 17 not. Of the 17, 15 gave more correct answers in the verbal task and two in the visual. From these results we were able to draw the following conclusions:

a failure to see that verbal messages can be ambiguous is not peculiar to problems involving communication;
b this failure appears to be a symptom of a more general absence of the idea that information of a verbal or visual nature can be insufficient for appropriate interpretation;
c the idea that information can be inadequate may occur first to children in activities involving communication with other people.

One direction in which we might proceed from these experiments involves probing the idea that to cope intelligently and adaptively with problems of perceived ambiguity in stimulus input, the child has to develop a strategy of *refusing to interpret that input*. The child needs to become aware of what kind of information is needed and to know how to acquire it, for example, asking questions of others, performing tests of some kind. So far we have not made a thorough examination of all the potentially relevant evidence in the literature, but we think it is consistent with the hypothesis that from birth children behave as though they have at their disposal *sufficient information for action*. The imperatives are to act. This requires design characteristics in the child that make the best interpretation of the evidence available for decision-making and taking. If the initial design characteristics of young children do oblige them to treat stimulus intake as true reflections of reality, no peculiar problems arise. Errors will occur, but these will not be diagnosed as residing in the ambiguities in the perceived information.

One exciting possibility along that line of thinking is that it may be in verbal interaction with others that children first come to realize the significance of feelings of uncertainty. This context of learning may then serve as a point of departure for a more general orientation to the rest of perception as providing 'clues' to reality rather than being a direct reflection of it. Whilst it would be theoretically possible, if empirically improbable, for children to invent such ideas in respect of physical phenomena, we cannot see how they could do the same with the saying/meaning distinction. If a person has an intention to communicate a message and formulates a wording to represent it, there is no internal standard against which to evaluate the adequacy of the wording. It can only be through the behaviour of other people that the idea of a disassociation could be generated.

The imperatives for children to act are as imperative in the social as in the physical world. Joint activities with caretakers have been 'scaffolded' into the child's repertoire from early days. Requests have been made and acted upon within a social order initially defined by caretakers so that very young children become accustomed to notions of whose turn it is to do what. If caretakers ask questions or issue instructions young children know at which points in the interaction they are obliged to react, and they have also become accustomed to adults reacting in similar fashion in response to their own initiatives. As Piaget argued, younger children may be protected from having to accommodate to ambiguities of speech by caretakers interpreting their intentions from 'inadequate' messages. Our analysis of natural recordings is consistent with this view. Misunderstandings between mother and child were generally followed by pragmatic solutions, and not by semantic inquiries.

For young children to become aware of the issues of ambiguity and the saying/meaning distinction they will need experiences that both activate the specific strategies appropriate to solutions of immediate problems and promote the understanding of why those strategies are necessary. Whilst the former might be achieved via associative and observational learning processes constructed into action schemes and rules of procedure, the latter will require a superordinate structure. Children will have to come to know that they do not know – more generally they will have to come to appreciate that the possibilities of 'not knowing' can apply to them.

Perhaps, to have that idea presupposes the existence of an 'I' that can experience the distinction.

In respect of the particular problem of message ambiguity, the following steps could be abstracted as a developed sequence for handling referential communication problems. Faced with a message that is observed to refer to more than one item in an array the child has to:

  a experience feelings of uncertainty and recognize them as such;
  b understand that messages can be ambiguous and see that this one is;
  c relate the feelings of uncertainty to the ambiguity of the message;
  d decide what to do.

One strategy would be to formulate a general or specific question. Another would be to state the problem of choice. The child could also wait for further information or tag a provisional interpretation with a marker of uncertainty.

Results have been obtained showing that younger children can be capable of making discriminating comparisons, notice more than one possible referent and yet make a choice and then answer questions about mismatches without referring to the multiple reference of the verbal message (Robinson and Robinson, 1978b; Whitehurst and Sonnenschein, 1981). Furthermore they can diagnose their uncertainty; they will say they are unsure what the speaker means, but will still judge that the speaker has told them enough (e.g., Beal and Flavell, 1982; Robinson and Robinson, 1983). How then do they come to understand that messages can be ambiguous? What further ideas do they have to grasp? They have to develop from active thinking creatures deciding what to do and doing it, to become creatures who know both that they do not know what to do and why they do not – they have not only to think about the problem, but think about themselves in relation to that problem. It would be a highly improbable coincidence of our research if the child's solution to the problem of communication failure arising from message ambiguity were the first issue requiring the child to construct ideas about the inferential nature of perception and to conclude from reflection in appropriate circumstances that 'I know that I do not know.' On the other hand it would not be surprising if the eventual primary candidates are cultural rather than physical and concerned with interpersonal communication via language. To date we have concentrated on conditions of learning promoting development, which will be considered more fully in the following section.

Conditions promoting understanding about ambiguity

We have some relevant evidence from our various efforts to advance children's understanding about ambiguity in speech and from our studies of factors associated with naturally arising individual differences in the onset of such understanding. In *intervention* and *natural* studies (Robinson and Robinson, 1981) we discovered associations between induced or early achievement of such understanding and adult use of the reaction, 'I don't know what you mean', on occasions when the child had offered an ambiguous instruction or request to another person. Observational data, however, had shown that this was a comparatively rare adult reaction, both in homes and schools, and this rarity alerted us to the possibility of other treatment and reactions being significant.

This possibility became a more urgent challenge when we had to explain results obtained in a longer experimental intervention study spread over six half-hour sessions in a pre-school. In that study (Robinson and Robinson, 1982a) we found that we were able to advance understanding and verbal performance of pre-school children quite strongly by reacting with 'I don't know what you mean', combined with detailed statements of the listener's reasons for not being able to select actions or items. Also in that study, however, a second set of non-understanding children was accorded a different treatment. The adult never explained why she or other children could not make choices, but did

  a *model* appropriate speaker and listener behaviour at the beginning of
    each activity, and
  b *intervened* to encourage listeners to *ask* speakers questions if they did
    not know enough to choose.

This group also made advances in understanding and performance relative to their own initial scores and those of independent controls. How? A secondary analysis showed that modelling could not be used to explain the result. We suggested that these children were being treated *as if* they already understood about ambiguity of reference and could observe the experimenter's refusal to act before asking questions. The response of asking for more information in fact draws attention to the message and presumes that the original speaker may be able to diagnose what was inadequate in this message and can improve it. We can also argue incidentally that while saying 'I don't know what you mean' in the first treatment condition is rendering more explicit what the problem is, it *also assumes* the speaker may be able to diagnose the fault in the message and correct it.

To test the proposition more thoroughly, three varieties of intervention were compared (Robinson and Robinson, 1985). All the chidren included were ones who did not understand about message ambiguity in the communication evaluation task. The materials and procedure involved the choice and specification of individual 'playpeople' in arrays whose members varied in dress and equipment. The listener's task was to identify the item the speaker had in mind.

In one condition the experimenter as listener provided information relevant to target identification, but only *after* she had made her choice. Hence, after an ambiguous message from the child and a guessed identification by the experimenter, she said 'I didn't really know which one you meant, because there were three like that (pointing to the three). I just guessed. I needed to know some more'. In this statement the experimenter indicated her difficulty of identification, illustrated the range of difficulty, but did not refer to the child's message *per se*. Neither did she refer to the child's control over the quality of the message. She has not treated the child as though he or she understands about message ambiguity.

In the second condition, when needing to react to an ambiguous message, the experimenter looked puzzled, moved her hand around possible target playpeople, muttering, 'I can't really choose yet'. In this case, she did not mention the message, but was *behaving* as if she expected the child to understand her difficulty and to help her.

In the third condition, the experimenter added to the second by saying 'I don't know which one you mean. It might be this one, or that one or that one (moving potential referents forward). There are three like that. I don't know which one you mean yet.' Whilst there is still no explicit reference to the message, the experimenter has both behaved and spoken as though she is expecting the child to help.

Children were post-tested on understanding about ambiguity and on two other tasks: refusals to interpret ambiguous messages and competence to give 'easy' and 'hard' messages. The results clearly demonstrated the superiority of the last two treatments as means of enhancing understanding. Post-identification speech did not help. Speech plus behaviour was not significantly more efficacious than behaviour alone.

In a related study Sonnenschein and Whitehurst (1984) utilized six strategies for training children to deal with ambiguous messages, and to evaluate the quality of speaking or reactive behaviour of a doll performer. Each child was either a performer or an observer, was required to give judgements about performance or not, and was given explicit post-trial feedback about the trial or not. If given feedback, this could be for both roles, for the speaker only or for the listener only. Post-intervention testing on different materials assessed children's capacity to give unambiguous messages when speakers, to react with 'I don't understand' to ambiguous messages when listeners, and to evaluate the speaking or reactive behaviour of a doll performer in both roles. Children who were assigned to be observer judges and given explicit feedback about the adequacy of their judgements (with reasons) in respect of doll performers in both speaking and listening roles made near perfect scores on all three criterion measures. Other conditions were efficacious *only* within the parameters trained, for example, children judging the speaking performance of a doll and given explicit feedback became more efficient speakers, but were not more likely to be more effective listeners or evaluators. Sonnenschein and Whitehurst conclude that 'evaluation of others is superordinate to speaking, listening, and self-evaluation'. I would suggest that they could express this conclusion by saying that coming to understand about ambiguity is superordinate to the detailed skills encouraged in their other manipulations. They also note the power of such systematic intervention to accelerate children's performance far beyond what is likely to happen in their everyday lives.

Are treatments such as those used by Sonnenschein and Whitehurst or Robinson and Robinson (1985) used by parents, teachers, or peers in the everyday world?

Robinson and Whittaker (in press) examined two bodies of data for such evidence: Wells's (1981) collection of transcripts of natural interaction at home and at school and Cambourne's (1971) transcripts of the playground activities of Australian six year olds. No evidence was found to suggest that in school children were expected to reformulate ambiguous utterances or to evaluate the speech of themselves or others in this kind of respect. In the homes there was no indication that parents were increasing such implicit demands once children had started school. Cambourne's transcripts of child-child interaction in playgrounds revealed very few information exchanges between children. Switching strategy to a more general examination of home/school differences with the Wells data, Robinson and Whittaker confirmed Wells' (1985) observation that topics, the incidence of instruction giving, and the kinds of questions asked by adults did differ: at school topics were more likely to be initiated and sustained by adults, instructions with three or more components were commoner, and there were more questions asked to which the adult already knew the answer. Question sequences funnelling down to a specific answer were also more frequent in school. Robinson and Whittaker argue for possible indirect ways in which these activities might enable a child to construct the idea of a meaning/message distinction. They do not focus upon understanding about ambiguity as such, but upon the message/meaning distinction more generally.

The natural samples are, of course, but drops in the ocean of reality; if the children recorded were awake for 12 hours a day then Wells's procedure was capturing approximately one-two thousandth of each child's waking life. While this may be sufficient for the examination of general trends in development, it will not reveal relatively rare events. An extreme position to adopt would be one that posited single-trial learning about speech being potentially ambiguous. This is not absurd. Insight differs from classical or operant conditioning in its rapid change of state. Sonnenschein and Whitehurst report *near perfect* performance and evaluations by children rising six who were accorded their most powerful intervention. Robinson and Robinson (1981) switched seven out of nine children into understanding about ambiguity with six trials, and found a similar number of trials efficacious in the 'as if' intervention study (Robinson and Robinson, in press). In the first analysis of natural data the 16 mothers who registered an explicit statement of non-understanding of a child's utterance did so with a modal frequency of one only in the three and a half hours of recording analysed: all 16 of their children had achieved understanding by age six.

On the evidence currently available I would agree with the conclusion of Robinson and Whittaker that 'we still have much to learn about how children make these advances in their everyday lives', but do not feel obliged to abandon the 'as if' hypothesis. Relatively rare applications of this treatment may be sufficient to promote understanding about ambiguity.

The nature of this suggestion is likely to be misunderstood. I am not proposing that at one moment children enjoy a revelation that provokes an immediate and dramatic reconstruction of their world. They are unlikely to sit down and explore the full psychological and logical implications of their insight; more likely they will simply eat the specific cake they were trying to obtain. They will, however, have a new idea in their minds, an idea that can be recalled and applied to circumstances when communication problems arise, an idea whose wider implications can be gradually deployed across other contexts. The idea provides the potential for development; the impetus for that will probably continue to be provoked by the actions and reactions of other people and the physical environment. They may simply forget the insight and have to gain it afresh later, but if the cultural circumstances are conducive, the idea will become a stabilized basis for more general application.

I would like to suggest that the crucial more general transition is for children to become capable of saying as a result of reflection upon a problem, 'I know that I do not know' and for them to know why they do not know. In the case of message ambiguity in communication failure they can say that the speaker has not given enough information for a unique choice to be made. They know that messages have to be interpreted, that they are 'clues' and not the reality itself. But that stance seems to require a superordinate (transcendental) 'I' to be aware why the second 'I' does not know; it has to see that 'I' as a subject and object. The components require simultaneous conjunction and integration for the solution to the problem. Perhaps this thrust will become clearer if we examine other attempts to promote its significance.

The emerging 'I': general

What are the characteristics of young children's conceptions about themselves and how do these change? There has been a resurgence of speculative interest in Mead's (1934) views about children coming to turn round upon their own schemata. Harré (1983) and Shotter (1984) have argued cases for cultural conditions likely to promote the child's coming to conceive of itself as a self-reflective active agent. Persuasive, provocative and strong on theory as these stories are, as yet they lack detailed integrative empirical support.

Given the importance Harré (see chapter 13) ascribes to language use as the mediator of development, we can ask a host of questions about development in the use (and understanding) of, for example:

a personal pronouns, particularly in respect of 'I'/'other' contrasts, bearing in mind developmental changes in the meaning of 'I';
b verbs of cognition, affect and conation, especially in the first person;
c epistemologically significant markers indicative of discrepancies between appearance and reality, possibility and certainty, etc.;
d metacognitive claims in relation to (*b*) and (*c*).

Harré cites such work as exists, but thorough and comprehensive studies have not so far been designed to answer the kinds of questions for which Harré is offering theoretically plausible explanations.

More generally, studies of 'selfhood' have been concerned mainly with matters other than those of immediate concern here, although it is possible to extract the idea of significant changes in self-perception occurring around the age of seven. In a timely review of the development of self-understanding from infancy through adolescence, Damon and Hart (1982) draw attention to some of the conceptual analyses that have so far guided research in this area. They repeat James's (1892) distinctions between 'Me' (self as known) and 'I' (self as knower), accept Mead's (1934) proposal that human beings have knowledge of both, and use that definition to frame their review. (My suspicion is that Kant's distinctions between self as object, self as subject, with a transcendental 'I' exercising superordinate surveillance and power over both will eventually prove to be a better basic framework, but that is a problem for the future.) Within their framework, they note that of the 151 studies cited in Wylie's (1979) review of self-concept, over 80 per cent are concerned primarily with self-evaluation. Of those studies which have pursued perception and conception of self from a descriptive rather than an evaluative perspective, not all have treated perception of self as importantly different from perception of others. Bias has been created by the methods of investigation: techniques which are open-ended may fail to elicit what the subject does not see as worthy of comment; techniques which emphasize distinctiveness from other people will fail to evoke information about similarities with others; techniques which encourage the mentioning of static features will not evoke comments about actions.

Relying heavily on the work of Broughton (1978), Guardo and Bohan (1971), Keller, Ford and Meacham (1978), Livesley and Bromley (1973), Secord and Peevers (1974) and Selman (1980) for results relevant to childhood, Damon and Hart (1982) are able to integrate the findings with each other and set them into a more comprehensive four-level ontogenetic model. The authors see their construction as being in no more than a germinal phase, but what could be relevant for the present purpose is the second level with its alleged transition age around seven or eight. Broughton (1978) claims that distinctiveness of identity begins then to be defined in terms of personal thoughts and feelings rather than personal appearance and possession. Selman (1980) suggests that children realize there is a difference between psychological and physical experience around six, but that it is not until eight that they realize they can fool others by saying one thing while feeling something different. Guardo and Bohan (1971) found psychological characteristics appearing in the descriptions of personal distinctiveness in eight and nine year olds that were not present in those of six and seven year olds. Whilst much of the work has been set in contexts encouraging statements about identity in the sense of uniqueness rather than about the characteristics of the child *per se*, these beginnings of the *appreciation* of the psychological around the age of seven or eight for purposes of comparison presuppose the prior emergence of beliefs about the mind, the body and the outside world, and relationships between them. That children will in fact have been using appropriate psychological terms much earlier in a pragmatically successful manner is not to be doubted, as Dunn (chapter 5) illustrates. What may be missing at the younger ages is an appreciation of the epistemological implications and presuppositions of that usage.

Damon and Hart offer an attempt at pragmatic systematization of the development of understanding about the self relating themes to levels, but do not elaborate a thoeretical basis beyond reference to James and Mead and do not refer to the dynamics of development at all. Such writers as Harré and Shotter offer a grander theory, begin to refer to contexts of development, and elaborate on these in terms of general processes. What is missing is the detail of specific achievement in terms of sequence, content, and mechanisms.

Children's beliefs about 'I'

To begin to find out more about children's conceptions of 'I' in the sense of being an individual who can reflect upon himself or herself in relation to the world and in particular as an organizer and agent of his or her own biography, I have had conversations with a number of five to eight year old children in a number of primary schools. What has struck me most is the range of conceptions children have expressed.

At one extreme are children who have a well-defined past and present –
and a vision of possible futures stretching before them. They can talk
about their biography in space/time. Moreover, they claim to be able to
direct their attention, learning and remembering – they have tactics for
helping themselves to control these. They can discriminate between what
they know (believe they know) and what they do not know, what they
think they understand and what they think they do not understand. They
believe they can exercise some control over their emotional and moti-
vational states, particularly by changing their immediate context of situation. These children appear to have a conception of themselves which
includes a transcendental 'I' deciding and controlling what kind of person
they may become in terms of both capacities and dispositions.

At another extreme are children whose 'I' is very faint. Their immediate
past is difficult to retrieve, the more distant past a blank. What is retrieved
is not ordered sequentially. Their future is vague and unconsidered rather
than indeterminate. They appear to have difficulty directing and maintaining attention. Learning and remembering happens to them (or not, as the
case may be). They do not comment on ways of eliminating unhappiness
or fear.

To caricature them, I would say their model of themselves is rather
Skinnerian; they are victims of an environment whose contingencies are
difficult to calculate. They do calculate, seemingly using a principle of
minimizing trouble in the short run. The self making these calculations is
tightly constrained in space/time.

If these impressions can be rendered into acceptable data, they will raise
questions about development in stark and dramatic terms. As well as
perhaps needing to answer questions about the conditions of learning that
facilitate the development of children with the apparently strong embryo-
nic transcendental 'I' that can. delimit, explore, develop and test the
boundaries of their own beliefs about self-determination, we shall also
have to attend to the conditions which do not act in this way.

One immediate problem is the possible linkage between the specific issue
of the child coming to understand about the message/meaning distinction
and possible correlated important transformations in the child's self-
concept. A potentially very important set of related distinctions, of which
Selman's (1980) observation that children come to realize that they can say
one thing while feeling something different is one example, concerns the
gap between inner experience and presentation of self. Children who have
mastered the message/meaning distinction are in a position to generalize
this to the whole range of behaviour/inner experience distinctions, both
for themselves and others. Theoretically at least they should know that
they can display fearlessness while being frightened, look happy when they
are sad, look attentive when they are not. They should realize that reality
can be disguised. The displays of others can be treated as clues to inner

reality and not that reality itself. The 'I' reflecting upon the self in relation to its situation can exert its will and skill to disguise the inner states. Individuality can be an island.

This is not simply a matter of role-taking in play. Imaginative play is not intended to deceive either oneself or others. The exercise of the competence requires the simultaneous dissociation of the display and the inner reality; it is intended to hide that reality from the outside world.

How the emergence of these ideas and capacities is in fact related to the appreciation of the message/meaning distinction we do not know. How both are linked to the observations made in the conversations with five to eight year old children we do not know.

That the 'as if' principle of treatment may apply is not particularly interesting, if the actual components of behaviour to which they are applied are not related to each other and if there is no internal linkage in the child's thinking. It is easy to posit a general transformation in the child's thinking (Piaget has already proposed the concrete operational stage beginning around the relevant age), and no doubt empirical investigations would show the customary mess of decalage, horizontal and vertical. Appreciating the biological, psychological and historico-cultural limits of the self and framing one's decisions accordingly can last until the final breath; the very first occasion on which a child first thinks in terms of a self-conscious and agentive 'I' may pass almost unnoticed by the child itself, as I have mentioned above.

Children do not sit down and work out the full potential implications of their discoveries or ideas, asking themselves questions about the range of applications of their insights; they have other things to do. Clearly, however, there may well be developmental sequences in the domains and degrees of perceived application of the idea of control of self. The experiment reported here purporting to demonstrate that their understanding about ambiguity in speech precedes somewhat their realization that they can have insufficient information to judge the size of balloons is one small step into the maze, but many more and better investigations are needed to examine these issues. Harré (1983) writes out research menus for work in the general area, but does not see especial difficulties surrounding this particular issue. He accepts and develops Vygotsky's (1962) argument for speech originating as public and collective, becoming private and collective and finally bifurcating into private and individual on the one hand and remaining public and collective on the other. As far as I know this most important set of ideas has not yet been systematically explored, and it is not yet clear how it may best be tested. Such testing is, however, crucial for the questions posed here (and by Harré).

We would hope that, at least along the thin strand we have investigated, we are beginning to be able to fill in a few of these gaps to some degree. We have tried to demonstrate the usefulness of the 'as if' principle as

230 *Children of social worlds*

a means for promoting understanding about ambiguity in referential communication, and I have tried to illustrate some possible links between this and children's emergent 'I'. We hope that our theoretical premises are also valid: to grasp the saying/meaning distinction presupposes that children distinguish between what is immediately available to them and what is intended by another speaker (and more generally between the world of experience and the real world). This may also require some conception of 'I' as an agent who can monitor his or her psychological processes and, to some extent and in some domains, choose what to say or do.

Note

1. I should like to acknowledge the helpful criticism of Sara Meadows, Elizabeth Robinson and Steven Whittaker.

References

Beal, C. R. and Flavell, J. H. 1982. The effect of increasing the salience of message ambiguities on kindergartner's evaluations of communicative success and message adequacy. *Developmental Psychology*, **18**, 43–8.

Broughton, J. 1978. Development of concepts of self, mind, reality, and knowledge. *New Directions for Child Development*, **1**, 75–100.

Cambourne, B. L. 1971. A naturalistic study of language performance in grade 1 rural and urban school children (Ph.D. dissertation, James Cook University, Queensland, Australia).

Damon, W. and Hart, D. 1982. The development of self-understanding from infancy through adolescence. *Child Development*, **53**, 841–64.

Flavell, J. A., Botkin, P. T., Fry, C. L., Wright, J. W. and Jarvis, P. E. 1968. *The Development of Role-taking and Communication Skills in Children*. New York: Wiley.

Flavell, J. H., Speer, J. R., Green, F. L. and August, D. L. 1981. The development of comprehension monitoring and knowledge about communication. *Monographs of the Society for Research in Child Development*, **46**, serial no. 192.

Guardo, C. J. and Bohan, J. B. 1971. Development of a sense of self-identity in children. *Child Development*, **42**, 1909–21.

Harré, R. 1983. *Personal Being*. Oxford: Basil Blackwell.

James, W. 1961. *Psychology: the briefer course* (originally published 1892). New York: Harper.

Keller, A., Ford, L. H. and Meacham, J. A. 1978. Dimensions of self concept in pre-school children. *Developmental Psychology*, **14**, 483–9.

Krauss, R. M. and Glucksberg, S. 1969. The development of communication competence as a function of age. *Child Development*, **40**, 255–66.

Lefebvre-Pinard, M., Charbonneau, C. and Feider, H. 1982. Differential effectiveness of explicit verbal feedback on children's communication skills. *Journal of Experimental Child Psychology*, **34**, 174–83.

Livesley, W. J. and Bromley, D. B. 1973. *Person Perception in Childhood and Adolescence*. New York: Wiley.

Mead, G. H. 1934. *Mind, Self and Society*. Chicago: University of Chicago Press.

Patterson, C. J. and Kister, M. C. 1981. The development of listener skills for referential communication, in W. P. Dickson (ed.), *Children's Oral Communication Skills*. New York: Academic Press.

Roberts, R. J. and Patterson, C. J. 1983. Perspective taking and referential communication: the question of correspondence reconsidered. *Child Development*, **54**, 1005–14.

Robinson, E. J., Goelman, H. and Olson, D. 1983. Children's understanding of the relation between expressions (what was said) and intentions (what was meant). *British Journal of Developmental Psychology*, **1** 75–86.

Robinson, E. J. and Robinson, W. P. 1977a. The young child's explanations of communication failure: a re-interpretation of results. *Perceptual and Motor Skills*, **44**, 363–6.

Robinson, E. J. and Robinson, W. P. 1977b. Development in the understanding of causes of success and failure in verbal communication. *Cognition*, **5**, 363–78.

Robinson, E. J. and Robinson, W. P. 1978a. Explanations of communication failure and ability to give bad messages. *British Journal of Social and Clinical Psychology*, **17**, 219–25.

Robinson, E. J. and Robinson, W. P. 1978b. Development of understanding about communication: message inadequacy and its role in causing communication failure. *Genetic Psychology Monographs*, **98**, 233–79.

Robinson, E. J. and Robinson, W. P. 1981. Ways of reacting to communication failure in relation to the development of children's understanding about verbal communication. *European Journal of Social Psychology*, **11**, 189–208.

Robinson, E. J. and Robinson, W. P. 1982a. The advancement of children's verbal referential communication skills: the role of meta-cognitive guidance. *International Journal of Behavioural Development*, **5**, 329–55.

Robinson, E. J. and Robinson, W. P. 1982b. Knowing when you don't know enough: children's judgments about ambiguous information. *Cognition*, **12**, 267–80.

Robinson, E. J. and Robinson, W. P. 1983. Communication and meta-communication: quality of children's instructions in relation to judgements about the adequacy of instructions and the locus of responsibility for communication failure. *Journal of Experimental Child Psychology*, **36**, 305–20.

Robinson, E. J. and Robinson, W. P. 1984. Coming to understand that referential communication can be ambiguous, in W. Doise and A. Palmonari (eds), *Social Interaction in Individual Development*. London: Cambridge University Press.

Robinson, E. J. and Robinson, W. P. 1985. Teaching children about verbal referential communication. *International Journal of Behavioral Development*, **8**, 1–15.

Robinson, E. J. and Whittaker, S. J. In press. Children's responses to ambiguous messages and their understanding of ambiguity (paper submitted to *Developmental Psychology*).

Secord, P. and Peevers, B. 1974. The development and attribution of person concepts, in T. Mischel (ed.), *Understanding Other Persons*. Oxford: Basil Blackwell.

Selman, R. 1980. *The Growth of Interpersonal Understanding*. New York: Academic Press.

Shotter, J. 1984. *Social Accountability and Selfhood*. Oxford: Basil Blackwell.

Sonnenschein, S. and Whitehurst, G. J. 1984. Developing referential communication: a hierarchy of skills. *Child Development*, **55**, 1936–45.

Vygotsky, L. S. 1962. *Thought and Language*. Cambridge, Mass.: MIT Press.

Wells, C. G. 1981. *Learning through Interaction: the study of language development*. Cambridge: Cambridge University Press.

Wells, C. G. 1985. *Language Development in the Preschool Years*. Cambridge: Cambridge University Press.

Whitehurst, G. J. and Sonnenschein, S. 1981. The development of informative messages in communication: knowing when vs. knowing how, in W. P. Dickson (ed.), *Children's Oral Communication Skills*. New York: Academic Press.

Wylie, R. C. 1979. *The Self Concept: theory and research on selected topics*. Vol. 2. Lincoln, Nebraska: University of Nebraska Press.

Part 4

Some broader issues

Introduction

The issues raised in this final part are 'broad' in several rather different senses. Barbara Tizard's chapter shifts the focus of attention beyond the daily realities of the home or the school towards consideration of a major contemporary threat to children's very existence – nuclear war. She seeks to establish the extent to which children are worried by, or are afraid of, nuclear weapons, and to examine the relationship between their levels of anxiety and their understanding of the issues involved. There are echoes here of Dunn's earlier chapter, both in the emphasis on emotions and their relation to understanding, and in the suggestion that the child's inter-actions in the family may mediate the effects of outside threats.

The developmental role of emotion is one of the central concerns of Cathy Urwin's chapter. She sees, not only in Piaget but also in recent 'social cognition' research, clear signs of an over-rationalized approach to development. Emotional processes are given no real role, and little room is left for imagination. By contrast, the psychoanalytic perspective on devel-opments highlights emotional conflicts and costs, and the workings of phantasy and desire are seen as central to the processes of developmental change. By tracing the early development of Piaget's ideas in the context of the wider history of the Child Study Movement, Urwin illustrates the progressive splitting of emotion and rationality. Turning to contemporary issues in developmental psychology and to recent psychoanalytic thinking, Urwin sketches out some possibility for productive interchange between these traditions and identifies some methodological problems that might arise in pursuing them.

The two final chapters, by Rom Harré and by David Ingleby, are con-cerned with the articulation of some broad theoretical issues that underlie many of the contributions to this volume. Harré, seeking an alternative to the dualisms and individualistic emphases of much contemporary psychology, offers a characterization of development in 'social construc-tionist' terms. Development is seen as a process of appropriation from a common public realm; indeed of successive appropriation from the social through the subjective and personal to the objective, and thence to the social again. This scheme, reminiscent as it is of Vygotsky, encompasses many of the specific ideas offered by Light, Wood and Robinson in the previous section. Robinson's chapter finds even clearer resonances in

Harré's treatment of the formation of the self. The structure of language, and in particular the grammar of typical forms of self-commentary, is examined for the light it casts on the nature of 'the embedded I'.

The task Ingleby takes on in the final chapter of this volume is not to advance any one particular 'social constructionist' account of development, but rather to survey the range of such approaches and to evaluate their potential as foundations of a new paradigm for developmental psychology. Starting with the critical movement of the late 1960s and early 1970s he traces a variety of attempts to establish a truly social approach to development. He brings out the basic areas of agreement between symbolic interactionist and ethnomethodological stances, approaches based on Wittgenstein and on Vygotsky, and last but not least the 'post-structuralist' view which has surfaced not infrequently in this volume. He suggests, however, that divisions and disagreements between proponents of these various approaches may well jeopardize any prospect of real achievement. None of the approaches is free from shortcomings, he argues, but between them they command rich resources, both theoretical and empirical.

11

The Impact of the Nuclear Threat on Children's Development

Barbara Tizard

This book's predecessor (Richards, 1974) marked an important shift by British psychologists towards understanding the social development of the child in terms of an interactive system. In the earlier paradigm, social-ization tended to be seen as a one-way process, in which adults impose social practices and knowledge on pre-social beings. In the succeeding decade, the focus of much child development research (including my own) has been the analysis of face-to-face mother-child and sibling interactions, and in particular the exchanges of meanings that take place in these inter-actions, and that lead to the child's development.

What we have tended to neglect is the obvious fact that such interactions do not take place in a social vacuum. Both parents and children are affected by events originating outside the family, including government decisions on housing, income and hours of work; unemployment, strikes and civil strife; international crises and wars. It is true that some psychologists have studied the relationship between child development and more or less constant characteristics of the family's broader social context, such as the social class and ethnic group of the parents, but very few have looked at the impact of specific societal policies and events on the child's develop-ment.

This neglect may be in part because in a sense most psychologists *do* believe that family interactions occur in a social vacuum – after all, the major theorists in developmental psychology have not taken account of societal influences. It may also be that psychologists are wary of studying issues that have political implications. Usually, those who do study the impact of a particular policy are those actively opposed to it. Further, there are methodological difficulties in such studies. There is often no 'control' group available – virtually all young people in a society are exposed to the threat of war, or to a high level of unemployment. (In the same way, in a country with universal education, the impact of going to school on children's general development cannot be assessed.) The psychologist can therefore only assess the impact of these factors if there are baseline data from a preceding period. However, the interpretation of changes in baseline data is complicated by the fact that societal factors rarely change in isolation – for example, unemployment and the threat of war may increase together. Occasionally, it is possible to study the impact of a planned social event, as when television is introduced on a large scale into a new region.

A more fundamental difficulty in assessing the impact of societal factors on development arises from the absence of any theoretical framework in which the issues can be studied. By what psychological processes do events in society influence the development of the child? Because of the lack of a theoretical framework, psychologists have tended to fall back on a very outmoded, and probably implicit, paradigm. External events are described as having certain impacts on the child, but the contribution made by the child himself or herself in mediating the impact, or the mediating influence of parents and other adults and children is not analysed. Thus, whilst an advance is made in one direction, in extending the social context in which the child develops, a step back is taken in another direction, towards the older notion of the child as a passive individual, moulded by external social pressures.

As will become clear in this chapter, research on the impact of the nuclear threat on children's development illustrates very well both the neglect of societal factors by most psychologists, the use of an outmoded paradigm, and the difficulties involved in such research. The small volume of research testifies to the neglect – virtually no research on this topic has been carried out in the UK. Yet one has only to talk to children to realize that they are aware of, and often frightened and pessimistic about, the possibility of a world-wide holocaust. What impact does this have on their development? Most of the research that has taken place has been carried out by psychologists and child psychiatrists who are themselves involved in the peace movement. The volume of research has closely paralleled the level of public anxiety about nuclear weapons. The first research peak accompanied the 1961 Berlin and the 1962 Cuban missile crises. This was followed by a long period of relatively low public anxiety about nuclear weapons, and little research. Since the late 1970s, public anxiety, the activities of the peace movement, and the volume of research have all greatly increased (Kramer et al., 1983).

The bulk of the research has been carried out in the USA, latterly under the aegis of a Task Force of the American Psychiatric Association. No doubt because of their psychiatric orientation, these researchers have tended to concentrate on the issue of children's anxiety, and their fears about their future and about personal survival. Most of the studies have involved young people aged 12–18 years, and virtually no research has been done with children under ten.

Anxiety about nuclear war

The first two studies were carried out in US high schools soon after the 1961 Berlin and the 1962 Cuban missile crises (Escalona, 1963; Schwebel, 1965). Both concluded that the majority of high school pupils were deeply worried about the danger of nuclear war. After the accident at the Three Mile Island nuclear reactor plant in 1979, Schwebel again studied young people's responses by interview and questionnaire. He found that 70 per cent of the high school pupils surveyed thought that there would be a serious nuclear accident in the future, and almost all saw the prospect as very frightening (Schwebel, 1982).

Children's assessment of the likelihood of nuclear war appears, not surprisingly, to be related to the current general level of public anxiety on this issue. In a study carried out in the mid-1960s, several years after the Berlin and Cuban crises, with English children aged seven to 16, the majority of the older children stated that nuclear war would never happen (Cooper, 1965). However, if it did occur, they rated their chance of survival as only one in ten. The younger children were more likely to believe that nuclear war would occur, but they were more optimistic about their chances of survival. Studies since the late 1970s by the Task Force and others have come up with higher, although varying, estimates of the amount and type of concern. Findings about the proportion of US high school pupils who believe that nuclear war will occur in the next 20 years range from 34 per cent in one study to 80 per cent in another (Mack, 1983). A large survey of teenagers in a Southern US state found that 33 per cent believed there was a great probability of human civilization being destroyed in their lifetime, whilst a further 49 per cent thought there was a moderate possibility (Blackwell and Gessner, 1983).

A cross-country comparison of the views of somewhat younger children, aged ten to 15, was recently carried out in the USA and the Soviet Union by two US psychiatrists, John Mack and Eric Chivian, and has since been extended to Sweden (Chivian and Mack, 1983; Holmborg and Bergstroem, 1984). More US (39 per cent) than Soviet (12 per cent) children thought that a nuclear war would occur in their lifetime, but more Soviet children thought that if a war did occur they and their families would not survive (Soviet, 81 per cent; US, 42 per cent). The Swedish children's views fell midway between those of the US and Soviet children on almost all issues.

Most of these studies can be criticized for their methodological limitations. In particular, some samples were biased, being apparently composed of volunteers, others were opportunistic, that is, one or more schools were surveyed, with no indication of why they were selected or whether the children in them were in any sense representative of a wider population. Sometimes the questions were asked in a loaded way, and sometimes no attempt was made to conceal the fact that the surveys were being carried out by enthusiastic peace workers. Several studies, however, have been carried out that are not open to these criticisms. The Institute of Social Research at the University of Michigan, as part of a study of adolescent attitudes towards the military and the draft, surveyed high school seniors each spring for seven consecutive years, from 1975–1982. The pupils were drawn from 130 schools in 48 states. The survey included a series of questions about 'monitoring the future'. It found a steadily increasing trend for these young people to agree or mostly agree with the statement 'Nuclear or biological annihilation will probably be the future of all mankind within my lifetime'; in 1976 23 per cent did so, in 1982, 35 per cent (Bachman, 1983).

There is evidence that British young people tend to be even more pessimistic. This comes from a carefully carried out market research study in 1983 of 422 teenagers, aged 15–18, with quotas set on age, sex, and social class (Business Decisions Ltd, 1983). Overall, 52 per cent thought that it was either extremely or quite likely that nuclear war would occur within their lifetime, and 61 per cent thought that the presence of nuclear weapons in the UK did not protect us from attack. On both issues girls were more pessimistic (or realistic) than boys. A methodologically less satisfactory survey of comprehensive school pupils in Bristol reported very similar findings (Jones and Saunders, 1984). One-fifth of the pupils thought that a nuclear war was likely to happen at any minute, and 91 per cent did not expect to survive a nuclear war.

If somewhere between a third and a half of young people in the West expect that a catastrophic nuclear war will occur, it is not surprising to find that about the same proportion are seriously worried about the threat. In the survey of high school seniors' attitudes between 1976 and 1982, referred to above, one question was 'Of all the problems facing the nation today, how often do you worry about each of the following?' There was a steady rise in the proportion of those who said they *often* worried about the nuclear threat, from 7 per cent in 1976 to 31 per cent in 1982. A more recent study in California found that 58 per cent of 11–19 year olds were 'worried' or 'very worried' about nuclear war (Goldenring and Doctor, 1984), whilst in a Canadian study, nuclear war was rated as a very important worry by 63 per cent of high school pupils (Sommers et al., 1984). A Finnish survey of over 5,000 12–18 year olds is of particular interest because of its good methodology (Solantaus, Rimpelä and Taipale, 1984). The sample was drawn from the National Population Registry, and there was an 81 per cent response rate. Like the Swedish study cited above, it shows that anxiety about war is widespread in a neutral country without nuclear weapons. As part of a postal questionnaire about health habits young people were asked in an open-ended question to name their three major fears. The great majority of 12 year olds (79 per cent) and 48 per cent of 18 year olds named a probable future war as their major fear.

How salient are these fears?

In all these studies the terms fear, worry, and anxiety seem to have been used interchangeably. In clinical writings, however, distinctions are often drawn between them, although the basis of the distinction varies from one author to another. Some regard anxiety as a compound of fear with other emotions, particularly distress or shame. Others regard anxiety as a mild chronic fear, whilst others again consider that anxiety is a more diffuse and less focused state than fear, and one that, unlike fear, does not involve an avoidant response (cf. Izard, 1977; Johnson and Melamed, 1979; Rutter and Garmezy, 1983). Subjective experience certainly suggests that there are a variety, possibly a continuum, of fear-like states which vary in intensity from terror to mild apprehension, and also vary in duration and chronicity. All involve physiological reactions and unpleasant subjective experiences of different kinds and degrees, but not all are accompanied by attempts to avoid or escape.

Because of the lack of agreement on the differentiation between fear and anxiety, these terms will be used interchangeably in this chapter. Nevertheless, in order to understand the significance of the survey findings on children's fears about nuclear war, it seems important to know how intense the fear or anxiety is, and how salient it is in their lives. After all, most adults, if asked, would agree that they were afraid of lions, but unless confronted by an uncaged lion, the fear is more in the nature of an intellectual judgement than an emotional state, and has minimal salience. The only research which appears to have addressed the issue of intensity is the Finnish study referred to above. A subset of the sample (N = 2167) were asked eight structured questions about peace and war. These included questions about the intensity of their anxiety about war. Of the girls, 37 per cent, and of the boys, 15 per cent, said that they had experienced intense fear or anxiety about war during the preceding month. Of the girls, 13 per cent, and of the boys, 6 per cent, also said that they had nightmares about war (Solantaus, Rimpelä and Taipale, 1984).

The frequency with which the anxiety or fear is experienced is a different issue, but one relevant to salience – a mild anxiety may be very salient, if frequently experienced. Both the Canadian and the California projects included questions about the frequency of the children's anxiety. In the Canadian project, 24 per cent said that they worried about nuclear war 'at least once a week' (Sommers et al., 1984). In the Californian project 33 per cent 'often' worried, and 57 per cent did so 'sometimes' (Goldenring and Doctor, 1984).

Another approach that has been made to the issue of salience is to ask young people to construct a list of their anxieties and rank order them, or to state in answer to an open question what is their main anxiety. Again, there is evidence of the greater salience of anxiety about the nuclear threat amongst Europeans than Americans. Asked to name their three greatest fears in an open-ended question, Finnish young people mentioned war as their first fear at all ages from 12 to 18 (Solantaus, Rimpelä and Taipale, 1984). Given a list of 14 possible worries, and asked to rank their top three, Swedish teenagers rated nuclear war first, and a parent dying second (Holmborg and Bergstroem, 1984). Given the identical list, however, Californian teenagers rated both the fear of parents dying, and getting bad grades, above the anxiety of nuclear war (Goldenring and Doctor, 1984), and Canadian teenagers also placed the fear of 'my parents' death' above the fear of nuclear war (Sommers et al., 1984). Another US researcher recently asked high school pupils to rank in order the following public concerns – the economy, unemployment, energy, marriage, and nuclear conflict. Less than half (40 per cent) rated nuclear conflict as their major concern, although at some point in the questionnaire the great majority expressed some anxiety about the issue (Haas, 1983). On balance, therefore, the evidence suggests that a minority of young people, perhaps as many as a quarter, experience intense and/or frequent anxiety about nuclear war.

The characteristics of those who worry most

Most researchers have not analysed their findings by age, sex, and social class background. Those few who have done so have found that girls express more intense and more frequent worries about nuclear war, and are more pessimistic about its probability than boys (Beardslee and Mack, 1983; Business Decisions Ltd., 1983; Holmborg and Bergstroem, 1984; Solantaus and Rimpelä, 1984; Schwebel and Schwebel, 1981). When age effects have been analysed, younger adolescents have always been found to express anxiety about nuclear war more often and more intensely than older adolescents (Beardslee and Mack, 1983, Goldenring and Doctor, 1984; Schwebel and Schwebel, 1981; Solantaus and Rimpelä, 1984). Because of the virtual absence of studies of children under the age of 11 or 12, we do not know at what age anxiety about nuclear war begins, or when this fear peaks.

A number of US studies have found that children and adolescents from lower social classes admit to more fears in general than those from a higher socio-economic level (Angelino, Dollins and Mech, 1956; Croake, 1969; Croake and Knox, 1973; Jersild and Holmes, 1935, Jersild, Marley and Jersild, 1933), although this difference has not always been found to be statistically significant (Lapouse and Monk, 1959). Others have found that in the US black children have more fears and anxieties than white children (Lapouse and Monk, 1959). So far as fear of nuclear war is concerned, Solantaus appears to be the only author to have analysed her findings by social class. She found a tendency, not statistically significant, for anxiety to be greatest at the two social class extremes (Solantaus and Rimpelä, 1984). Only one US study seems to have looked at race differences in fear about nuclear war. The survey of 1,500 teenagers in a Southern US state found that black young people were more fearful of nuclear war and pessimistic about its probability than whites (Blackwell and Gessner, 1983). Social class was not controlled, however, so it is not clear whether this is an ethnic or a class difference.

A few researchers have attempted to throw light on the issue of whether young people who worry about nuclear war have particular personality characteristics. Is it the case that they are unusually neurotic or fearful? Goldenring presented high school students with a list of 20 possible worries, and asked them to rank order their top five worries. He found that those who ranked nuclear war as a major worry also tended to worry more than other students about other environmental concerns, for example, pollution and Third World starvation. They did not, however, worry more about personal concerns (people not liking you, parents divorcing, etc.), or personal dangers (possible illness or death, etc.) than the other students. Moreover, on a test designed to measure good adjustment and self-esteem the 'nuclear worriers' scored higher than the other students (Goldenring and Doctor, 1984).

Wrightsman found no relationship between the degree of high school students' fear of nuclear war and several measures of personality adjustment (Wrightsman, 1970). Both these studies, however, as well as one by London (1984), found a relationship between the degree of child and parental anxiety on the issue. Goldenring and London obtained information on the degree of parents' anxiety by asking their children, Wrightsman posted questionnaires to parents one month after their children had filled out questionnaires at school. (A tendency for parents and children to hold similar fears has often been noted in research concerned with children's fears in general, cf. Johnson and Melamed, 1979.) Together, therefore, these findings suggest that those young people who worry a lot about the nuclear threat are not excessive worriers or particularly neurotic, but are rather people with broad political concerns, who come from families who share their anxieties.

There is some evidence that those young people who express most anxiety about the nuclear threat are not those who feel most fatalistic and helpless about it. Solantaus found that girls, although more worried about the threat of war than boys, discussed it more often and were more likely to believe that they could help to prevent war. This tendency increased with age, and was also related to the level of educational achievement of both the girls and their mothers (Solantaus and Rimpelä, 1984). Goldenring also found that the more worried pupils had talked more to their parents about nuclear war than the less worried, and were more hopeful than other pupils that war could be prevented (Goldenring and Doctor, 1984).

The age and sex trends found in anxiety about nuclear war raise some intriguing questions. Why do girls worry more about nuclear war than boys, and younger children more than older children? Solantaus, the only researcher to examine sex and age effects together, has reported an interaction between sex and age in relation to intense anxiety about war. Whilst at age 12 she found a relatively small sex difference, thereafter the number of boys expressing intense anxiety decreased, whilst the number of girls doing so increased. She attributes this to the increasing tendency of boys during adolescence to identify with the traditional male role of mastery of war, whilst girls tend to identify increasingly with the adult female role of a victim of war, rather than a conquering hero. She also suggests that the adolescent male predilection for computer war games adds to their feeling of mastery over war situations (Solantaus and Rimpelä, 1984). Others have argued that older adolescents develop strong defence mechanisms that enable them to deny or distance themselves from anxiety about the nuclear threat, but this does not explain the sex difference.

Sex and age trends in other worries

These and other explanations could obviously be explored in small-scale investigations. In attempting to formulate hypotheses it should be borne in mind that fears of all kinds are more frequent in girls than in boys, and that, for fears of all kinds, this sex difference widens during adolescence (Cummings, 1944; Lapouse and Monk, 1959; Simon and Ward, 1982). Moreover, younger children have more fears and more intense fears, of all kinds than do older children and adolescents (Coleman, Wolkind and Ashley, 1977; Mcfarlane et al., 1954). These sex and age trends are found not only in self-reports, but also in teachers' and parents' accounts of children's fears. It may be, therefore, that one should first consider more general explanations of sex and age trends in fears before attempting to explain those found in relation to the fear of nuclear war. Unfortunately, most theoretical accounts of fear formation, for example, psychoanalytic and conditioning theories, or those invoking innate or constitutional factors, do not account for these trends or for many other well-established empirical findings about fears (this point is discussed in Rutter and Garmezy, 1983).

In order to account for age and sex trends in fears, it seems necessary to postulate factors that do not form part of the classical theories about fear. In particular, it seems necessary to take into account the differential socialization of girls and boys, and children's own understanding of the situation. This would include the extent to which they perceive themselves as able to master dangerous situations, their cognitive level, and also the extent of their knowledge, which may limit their ability to understand and assess a fearful situation. Gender socialization seems likely to be involved in the greater number of fears expressed by girls than boys. Stress is laid in our society on the importance of boys overcoming, or at least concealing, their fears, but the feminine role is still one of relative passivity, with girls and women encouraged to avoid danger and to look to men to defend and protect them. This differential socialization probably affects not only attitudes, but coping abilities. Because it is unacceptable for boys to express fear, they have to learn to face dangers that girls can avoid. By putting themselves into dangerous or feared situations they are likely to increase their ability to overcome their fears, since all clinical treatment of fears have one thing in common – repeated exposure to the phobic situation (cf. discussion in Johnson and Melamed, 1979). Hence, girls are likely to perceive themselves to be, and in fact to be, less able to master frightening situations than boys.

Cognitive factors in fears

The ability to cope with fearful situations as a consequence of greater experience of them may be a factor in age as well as sex trends in fears. However, the well-attested finding that the content of fears changes during development, and that fears are more frequent and more intense in younger children, seems likely also to be related to the cognitive limitations of younger children. It is generally agreed that the emergence of a fear of strangers between the ages of six and nine months is linked to a specific stage in cognitive development (Kagan, Kearsley and Selazo, 1978). Fear of animals, especially dogs, reaches a peak at about three years (Jersild and Holmes, 1935); as Bowlby has pointed out, learning how to assess and cope with dogs is by no means a simple matter, and involves attending to and synthesizing a number of cues, a process that takes time and experience (Bowlby, 1973). Fears of the dark peak at four or five years, and fears of monsters and imaginary creatures intensify slightly later, but both have almost disappeared by the age of 11. They are replaced by more realistic worries to do with school marks, friendships, personal appearance, and, from the mid-teens, anxieties about jobs, money, and world affairs (Maurer, 1965; Lapouse and Monk, 1959; Angelino, Dollins and Mech, 1956).

The intense fears of early to mid-childhood are akin to adult phobias in that the fears appear to adults to be out of proportion, beyond voluntary control, and not amenable to reasoning. Like phobias, they lead to marked avoidance responses. It seems likely that the intensity of these early fears is in part grounded in children's uncertainty about what is a realistic possibility – whether monsters really exist, or whether lions might appear and attack them. They are also aware of their own powerlessness. Adults may, indeed, help to create these fears, by frightening stories, mock threats – 'I'll eat you up' – and real displays of frightening anger, and physical punishment. They also frequently help to create fears by their deliberate or unintentional ambiguity about the reality of witches, monsters, ghosts and so on. Some would argue that psycho-dynamic factors are also involved. Children struggling with their own strong, but unacceptable, aggressive feelings towards their parents, may project them on to monsters, witches, etc.

In any event, with their very limited knowledge of what is likely and possible, and their real experience of parental anger, it is hardly surprising that children respond with fear to situations in which they are uncertain about the nature of the danger stimulus. Games may help them both to master their fears, and to enjoy the sensation of fear. The Opies have documented many traditional children's dramatic games, which involve children being captured and frequently eaten by a witch or other sinister adult. The frightening element for the children in the games is relieved by slapstick, and by the knowledge that they are playing a game with rules, in which the roles can be reversed. As the Opies point out, however, the players may, nonetheless, shiver with fright (Opie and Opie, 1969). Parents are rarely aware of the pervasive nature and intensity of their children's fears. Whilst writing this chapter I discussed informally with several adolescents their recollections of childhood fears. Two described a secret anxiety that their mothers turned into witches at night, or at times when they were not present. Others admitted searching under the beds every night before daring to climb in. None had ever mentioned these fears at the time to anyone.

With such basic and frightening uncertainties in their daily lives, it is not surprising that young children are likely to be more frightened by disturbing events in the adult world than are older children or adults. One US study, for example, showed that ten year olds were much more disturbed than 18 year olds by the assassination of President Kennedy. Many of them developed headaches, lack of appetite and insomnia (Sigel, 1970). Given the US school context, where the President is portrayed as a supremely powerful and benevolent father figure, his assassination must have been devastating for young children who had no understanding of the possible antecedents or consequences of this event.

It may be for very similar reasons that younger children are more fearful of nuclear war than older children. Whilst an adolescent will appreciate, for example, that nuclear war is unlikely to start without a build-up of international tension and precipitating international events, a younger child does not understand this. One six year old that I know was terrified when he heard that Cruise missiles had come to Britain. It turned out that he thought that Cruise missiles *had come* to Britain meant that the missile had been *used* on Britain. Again, an older child would have realized that such an event could not have occurred without tremendous repercussions. It is my impression from studying videotapes of groups of six and seven year olds discussing nuclear war that they have no clear understanding of the distinction between nuclear and conventional weapons. They may therefore have their fears reinforced by news or media presentation of conventional warfare.

If cognitive factors are involved in appraising the nature of dangerous situations, it might be expected that a relationship of some kind exists between the extent of a person's knowledge of nuclear issues and the level of their anxiety. There appear to be no studies that have analysed this relationship, and very few that have attempted to probe the extent of children's knowledge or understanding of nuclear issues. Such studies as exist suggest that most young people are very ill-informed. One US researcher found that 30 per cent of high school pupils did not know which country had used nuclear weapons in war; their average estimate of the time a Soviet missile would take to reach the US was 192 minutes (Mack, 1983).

A British market research survey found that only 58 per cent of 15–18 year olds knew that nuclear weapons were used in the Second World War, and only half the sample knew that Polaris was a weapon of some kind. However, 70 per cent knew that CND stands for the 'Campaign for Nuclear Disarmament' (Business Decisions Ltd., 1983). Boys were much more knowledgeable than girls, young people with higher educational qualifications were better informed than those with fewer qualifications, and older adolescents were better informed than younger adolescents. Unfortunately, this survey did not ask about fears, so it is not possible to relate the young people's level of knowledge to their level of anxiety. In another British survey carried out in secondary schools, only 11 per cent of pupils correctly identified the number of countries with nuclear weapons. Two-thirds of the pupils thought that between 30 and 102 countries had nuclear weapons (Jones and Saunders, 1984). Two studies reported that adolescents feel themselves ill-informed about nuclear issues, that they would like to be given more information, and that TV is their main source of information (Goldenring and Doctor, 1984; Holmborg and Bergstroem, 1984).

The ignorance of most children and adolescents about international and defence issues is seen by a Finnish researcher, Engeström, as an essential ingredient of their concepts about nuclear war. In an attempt to explore and analyse these concepts in depth, he distinguished three important characteristics commonly found: compartmentalized thinking, fatalism, and ignorance (Engeström, 1984). Compartmentalized thinking was exemplified by the frequent tendency for the same person to describe war in opposing ways, on the one hand as heroic and adventurous, on the other hand as disaster. Concepts of nuclear war also commonly included the view that it is inevitable and uncontrollable. Engström argues that this fatalism rests on ignorance, and that young people cannot think in a realistic or constructive way about nuclear issues because they are so ill-informed. In fact, he suggests that their thinking about nuclear war is on the same level of abstract fantasy as the video games they play. He therefore sees education about nuclear issues as an important way of helping children to overcome feelings of fatalism and helplessness.

It might reasonably be hypothesized that the greater fears about nuclear war of younger children, girls, and adolescents with relatively low educational qualifications are related to their more limited knowledge, since there is a good deal of evidence that these groups are also less well-informed (cf. references above). There is virtually no evidence, however, about the relation between the level of knowledge of young people about nuclear issues and the level of their anxiety, nor of the effect on anxiety of increasing knowledge.

Parental ignorance of children's fears

Parents and teachers are often unaware that fears of nuclear war are so widespread amongst children. This is not surprising, given that adults are often unaware of the extent and the intensity of children's other fears. In one study, children aged eight to 12 and their mothers were interviewed separately about the children's fears. In comparison with what their children said, the mothers under-reported the children's fears by 41 per cent. They were most likely to report fears that they had personally observed, for example, fears of the dark, of staying alone at home, or crossing the street alone. They were much less likely to know about fears of unusual events (wars, floods, murders), or fears about the safety of the family (the child or others in the family getting ill, having an accident, dying, being kidnapped) (Lapouse and Monk, 1959).

Several studies have shown that adolescents do not, in fact, often discuss the threat of war with their parents. Solantaus found that, whilst 84 per cent of girls and 77 per cent of boys stated war as one of their three main fears, only a third had discussed this at home. However, 63 per cent of girls and 50 per cent of boys had discussed the issue with friends. Similar findings emerge from other recent studies (Goldenring and Doctor, 1984; Holmborg and Bergstroem, 1984). Parental silence on this topic may be interpreted by their children as lack of concern. In the Swedish survey, 56 per cent of the young people stated that 'adults seem very little concerned about, or are totally indifferent to' the issue of nuclear war (Holmborg and Bergstroem, 1984). Yet in a Swedish public opinion poll in 1982, in which adults were asked to state their three greatest worries, 78 per cent named nuclear war.

Is anxiety about the nuclear threat a matter for concern?

Most researchers have been distressed to discover the extent of anxiety about nuclear war amongst young people. Others, however, have argued eloquently that some degree of anxiety is needed to ensure our survival; lack of anxiety in this situation can only be due to powerful and potentially dangerous denial mechanisms (Humphrey, 1981; Lifton, 1982). The issue is complex; denial may have an important protective function in the short run for the individual, yet an adverse effect on the long-term chances that society will survive.

Others have argued that the widespread anxiety about the nuclear threat amongst children should not be taken too seriously, since if children do not worry about one thing, they will worry about another. It is certainly true that the prevalence of different types of fear changes from one decade to another (Croake and Knox, 1973). From the 1930s to the 1950s numerous surveys of eight to nine year olds found that the most often cited fears concerned personal safety (e.g., getting lost or kidnapped), animals, supernatural beings, thunder and lightning, and the dark (Winker 1949; Lapouse and Monk, 1959; Angelino, Dollins and Mech, 1956). But by the late 1960s and early 1970s, 'political' fears (e.g., of war, or communists taking over) were those most frequently mentioned in the USA, both by children within this age group, and also by 15 year olds (Croake, 1969; Croake and Knox, 1973). Croake suggests that this change was caused by the widespread TV coverage of the Vietnam war.

There is an important sense, however, in which anxiety about nuclear war is not interchangeable with, or equivalent to, anxiety about thunderstorms or bad school marks. The threat is real, and its implications are even more overwhelming than the threat of personal death or parents' death. More important, it is not possible for parents honestly to help children overcome this fear by showing them that it is unrealistic, or relatively unimportant, or that they can take steps to avoid it, or that they can confront and master the danger. It is probably for this reason that many parents find the subject too painful to discuss with their children. Peace activists have an advantage, in that they can involve their children in activities that they believe will help to overcome the danger. At the same time, studies quoted above suggest that their children are likely to be more worried than others about the nuclear threat. Perhaps this is the most advantageous solution for both children and society – a degree of anxiety, coupled with a positive approach to mastering the danger.

Young people's attitudes to defence policies, war and peace

The fact that many young people worry about nuclear war, and expect a nuclear holocaust in their lifetime, does not necessarily mean that they oppose a defence policy based on nuclear arms. Such studies as there are suggest that young people's views in each country at any particular time resemble those of their parents. For example, shortly after the Three Mile Island accident, 70 per cent of the high school pupils interviewed in New Jersey said that they feared another serious accident but only a third were in favour of closing these plants or relying on other forms of energy (Schwebel and Schwebel, 1981). The majority of a Canadian teenage sample in 1983 were in favour of refusing to manufacture and test nuclear weapons, but against withdrawing from NATO (Sommers et al., 1984).

The most extensive study of young people's views on defence policy was carried out in the UK by a market research firm with a sample of 15–18 year olds (Business Decisions Ltd., 1983). They appeared to be sceptical about a policy of deterrence, since 61 per cent stated that the UK's possession of nuclear weapons did not make it less likely that Russia would attack us, and 58 per cent considered that the presence of Civil Defence encouraged war. On the other hand, 70 per cent said that it would have no effect at all on other countries if the UK abandoned its nuclear weapons. In all 87 per cent had heard of the Greenham Common women peace protesters, who camp round the perimeter of a Cruise missile site. Of these 46 per cent made unfavourable comments about them (e.g., 'wasting their time'), 41 per cent expressed favourable attitudes (e.g., 'standing up for what they believe'), whilst 22 per cent had mixed feelings (e.g., 'right idea, but wrong method'). There were no age or social class differences in attitudes but girls made more positive comments about the Greenham Common women than boys.

Children's views on nuclear defence policies are clearly related, like those of their parents, to their conceptions of potential enemy states, to their general attitudes to war and peace, and to the best methods of reconciling international disputes. There have been very few studies of children's general political attitudes and concepts. During the 1960s there were several studies of children's concepts and moral judgements about war (Cooper, 1965; Ålvik, 1968; Rosell, 1968). Cooper's study, which influenced the design of the others, included children from six to 16 years. Both questionnaires and individual interviews were used. He found that at the youngest age at which a concept of war is articulated, around five or six years, war was seen in terms of personal fighting with guns, and quarrelling. It is only by the age of nine to ten that war was seen as an activity of nation states. Younger children tended to describe war more in terms of weapons and exciting events – fighting and battles – older children more in terms of the negative consequences of war, for example, killing and dying.

Despite the fact, however, that they had more negative associations to war, Cooper found that 15 year olds were more likely to see war as justified and necessary than younger children. Specifically, the older children were unanimous in stating that the UK was right in entering the Second World War, whilst most thought that Japan was wrong. Younger children had less clear-cut views, and some stated that both countries were wrong. This age trend may in part have reflected a greater ignorance about the last world war on the part of the younger children. In answer to a more general question, however, 70 per cent of eight year olds, and only 10 per cent of 15 year olds, said that war can never be justified. At all ages girls described war more in terms of killing and dying than in terms of weapons and battles, and were less likely to see war as justifiable. The children had many fewer ideas about peace than war. Peace was usually seen in negative terms of not being at war. Very few children of any age saw war in terms of an international conflict of interest, or peace in terms of reconciling these conflicts.

The age differences in attitudes to war were interpreted by all three authors in a Piagetian framework. According to Piaget, morality means for the young child adhering to rigid rules fixed by adults: hence their judgement that war is always wrong. Only from the age of about 12 does the child understand that rules are alterable by consensus, and must be viewed in relation to the particular total circumstances of events (Piaget, 1932). Hence by the age of 15 the child realizes that war can be justified as necessitated by the enemy's aggression.

This interpretation of the data, however, fails to account for the fact that girls' judgements about war and peace tend to resemble those of younger children. Moreover, Piaget's views on the development of moral judgements are now disputed. In a recent review of research on children's moral judgements, Turiel cites several studies showing that even very young children do not blindly apply adult rules when making moral judgements, but take into account the consequences of actions, especially those that relate to harming others. As children get older, the main change in the basis of their judgements appears to be in the number and type of factors they take into account when assessing the morality of an action (Turiel, 1983). A more likely explanation of the age trends reported by Cooper and others is that as they get older, children are increasingly exposed, both at school and in the media, to prevailing political attitudes, and to patriotic, militaristic attitudes and values. These are overwhelmingly presented in terms of male heroes, with whom boys are more likely to identify.

The impact of the nuclear threat on young people's personalities

An issue of great concern to many parents, teachers, and psychiatrists, is the effect on children's personalities of growing up in the shadow of the nuclear threat. If, as we have seen, a substantial proportion of young people believe that mankind will be annihilated in their lifetime, how does this belief affect them? Are there pervasive effects on development, which are much more sinister than feelings of anxiety? A number of US psychiatrists have argued that the nuclear threat has led to a widespread feeling of helplessness and incompetence (Escalona, 1982; Schwebel, 1982; Beardslee and Mack, 1983). Young people's trust in adults has been undermined, leading to cynicism and unhappiness. A sense of futurelessness leads to a reckless orientation in the 'here and now', to impulsive problem behaviour and a failure to adopt long-term goals. Children may be overwhelmed by the fact that their unconscious fantasies of destruction are likely to be actualized.

These assumptions seem reasonable, but they are extremely difficult to validate. It is true that several studies have shown that young people often say that the nuclear threat affects their plans and thinking about the future. In one such study, 31 Boston high school students aged 14 to 19 were interviewed in depth about this and related issues (Goodman et al., 1983). The sample was probably biased in unknown ways, since the pupils were located by the help of teachers, parents and counsellors. The authors report that many of the adolescents lived on two levels. They felt the future was doubtful, yet most made plans for it, despite their fears. Some said that the threat of nuclear war forced them to live for the present, others that the threat was responsible for their use of drugs. Many expressed feelings of disillusion about the world in general, the USA in particular, and even about human nature. The authors conclude that these adolescents were acquiring a sense of powerlessness and resignation and in many cases a tendency to impulsivity and immediacy in personal relationships.

But there is very little evidence, in the UK at least, of the behavioural consequences that could be expected to accompany such effects. For example, one might predict that trends in juvenile crime, drug and alcohol abuse, would in some way match the peak periods of anxiety about nuclear war, especially the 1961–2 crises and 1979 onwards. One might also predict that young people would fail to enter higher education at these times. Heroin and alcohol use have certainly increased rapidly amongst young people in the UK in recent years, but this seems to be a consequence of their greater availability at lower prices than in the past. On some indices the trend is the reverse of what might be predicted. In the UK there has been a steady increase since 1979 in the level of examination successes amongst school leavers, and in the number of young people entering tertiary education. A plausible interpretation is that they are responding in a positive way to the current situation of high youth unemployment, and that they are not overwhelmed by despair about the future.

Evidence from Northern Ireland suggests that one should be cautious in making assumptions about the impact of societal stresses on young people's behaviour. It is widely believed that 16 years of violence, inter-communal tension and conflict in Northern Ireland must have had a damaging impact on the children growing up in the province. Yet numer-ous research studies have failed to find evidence of such damage, despite the coexistence of civil strife, high unemployment, and great poverty. Educational standards in the province are above those in most of Eng-land and Wales, levels of juvenile crime are much lower than elsewhere in the UK, truancy rates in Belfast are similar to those in other UK cities, child referrals to clinics for emotional disorders have not increased since civil strife began in 1968. Children's views of themselves, and their relationships with their peers and their parents seem unaffected (Harbison, 1983).

This is not to say that there has not been serious psychological damage to individual children in Northern Ireland, but that in general they seem remarkably resilient and adaptable to stress arising outside their family. Throughout history, after all, both young and old have lived with fear. During the Middle Ages bubonic plague killed a quarter of the population; for centuries fear of damnation and hellfire must have been very real. A supportive family seems largely able to buffer children from psychological damage by outside threats – a poignant and extreme example of this is preserved in the diary of Anne Frank. Of course, this conclusion in no way minimizes the seriousness of these threats.

It is possible that there are subtle effects of the nuclear threat on young people's personalities that are not easy to demonstrate. But even if such effects did occur, it would be extraordinarily difficult to show that they were due to the specific impact of the nuclear threat, as distinct from other stresses in society.

This said, many teachers and parents would like guidance in helping young people to live with the nuclear threat. The studies reviewed here have thrown up some leads from young people themselves, notably their feeling that adults are indifferent to the threat, and their desire for more information and discussion. Discussion at home, and courses on nuclear issues at school, may help adolescents. Knowing that their parents and teachers are concerned about these issues may change their perception of adults as ineffective and uncaring about the future, whilst greater intel-lectual understanding and more information may help to relieve their anxiety. There has as yet been little or no research about the best way to conduct such education.

Conclusions

It seems reasonably well established that between a third and a half of young people in the West over the age of ten believe that a nuclear holocaust in their lifetime is probable (there has been virtually no research with children under this age). About half, or more, say that they worry about this prospect, and perhaps a quarter suffer intense or frequent anxiety. The level of anxiety is higher in Europe than in North America. Girls and younger adolescents worry more than boys and older children. Those who worry most are not usually neurotic or disturbed, but tend to be those who are concerned about other broad social issues.

If half the young people in Europe believe that a nuclear holocaust is likely, how do they live with this belief? This question has received little study. There is some evidence that those young people who discuss nuclear issues more often with family and friends are more worried, but also more optimistic that war can be prevented. Powerful defence mechanisms must protect most young (as well as most older) people from extreme anxiety. It is not clear whether the widely noted decrease in anxiety in older adolescents, especially boys, is due to a strengthening of their defence mechanisms, or to attitudinal and cognitive changes. There have been virtually no studies of the relation between the level of anxiety in young people about nuclear issues and their level of understanding of them. Moreover, it is not clear whether the nuclear threat has resulted in an overall increase in their anxiety and unhappiness. It has also not been established that the nuclear threat has affected personality development, although many psychiatrists believe this to be the case.

Most of the research reviewed has been concerned with answering a few simple, descriptive questions. As I pointed out at the beginning of this chapter, in order to go further a more sophisticated research paradigm is required. We know that the main channel by which the nuclear threat reaches children is TV. We also know that the impact of the threat is mediated by certain characteristics of the child (age, gender, interests), and of the child's family. We do not know *how* this mediation occurs – for example, how and to what extent the child's cognitive understanding, stock of information, self-perceptions, and attitudes to war and politics are involved. So far as family influence is concerned, numerous studies have shown that the majority of children and teenagers share their parents' moral, political and religious beliefs (cf. a discussion in Coleman, 1980). One specific and relevant example is a study by Tolley of children's attitudes to the Vietnam war (Tolley, 1973). He found children's attitudes to the war were closely related to their parents', but that their degree of knowledge about it was more dependent on their age and sex, and also on their newspaper reading and TV watching habits.

254   *Children of social worlds*

The research question discussed in this chapter is seen by most psychologists as marginal, and perhaps politically suspect. Yet, as I have tried to show, apart from its intrinsic importance, it raises in a concrete form some of the most fundamental issues with which developmental psychology is concerned – notably, the relationship between the child, the family, and the wider society, and the interaction between cognitive and affective factors. Perhaps in the next decade we shall see an increased understanding of child development through the analysis of the impact of societal events of this kind on the child.

References

Ålvik, T. 1968. The development of views on conflict: war and peace among school children. *Journal of Peace Research*, **2**, 171–95.

Angelino, H., Dollins, J. and Mech, E. 1956. Trends in the fears and worries of schoolchildren as related to socio-economic status and age. *Journal of Genetic Psychology*, **89**, 263–76.

Bachmann, J. 1983. How American high school seniors view the military. *Armed Forces and Society*, **10**, 86–104.

Beardslee, W. R. and Mack, J. E. 1983. Adolescents and the threat of nuclear war. *Yale Journal of Biology and Medicine*, **56**, 79–91.

Blackwell, P. L. and Gessner, J. C. 1983. Fear and trembling: An enquiry into adolescent perceptions of living in the nuclear age. *Youth and Society*, **15**, 237–55.

Bowlby, J. 1973. *Attachment and Loss*, Vol. 2. *Separation, Anxiety and Anger*. London: Hogarth Press.

Business Decisions Ltd. 1983. Nuclear weapons study: a summary report (unpublished manuscript of a private report carried out for the *TV Times*, London).

Chivian, E. and Mack, J. 1983. What Soviet Children are Saying about Nuclear War. *Washington Post*, 14 October 1983.

Coleman, J. 1980. *The Nature of Adolescence*. London: Methuen.

Coleman, J, Wolkind, S. N. and Ashley, L. 1977. Symptoms of behaviour disturbance and adjustment to school. *Journal of Child Psychology and Psychiatry*, **18**, 201–10.

Cooper, P. 1965. The development of the concept of war. *Journal of Peace Research*, **2**, 1–18.

Croake, J. W. 1969. Fears of children. *Human Development*, **12**, 239–47.

Croake, J. W. and Knox, F. H. 1973. The changing nature of children's fears. *Child Study Journal*, **3**, 91–105.

Cummings, J. D. 1944. The incidence of emotional symptoms in school children. *British Journal of Educational Psychology*, **14**, 150–61.

Edwards, G. 1976. Psychiatric aspects of civilian disasters. *British Medical Journal*, **1**, 944–7.

Engeström, Y. 1984. Multiple levels of nuclear reality in the cognition, fantasy and activity of school-aged children. *Proceedings of the 4th Congress of International Physicians for the Prevention of Nuclear War*.

Escalona, S. K. 1963. Children's responses to the nuclear war threat. *Children*, **10**, 137–42.

Escalona, S. K. 1982. Growing up with the nuclear war. *American Journal of Orthopsychiatry*, **52**, 600–7.

Goldenring, J. M. and Doctor, R. M. 1984. California adolescents' concerns about the threat of nuclear war. *Proceedings of the 4th Congress of International Physicians for the Prevention of Nuclear War*.

Goodman, L. A., Mack, J. E., Beardslee, W. R. and Snow, R. M. 1983. The threat of nuclear war and the nuclear arms race: adolescent experience and perception. *Political Psychology*, **4**, 501–3.

Haas, S. 1983. cf. W. R. Beardslee and J. E. Mack, Adolescents and the threat of nuclear war. *Yale Journal of Biology and Medicine*, **56**, 79–91.

Harbison, J. (ed.) 1983. *Children of the Troubles*. Belfast: Stranmillis College Learning Resources Unit.

Holmborg, P. E. and Bergstroem, A. 1984. How Swedish teenagers, aged 13–15, think and feel concerning the nuclear threat. *Proceedings of the 4th Congress of International Physicians for the Prevention of Nuclear War*.

Humphrey, N. 1981. Four minutes to midnight. *The Listener*, **29**, 493–9.

Izard, C. E. 1977. *Human Emotions*. New York: Plenum.

Jersild, A. T. and Holmes, F. G. 1935. *Children's Fears*. New York: Teachers College Press.

Jersild, A. T., Marley, F. V. and Jersild, C. L. 1933. Children's fears, dreams, wishes, daydreams, likes, dislikes, pleasant and unpleasant memories. *Child Development Monograph*, **12**, 144–59.

Johnson, S. B. and Melamed, B. G. 1979. The assessment and treatment of children's fears, in B. B. Lahey and A. E. Kazdin (eds), *Advances in Clinical Child Psychology*. Vol. 2. New York: Plenum.

Jones, S. and Saunders, H. 1984. Growing up in the nuclear age: an interim report on a survey of schoolchildren's attitudes to nuclear weapons. Bristol: Avon Peace Education Project.

Kagan, J., Kearsley, R. B. and Selazo, P. R. 1978. *Infancy: its place in human development*. Cambridge, Mass.: Harvard University Press.

Kramer, B. M., Kulick, S. M., and Milburn, M. A. 1983. Attitudes towards nuclear weapons and nuclear war 1948–1982. *Journal of Social Issues*, **39**, 7–24.

Lapouse, R. and Monk, M. A. 1959. Fears and worries in a representative sample of children. *American Journal of Orthopsychiatry*, **29**, 803–18.

Lifton, R. 1982. The political and psychological case against nuclearism, in R. Lifton and R. Falk (eds), *Indefensible Weapons*. New York: Basic Books.

London, D. B. 1984. Anxiety and attitudes in high school students before and after an educational workshop on nuclear war issues. *Proceedings of the 4th Congress of International Physicians for the Prevention of Nuclear War*.

Macfarlane, J., Allen, L. and Honzik, M. 1954. *A Developmental Study of the Behavior Problems of Normal Children*. Berkeley: University of California Press.

Mack, J. 1983. The psychological impact of the nuclear arms competition on children and adolescents (testimony to Select Committee on Children, Youth and Families, US House of Representatives).

Maurer, A. 1965. What children fear. *Journal of Genetic Psychology*, **106**, 265–77.

Opie, I. and Opie, P. 1969. *Children's Games in Street and Playground*. Oxford: Oxford University Press.

Piaget, J. 1932. *The Moral Judgement of the Child*. London: Routledge and Kegan Paul.

Richards, M. P. M. 1974. *The Integration of a Child into a Social World*. London: Cambridge University Press.

Rosell, L. 1968. Children's views of war and peace. *Journal of Peace Research*, 5, 268–76.

Rutter, M. and Garmezy, N. 1983. Developmental psychopathology, in P. H. Mussen (ed.), *Child Psychology*. Vol. IV. New York: John Wiley.

Schwebel, M. 1965. Nuclear cold war: student opinion and professional responsibilities, in M. Schwebel (ed.), *Behavioral Science and Human Survival*. Palo Alto, California: Science and Behavior Books.

Schwebel, M. 1982. Effects of the nuclear war threat on children and teenagers. *American Journal of Orthopsychiatry*, 52, 608–18.

Schwebel, M. and Schwebel, B. 1981. Children's reactions to the threat of nuclear plant accidents. *American Journal of Orthopsychiatry*, 5, 260–70.

Sigel, R. S. 1970. An exploration into some aspects of political socialisation: school children's reactions to the death of a president, in R. S. Sigel (ed.), *Learning about Politics*. New York: Random House.

Simon, A. and Ward, L. O. 1982. Sex-related patterns of worry in secondary school pupils. *British Journal of Clinical Psychology*, 21, 63–4.

Solantaus, T. and Rimpelä, M. 1984. Young people and threat of war: anxiety versus optimism about prevention. *Proceedings of the 4th Congress of International Physicians for the Prevention of Nuclear War*.

Solantaus, T., Rimpelä, M. and Taipale, V. 1984. The threat of war in the minds of 12–18 year olds in Finland. *Lancet,* 1, 784–5.

Sommers, F., Goldberg, S., Levinson, D., Ross, C., LaCombe, S. 1984. Children's Mental Health and the Threat of Nuclear War: a Canadian pilot study. *Proceedings of the 4th Congress of International Physicians for the Prevention of Nuclear War*.

Terr, L. C. 1981. Psychic trauma in children: observations following the Chowchilla school-bus kidnapping. *American Journal of Psychiatry*, 138, 14–19.

Tolley, H. 1973. *Children and War: Political socialisation in international conflict*. New York: Teachers College Press.

Turiel, E. 1983. *The Development of Social Knowledge*. Cambridge: Cambridge University Press.

Winker, J. B. 1949. Age trends and sex differences in the wishes, identifications, activities and fears of children. *Child Development*, 20, 191–200.

Wrightsman, L. S. 1970. Parental attitudes and behaviors as determinants of children's responses to the threat of nuclear war, in R. S. Sigel, *Learning about Politics*. New York, Random House.

12

Developmental psychology and psychoanalysis: splitting the difference

Cathy Urwin

Introduction

Like many disciplines, developmental psychology has proceeded in relative ignorance of its own history. It embodies particular priorities, conceptions of 'the child', of appropriate methodology, and of what development itself is, and seldom asks how and why these assumptions have come about. Even less attention is given to how they maintain and produce divisions and connections with other practices in which relations to children are central, such as those of the school, social welfare, medicine and the law. This ignorance of where we come from and how the intellectual discipline has both affected and depended on other practices makes it difficult to examine critically what Ingleby (chapter 14) describes as the productive power of psychological knowledge and its role in the processes of social regulation that circumscribe our daily lives. As important, an unquestioning attitude towards our own roots also constrains the kinds of questions that can be asked from within what developmental psychology takes as its own intellectual frame of reference.

In this chapter I am concerned with the relation between developmental psychology and a body of knowledge, assumptions and forms of practice that in many ways appear to be in direct opposition to the priorities of developmental psychologists: the psychoanalytic tradition and forms of play therapy with children whose developmental difficulties are viewed as predominantly emotional. Again, Ingleby refers to this opposition, and several reasons for it suggest themselves. These reflect different purposes and populations of concern – the 'normal' and the 'pathological' – and different assumptions about methodology and scientific truth. The latter centre on an opposition between clinical and interpretive methods and the search for objectivity. Less obviously, the traditions embody different notions of cause and effect, of relations between past and present, and of developmental processes themselves. For example, psychology has a preference for specific events or processes which can be taken as causal and predictive of later outcomes. This is linked to a view of development which, broadly speaking, progresses 'upwards', whether this is achieved

stepwise through stages, as a gradual linear accumulation, or, more adven-
turously, in a series of cycles. But these accounts contrast markedly with
the view of development which, I suggest, must follow from psychoanalytic
material. Here the message is not simply that the past is never lost, as is
witnessed most clearly in the phenomena of regression and the compulsion
to repeat, but that the relation between the past and present is never one of
simple determination. It is not that there is no relation between life events
and mental concomitants, but the psychic implications of environmental
contingencies cannot be read off directly, nor can they be entirely predicted. The subjective consequences are a complex product of meanings
produced through previous life history, present circumstances and constructions engendered through the individual's own phantasies. These
serve to produce our relation to our pasts, and also to screen us from
them.

Gross differences in methodology and assumptions about development
would seem to confirm that the discourses and practices of psychoanalysis
have little contact with developmental psychology. But this lack of contact
may be more apparent than real. First, considerable borrowing has taken
place between the two traditions. This borrowing has, however, been
remarkably selective, reflecting each tradition's contribution to social
regulatory processes and their role in maintaining dominant ideologies.
An obvious example of psychology's uptake is the preoccupation with the
mother-child dyad and the influence of Bowlby (1952, 1953). Yet he himself, originally a psychoanalyst, eventually 'borrowed' from psychology
(Bowlby, 1969), and the influence of his work has depended on the fact
that its popularization took place in a period of rapid expansion in various
social practices that regulate the family (Riley, 1983; Urwin, 1985).
Secondly, as I shall show, this selective borrowing is itself facilitated by
the fact that, despite the apparent division, psychoanalysis and developmental psychology share several assumptions. This is largely because both
fields originally developed within the same intellectual tradition and held
related practical concerns. Thirdly, the apparent division in interest,
theoretical assumptions and realms of practice may itself have contributed
to certain phenomena being marginalized, occluded or rendered inaccessible within developmental psychology. Here I am thinking particularly of
the ways in which emotional processes have been excluded from the study
of 'normal' children. For example, clinicians can point to many children
who have found their way into child therapy who go on to cope considerably better with school tasks such as reading and mathematics, as one
consequence of the clarification of emotional problems. This indicates a
clear relation between emotional and cognitive processes. Is it not remarkable, then, that a developmental psychology of normal development has
not managed to specify the relation between emotion and cognition in any
satisfactory way?

This is but one illustration of developmental psychology's tendency to take for granted processes which psychoanalysis suggests are central if deeply problematic. In this paper my aim is not to bring psychoanalysis and developmental psychology together in any grand scheme, which may be neither possible nor ultimately desirable. Rather, I shall indicate areas where I feel that the introduction of some psychoanalytic assumptions about development may illuminate some current concerns in developmental psychology, concentrating on the pervasive split between emotion and cognition and how this has come about. In the first section I shall illustrate the implications of this split with reference to two contemporary research fields: work aiming to place young children's reasoning in a social context, and the study of pre-verbal communication and the emergence of language. But while I shall indicate why such work might usefully engage with psychoanalysis, there are fundamental problems and limitations in any integration. Some of these are explored in the second major section, which is historical and includes a re-examination of the early work of Piaget. This was far more influenced by psychoanalytic ideas than is commonly realized. The final section discusses possible future directions for developmental psychology. What emerges is the need for a reworking of the relation between rationality, phantasy and social practices and a renewed interest in children's mistakes.

Social cognition and self–other awareness

I have suggested that developmental psychology is largely unreflexive in relation to its own history. But the publication of this book a decade or so after *The Integration of a Child into a Social World* does provide the impetus for historical review. As Ingleby (chapter 14) suggests, this period has produced a distinct shift in emphasis resulting from the recognition of the importance of placing children's development and the way we study it in a social context. But how far has this shift fundamentally altered the nature of psychologist's enquiries? Unsurprisingly, the degree of theoretical innovation has varied considerably. For example, in some cases social phenomena like children's social relationships and understanding of social rules and regularities are studied alongside more familiar processes, such as perception and cognition, which are taken as being somehow more fundamental. Cognitive processes are then drawn in to 'explain' the emergence of social phenomena or age-related changes. On the other hand, other researchers are committed to the more radical view that it is from an understanding of social processes that an account of cognitive development is most appropriately derived, a position that regards individuals as produced through social relations rather than the other way around. From this viewpoint, integrating social and cognitive processes requires a theoretical orientation which challenges the individualistic basis of psychology. Like most Western philosophy, this takes the unitary individual as the starting-point, ascribes to him or her pre-given character- istics or tendencies, and uses these to account for social relations and ultimately social life as a whole. One of the political implications following from this is that social relations rapidly reduce to consequences of indi- vidual tendencies which are viewed as inbuilt and/or as more or less inevitable (see Henriques et al., 1984).

Finding ways of thinking about the social production of individuals, which avoid crude determinism and allow for tensions between 'individual' and 'social', is a complex task and it is a moot point as to how far this has yet been achieved. But this does not mean that developmental psychology can- not make considerable gains through redefining its terrain in both theory and practice. In this endeavour a major target must be to challenge what one might call 'cognitive reductionism', or the ubiquitous tendency to attempt to explain social developments in terms of inbuilt capacities or universal emer- gent cognitive structures. It is particularly relevant to consider the major inroads which have come through challenging Piaget's theory of develop- mental stages and the emergence of operational structures which are assumed to underly and make possible logical thought. This challenge to Piaget's universalism has been fuelled by work on reasoning and problem- solving in adults. For example, Wason (1965) has questioned the assump- tion that formal logic is a useful model for cognitive processes even in Westernized adults and several researchers have stressed the historicity and cultural specificity of this sort of reasoning and its dependence on very particular practices and technologies (see Olson, 1977; Walkerdine, 1982). In the developmental field, one of the most influential attacks on the Piagetian hegemony has been that of Donaldson (1978) and her colleagues. Broadly speaking, this work relies on introducing various modifications into the traditional Piagetian experiments, in order to explore, for instance, the possible meaning of the testing situation to young children, and how they may construe the experimenter's questions or definition of the task at hand. Many modifications consist in presenting problems related to the familiar Piagetian tests, but which draw on activities or procedures which can be assumed to be familiar to young children. This has given rise to some very ingenious experiments which have become classic studies in their own right, for example, Hughes's (1975) perspective-taking task involving a boy doll hiding from a policeman doll, or McGarrigle and Donaldson's (1975) 'naughty teddy' version of the conservation task. (See Light, chapter 8, for a detailed account of some of these tasks.) Taken together, these kinds of experiments clearly suggest that young children have considerable abilities to 'put themselves in other people's shoes' and to reason in contexts that involve materials and procedures which are familiar to them. They also suggest that they are particularly sensitive to the form of the experimenter's questions. In Donaldson and Hughes's terms the children can solve these problems because they 'make human sense' and they 'make human sense' because 'the motives and intentions of the characters are entirely comprehensible' (Hughes and Donaldson, 1983, 253).

In emphasizing social context, this work has thus profoundly challenged the conservative estimate of young children's reasoning abilities that has been produced through the Piagetian paradigm. It also suggests the beginnings of a social account of cognitive functioning. If, as Donaldson argues, the child's true cognitive abilities will only be revealed in situations that make human sense to the child, we might infer that it is within such contexts that cognitive development itself takes place. But how far has this account actually shifted the emphasis onto social processes, and to what extent is it an account of development at all? There are problems with this work, not the least of which is the fact that children succeeding in the modified tasks still fail the standard Piagetian tasks. It is arguable that in most cases the modified and original tasks are not testing the same thing. The modified perspective-taking task and the Piagetian 'three mountains' tasks are clearly not equitable in terms of level of inference, for example (Light, 1985 and chapter 8). This apart, we may assume that young children will eventually succeed in solving Piaget's problems, when they get older. But how does this development come about? Although Donaldson has been able to provide plausible explanations for young children's errors, rendering them 'sensible', it is not clear how the concept of 'human sense' is relevant to children's eventual achievement. This ambiguity invites two kinds of conclusions. Either Piaget's account of how development takes place is correct after all, particularly if it is admitted that the modified tasks are not genuine tests of conservation or other operations. In consequence, social transactions and context are irrelevant to the process of cognitive development. This, of course, is very similar to Piaget's own view, in that, although he stresses the importance of environment and social interactions in his account, their relation to cognition is a functional one; they speed up or slow down the emergent cognitive processes but do not actually enter into the structuring of cognition itself (Ingleby, 1983). Alternatively, we are invited to conclude that cognitive categories eventually emerging in operational thinking are inbuilt, merely requiring appropriate situations for their expression. This again renders the contribution of social processes to the structuring of cognition and the developmental task itself relatively trivial and reifies a normal course underlying these transformations. We are pushed back into a nativist or predeterminist position with the individual at its core and logic privileged as the naturally emerging pinnacle of adult thought.

As Walkerdine (1982) points out, accounting for cognition as a social process requires a rather different analysis of social context. Walkerdine

(1982, 1984) herself has put forward one of the most promising new theoretical positions. She points out that in most psychological accounts social context is grafted onto or outside the child, leaving a 'common core' rationality to emerge untouched by the specifics of social processes. In contrast, her analysis replaces this notion of context with an emphasis on historically specific social practices and signifying relations which have a dynamic and constitutive role in the development of thinking. From this perspective, formal logic may be regarded as a practice supported and maintained as an activity between people, dependent on particular forms of discourse, notably in this case those associated with school and literacy (Walkerdine, 1982). By extension Light argues in chapter 8 that conservation concepts, too, can be thought of not so much as transcendental logical entities, but as products of shared human functional interests. This view is consistent with cross-cultural research (see, for example, Cole and Scribner, 1974).

But the problems are not just to do with the content of children's thinking, but also with what motivates their development and engagement in the learning process. Here, I suggest, there are as many limitations with Donaldson's notion of 'human sense' as a description of children's motivation and involvement in the experiments she describes as there are with the concept as an explanation of children's relative success or failure. Donaldson suggests that children are not only skilled in reading the intentions, motives and wishes of other people but that they are positively preoccupied with doing so. How could this come about? Donaldson's emphasis on the importance of the child's intentions is consistent with recent work on pre-verbal communication, and the emergence of language, such as that described in the volume edited by Lock (1978) and by Bruner and his co-workers (Bruner, 1975, 1978, 1983). Much of this work on infant development and early language has been implicitly or explicitly influenced by the theories of Mead and Vygotsky and, again, several researchers aim to move towards an account of the social basis of language and eventually of mental life as a whole. But despite this aim, there is a pervasive tendency for these accounts of the social to reduce to cognitive categories, or to discussion of what the baby does or does not know. For example, a great deal has been made of experimental evidence purporting to show that newborn infants are endowed with neurological equipment that makes them particularly sensitive to perceptual features, like particular sound frequencies or properties indicating 'animation', which are likely to be found in other people (see, for example, Schaffer, 1984). Interpretations of this evidence vary from those which stress that people are likely to be interesting to babies because they embody so many of these attractive or attention getting properties, to those which see this correspondence as evidence of an innate predisposition towards social life as a whole. In line with the latter interpretation, perhaps the most extreme views have been put forward by Trevarthen and his collaborators (Trevarthen, 1975; Trevarthen and Hubley, 1978). On the basis of video records comparing young babies' interactions with their mothers with their interactions with a suspended inanimate object, Trevarthen has argued not only that young babies in some sense 'know' the difference between people and things, but that they are equipped with two distinct modes of psychological action and forms of intentionality, one directed towards acting on inanimate objects, the other towards communicating with persons. More recently, Trevarthen (1982) has added a catalogue of emergent motives which unfold according to predetermined biological principles. Although this emergence may require some environmental support, notably the presence of an attentive mother, this does not enter into the structuring of the babies' sociability. The contribution of social context is thus trivialized, and the problem of what 'sociability' may actually be is occluded by an emphasis on universal properties.

Turning to somewhat older infants, a very similar view to Trevarthen's has been put forward by Kagan (1981) who uses socio-biological assumptions in arguing for the emergence of 'self-awareness' as a unitary phenomenon in the second year. He supports this claim by illustrating various changes in infants' executive powers. These developments include the emergence of language and symbolic play, infants' unwillingness to engage in tasks which are too difficult for them, and signs of upset, often extreme, over their own or others' transgressions, or about things out of place or damaged in some way. Kagan groups these disparate phenomena together and claims that they are biologically pre-programmed. He provides no examination of developmental preconditions or of individual differences and ignores the contribution of specific social events that, for example, obviously enable children to learn what is out of place. Again, sociability is reduced to what the baby 'knows', and its development in accordance with a pre-given scheme.

In contrast, other researchers who have been more directly influenced by the work of Mead and Vygotsky, such as Newson (1978) and Shotter (1978) have put forward a view which Ingleby describes as 'social constructivist'. These researchers have apparently been more cautious, and, for example, are loath to ascribe intentionality to very young infants. Instead, in discussing the early months, they give the supportive adult a far more fundamental role, stressing the adult's ability and willingness to interpret the baby's behaviour as indicating intentions from way before the baby may be properly said to 'know' what his or her actions mean. This process of interpretation is said to provide a framework for the baby to learn the conventional significance of his or her actions, laying the groundwork not only for the learning of meaning systems such as language but for the social production of the self and individual consciousness. Similarly, following Ryan (1974), Bruner (1975, 1978, 1983) emphasizes

the importance of mothers' consistent interpretation in providing a scaffold for learning language within familiar shared activities like games and
caretaking.

Here there is a clear correspondence between this work on infant intentionality and regularized contexts and the 'human sense' which Donaldson
sees operating in pre-school children. One is tempted to speculate that the
reading of intentions and purposes and the establishing of shared contexts
between mothers and babies sets the groundwork for the later emerging
context dependent reasoning in the child. Indeed Donaldson (1978) specu-
lates along these lines. There are limitations, however, in the infancy work,
which I have touched on elsewhere (Urwin, 1982, 1984). For example, in
contrast to Trevarthen's strong claims, this work is extremely hazy about
the baby's contribution, tending to put everything in the mother and
nothing in the baby. This invites a crude and unsatisfactory determinism.
Alternatively, by leaving the baby's contribution unspecified, a space
is left open for assuming that the baby contains all that is necessary to
account for his or her individuality; environmental conditions merely
facilitate the baby's becoming conscious of a pre-exist self. Again the
impact of the social environment is trivialized. We are also left with the
question of whether or not these rich observations of interpretations and
interactions have actually told us about anything that contributes to the
process of development itself.

This kind of impasse follows inevitably from many approaches attempting to give social processes a fundamental role. But it is important to stress
that my quarrel is not simply with the adequacy or otherwise of their
philosophical foundations and their political implications. Though not
unrelated, it is also with the view of development which this work presents.
Putting together the work on pre-school children and infants, we are
presented with a view of development which on reflection may appear as
somewhat extraordinary. The demonstration of young children's considerable reasoning abilities and the 'sensibleness' of their errors presents, I
suggest, an over-rationalized view of young children. In an environment
of consistent interpretation, of familiarity and predictability, where everything the child does can be 'explained', there is little room for making
mistakes, confusing the perspectives of self and others, or for confusing
animate and inanimate. Above all, in the realm of human sense there is
little room for imagination and no role given to emotional processes. This
rationalized view of the young child is coupled with an idealized but also
grossly impoverished view of mother-child relationships. Turning to the
infancy work, before the child goes to school, we are presented with
the mother-child dyad as a unit of perfect harmony, in which adults'
readings scaffold the child's intentions within an increasingly familiar
world. Not only is the social world limited to the dyad, but in this world
there appears to be little room for pleasure and distress, or for conflict

or aggression. It is significant, for example, that psychologists' recognition of the ubiquitousness of aggression within mother-child relationships has come from studies also embracing relationships outside the dyad, for example, between siblings and peers (Dunn, chapter 5; Urwin, 1983a).

It may require some effort of introspection to perceive a relationship between emotionality and human reasoning. For adults, the relationship becomes clearer when our powers of reasoning break down. However, it is perhaps easier to illustrate what is occluded by this view of children's development. While I suggest that the picture of harmony and complete comprehension between mother and child does not square with anyone's experience, neither, I think, does the view of the young child's ability to take the perspective of the other. It is clear that young children can and do 'decentre' from an early age, in relatively familiar contexts at least. But it is questionable how far we, as adults, consistently exercise our abilities in this sphere. Knowing what other people think, feel or will do in particular situations remains a lifelong problem. This is not simply a question of a deficiency in experience, though we may do better with people we know well and whom we have seen react before in proto-typical situations. Rather, although we may want to understand the feelings and motives of others, we also have an ineffable tendency to confuse our motives with theirs, to impute to them what we wish, in order to have them conform to our own purposes, or to shift the blame somewhere else. Alternatively we may be unable to perceive what other people want because this implies demands on ourselves which are too difficult. Hollway's (1984) discussion of various misrecognitions in couple relations provides vivid examples of this. These facts of social and psychic life render the notion of 'perspective-taking' as currently formulated somewhat inadequate. In the infancy work, there are similar problems with the assumption that very young infants 'know' the difference between people and things. Apart from the fact that the empirical evidence does not actually support this claim, (Sylvester-Bradley, 1985), taking this distinction as some defining criterion of sociability renders inaccessible certain phenomena that are fundamental to how we are. I am thinking here of pervasive processes through which our own emotional reactions or states of mind colour our interactions with the inanimate as well as animate world or our attempts to control it. This process includes the imputation of feeling states or personal characteristics to inanimate objects such as well-loved possessions, and even the imputation of agency to them: the car that consistently breaks down at the least opportune moments, or the tools that the bad workman is supposed to blame. Less obviously, the relation between inanimate materials, emotions and parts of ourselves emerges in art, our reactions to it, and in variations in how we see pictures, sculptures and even shop-windows from day to day.

These kinds of phenomena are the stuff of the theory and practice of psychoanalysis. This fundamentally challenges the notion of the unitary, self-determining individual, simultaneously embracing the irrational and giving emotionality a central role. It stresses that unconscious processes indicating the workings of desire underpin all psychic life in both adults and children, contributing to the precarious instability of many apparent developmental achievements such as being able to differentiate between 'self' and 'other'. It also emphasizes the role of various mechanisms of defence that operate in relation to internal and external threats. Although these processes can colour our relation to the external world or other people in ultimately destructive ways, at the same time the restitution of the internal world through the workings of phantasy makes it possible to move forward in the face of external constraints. Given these assumptions and priorities, it seems reasonable to look to the psychoanalytic tradition for tools for bringing together emotion and cognition within a social approach to development. But there are pitfalls as well as possibilities here. In the next section I explore historical processes that have contributed to developmental psychology's neglect of emotion and look in detail at one foray developmental psychology has already made into psychoanalysis.

The splitting of emotion and rationality in the Child Study Movement

It is misleading to assume that developmental psychology's relative neglect of emotionality represents a new problem. Indeed, at its simplest the difficulty is a result of a pervasive opposition between emotion and reason which itself has a long history. This opposition was inscribed in the tradition from which developmental psychology as we know it first began in the middle of the last century. Of course, philosophical speculations about the state of the newborn infant, as a blank state or equipped with faculties of reason, had already had implications for education and child care before this, Rousseau and Locke being well-known examples (see Hardyment, 1983). But the scientific observation and cataloguing of child behaviour depended crucially on the emergence of a particular tradition, the Child Study Movement, which began with the work of Charles Darwin, whose theory of evolution made the development of the human infant a subject of scientific importance. Indeed Darwin's own autobiographical account of his son's development set the tone both for how development should be studied and for identifying what was of interest (Darwin, 1877). Here, the concern was with describing patterns of growth and behaviour with the aim of likening human infants to the rest of the animal kingdom, and at the same time demonstrating species specificity and adaptation and fitness to the environment. This scientific endeavour carried with it certain implications for how child development was to be observed. Principally,

observation was to be 'objective', precluding any interference from sentiment or emotion in the process of observation itself. This division was not
simply one of exclusion, embracing some phenomena and discounting
others. It involved a more fundamental denial of emotionality, with
certain social and political implications. At this time women in the middle
classes were, in general, firmly confined to the domestic sphere (Hall,
1985; Hardyment, 1983) and it was men, not women, who produced the
new knowledge of child development. As Riley (1983) points out, in the
interest of scientific scrutiny, the infant was prised from its familial
context. In the process the opposition between scientific rationality and
sentiment was split between fathers and mothers. For example, many early
diarists gave guidance to other 'psychological papas' that contrasted the
objectivity required of the father with the sentiment of the mother. According to Sully (1881) the mother's involvement with her children

> unfits her from entering very cordially into the scientific vein. She rather
> dislikes [her children] being made the objects of cold intellectual scrutiny and
> unfeeling psychological analysis. To suggest a series of experiments on the
> gustatory sensibility of a small creature aged from twelve to twenty-four
> hours is likely to prove a shock, even to the more strong-minded of mothers.
> (Sully, *Cornhill Magazine*, 539–54. Cited in Riley, 1983)

In contrast, the father could be 'trained' in accurate observation, which
was deemed anathema to the sensitive mother.

> If the mother gets herself in time infected with the scientific ardour of the
> father, she may prove more of an auxiliary than he desires. Her maternal
> instincts impel her to regard her particular child as phenomenal in an extra-
> scientific sense. She . . . is disposed to ascribe to her baby a preternatural
> degree of intelligence. (Sully, *Cornhill Magazine*)

The father, of course, 'is compelled to suspect the accuracy of these
observations'.

Now the importance of this reference to the founding fathers of our
discipline is not merely polemic or of academic interest. The Child Study
Movement provided us with assumptions about development and how to
study it which are still with us (see Walkerdine, 1984). Rooted in biology
and the evolutionary theory of the day, it is this tradition that provides us
with the assumption of a normal core of development which unfolds
according to predetermined biological principles. Though this is most
obvious in the work of the early maturationists such as Gesell, and more
recently in that of Kagan and Trevarthen, described previously, it under-
pinned Piaget's thinking, giving rise to his notions of assimilation, accommodation, adaptation and stages representing structural changes in
organization. This tradition also fundamentally influenced Freud's early

work, providing the maturationist assumptions behind the theory of 'erotogenic' zones – the mouth, the anus and the genitals – which has often been interpreted as a normative theory of developmental stages (Sulloway, 1980; Urwin, 1983b).

But the emphasis on biology was not the only influence on the priorities of the Child Study Movement. Nor were questions of emotionality entirely neglected. The movement flourished at a time of great optimism about what could be achieved through scientific endeavour. It was also a time when scientific knowledge became integral to the formation of new forms of social regulation that emerged in the wake of the problems of civil unrest, poverty, illness and crime that had accompanied the development of industrialization under capitalism (Foucault, 1973, 1977; Walkerdine, 1984). By the turn of the century, the emerging science of population studies, with its demographic and statistical surveys, had joined with the new science of child development, which was seen as a source of knowledge relevant to the developing practices of education, welfare and medicine (Riley, 1983).

With hindsight, the 1920s stand out as a particularly productive period in both the study of child development and its incorporation into social practices both in Europe and in the USA. In the UK it was a time when there was considerable concern over problems of infant mortality and, eventually, maternal mortality, child health, delinquency and educability. Some of the figures of influence in this period are well known. For instance, Burt began his work on delinquency and intelligence testing which was to become so significant later on (Rose, 1979). It was also the time when the possibility of child analysis and psychotherapy first became actualized, notably through the work of Melanie Klein and Margaret Lowenfeld. By the 1930s Anna Freud had also arrived in this country. What is striking, now, is how much new activity was centring on children, with tremendous optimism and, in some cases, philanthropic zeal. But there was also considerable cross-fertilization of ideas between what we now take to be distinctly different traditions or orientations. Professional boundaries which we now take for granted, between clinical psychology, educational psychology and academic developmental psychology, for instance, had yet to be firmly established. Furthermore there was also an active engagement with psychoanalysis on the part of other developmentalists, even if they were wont to reject its findings. At that time, too, some child analysts were optimistic that practical implications for child-rearing and education could be derived from psychoanalysis, a view espoused particularly by Susan Isaacs (1930, 1933; see also Walkerdine, 1984).

This cross-fertilization was facilitated by the fact that some basic assumptions about child development, stemming from the Child Study Movement, were shared. Both the engagement with psychoanalysis and shared assumptions are particularly evident in the early work of Piaget, which began in the same historical period. Indeed I would go so far as to suggest that the similarities between psychoanalytic thinking and Piaget's early work were stronger than the differences, contributing to the fact that at that time Piaget explicitly acknowledged the role of emotion in development even if this emphasis subsequently was diluted. *The Child's Concept of the World*, first published in English in 1929, provides a particularly clear example. In this work Piaget explores young children's notions of causality. In line with his general emphasis on young children's egocentricity, or the way they assume that the world revolves around them, Piaget discusses their preferences for 'magical' explanations, for making 'superstitious' connections, and the phenomenon of animism: attributing thoughts, feelings and motives to inanimate things. Particularly interesting is the fact that the work is sprinkled copiously with references to Freud, Freud's protégé Ferenczi, Klein and other psychoanalysts. An explicit acknowledgement of common interests also included questions of methodology, reflecting debates which were current within child psychology at the time. His arguments against pure observation and the use of the newly emerging standard developmental tests, for example, were almost identical to those put forward subsequently by Susan Isaacs (1933) in presenting her psychoanalytic account of children observed in a school setting. It is interesting, too, that Piaget's (1929) own ideas of what the clinical method should consist of was based on the model of the psychiatric interview.

These points of connection were far from superficial. Indeed the way Piaget saw the child's situation and the developmental programme was strongly influenced by recent psychoanalytic writing. in *The Child's Conception of the World* there is an obvious correspondence between the phenomenon he was concerned with and the phenomenon rendered important by psychoanalysis. The interest in magical thinking, for instance, and how or why very young children may locate the causes of things in themselves as opposed to the external world, is clearly related to the problem of delusional states with which psychoanalysis was trying to grapple (Freud, 1911a). Children's beliefs that they can 'wish' things into being is related to Freud's (1900) idea of wish fulfilment; children's tendencies to displace the blame for something for which they are in fact responsible onto inanimate objects or other people are indicative of mechanisms of defence, such as 'denial' or 'projection'; and acting in superstitious or ritualistic ways suggests the origins of the kind of processes that may eventually become obsessional. Like Freud, Piaget also showed considerable interest in children's dreams, which he later developed in *Play, Dreams and Imitation* (Piaget, 1962), and in the kinds of questions children ask about where babies come from. In the *Child's Conception of the World* Piaget even gives attention to children's rituals around masturbation. The following example of 'superstitious' behaviour illustrates what Piaget describes as confusion between thinking and reality, or a lack of differentiation between psychical and material characteristics:

> CLAN, like all masturbators, was in fear of losing his intellectual faculties and becoming 'lazy'. Whence the following rite: 'When accompanying a particularly lazy boy I sometimes chanced to walk hand in hand with him. Then when I was home again I would say to myself that to hold hands with a lazy boy will make me lazy too, and I must do something against it.' Clan would then rub his hands vigorously. (Piaget, 1929, 141–142)

Piaget then goes on to describe this as a case of simply thinking of something to make a particular event happen or not, adding 'This is Freud's "all powerful nature of thought".' I shall return to this example later. But it illustrates that Piaget was fundamentally concerned at this time with the relation between psychic reality and external reality that psychoanalysis had rendered significant.

How did Piaget use these particular ideas? Of particular importance to the way Piaget thought about developmental questions was a little known but also highly significant paper written by Ferenczi in 1913 called 'The Development of a Sense of Reality in the Child'. It is to this paper that Piaget alludes when he uses the notion of the young child's omnipotence and tendency towards animistic and magical thinking. In this paper Ferenczi followed the view of the infant's state at birth which was currently dominant within the Child Study Movement: that the infant is initially in an adualistic state, with no self-other distinction and little differentiation between itself and the outside world. But Ferenczi's insight was to point out that this was also a developmental period where, in actuality, the world hovers around the immature and dependent infant as the mother caters for his or her every need.

At first, Ferenczi speculated, the infant may perceive little or no connection between the internal need state, or even a memory trace of previous satisfaction, and the caretaking operations leading to their satisfaction. The connection might be perceived as purely 'magical'. But gradually, as the infant learned that crying could bring about the necessary ministerings, the infant could acquire a sense of 'omnipotence', based on the relatively complete control of his or her need states. This developmental shift is mirrored in Piaget's account of the infant's move from an 'autistic' to an 'egocentric' frame of mind. The concept of magical thinking in infancy appears to have remained in Piaget's later accounts of the development of causality (see Piaget and Inhelder, 1969). Ferenczi's own account contributed to Freud's formulation of the concept of narcissism, and the developmental and clinical significance of taking the self as a love object, published a year later (Freud, 1914).

But before this, both Ferenczi and Piaget's accounts of the young child's state of mind and the opposition between 'magical' and 'realistic' thinking were governed by the way in which Freud (1911b) discussed the problem of the relations between psychic and external reality in his speculative but highly influential paper, 'Formulations on the Two Principles of Mental Functioning'. This followed not only considerable clinical work but also, of course, *The Interpretation of Dreams* through which he sought to demonstrate that unconscious life was governed by a process basically concerned with gaining pleasure and avoiding pain (Freud, 1900). Freud called this process, which he perceived as an archaically primitive form of thinking with roots in infancy, 'primary process' and contrasted it with the 'secondary process', a more complex thought process which was concerned with the testing of external reality and which was under the sway of the ego, the monitor of conscious thought. In the 'Two Principles' Freud explored how the secondary process might emerge, and why the infant might not forever remain governed by the pleasure principle rather than adapting to the demands of the outside world.

I shall discuss this paper of Freud's in more detail later. In the *Child's Conception of the World* there are further instances of Piaget's use of psychoanalytic ideas, which is unsurprising given the phenomena he was dealing with. For example, he was obliged to introduce into the discussion of 'animism' and children's tendencies to impute agency to things, or to confuse properties of things with parts of themselves, the psychoanalytic concepts of 'projection' and 'introjection', albeit somewhat loosely. Similarly, although he was not ostensibly concerned with the place of emotionality, its centrality becomes apparent in examples where he was obliged to invoke deeper anxieties to explain the fact that, as is common in childhood, some of the children feared that objects were out to get them, or, for example, that the moon knew their thoughts. What is also striking about this work is that, even though he was organizing his material into age periods, pre-figuring the notion of stages, he stressed the lack of absolute fixity, either in age or definitive order. There were children who lapsed in their ability to see things as adults see them, or who held onto entrenched beliefs when other aspects of their functioning suggested that they were capable of seeing the situation differently. Furthermore, he gives several examples of adults showing similar animistic, superstitious or omnipotent views, a position echoed in *Play, Dreams and Imitation* (1962) published more than 30 years later. There he points out that we all remain 'egocentric' to some degree, an untidy observation in relation to the hierarchical model of developmental stages that had crystallized by this time.

The concordance between Freud and Piaget raises the question as to whether Piaget saw himself as part of a similar endeavour and, indeed, whether a re-examination of Piaget can help to produce accounts of the relation between emotionality and reasoning. On the former point Piaget himself seems somewhat equivocal. In the early period of his work, he delivered a paper called 'Psychoanalysis and its relations to child psychology' (Piaget, 1920). There he proposed a joint venture, stressing the importance of the enterprise on several occasions subsequently (see, for example, Piaget and Inhelder, 1969). Yet there are crucial omissions or misunderstandings in Piaget's use of psychoanalysis which put considerable constraints on the kind of amalgamation he proposed. First, although Piaget acknowledged unconscious processes, his work does not seriously grapple with them. He concentrates instead on the contents of conscious thought and its distortions. In the example of Clan cited previously, for instance (Piaget, 1929), Piaget identifies faulty reasoning. But he does not explore the unconscious processes which psychoanalysts might presume are operating, accounting for the form of the 'symptom' or obsession. These might involve unconscious connections between touching the genitals and touching the hand and the displacement of the fear of damage or retribution into a fear of contamination. Secondly, in spite of Piaget's acknowledgement of psychoanalytic findings, on the extensiveness of early anxieties, for example, he fails to appreciate the significance of the psychoanalytic notion of 'defence'. He views it simply as evidence of error and ignores the tensions which psychoanalysis proposes as necessary concomitants to development. In contrast, although Piaget (1971, 1977) proposed that conflict may play an important role in the child's moving from one stage to another, the view of development which Piaget takes from biology is a harmonious one, of adaptation and equilibrium, even if dynamic. This harmonious relation to the environment is linked to what one might almost describe as a visionary view of the importance of rational thinking, or belief in a particular view of science. This has been well described by Walkerdine (1984) who has used autobiographical material to argue that, like many of his contemporaries, Piaget saw the human dilemma in terms of an opposition between passion and reason. From this position, he came to the conclusion that the scientific imperative was to facilitate the development of knowledge which would help to free us from our passions, or emotional vestiges of our animal pasts. This opposition between emotionality and rationality clearly influenced the way he understood psychoanalysis. Rather than viewing phantasy as a mode of functioning, which could facilitate our relation to reality, the early paper suggests that even then he saw it in terms of a developmental phase. That is, in his terms, although phantasy life has its value, it is necessarily in opposition to the development of reasoning, and hence is something that we should be encouraged to outgrow.

It is the prioritizing of reason, in the form of logicomathematical thought, that we have come to associate with latter-day Piaget. By now, of course, the theory of stages and universal cognitive structures has become the fulcrum of the account. In this process forms of thinking about the external world have been identified with cognitive structures and then reduced to logical mathematical operations themselves (see Light, chapter 8). The production of this account was perhaps what led him, or enabled him, to avoid re-examining the role of emotion, ever present in his early work, though inadequately conceptualized. Like social interaction, it remains as 'energetics', (Piaget and Inhelder, 1969) speeding up or slowing down the developmental process, but not entering into the structuring of cognition itself.

Piaget's later account, then, is not only universalistic and normative. By privileging logic and a particular kind of reasoning, it epitomizes the split between emotion and rationality characteristic of developmental psychology as a whole. But it is clear that this tendency is not Piaget's alone. The denial of emotion was inscribed in the way that the scientific study of children first began. Furthermore, the privileging of a particular kind of rationality can also be identified in some branches of psychoanalysis, particularly in the early work of Freud on which I suggest Piaget drew heavily. It is useful to re-examine the 'Two Principles' in this light, since this will illustrate how Piaget's selective uptake may have come about, and also highlights problems that we may have to circumvent. First, the way this paper suggests a transition from a more primitive to a 'higher' form of mental functioning is concordant with a view which was general within scientific circles in Freud's time. Fuelled by evolutionary theory, this view separated Rational Man not only from his anthropoid ancestors but also Primitive Man who was assumed to be more closely governed by the forces of nature. Both Piaget's (1929) and Freud's (1912, 1930) forays into anthropology reflect this orientation. Notably Rational Man was not only masculine; he was also white. Secondly, in this paper Freud in fact presents us with not one but several accounts of both the nature of reality and of the emergence of the reality principle. Some confusions and ambiguities were resolved in later work by Freud or later psychoanalysts, but this multiplicity invites selective uptake. For example, sometimes Freud uses the notion to refer to the infant's having to learn what is possible within the limits set by caretaking adults. He is thus using 'reality' in a social sense. On other occasions, the account equates 'reality' with limits imposed by the material rather than the social world. In yet other instances, 'reality' is inferred or identified through its difference from 'phantasy', but what its nature is is left unexplored. On the reality principle itself, Freud's speculations varied according to whether he was discussing developmental issues or the function of the principle in adult life. In development, he postulated that the development of a process which perceives a disjunction between phantasy and something real in the external world might depend on the infant's recognition of an *absence* of satisfaction, as distinct from an hallucination of satisfaction or a wish-fulfilment phantasy. When referring to adults, Freud is more concerned with what facilitates recognizing the difference between phantasy and reality. Here he discusses the reality principle in terms of an ego function concerned with 'an impartial passing of judgement', or with deciding whether a particular idea was 'true' or 'false', or in agreement with reality or not. In contrast to the pleasure ego, which is dominated by wishes, the reality principle is concerned with what is useful. Although Freud stressed that there is an essential tension between the two processes and that the domination of pleasure was never entirely lost, he also proposed that it was in *science* that the conquest of the pleasure principle was most successful. By the time this account was re-rendered by Ferenczi, this idea was taken even further. Now scientific thinking was described as epitomizing the mind at its most 'objective' (as opposed to subjective) and the reality principle identified with scientific thought itself. Though this shift was Ferenczi's, it is significant that by the time that Freud (1930) came to write *Civilization and its Discontents* late in his life, he argued that the power of reason, seen in the capacity for scientific thought and objective judgement, may be the only potential saving grace of humankind. Though his viewpoint is pessimistic in contrast to Piaget's optimism, in the belief in and privileging of scientific reasoning, his position appears remarkably similar to Piaget's.

Given their shared intellectual heritage, this similarity is hardly surprising. It is still important, however, to stress crucial differences between the two positions. For Piaget, constraints of the material world give rise to cognitive structures through action, which become identified with rational thought itself. Emotional processes speed up or slow down the transition from earlier to later forms of thought, but they are not interwoven into the thinking process. In Freud, rational thought, concerned with monitoring the external world, emerges developmentally. But its functions always remain connected to the regulation of emotional life, which enters into the thinking process itself. In the final section I shall consider whether there are ways of retaining the latter emphasis in opening up the role of emotion and phantasy in the development of social reasoning.

Some theoretical and methodological possibilities

It is clear from the previous account that there are intrinsic problems in using psychoanalysis to bring emotion into a social approach to the study of development. The endeavour requires more than a simple addition, or a translation between psychological and psychoanalytic frames of reference. As I have shown, there are points of contact between the two traditions already, reflecting shared epistemological and political assumptions and/or practical concerns. For example, the previous section illustrates that the notion of a biologically based core of normal development, and the privileging of scientific reason, were integral to Freud's early work.

But as I have argued in an earlier section these assumptions are precisely those which we must displace as fundamental givens or starting-points if we are to obtain a radically different approach to the role of social processes. It is significant that many of the attempts to combine psycho-analysis and developmental psychology have explicitly or implicitly relied on these assumptions, producing normative accounts which reduce to the lowest common denominator and exclude fundamental aspects of psychoanalytic thinking in the process. For example, attempts to combine psychoanalytic accounts of the object relationship between mother and infant with Piaget's theory have concentrated on the emergence of phenomena such as stranger anxiety and separation protests, plotted against Piagetian sensorimotor stages (e.g., Bell, 1970; Gouin-Decarie, 1966). In consequence, the relationship to the mother has been reduced to a question of representation, and re-rendered in cognitive terms: 'knowledge of' the mother replaces the infant's relationship to her, and emotionality is marginalized. Similarly, Bowlby's (1969) theory of attachment is, on his account, an attempt to render psychoanalysis scientific and compatible with empirical psychology. In addition to the usual criticisms of this account, that the mother is over-emphasized and the role of the father and the Oedipus Complex are discounted (Riley, 1983) the psychologistic enterprise has dismissed the problem of the inner world, or the phantasy life of the baby.

But it may be both misleading and pessimistic to assume that we must be tied solely by the assumptions which the two disciplines share. There is much to be gained by exploring the tensions which keep them apart and the factors which contribute to psychology's selective uptake. Here a major part must be given to the establishing of professional boundaries and the ways in which psychoanalytic ideas have been incorporated into social regulatory practices such as social welfare and the legal apparatus (Donzelot, 1980). In so far as these practices rely on producing a distinction between 'normal' and 'abnormal', they tend to render as pathological what psychoanalysis takes as fundamental to all of us. The disappearance of aggression from the harmonious, tension free account of the 'normal' mother-child relationship which has dominated developmental psychology since Bowlby is an obvious case in point (see Sylvester-Bradley, 1983).

Looking again at the psychoanalytic tradition, here I have drawn attention to limiting implications of Freud's account. But elsewhere I have also illustrated that Freud's own case history material gives a far richer perspective on developmental processes than does his stage account of development which is usually presented in psychology textbooks (Urwin, 1983b). Furthermore Freud's views constantly changed as clinical material forced him to recognize the oversimplicity of some of his early ideas, and since his time, of course, alternative emphases have been put forward by other theorists, notably by Melanie Klein and the British Object Relations school, and also by the French psychoanalyst, Jacques Lacan. In investigating what these different traditions offer, and how far they may enable us to circumvent the problems with Freud, their potential must be judged in relation to the kinds of questions we wish to ask. Here it is relevant to consider the issues which emerged in the discussion of the social cognition and pre-verbal communication work at the beginning of this chapter.

It is clear that it is largely because of the work on social cognition that developmental psychology has reached a position from which to question the validity or usefulness of privileging scientific or logical reasoning as a natural pinnacle. As Light (chapter 8) argues, these forms of reasoning can now be seen as an outcome of historically and culturally specific social practices. But to move beyond this requires that we do more than re-examine the 'content' of thought. It is insufficient, for example, to substitute the emergence of logic with the 'acquisition' of other forms of knowledge or social procedures, leaving the assumption of the individual untouched. A more radical shift requires that we penetrate the inter-relationships between these socially produced forms of truth and the psychic life of children, in order to understand how children may eventually think through, or in terms of, these forms of truth themselves. As important, we must begin to specify the role of emotion in this.

Some of the most important work in this direction has been carried out by Walkerdine (1982) in exploring how children are introduced to mathematics through the social practices of the primary school. Walkerdine's framework uses Lacan's (1949, 1953) psychoanalytic account. One of the most attractive features of this account is that Lacan explicitly undermines the notion of the unitary rational subject, the 'I' of the cogito which underpins traditional psychology, and proposes instead that subjectivity and consciousness are produced through entering into language or signifying systems more broadly. But this process of entry not only makes possible conscious thought; it also structures unconscious thought at the same time. According to Lacan this process is in the first instance concomitant with the resolution of the Oedipus Complex. As in Freud, this involves considerable emotional conflict and repression is an inevitable price to be paid for the gains involved in active participation in social life. Lacan's psychoanalytic account differs, however, from Freud's in several respects which are particularly relevant here. First, in Lacan's account, the maturational and normative theory of stages in libidinal organization is of relatively little significance as a driving force in development. Secondly, Freud and Lacan put forward different emphases in discussing the Oedipus Complex. Freud's account centres around the presence or absence of the penis, such that biological difference accounts for differences in the psychological development of boy and girl children. Lacan, however, emphasizes the phallus not the penis, or the sign of sexual difference rather than anatomical difference *per se*. That is, Lacan is concerned with the meaning given to sexual difference in culture, escaping some of the implications of the implicit biological reductionism in Freud. Here Lacan follows Lévi Strauss in arguing for universals in socio-cultural laws which privilege the position of the phallus. Thirdly, Lacan's reading of Freud and elboration of it puts particular emphasis on the part played by sign systems in regulating both conscious and unconscious life. In so far as sign systems are socially produced, by focusing on how signifying relations operate in social practices, the possibility is open for exploring relations between social processes and psychic ones without assuming that one simply determines the other. It is the latter aspect of Lacan's work which Walkerdine has taken up. She herself, however, has introduced an important change in Lacan's account which draws on Foucault's (1977, 1979) analysis of power/knowledge relations. To avoid the universalism which one may argue follows from Lacan's use of Lévi Strauss, and the implications of inevitable subordination of women which this implies, Walkerdine has replaced Lacan's universal laws of culture with an emphasis on discursive relations and the culturally and historically specific production of particular forms of truth. This production itself presupposes relations of power. Using this framework and the notion of 'subject positions' established through discourses, she has put forward an approach to children's mathematics learning which not only cuts across the individual/context distinction underlying the social cognition work described earlier, but also gives children's emotional engagement in the learning process a major role. For example, in examining how teachers facilitate children's entry into mathematical discourse, an historically specific product, by establishing metaphorical links between the practices of home and school, Walkerdine also argues that children's ability to take up subject positions in the discursive practices of school depends on a prior and ongoing social-emotional history and subsequent identification with teachers (see Urwin, 1984; Walden and Walkerdine, 1981). Moving to younger children, I myself have also explored how some of the processes which she describes may begin. In looking at early relationships between mothers and babies, I have illustrated, for example, how normative notions of 'good mothering' which are embedded in the social practices which regulate family life may enter into mothers' own aspirations and fears in relating to their babies (Urwin, 1984, 1985). I have also produced a modified version of Lacan's (1949) account of the 'mirror phase' of infant development which is consistent with Walkerdine's orientation (Urwin, 1984). The result is a view which is in marked contrast to the harmony put forward by the mother-infant interaction studies described earlier.

Though not without limitations, this work suggests the potential value of Lacan's emphasis on signification in finding new ways of thinking about relations between individual and social practices and of opening the possibility of a fuller examination of the role of emotional processes.

However, to move beyond this in encompassing emotion is not easy. Here the problems and questions are not simply about what theory to 'choose', or indeed what changes, amalgamations, omissions or recastings are more legitimate than others. They are also about methodology, and how to encompass those phenomena which psychoanalytic insights show to be of fundamental importance but which developmental psychology has systematically excluded. These phenomena include not only the role of emotion *per se*, but also the workings of unconscious processes, particularly phantasy and mechanisms of defence. In the long term I believe that the most fruitful kinds of exchanges between psychoanalysts and developmental psychologists will depend on the latter group having a greater understanding of the psychoanalytic method, the relation between theory and technique, what counts as evidence in this tradition, and the part played by developmental assumptions in the course of particular patients' analyses. Nonetheless, it is important to recognize that any use which developmental psychologists make of psychoanalysis will necessarily involve some transformation of the truth produced by psychoanalysis as it is removed from its original field of practice. But there is also an intermediary ground already available, and several implications for methodology and new orientations follow directly from the account I have given of how emotion and cognition became split apart in the history of child study.

First, it is clear that the way we insist on observing babies and young children 'objectively' within developmental psychology is a direct descendant of the assumptions about scientific method with which the Child Study Movement began. Ethology, which aims to provide taxonomies of behaviour illustrates this particularly clearly. It is not that this tradition does not encompass emotional states. 'Cries' and 'smiles' for instance can be described, counted and correlated with other variables. But as Dunn's work (chapter 5) shows, allowing what the child may be feeling and experiencing to become part of the investigation requires a different kind of engagement on the observer's part, an openness to the emotional aspects of the situation, which is generally diffused or disguised through the use of pre-established categories for recording behaviour.

To move forward, it is thus necessary to accept back within the methodology that 'sentiment' which was historically split off and projected into mothers. This will require new forms of observation. But if it is difficult for psychologists to encompass emotion within their methodology, phantasy and mechanisms of defence perhaps present even greater problems. In referring to 'phantasy' I am referring to unconscious processes. It is to be distinguished from 'fantasy', which of course developmental psychologists study when they look into make-believe and play. There, however, the emphasis has been on using these phenomena as indicative of what children 'know', whether as evidence of general cognitive level, or knowledge of social roles, rules, or language skills. Rather less attention is given to the emotional functions of the play for the children, which in psychoanalytic terms are related to unconscious processes and phantasies. Though these are theoretical concepts, their workings are inferred from behaviour. A particularly clear illustration of this is to be found in Freud's (1920) well-known example of the 'cotton reel' game. This involved an 18 month old boy child who, we are told, was having considerable problems in separating from his mother. Freud tells us that his working through this problem was greatly facilitated by the invention of a game in which the child would throw the cotton reel away from him with a cry of 'Fort' (the German for 'gone'), bringing it back to himself with a joyous 'Da' ('there'). According to Freud the game facilitated the child's first cultural achievement, separating from the mother. The cotton reel symbolized the mother over whose departures, in phantasy, he now had perfect control. (Lacan adds a rather different emphasis to this account, see Urwin, 1984.) Games like this which involve 'disappearance' are very common in children of this age. For Freud it illustrates how, in play, children may go over difficult experiences, mastering or displacing the underlying anxiety and achieving a new relation to external reality. In this case the 'reality' notably includes the social world of adult permissions and sanctions.

Here, Freud's interpretation of the unconscious phantasy underlying this game was based on what he knew of the child and subsequent events. Strictly speaking in psychoanalytic play therapy, the appropriateness of the particular interpretation could be confirmed or disconfirmed according to the subsequent phantasy material which it produced. But the expression of phantasy is not itself tied to psychoanalytic sessions. If it is a perennial fact of psychic life, can we perceive it in young children even within the limits of our observations or experimental methodologies?

I suggest that the material we collect for other purposes is replete with indications of the workings of phantasy, and also of mechanisms of defence, if we only knew how and where to look. To clarify how we might do so it is useful to return to Freud's 'Two Principles of Mental Functioning'. As I have pointed out, Freud in fact gave several descriptions of 'reality'. The reason for this multiplicity is in part due to the way in which analytic practice relies on distinguishing the workings of the pleasure principle from the reality principle. In practice, one of the most important functions served by the analyst's interpretations is to facilitate the patient's own ability to distinguish between what is 'real' and what is phantasy. Is, for example, the analyst 'out to get' the patient, or is this a product of the patient's phantasy? Once this distinction is perceived, the patient's defences, anxieties and desires underlying the phantasy can be revealed and explored. An example from Freud's (1909) Ratman case may make this clear. This person came to Freud knowing, at one level, that his obsessional behaviour was 'irrational'. A turning-point occurred in the case when Freud interpreted to him that his refusal to lie down in the consulting room reflected his considerable fear of Freud. Now the rational side of the patient accepted the 'reality' that this fear was unjustified. Once the Ratman perceived this disjunction, he was open to appreciating that his fears were related to phantasies stemming from a strong but unacknowledged ambivalence towards his father, a person whom he loved but also hated at the same time. The unacknowledged aggression towards his father had rebounded in terms of intense internal persecution, and it was this fear of the father's retaliation to his own phantasized attacks that he was now experiencing in relation to the person of Freud.

The importance of the distinction between phantasy and reality here is twofold. First, the identification of phantasy depended on the fact that the Ratman's emotional reactions – his intense fear – and behaviour were 'inappropriate' to the reality of the situation. Secondly, Freud's interpretations could gain no purchase if the patient was not himself able to distinguish between the person Freud and the phantasies and projections which he put on him. (It is for this reason that psychoanalytic work with psychotic patients poses particular problems.) But what is this reality against which phantasy is compared? In constituting this reality, aspects of habitual psychoanalytic practice, such as the stability of the analytic session and the physical location of analyst and patient play a major role. Thus the 'reality' that is at issue here is not a timeless scientific truth. It is a social reality produced by analytic practice and the social positions of analysts and patients and the relations of power which this implies.

This reading of the psychoanalytic situation brings us closer to the orientation that follows from Walkerdine's work and to the possibility of incorporating further psychoanalytic insights into our developmental observations. I suggest that the general principle that the workings of phantasy can be identified with reference to a social reality which is in some way altered or transformed through inappropriate reactions is a useful way into exploring psychic concomitants of children's participation in social practices, giving access to their motivations and preoccupations, their anxieties and desires. What becomes striking immediately is how much use psychologists already make of 'inappropriate' reactions or processes of transformation, but for different purposes. For example, Kagan's (1981) argument for 'self-awareness' in the second year, cited earlier, uses as evidence children's over-reactions to their own or other people's transgressions, extreme upset at things out of place or broken, and irrational unwillingness to attempt difficult tasks. I have described similar kinds of 'over-reactions' to transgressions and damage in the beginnings of the second year (Urwin, 1984), linking this to equally over-the-top signs of omnipotence becoming particularly clear at the same time. There I drew attention to the knowledge of social practices which the distress reactions presuppose. But they also indicate extremely powerful judgements which the children are exerting over themselves which are out of proportion to the adults' intentions in imposing these sanctions in the first place. That there is no direct read-off from the relative severity of parental discipline and the strictures which children impose on themselves was pointed out by Freud (1930), and is of course well known (see, for example, Newson and Newson, 1968). In psychoanalytic terms, the strength of the anxiety is related to the children's own destructive phantasies and the early workings of a super-ego which is relatively severe. In the usual course of events one might speculate that some release from self-judgement is achieved through emotional dynamics of relationships with other family members, as the child meets actual consequences of acting out destructive impulses. Working through is also achieved through play. Psychologists generally use play as evidence of how much children know about social practices. But again what is striking is that play also gives evidence of remarkable alterations of current social practices. For example, children's dolls and teddy bears may be subjected to extreme forms of punishment and retribution, unlike anything to which they had actually been exposed.

In such play several parts of the self are represented (the 'mother' who rebukes in play stands as a severe internal parent or super-ego, the animated toy as the bad self), and for the child it has the positive function of providing the opportunity for projecting or displacing bad feelings about himself or herself. Children's fascination with the social cognition experiments described earlier, involving the 'naughty teddy', 'chipped beakers' (Light, chapter 8), and hiding a boy doll from a policeman reflects, I suggest, not only the fact that the experimental tasks make sense but also their appeal to children's ongoing emotional preoccupations. Of course, the alterations in children's play are not only related to transgressions. The same children who rebuke their dolls vehemently will on other occasions exhibit near perfect tenderness. The perfect depictions or idealizations which are common in early role play, being shopkeepers, fathers, mothers, or doctors, for instance, may have many functions related to different desires, conflicts or other developmental preoccupations thrown up in the struggle to move from being a baby towards taking up an active position within social practices. These include taking care of the infantile parts of the self. It is interesting to speculate on the possible emotional functions at work in the famous example given by Vygotsky (1978) in which two sisters spontaneously decided to play at 'being sisters'. This enactment of perfect sisterly behaviour included no expression of sibling rivalry. The idealization perhaps allowed them to split off aggressive or jealous feelings, and provided opportunities for expressing affection which were too loaded to show elsewhere.

What I have proposed, then, is that the workings of phantasy may be identified in relation to a social reality, defined in terms of specific social practices which are themselves regulated through systems of power.

282 *Children of social worlds*

Several implications follow from this orientation. First, in forefronting phantasy underlying children's play, it becomes clear that their engagement in play cannot be adequately explained as simply learning social roles. At the same time the material supporting the child's phantasy and associations consists of cultural forms, and the identifications reflect potential positions in the adult world. Secondly, the social cognition work has, as I earlier argued, produced an over-rationalized view of the child. This is in part due to the way in which questions have in effect been designed to render their errors explicable or to allow them to make no mistakes. But what now becomes interesting again is precisely children's errors. While I have given examples indicating alterations of social practices in play, access to children's phantasies may also be gained through looking at the pieces they fill in themselves. Consider, for example, an example involving illness given by Wilkinson (1984) in a study of young children's theories about the causes of illness. In answering questions concerned with what 'germs' were and how they were caused, a four year old child, like many of his age-mates, answered that germs were about nine inches high and bright blue, reflecting a recent television advertising campaign for Domestos! The child's ability to think about 'germs' shows both the importance of signs mediating cultural practices, and also a pragmatic attitude towards illness and how to combat it which is particularly common in adults dealing with illnesses for which science has yet to produce a cure, like the common cold (Prout, 1984). But in being probed more closely on how you 'catch' illnesses, the child showed a common tendency (again found in adults) to relate illness to failure or badness, and to relate this not only to social sanctions but also his own current emotional preoccupations which in this case included sexuality. Germs, he thought, could be caught by 'kissing people', and the outcome would be particularly bad if the people concerned were not married!

This example illustrates the complex interplay between phantasy, signification and its role in the social practices which regulate human action. The focus on shifts in emphasis, errors, or the pieces children fill in themselves will, I suggest, reveal the powerful presence of phantasy. Such an orientation must at the same time lead us to question the reality which we take for granted and how that truth is produced.

But given that I have used children's participation in social practices as a way into underlying phantasy, one may well ask how we can approach the infancy period, when by definition some of the essential transitions towards participation in socio-cultural life have yet to be made. Again, I suggest that there is abundant material on the role of emotion in infancy. For example, it is remarkable how much the expansion of infant cognition studies has relied on emotionality in very young babies, but has used it as a way of gaining access to perceptual abilities or cognitive status. For example, indexes of 'surprise', 'pleasure' or 'distress', seen in crying or turning away, are taken to indicate that the baby has detected a difference, to enable the experimenter to make inferences about knowledge of perceptual constancies or object permanence (see, for example, Bower, 1974). But the emotional consequences which the baby's behaviour suggests are totally discounted. Nor is their contribution to cognitive development explored. Yet in the detection of difference in relation to a previous perception or absence, are we seeing the beginnings of reality testing as described by Freud? In looking at babies' avoidance reactions to unpleasant stimuli and their selective attention, we may also be seeing the beginnings of systems which are identifiable later as necessary mechanisms of defence. Infants' lack of concern over mothers multiplied or displaced in space (see Bower, 1974), and their early imitations (Meltzoff, 1976), suggest the early operation of processes recognizable later in denial, splitting and various forms of identification. But as far as the phantasy life of very young babies is concerned, can our present methods allow or embrace this possibility? The examples given earlier, of 'over-reactions' to transgressions at the beginning of the second year were discussed in terms of infants' phantasies about their own destructive impulses. They suggest that phantasy has a very early origin indeed, and that in this case phantasy precedes knowledge of social regularities, accounting for the direction of the inappropriate reaction. Phantasy cannot be equated with cognition, and reduced to the same cognitive structure. But where does it come from? To push the process back further into infancy might not be an enquiry which psychology can undertake on its own. It might require a more active engagement not only with psychoanalytic practice and the knowledge produced through working with very ill patients, but also with autistic, psychotic, and infantile parts of ourselves.

References

Bell, S. 1970. The development of the concept of object as related to infant-mother attachment. *Child Development*, **41**, 291–311.

Bower, T. 1974. *Development in Infancy*. San Francisco: Freeman.

Bowlby, J. 1952. *Maternal Care and Mental Health*. Geneva: World Health Organisation.

Bowlby, J. 1953. *Child Care and the Growth of Love*. London: Penguin Books.

Bowlby, J. 1969. *Attachment and Loss*. Vol. 1. *Attachment*. London: Hogarth Press.

Bruner, J. S. 1975. The ontogenesis of speech acts. *Journal of Child Language*, **2**, 1–19.

Bruner, J. S. 1978. From communication to language: a psychological perspective, in I. Markova (ed.), *The Social Context of Language*. Chicester: Wiley.

Bruner, J. S. 1983. *Child's Talk*. Oxford: Oxford University Press.

Cole, M. and Scribner, S. 1974. *Culture and Thought*. New York: Wiley.

Darwin, C. 1877. A biographical sketch of an infant. *Mind*, **2**, 285–94.

Donaldson, M. 1978. *Children's Minds*. London: Fontana.

Donzelot, J. 1980. *The Policing of Families*. London: Hutchinson.

Ferenczi, S. 1913. Stages in the development of the sense of reality, in *First Contributions to Psychoanalysis*. London: Hogarth Press, 1952.

Foucault, M. 1973. *Birth of the Clinic* (trans. A. M. Sheridan). London: Tavistock Press.

Foucault, M. 1977. *Discipline and Punish* (trans. A. M. Sheridan). London: Allan Lane.

Foucault, M. 1979. *The History of Sexuality*. Vol. 1. *An Introduction* (trans. A. M. Sheridan). London: Allan Lane.

Freud, S. 1900. *The Interpretation of Dreams*. London and New York: Hogarth Press. Standard Edition. London: Penguin Books. Freud Library. Vol. 4.

Freud, S. 1909. *Notes upon a Case of Obsessional Neurosis*. London and New York: Hogarth Press. Standard Edition. London: Penguin Books. Freud Library. Vol. 9.

Freud, S. 1911a. *Psychoanalytic Notes on an Autobiographical Account of a Case of Paranoia (Dementia Paranoides)*. London and New York: Hogarth Press. Standard Edition. London: Penguin Books. Freud Library. Vol. 9.

Freud, S. 1911b. *Formulations on the Two Principles of Mental Functioning*. London and New York: Hogarth Press. Standard Edition. London: Penguin Books. Freud Library. Vol. 9.

Freud, S. 1912. *Totem and Taboo*. London and New York: Hogarth Press. Standard Edition. London: Penguin Books. Freud Library. Vol. 13.

Freud, S. 1914. *On Narcissism: an introduction*. London and New York: Hogarth Press. Standard Edition. London: Penguin Books. Freud Library. Vol. 11.

Freud, S. 1920. *Beyond the Pleasure Principle*. London and New York: Hogarth Press. Standard Edition. London: Penguin Books. Freud Library. Vol. 11.

Freud, S. 1930. *Civilisation and its Discontents*. London and New York: Hogarth Press. Standard Edition. London: Penguin Books. Freud Library. Vol. 12.

Gouin-Decarie, T. 1966. *Intelligence and Affectivity in the Young Child*. New York: International Universities Press.

Hall, C. 1985. Private persons versus public someones: class, gender and politics in England 1780–1850, in C. Steedman, C. Urwin and V. Walkerdine (eds), *Language, Gender and Childhood*. London: Routledge and Kegan Paul.

Hardyment, C. 1983. *Dream Babies: baby care from Locke to Spock*. London: Cape.

Henriques, J., Hollway, W., Urwin, C., Venn, C. and Walkerdine, V. 1984. *Changing the Subject: psychology, social regulation and subjectivity*. London: Methuen.

Hollway, W. 1984. Gender difference and the production of subjectivity, in J. Henriques, W. Hollway, C. Urwin, C. Venn and V. Walkerdine, *Changing the Subject: psychology, social regulation and subjectivity*. London: Methuen.

Hughes, M. 1975. Egocentricism in pre-school children (unpublished Ph.D. dissertation, Edinburgh University).

Hughes, M. and Donaldson, M. 1983. The use of hiding games for studying coordination of viewpoints, in M. Donaldson, R. Grieve and C. Pratt (eds), *Early Childhood Development and Education*. Oxford: Basil Blackwell.

Ingleby, D. 1983. Freud and Piaget: the phoney war. *New Ideas in Psychology*, **1**, 123–44.

Isaacs, S. 1930. *Intellectual Growth in Young Children*. London: Routledge.

Isaacs, S. 1933. *Social Development of Children*. London: Routledge.

Kagan, J. 1981. *The Second Year: the emergence of self-awareness*. Cambridge, Mass.: Harvard University Press.

Lacan, J. 1949. The mirror stage as formative of the function of the I as revealed in psychoanalytic experience, reprinted in J. Lacan, *Ecrits* (trans. A. Sheridan, 1977). London: Tavistock Press.

Lacan, J. 1953. Function and field of speech and language, reprinted in J. Lacan. *Ecrits* (trans. A. Sheridan, 1977). London: Tavistock Press.

Light, P. 1985. Taking roles, in H. Weinreich-Haste and J. S. Bruner (eds), *Making Sense: the child's construction of the world*. London: Methuen (in press).

Lock, A. (ed.) 1978. *Action, Gesture and Symbol: the emergence of language*. London: Academic Press.

McGarrigle, J. and Donaldson, M. 1975. Conservation accidents. *Cognition*, **3**, 341–50.

Meltzoff, A. 1976. Imitation in early infancy (unpublished Ph.D. dissertation, University of Oxford).

Newson, J. 1978. Dialogue and development, in A. Lock (ed.), *Action, Gesture and Symbol: the emergence of language*. London: Academic Press.

Newson, J. and Newson, E. 1968. *Four Years Old in an Urban Community*. London: George Allen and Unwin.

Olson, D. 1977. From utterance to text: the bias of language in speech and writing. *Harvard Educational Review*, **47**, 257–81.

Piaget, J. 1920. Psychoanalysis and its relations with child psychology, in M. Gruber and J. J. Voneche (eds), 1977, *The Essential Piaget*. London: Routledge and Kegan Paul.

Piaget, J. 1929. *The Child's Conception of the World*. London: Kegan Paul.

Piaget, J. 1962. *Play, Dreams and Imitation*. London: Routledge and Kegan Paul.

Piaget, J. 1971. *Structuralism*. London: Routledge and Kegan Paul.

Piaget, J. 1977. *The Grasp of Consciousness*. London: Routledge and Kegan Paul.

Piaget, J. and Inhelder, B. 1956. *The Child's Conception of Space*. London: Routledge and Kegan Paul.

Piaget, J. and Inhelder, B. 1969. *The Psychology of the Child*. London: Routledge and Kegan Paul.

Prout, A. 1984. Science, health and everyday knowledge: a case study of the common cold (unpublished manuscript, Child Care and Development Group, University of Cambridge).

Riley, D. 1983. *War in the Nursery*. London: Virago.

Rose, N. 1979. The psychological complex: mental measurement and social administration. *Ideology and Consciousness*, **5**, 5–68.

Ryan, J. 1974. Early language development: towards a communicational analysis, in M. P. M. Richards (ed.), *The Integration of a Child into a Social World*. London: Cambridge University Press.

Schaffer, H. R. 1984. *The Child's Entry into a Social World*. London: Academic Press.

Shotter, J. 1978. The cultural context of communication studies: theoretical and methodological issues, in A. Lock (ed.), *Action, Gesture and Symbol: the emergence of language*. London: Academic Press.

Sulloway, F. 1980. *Freud, Biologist of the Mind*. London: Fontana.

Sully, J. 1881. Babies and science. *Cornhill Magazine*, **43**, 539–54.

Sylvester-Bradley, B. 1983. The neglect of hatefulness in psychological studies of early infancy (unpublished manuscript, Child Care and Development Group, University of Cambridge).

Sylvester-Bradley, B. 1985. Failure to distinguish between people and things in early infancy. *British Journal of Developmental Psychology* (in press).

Trevarthen, C. 1975. Early attempts at speech, in R. Lewin (ed.), *Child Alive*. London: Temple Smith.

Trevarthen, C. 1982. The primary motives for cooperative understanding, in G. Butterworth and P. Light (eds), *Social Cognition: studies of the development of understanding*. Brighton: Harvester.

Trevarthen, C. and Hubley, P. 1978. Secondary intersubjectivity: confidence, confiding and acts of meaning in the first year, in A. Lock (ed.), *Action, Gesture and Symbol: the emergence of language*. London: Academic Press.

Urwin, C. 1982. The contribution of nonvisual communication systems and language to knowing oneself, in M. Beveridge (ed.), *Children Thinking Through Language*. London: Arnold.

Urwin, C. 1983a. Observations of aggression between same aged infants (paper presented at Second World Congress on Infant Psychiatry, Cannes).

Urwin, C. 1983b. Freud's account of development (unpublishesd manuscript, Child Care and Development Group, University of Cambridge).

Urwin, C. 1984. Power relations in the emergence of language, in J. Henriques, W. Hollway, C. Urwin, C. Venn and V. Walkerdine, *Changing the Subject: psychology, social regulation and subjectivity*. London: Methuen.

Urwin, C. 1985. Constructing motherhood: the persuasion of normal development, in C. Steedman, C. Urwin and V. Walkerdine (eds), *Language, Gender and Childhood*. London: Routledge and Kegan Paul.

Vygotsky, L. S. 1978. *Mind in Society: the development of higher psychological mechanisms* (eds M. Cole, V. John-Steiner, S. Scribner and E. Souberman) Cambridge, Mass.: Harvard University Press.

Walden, R. and Walkerdine, V. 1981. Girls and mathematics: the early years. *Bedford Way Papers*, **8**, London: Heinemann.

Walkerdine, V. 1982. From context to text: a psychosemiotic approach to abstract thought, in M. Beveridge (ed.), *Children Thinking Through Language*. London: Arnold.

Walkerdine, V. 1984. Developmental psychology and the child-centred pedagogy: the insertion of Piaget into early education, in J. Henriques, W. Hollway, C. Urwin, C. Venn and V. Walkerdine (eds), *Changing the Subject: psychology, social regulation and subjectivity*. London: Methuen.

Wason, P. C. 1965. The context of plausible denial. *Journal of Verbal Learning and Verbal Behaviour*, **4**, 7–11.

Wilkinson, S. 1984. Children's views on the causality of illness (unpublished M.D. dissertation, University of Cambridge).

13

The step to social constructionism

Rom Harré

Rereading the text of my contribution to *The Integration of a Child into a Social World* (Richards, 1974) I am struck by the extent to which the researches adumbrated in that piece have been pushed through. The basic thesis of the original programme was that there existed childhood societies which differed from adult societies only in the content of their social forms. The techniques of the construction of social relations through rituals and ceremonials, so typical of all known adult societies, were, I claimed fully developed amongst children by the age of six or seven. But children used these techniques only when constructing social worlds independent of and impenetrable to adults. The same general claim covered such matters as the skilled presentation of acceptable selves, and the management of social identities. The best project, I suggested, for understanding the social development of children would be the exploration of these independent social worlds. With the publication of works such as Sluckin's (1982) study of the role of playground games in creating the conditions for and competence in the management of social order, and Davies's (1982) study of the child's view of the social world he or she inhabits jointly with adults, much of the programme of that earlier project has been achieved. Davies, in particular, has shown how mythical is the idea of 'moral development'. Children, post five years of age, like adults, make strategic, situationally differentiated uses of the whole gamut of those styles of moral reasoning that were supposed to be the rungs of a developmental scale. Furthermore in our world-wide study of nicknaming, Jane Morgan, Christopher O'Neill and I showed (1979) how children, when left to themselves, create distinctive social orders and maintain repertoires of acceptable social personas. The study of nicknaming practices enabled us to penetrate social orders which were normally so closed that the mere presence of an adult led to their temporary dissolution. Sociograms of nicknaming relationships turned out to be able to be used as maps of otherwise unobservable social structures. Once the working social categories and their relationships had been worked out in this way all sorts of otherwise mysterious phenomena became intelligible. Furthermore the demonstration by Marsh, (see Marsh, Rosser and Harré, 1977) that even such obscure and violent activities as the aggro enjoyed by adolescent football hooligans is a rulebound and largely ceremonial social event, went a long way to proving the general point of my earlier contribution, that social order, whether amongst children or adults is a matter of conventions and rules through the following of which certain social goods, such as face and honour are preserved or achieved.

Wittgenstein's philosophy of language has prompted, directly or indirectly, the daring suggestion, to be explored in this chapter, that much, perhaps all of the *fine grain* of human psychological functioning is a product of the language that a person has acquired. For that reason psychology must from now on be thought of as much a collective as an individual phenomenon. The revival of interest in the theories and empirical researches of Vygotsky has added further impetus to this movement. The point of view to be sketched in this chapter developed at first independently of these sources but has come to be influenced by them more and more. The ideas of G. H. Mead can also be detected in contemporary social constructionism, but they seem blunt by comparison with the cutting edge of the more overtly linguistically oriented theories. In consequence of all this a new research dimension has recently opened out (see particularly the contribution to this volume by Ingleby). Given that we are indeed well equipped with knowledge of rules and conventions, and in control of a taxonomy of social situations within which they are properly employed, how is our acquisition of these bodies of belief to be understood? The displacement of all but a trace of biologism from the theory of social psychology leaves a yawning explanatory gap. If our capacities for social interaction are not inherited, how are they acquired? Well, we learn them of course! But how? There is a Cartesian answer to this question which needs to be deleted from our theory if any way forward is to be possible. According to that point of view, there is a body of knowledge, known subjectively to an adult as a competent social being. The educative task is to accomplish the transfer of that knowledge through some channel into the subjective contents of another being, the incompetent one. We read of encoding and decoding. I believe that it has become clear that this picture is seriously misleading.

To uncover the hidden distortions in the above conception we must go very deeply into basic psychological theory. I think it is no exaggeration to say that the Cartesian polarity that dichotomizes reality between a subjective and an objective pole continues to dominate a great deal of psychological thinking. Classical behaviourism was born out of it, through the assumption that subjectivity was a closed realm to science, while phenomenology was in part the consequence of a search for that level of factuality which was to be immune from revision. Despite the fact that neither of these classical approaches to psychology now seems to command widespread assent the picture of a mental realm (encouragingly called the realm of 'cognitive' psychology) standing over against a physical realm seems to be invoked implicitly in most contemporary discussions amongst academic psychologists. But this is not the only deeply buried assumption in much contemporary work. There is also the quasi-political doctrine of individualism that plays an almost equally potent role. In such a concept as 'socialization' we have a joint use of the two leading ideas. To be socialized is something that is required of an individual and it is achieved by the acquisition of something essentially mental. Suppose we were to try for a new beginning by denying both these deeply buried 'axioms' of the contemporary approach. What would the conceptual space of psychology look like then?

What was it that seemed to make the concept of 'subjectivity' so attractive to the psychologist, to seem so obvious a mark of the mental? Descartes seems to have been struck by the fact that not only are my thoughts not routinely available to you but that they are routinely available to me. We could call this the fact of essential privacy. But once one reflects on how things are in ordinary daily life it becomes very clear that there is much that deserves the title of the mental that is just as readily observable by another as it is known to myself. For example, my emotions are often available for all to enjoy and my efforts at reasoning are as often conducted in public as they are in private soliloquy. Already in these few remarks we have a more fundamental polarity making its appearance, the duality between the public display of something mental and the private reservation of that same sort of thing to an individual. I propose to call this the axis or dimension of Display whose poles are Public and Private.

A rejection of the assumption of individualism gives us the opportunity to create an orthogonal axis. Again a moment's reflection on the doings of everyday life suggests that it is quite common for reasoning, moral assessments, identification of emotions and so on to be performed by some group or collective. For example, committees perform acts of reasoning, the results of which may be composed of the contributions of different members without the total structure of the collective argument reflecting the individual considerations that led to individual contributions. We can use these ideas to create an axis of Location whose poles are Individual and Collective.

These axes provide us with a powerful new scheme for formulating psychological concepts and at the same time can control a new kind of research programme in developmental psychology. Consultation of figure 1 reveals that there are four quadrants, reading clockwise we called these Social (quadrant I), Subjective (quadrant II), Personal (quadrant III) and Objective (quadrant IV). The main hypothesis of social constructionism is that development usually occurs by the appropriation of structure and content from quadrant I through quadrants II, III and IV, and finally by conventionalization, to quadrant I, the realm of social, that is public-collective activity once again. I have used the term 'appropriation' deliberately to suggest a connection with the development psychology of Lev

Fig. 1   PSYCHOLOGICAL 'SPACE'

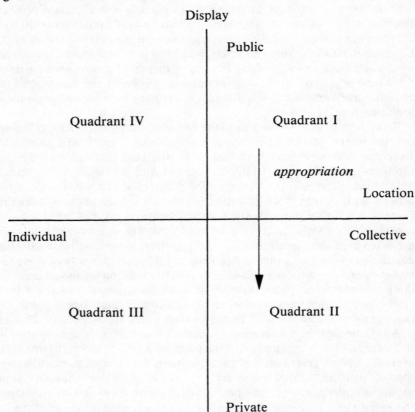

Vygotsky. My two-dimensional 'space', though not derived from the writings of Vygotsky, seems to me to express much of what he had in mind.

What is in quadrant I, the source of mind for a constructionist? For human beings the social realm contains at least the following: a cluster of conversations, at least one and perhaps more moral orders, and all sorts of intentional material practices. As a social constructionist sees it, becoming a competent person, indeed becoming a person at all, is not a matter of an injection of a dose of subjectivity from one mind to another, but rather the appropriation from a common public realm of whatever is needed to round out and inform the mind of the developing individual. Research then turns in two directions. What is in the public realm, that could be of the right sort to shape the mind; and what sort of shaping processes are there?

Conversations have two kinds of structure. There is the macro-structure created by the conventions governing the right to speak, turn-taking and the like. These rights are part of the moral order or orders obtaining in that society. For the purposes of this paper I propose to concentrate on the other kind of structure that is to be found in conversation, that is, the grammatical forms that convention confirms as the appropriate structures for expressing certain kinds of knowledge or belief. Developmentalists should be greatly interested in the formation of the self. By this I mean the permanent structuring of the forms of thought and feeling as a kind of 'pencil' centred on an inner ego. Philosophers were the first to point out that the 'inner self' cannot be a being presented in experience. Yet to most of us our physical location at the centre of a spatio-temporal 'sphere' of experience seems to be echoed by a similar kind of structure of thought and feeling. While the embodied person is a public object for all to see, and its location at the centre of the sphere of experience is a matter of simple observation, the centring entity upon which and to which our experience seems to belong is not so given. Ryle called it the 'systematically elusive' self. Vygotsky proposed that we should look for the organizing principles of thought and feeling in the structure of the language through which we come to express those thoughts and feelings. There we have a clue. Suppose we look at the structure of the grammar of typical forms of self-expression (see also the contribution of Robinson to this volume).

One notices immediately that in English there are two levels of complexity in such talk. There are simple sentences like 'I feel a draught' or 'I don't think you can be right about that' or 'I'm very cross with you'. We owe to Wittgenstein the insight that such sentences are not used to describe some inner state of the transcendental ego, but are public expressions of opinion, feeling or moral and other judgements. They are avowals not descriptions. In this they differ radically from similar forms in the third person, to which the ordinary assessments of putative descriptions apply; namely, there are criteria for whether we should take them to be true or false. The existence of this kind of talk in the conversation leaves us free of any demand for a 'real' inner being. The 'I' of such talk is indexical. It labels the opinion, the feeling or the judgement with the person who utters it.

But English and many other languages (though not all) have another level of complexity. There are expressions in which the reference to self is doubled up, so to speak. These appear very transparently in English or in French, languages with distinctive pronoun systems to express reference to persons. Thus we have sentences like 'I'm not sure whether I did see a fox in the covert' or 'I'm as sure as I can be that I felt a draught in your car' and so on. Such sentences seem to involve a commentary on the quality of the avowal embedded within them. Thus 'I saw a fox in the covert' is to make a claim about how the world seemed from the point of view of the speaker.

But to say 'I'm not sure whether I did' is to qualify that avowal. The form of such statements involves an embedded avowal and a commentary upon it. It is in these terms that one thinks about oneself, since it is in these terms that one comments upon one's own avowals. But what of the grammar of the pronouns? The form of mental organization that should arise to promote the possibility of this form of public (and later private) self-commentary should reflect the deep structure of the rules of pronoun grammar. The initial pronoun of any form of first person avowal will be an indexical marker, labelling the content of the speech act as pertaining to the person who uttered it. But the embedded pronoun follows a more complex grammar. To follow the steps towards the revelation of that grammar I need to introduce the idea of an exemplary episode. Not only are there grammatical models in the conversation of the public world but there are also model episodes. The commentary upon the avowals of a third or second person is set in episodes which have a certain definite character. The assessments of the avowals of others as sincere or insincere involve criteria, the bases of judgements as to whether what was avowed was true or false. The insincerity of a third person appears in public assessment as an appearance of falsehood. The moral condemnation of the speech-act arises because of the epistemic quality of the proposition embedded in it. Insincere talk is talk of which the content is false.

In the exemplary episodes in which self-commentary is picked up on the model of commentary upon the remarks of others the grammar of the comment upon avowal is that of the third person. In the later development of self-commenting speech-acts the embedded 'I' has something of the grammar of the third person. We can, in our overarching comment upon the epistemic quality of the embedded speech-act consider whether it truly or falsely represents the state of the speaker, namely ourselves. Thus a new referent, that to which the embedded 'I' refers, appears on the scene. In many cases this cannot easily be identified with the public person, since in exemplary episodes of self-concealment and lying there must appear an inner self whose attributes are different from those of the public person whose poker face and insincere speech-acts provide the public smoke-screen behind which a richer and more candid mental life has come to flourish. We learn to be liars by picking up the distinction between the public person and the inner self, but that distinction is modelled on the special distinction between the one who comments and the one whose speech-acts are the subject of the commentary. My self is modelled on the local concept of the public person. I have said all this in a very definite and forceful way, a rhetoric of established doctrine. But of course all of these remarks are hypotheses, proposals for a scheme for the understanding of the social origins of personal psychology, all of which can be subjected to empirical investigation. So far I have been developing a line of thought that closely resembles that of Vygotsky, with some important additions derived from Wittgenstein. But the process by which infant minds are shaped by the language games of their community is left open by this approach. We have reached, so to speak, evolutionary theory without the genetics. Vygotskyean 'appropriation' is a generic name for a process whose details are still obscure. A hint has already been given as to how we might go forward. In criticizing the Cartesian conception of education as 'transfer of subjective contents' I touched on the idea of a person learning to live in an ocean of public conversation. This idea or something very like it appears in the contribution to this volume by Light. The source from which the structure of mind is appropriated is that ocean. Some years ago now Shotter and Newson (1974) gave a special twist to the idea of psychological symbiosis. Watch carefully any group of people amongst whom are some couples who generally appear in public together, such as husbands and wives, mothers and daughters, teachers and pupils, and so on. One can be struck by the amount of psychological work each does for the other. This can take all kinds of forms. For instance there is 'face work', in which supplementary corrections to the public impression of the standing of the family or class, etc., are offered by one of the members of the group. Then there are supplementations of cognitive skills, subtle additions to the skilful use of words by one of the conversants to bring up the public performance of the other to the kind of level to which that couple aspires. There is even the wonderful example cited by Erving Goffman (1968), of the waiters who subtly coach unsophisticated clients to help them achieve the level of public behaviour that these waiters think proper for the clients of their class of restaurant. These are all examples of psychological symbiosis. We can define it in general as a continuing relationship in which one of the partners routinely supplements the psychological resources and public displays of competence or worth put on by the other, so as to sustain a level of public appearance that is in accord with what that couple, triad, etc., takes to be its proper level of attainment or value in that social milieu. Suppose we extend this idea 'backwards' so to speak, to the very early relationship between mother and infant. Studies of mothers' speech have shown how richly that speech was larded with high grade psychological concepts used to attribute states of mind, intentions and moral standing to the infant. Seen in this context a human infant is never presented in public as a merely organic being. It appears always in the form of a public person, any deficits that derive from its own nature being made up by the supplementations that appear in the mother's speech.

No more subtle or profound psychological process than imitation needs to be cited to explain how the relationship of psychological symbiosis can serve as the foundation of human development. But there is more to psychological symbiosis than mutual supplementation. It is worth remarking in passing that Trevarthen's work shows how much the infant's spontaneous actions are involved in calling forth the right kind of

supplementary speech and action from the mother or whoever else is involved. However, the theory I have sketched above implies that the infant's contribution must, at best, be generic rather than specific. Bruner has
demonstrated in various studies the extent to which the mother's way of
supplementing her infant's performance is controlled by some local theory
as to what sort of persons that society ought to have. There are vast differences in such theories, as a short time spent watching the differential
treatment of Indian boys and girls will soon make clear. These matters
noted and filed so to speak, we can turn to the second main feature of the
relationships I have called 'psychological symbiosis'. The symbiotic dyad
or triad, etc., is a social entity, structured and internally organized. The
early work on this idea by Shotter, Richards and Newson did not take into
account the internal order of the dyad, only its functional unity. But the
dyad is a human micro-order, and as such is structured by a moral system,
that is a system of rights and obligations, duties and responsibilities. This
feature of human relationships is also overlooked by Kohlberg, who treats
the developing child as passing through only cognitive stages of competence and knowledge. But developing human beings change not only in
respect to what they know they can do, but also and most importantly with
respect to what their society permits them to do, that is what they may do.
Certain classes of persons have certain rights and obligations to the display
of competences, while others, regardless of their state of knowledge are
forbidden to make public use of them. I have commented elsewhere on the
marvellously comic spectacle of the British Medical Association demonstrating public outrage on the occasion of a veterinary surgeon assisting at
an operation on a human being! Would the vets have been as outraged if
a doctor had assisted a vet? This amusing episode illustrates in particularly
vivid form a universal feature of the relation of human knowledge to
social order. Knowledge is a good and its display is morally regulated. Just
the same principles that govern the medical profession also reign in the
lives of those symbiotic dyads we find in the ordinary human family.
There are rights to display knowledge, moral judgement, practical skill,
and so on, and these rights are unevenly distributed with respect to age.
While on the one hand the law protects minors from the legal consequences
of their crimes, it also takes away from them any moral responsibility. In
a similar way our day-to-day moral system takes away certain rights of
display. I noticed this first in watching how on different occasions the
same child, sometimes with his or her mother, and sometimes with his or
her father was raised to different levels of social engagement by the very
same person. It became clear that in some relationships the child had
independent rights of social intercourse, in others he or she did not. But it
was apparent that the child was competent both at these social rituals and
at suppressing that knowledge when the moral order then reigning forbade
their display.

The traditional way of representing development could, I suppose, be simply laid out along a single polarized axis, running from low competence to high competence. The task of developmentalists such as Piaget and Kohlberg was simple: to find another polarized axis which could be mapped one to one onto the gradations expressed on that basic polarity. Thus Kohlberg's (1976) moral stages, which are defined by reference to a locally valid moral theory, are studied by attempting to map their pre-given order onto some other pre-given order, namely that of Piagetian cognitive development. Success or failure in the research enterprise is measured by the extent to which the mapping is achieved. Neither of the pre-given orders is itself subject to critical scrutiny. But it is not my purpose in this paper to rehearse the well-known difficulties that beset the standard theories of development. It is worth pointing out, however, that development must be seen in the light of the remarks I have made about moral rights, as a process which should be graphed on a two-dimensional plane. One axis represents the growing competence or knowledge and skill of an individual, the other the changing rights of that person as a social being to display that knowledge in well-specified public occasions. Failure to study the development of rights is perhaps another aspect of the incipient individualism that has dogged much of developmental psychology. It is as if the queer exigencies of the written examination ('No cheating there boys!') become the defining background against which all studies of development are to be designed. But most of life is a matter of adjusting what one can do to what one may do, and in the event of not knowing how, of knowing who is obliged to fill the gap and make up the deficit. With the members of one's family one has the very special right of psychological symbiosis wherein as a moral duty the deficits of the junior (and sometimes it is the senior members who are below par) are made up by others. So far this fascinating field of changing rights and duties has hardly been touched, with the exception of one remarkable piece by Davies (1981). She illustrated the ambiguities that the rights/competence orthogonality leads to in the way children and adults conduct moral disputes. Children are quite ready, at about the age of seven or eight, to engage in high level moral disputes with adults, using styles of moral argument of the Kohlberg post-conventionalist sort. Should they feel themselves to be in danger of being worsted they shift the ground of the dispute, accusing the adult of violating their rights as 'little children', to be immune from the force of adult logic. Feeling bad, the adult is as likely as not to concede the matter at issue in the original dispute.

These fragmentary case studies are sufficient, I believe, to show that the non-Cartesian theoretical framework, and the rather anti-Piagetian tone of the developmental theory sketched here, are on the right track. Once this framework is tentatively adopted a great many possibilities for further research suggest themselves (see the research menus in my 1983 book).

Just as in the physical sciences, the acceptability of the framework can be assessed only by the results of the smaller-scale research projects it inspires and controls.

References

Baker, G. P. and Hacker, P. M. S. 1982. The grammar of psychology. *Language and communication*, 2, 227–44.

Bruner, J. S. and Garton, A. 1978. *Human Growth and Development*. Oxford: Clarendon Press.

Davies, B. 1981. Children's accounts of adult interactions. *British Journal of the Sociology of Education*, 1, 1–36.

Davies, B. 1982. *Life in the Classroom and Playground*. London: Routledge and Kegan Paul.

Goffman, E. 1968. *Facework*. London: Penguin.

Harré, R. 1983. *Personal Being*. Oxford: Basil Blackwell; Cambridge, Mass.: Harvard University Press.

Harré, R. (ed.) 1984. Special issue: Piaget, Kohlberg and developmental psychology. *Oxford Review of Education*, 10, 249–304.

Kohlberg, L. 1976. Moral stages and moralisation. In T. Lickona (ed.) *Moral Development and Behavior*. New York: Holt, Rinehart and Winston.

Marsh, P., Rosser, E. and Harré, R. 1977. *The Rules of Disorder*. London: Routledge and Kegan Paul.

Morgan, J., O'Neil, C. and Harré, R. 1978. *Nicknames*. London: Routledge and Kegan Paul.

Richards, M. P. M. (ed.) 1974. *The Integration of a Child into a Social World*. London: Cambridge University Press.

Shotter, J. 1984. *Social Accountability and Selfhood*. Oxford: Basil Blackwell.

Shotter, J. and Newson, J. 1974. How babies communicate, *New Society*, 29, 346–7.

Sluckin, A. 1982. *Growing Up in the Playground*. London: Routledge and Kegan Paul.

Trevarthen, C. 1979. Communication and cooperation in early infancy, in M. Bullowa (ed.), *Before Speech: the beginning of interpersonal communication*. Cambridge: Cambridge University Press.

Vygotsky, L. 1962. *Thought and Language*, Cambridge, Mass.: MIT Press.

Wittgenstein, L. 1952. *Philosophical Investigations*. Oxford: Basil Blackwell.

14

Development in social context

David Ingleby

Introduction

Since the publication of this volume's forerunner (Richards, 1974), the landscape of developmental psychology has changed considerably. Many of the approaches argued for in that book have become almost a new orthodoxy; and in the field as a whole, the way in which psychologists discuss the relation between development and its social context has changed so much as to inspire talk of a 'paradigm shift'. Whereas it once seemed enough to throw in 'social factors' simply as more variables in the inter-actionist equation, what is being argued for today is nothing short of a fundamental revision of theory and methodology. In this chapter, I will try to trace the origins of this change in perspective, and to decide whether enough consensus underlies it really to justify calling it a 'paradigm shift'.

But before I attempt this, I must make two disclaimers. First, in describing the emergence of these ideas, I am not claiming to give an objective, unbiased account of developmental psychology's recent history. The identification of a 'developmental trend' is always a selective and biased process, creating rather than discovering a coherence in events. Moreover, in what follows, changes in the English-speaking world – in particular, those I happen to have had contact with – may be drawn exaggeratedly large.

Secondly, I am not going to attempt any simple causal explanations of why these changes occurred. Despite the fact that I will use the Richards book and other texts as 'landmarks' in surveying the scene, I do not wish to suggest, after the fashion of 'history of ideas', that books and articles are the generators of change. Rather, I see these texts as *symptomatic* of deeper changes, taking place on several different levels. What I am after are the 'conditions of possibility' of this shift in perspective.

At the intellectual level, these conditions include not only the availability of new ideas, but a loss of confidence in the old. But underlying these changes, I shall argue, is a changed attitude to psychology's place in society, and for this reason I will devote considerable space in this chapter to this theme. It has become increasingly difficult to maintain the traditional distinction between discussions about development on the one hand, and about developmental psychology on the other. Not only do the social functions of psychology play a role in shaping theory, but the activities of psychologists are increasingly seen as important factors in the developmental process itself (witness the amount of space devoted in the present volume to them by Dingwall and Eekelaar, Lewis, and Oakley). Looking a little closer, we see that a single idea unites recent thinking both *in* and *about* psychology: namely, the idea that 'mind' is situated in practical activity, and cannot be understood outside of its social and historical context.

The critical movement

In keeping with this, Richards's book was both a discussion about children, and about psychologists. Those who contributed to it were all, to a greater or lesser extent, influenced by the critical movement which had swept the universities in the late 1960s. Although this movement took different forms in the UK, the USA, and continental Europe, common to all its forms was a questioning of the role in society played by the intellectual labour-force, and this questioning has had profound effects on the direction psychology has taken in the more austere climate of the last ten years.

In saying this, I do not want to claim a direct causal link between the critical movement and certain new approaches in developmental psychology. Nobody came home from a sit-in to rewrite the theory of cognitive development. What the movement did do, however, was to open up a space in which certain long-suppressed issues could be argued out. Even though the more florid manifestations of student radicalism seem to be a thing of the past, the search for new ideas continues to be motivated by the alienation felt by younger developmentalists from psychology's traditional role, and from the attitudes that go with it. In this connection, I would point to the substantial contribution made by feminists to the ideas I shall discuss in this chapter.

Neither do I want to claim that anything particularly new was being said by those who saw themselves as radicals within psychology. Rather, what they were doing was to articulate latent contradictions within the mainstream of social science itself. In that sense, the critical movement was 'the return of the repressed' – and as I will show, some of the approaches being argued for were very old-fashioned indeed (though none the worse for that).

What was the kernel of the critique, and what were its implications for developmental psychology? In my own contribution to the Richards volume, I tried to spell this out. Basically, the message was that science was not neutral but value-laden, and we did not like the values it was laden with. The functions of developmental psychology were likened to those of psychiatry: following the model of 'anti-psychiatry', it was argued that psychologists were employed to bring children into line, to adapt them to their situations instead of vice versa, and to maintain a wholly artificial 'normality'. The goals of sorting, grading and straightening children out had deformed the vision of psychology.

This was not simply a critique of the *applications* of developmental psychology. The theory itself was seen as 'ideological': psychology was regarded as a set of myths whose existence was explained by their function, that of legitimating the existing social order. Three main themes can be singled out in this critique, and each of them found a response in the new perspectives that I shall discuss in this chapter.

First, in keeping with its task as an apparatus of social regulation, psychology was seen as propagating spurious norms of development: cultural values were presented as facts of nature. In the jargon of the times, psychology 'reified the status quo', transforming historical flux into timeless laws. Textbooks talked glibly and ethnocentrically about *the* child, *the* family, or *the* mother-infant relationship. They also treated mental abilities as something 'out there' waiting to be measured – measurement being just a matter of developing the right test: the sense in which both the abilities and the tests were social constructions was completely lost. By treating their own social order as a given, these textbooks implied that it was the only possible or desirable one.

Underlying this approach was a philosophical commitment to a particular view of psychology as a science. Science was taken to be the discovery of unchanging laws; the laws which developmental psychology discovered being those of individual development. From this standpoint, social factors could only be seen as a source of contamination – as variance to be partialled out. The true object of psychology was the individual considered in abstraction from culture: the social was something that had to be stripped away to reveal this object. In contrast, argued the critics, if you stripped away the social, you would have nothing left.

The second theme concerned the *individualism* of psychology. Because it focused on the single case, psychology tended to treat only the properties of the individual as variables; the culture became, in effect, a constant. Social inequalities tended to be explained in terms of psychological ones ('blaming the victim'). This critique did not only refer to those latter-day eugenicists who explained class, race or sex differences in terms of genetics. Environmentalism was also seen as 'individualistic', because in it the basic predictors of behaviour remained *dispositions* (abilities, attitudes, personality); though capable of being modified by the social context, dispositions remain logically distinct from it, and located firmly 'inside' the child's immediate environment, and thus to occlude social structure almost as effectively as the hereditarians.

A third line of criticism, whose target was the 'positivist' programme of basing psychology on natural-scientific methods and concepts, concerned the 'reification' of meaningful, purposive activity in a deterministic framework – the reduction of 'praxis' to 'process'. Positivism was attacked for its methodological denial of *agency* (a critique which has obvious connections with the humanist 'third force' movement in mainstream US psychology). This neglect of agency had helped to obscure the fact that growing up was not simply a matter of acquiring skills, but the site of complex political tensions between children, parents and the state.

These, then, were the three cental criticisms of psychology which were current at the time of the Richards volume. We are not, however, dealing here with a static body of ideas, but a movement which has itself undergone several upheavals since that time. The most significant of these, in my view, was brought about by the 'post-structuralists' (see Henriques et al., 1984), who charged that the critical movement was a prisoner of the very framework it was attempting to dismantle. This led to a very different analysis of psychology's defects, and a very different programme of reconstruction – much of it opposed to the received wisdom of the 'radicals'.

I shall return to this theme, however, later: for the moment, so as not to get out of step with ourselves, let us consider the changes in developmental psychology which the above three criticisms led to. I shall divide these changes into two phases: in the first of these, 'cultural relativism' attempted to deal with the charge that psychology paid insufficient attention to the varieties of development. This programme, however, failed to deal with the problems of 'individualism' and 'reification'; for this, a more radical programme was required, to which I have given the name (following Gergen, 1985) 'social constructionism'. In fairness to the 'cultural relativists', I must point out that some of them were aware of the need for more drastic revisions; the division between my first and second phases should therefore be seen as a distinction between ideas, not between authors.

Cultural relativism

The framework for what I call the 'relativist' approach already existed under the banner of environmentalism: what this approach insisted was simply that social factors are more influential and pervasive than the textbooks supposed, and more culturally variable. Examination of development in other times and places showed that many of its supposed constants were in fact variables – the structure of mental abilities, the position of children in society, and so on. The sources for these notions were of course history and anthropology, and apart from citing a few obvious names (Ariès, Elias, Van den Berg, Margaret Mead, Ruth Benedict) I shall not detail this work here.

The lesson of history and anthropology was that many varieties of development are possible, and that our notions of maturity, attachment, abilities, stages of development – even the notion of childhood itself, are very specific to our culture. A landmark text here is perhaps the proceedings of the Fourth Houston Symposium, entitled *The Child and Other Cultural Inventions* (Kessel and Siegel, 1983). What was said above about the lack of direct causal links is well illustrated by the fact that Richards (1974) is nowhere cited in this volume, though many of the same arguments were rehearsed.

A relativist approach in itself does not offer a new theorization of the object of psychology: but it does suggest a broadening of the *topics* of research. Textbook developmental psychology presented a stereotyped and idealized notion of 'normal' development, hardly representative even of its authors' culture. It overlooked the fact that a standard nuclear family was absent from the background of an increasing number of children's lives, and that for all the talk about mother-infant interaction, mothers were by no means the only ones who counted. The relativist approach opened up the topics of divorce, non-traditional households, fathers, and siblings: to select just one example, Dunn and Kendrick's work on siblings (1982) is enough to silence those who see only adult-child relationships as relevant to development.

Most historical and cross-cultural studies treated the individual/society relationship in terms of a 'socialization' model, in which social structures were embodied in *roles*, which were external to the individual and acquired by a process of learning. Behaviourist 'social learning theory' fitted most neatly with this model, though Erikson (1950) had adopted a psycho-analytic approach. Yet a relativist approach which was simply a super-charged version of traditional environmentalism could not meet all the demands of the critical movement. Adding more varied and powerful social factors did not really answer the second and third critical themes, that psychology was 'individualistic' and 'reifying'.

This was made abundantly clear in another 'landmark' article, 'Psychology, ideology and the human subject' (Adlam et al., 1977). This manifesto appeared in the first number of *Ideology and Consciousness*, a journal which was to have a substantial influence on younger British psychologists. In it, contributors to the Richards volume were dismayed to read that they were not the solution at all, but part of the problem: restoring the social context of development, argued the authors, was not achieved by positing a more labile individual, more easily 'filled up' with social influences – in other words, by making the '/' in 'individual/society' more permeable. This dualism itself – the idea of individual existence as something conceivable apart from the social – was seen as the root problem: simply privileging the 'social' would not remove it.

For the critics, then, the task of psychology was not to explore social influences on individual development, but to reconstruct its object in a way that transcended the dualism of individual and society. This, of course, was not a new idea: it had long been the project of Marxist psychologists (see Sève, 1975). But before psychologists could be interested in this project, it was necessary for their confidence in the ruling paradigm to be weakened. For a number of reasons, some of which had little to do with politics, this is precisely what was happening during the 1970s.

The crisis in mainstream psychology

As Bernstein (1976) shows, the collapse of confidence in traditional methods of theorizing and data-gathering within psychology was part of a wider crisis in the social sciences, which attacked the intellectual legitimation of the mainstream (the empiricist view of science) at the root. In this section, I shall ignore other disciplines and focus rather narrowly on certain changes within developmental psychology.

The central reason for the loss of confidence in the broadly behaviourist Anglo-American paradigm was that researchers were turning their attention to an object – *cognition* – whose non-existence was the fundamental premiss of behaviourism. The cognitive approaches which supplanted behaviourism, however (psycholinguistics, cybernetics and Piagetian theory), still did not provide a new theorization of the individual/society relationship: only when psychologists became disillusioned with these, in turn, did they become receptive to the call for a new paradigm. This could not occur until Chomsky's and Piaget's neglect of the social dimensions of language and cognition had been repeatedly pointed out.

How did the 'cognitive revolution' come about in the first place? Probably the immediate reason was the drive to 'optimize' the intellectual development of US children, which was part of the social engineering programme of 1960s psychology and had its concrete manifestations in compensatory education programmes such as Project Headstart. Underlying political motives here included fear of Soviet technological progress (in 1957 the first Sputnik started circling US skies), and a belief that equalizing educational opportunity would reduce class and race tensions. But behaviourism could not provide an adequate theoretical basis for this programme: indeed, up until the 1950s its strategy had been to avoid dealing with cognition altogether, on the basis that psychology should try to understand 'simple' functions first. More complex ones, including language, could be approached later, using the understanding thus built up. Unfortunately, US society could not wait.

It was on the battleground of language that behaviourism was decisively routed: the 'landmark' text here is, of course, Chomsky's (1959) review of Skinner's *Verbal Behavior*, with its devastating argument that it would take millions of years for a child to master language by processes of reinforcement. This critique restored 'mind' to its classical place as the object of psychological study, and thus created a methodological vacuum which was quickly filled by Piaget and by Chomsky himself.

But the revival of cognitive approaches did not immediately pose a challenge to the individualism of psychology: far from it, in fact, for neither Piaget, Chomsky, nor the proponents of 'artificial intelligence' gave a constitutive role to the social context in the development of cognitive processes. All these approaches took as their starting-point the 'epistemic subject' – the child being seen as a sort of scientific investigator, equipped with innate analytic skills, interrogating the outside world in order to infer the underlying structures of language and reality. For Chomsky, the 'deep structures' underlying cognition were not social artifacts, but inbuilt mechanisms. Piaget rejected such a rationalist approach, seeing the structures as *constructed* – but by the individual, and in a uniform way, which had to do with the physical, not the social, order (see Light, 1983). The initial thrust of cognitive developmental psychology, therefore, was away from, rather than towards, the study of mind-in-social-context. Indeed, the term 'cognitivist' has come to refer specifically to approaches which lack a social perspective (Haugeland, 1978; Sinha, 1985).

Awareness of this lack came from several sources. First, some of those who attempted to use the newly imported Piagetian research methods complained that important aspects of the social environment were left out of focus. The social psychologist Willem Doise undertook a systematic investigation of the co-operative aspects of cognitive development (see Doise (1978), Perret-Clermont (1980) and Doise and Mugny (1984)). Margaret Donaldson, in her now classic book *Children's Minds* (1978), showed that respect for the 'human sense' of the actions in which children demonstrate their cognitive abilities would result in a very different methodology from Piaget's own. The child in the conservation experiment, for example, has to be seen as making a social interpretation of the experiment, so that setting up the relation between tester and subject in different ways can have dramatic effects on conservation performance. As Elbers (1984) and Light (chapter 8) show, this kind of criticism of Piaget begins in a modest proposal to adjust the age at which conservation abilities should be credited to the child, as a function of situational variations (a kind of 'competence/performance' distinction), and ends in a fundamental questioning of the whole notion of 'competence' or 'structure'. In Elbers's words (1984): 'the experiment is not a window on competence, but an opportunity for learning.'

Much of this criticism of Piaget was stimulated by the new emphasis in US psychology on 'ecological validity'. This concept was elaborated by Bronfenbrenner (1979) in his influential book, *The Ecology of Human Development*. According to the latter, 'much of developmental psychology as it now exists, is the science of the strange behaviour of children in strange situations with strange adults for the briefest possible periods of time' (1979, 19). If the social context was important to development, this importance could never be revealed by traditional research methods. Tests and laboratory experiments had been devised in pursuit of the chimerical individual-abstracted-from-society. Recognition of the social context entailed studying the child in everyday life situations, and interpreting his or her behaviour by reference to that context. Unlike most 'ecologists', however, Bronfenbrenner did not rule out the laboratory as a valid setting for observing some kinds of phenomena.

Another line, which led ultimately to the rejection of both Piaget and Chomsky, was investigation of the role of language in cognitive development, and the role of social relations in providing the foundations of language. Bruner (1976) argued that it was non-verbal interactions that provided the 'scaffolding' for linguistic ones. Treating language as an acquired social skill created a tension with the Chomskian claim that the basis of language acquisition was innate. The idea that linguistic rules were entirely contained in languages themselves was undermined by the demonstration of indexicality – the fact that the *context of action* determines the meaning of an utterance. 'Speech act theory' and 'metalinguistics' (cf. Joanna Ryan's chapter in Richards, 1974) insisted that language could not be artificially abstracted from social interaction. Via these sorts of arguments, we see developmental psycholinguistics shifting away from a structuralist conception of language towards a pragmatic or dialectical one (for an excellent review of these developments see Hood, 1985).

These critical arguments directed at Piaget, Chomsky and the cyberneticists went much further than simply calling for a revision of the *content* of theory. At the same time, the very mode of psychological investigation was being called in question. This critique was similar to that mounted by ethnomethodologists against positivistic methods of measurement. According to Heritage (1976), scales constructed from questionnaires and tests could provide no more than a 'data soup', in which the intelligibility of individual items was obliterated; while Harré and Secord (1972) argued for a social psychology in which the agent's own frames of meaning were central.

In a similar fashion, Bronfenbrenner (1979) argued that different ways of seeing were required in order to study the meaning-in-context of what the child did. What mattered was not the 'objective' situation, but the way it was construed by the subject. Rom Harré and John Shotter, in their respective contributions to Richards's 1974 volume, argued for an interpretative approach to developmental psychology. One realization of this approach was the observational approach adopted by the 'Nottingham School' under John and Elizabeth Newson, which abandoned behaviouristic categories for a frankly mentalistic account of children's conduct. Jerome Bruner, in a controversial lecture given at Oxford in 1976, cast doubt on the exclusion of 'mind, intention, and culture' from contemporary psychology (Bruner, 1979).

The call by Bronfenbrenner, Bruner, Harré, Shotter and others for a return to interpretative approaches represented a fundamental challenge to psychology's view of itself as firmly located on the side of *Naturwissenschaften* rather than *Geisteswissenschaften*. It was as if the banished phenomenological tradition was returning, like Banquo's ghost, to haunt the positivist festivities. Yet for all the zeal with which psychologists went about demolishing the dominant approaches to cognition, all they succeeded in doing at first was to recreate the intellectual vacuum which had been left by the fall of behaviourism. Although ideas from many different sources were experimented with as possible foundations for a truly 'social' approach to development, there was no general agreement about which framework to adopt. Thus, at the present time, the *conditions* are right for the emergence of a 'social constructionist' paradigm in developmental psychology, but it is still arguable whether the critics share enough common ground for them to constitute, collectively, a 'paradigm'. 'Normal science' is in disarray – but so, as we shall see in the next section, are its critics.

Social Constructionism

In this section I will review the main schools of thought to which developmentalists have turned in order to provide a theoretical underpinning for the notion of 'social construction of mind'. The question I shall attempt to keep in focus is: do these schools constitute a 'paradigm'? Though there is much confusion about the meaning of the term, one of the undoubted properties of a paradigm is agreement between practitioners on the fundamental presuppositions that guide their enquiries. Can such agreement be found, despite the apparent diversity of these schools? In my view this question is not just of philosophical interest, for if agreement is not to be found, the danger is that 'social constructionism' will degenerate into a motley collection of sects.

What all these approaches have in common is that they break down the individual/society dichotomy via the following two-stage argument. First, human thought, perception and action must be approached in terms of *meanings*: secondly, the vehicles of 'meaning' are codes (especially language) whose nature is inherently intersubjective. Therefore, mind is an intrinsically social phenomenon. And if psychology is the science of mind, then the object of psychology is not individuals, but (to put it rather ineptly) *what goes on in the space between them*: that is, the codes which structure action. Different theories use different terms to refer to these codes (accounting systems, language games, meta-contracts, scaffolding, discourses, discursive practices), and offer different prescriptions about how they should be studied.

The theories I shall discuss here include pragmatism and symbolic interactionism; phenomenology and hermeneutics; ethnomethodology, linguistic and analytic philosophy; Marxism; and the descendants of De Saussure's structuralism. All of them, despite their apparent diversity, have a common origin in the philosophical and political reaction against Enlightenment notions which occurred during the late eighteenth and nineteenth century. The corner-stone of the Enlightenment was the conception of the individual which Descartes articulated – a conscious, rational agent whose existence was logically prior to that of the social world. In accordance with this notion, society was conceived of as a collection of individuals who happened to have struck a sort of bargain (the 'social contract') about how to coexist. It was this primacy of the individual that was rejected by the theories of mind which Charles Taylor (1985) labels 'romantic-expressive'. According to the German philosophers Herder and Humboldt, consciousness was embedded in language, and language was a *collective* invention; hence the individuals who were supposed to constitute society were already constituted *by* society. It is from this insight, according to Taylor, that all the schools I shall consider here originate.

Yet the mere fact of common ancestry is no guarantee that this family of ideas can be reconciled with each other today. In what follows I shall compare and contrast the different theories which 'social constructionists' have taken up. Of course, in the space available I cannot hope to provide a proper account of each school for those who are not already acquainted with them: for these purposes, the reader is referred to the literature cited. My aim, rather, is a tactical one. In place of a further deepening of schisms, what we need is a broadly based debate: my purpose is therefore to show that *none* of the currently available approaches constitutes 'the' way forward for developmental psychology. Each of these theories contains inherent difficulties, which their supporters tend to gloss over rather hastily: I want, therefore, to prompt second thoughts about these theories in the minds of their protagonists, while endorsing the basic project of all of them.

Pragmatism and symbolic interactionism

For contemporary developmental psychologists, the most influential figure in the pragmatic tradition has been G. H. Mead, who sought to analyse 'mental' phenomena in terms of social action (an approach that he termed, confusingly for us, 'social behaviorism'). Symbolic interactionism later drew on these ideas to analyse the way in which our subjective understanding of the world is socially built up.

The take-up of these ideas is well illustrated by Shotter (1974), who reworks the notion that motives are part of a 'social vocabulary', rather than residing in the individual. According to Shotter, the personal powers which emerge 'in' the child are essentially conferred by others. To give a familiar example, the mother gives meaning to a child's crying by interpreting it within a certain framework of conventions. Thus, subjectivity is something *afforded* by the ecology of the social world. Rom Harré (chapter 13) also elaborates this idea, showing how the 'rights' accorded to an agent define the space in which they manifest their being.

Following pragmatic principles, the framework which lends meaning to actions is seen as built up around practical contingencies. In this respect, the neo-Meadian approach resembles that of Piaget – for whom cognition also developed out of action-schemas: but the crucial difference is that for Piaget, these schemas were built up by the individual, whereas for the neo-Meadians they are *collectively* devised. Lock (1982) argues that gestures arise in the context of joint action (e.g., the child raising its arms in order to be picked up), and that symbolic activity is built up on the basis of this. The codes employed become more standardized as the idiosyncratic usage of the home is brought into line with broader conventions.

For developmentalists in search of an alternative to cognitivism, Mead's views have exercised a great attraction. However, there are certain endemic shortcomings in the neo-Meadian approach. As Morss points out in a penetrating study (in press), the interpreters of Mead tend to elide the 'generalized other' with *actual* others (principally, the mother), and to ignore Mead's 'social realism' – his insistence on the *impersonality* of knowledge. The neo-Meadians tend to focus on the 'Me' – the system of self-interpretations appropriated from the 'generalised other' – and tend to assimilate the 'I' to it: thus Shotter, in the above example, seems to be claiming that the mother *gives* the child motives. If this is taken as meaning that there can never be a clash of wills between mother and child, or that a mother can never *misinterpret* a child's intentions, then it is patently false. Mead's 'Me' requires a complementary 'I' – but once we accept this, we are landed with another dualism. The criticism appears to be warranted that Mead simply transforms the dualism of individual and society into an *internal* dualism of 'I' and 'Me'.

A further problem concerns the viability of the pragmatist analysis of language, in particular 'speech act theory'. It may be true that structural psycholinguists ignore the fact that utterances are *acts* which serve a social function: but to claim that their social function exhaustively defines their meaning is another matter. A large gap seems to separate hand-raising gestures and symbolic communication (to say nothing of formal logic), and the followers of Mead are in danger of being stranded on the wrong side of this gap.

Ethnomethodology

The fundamental project of ethnomethodology, as defined by Howard
Garfinkel, was to make our everyday procedures for making sense a
'topic' rather than simply a 'resource'. Thus ethnomethodologists focus
on the relation of actions to 'accounts', and on the nature of accounting
systems: this emphasis is again found in the work of Harré and Shotter
(though the latter's works show an increasing stress on the 'indeterminacy'
of social rules and the emergent properties of the self). One acts respon-
sibly, and thus counts as an agent, to the extent that one can 'account for
oneself' – that is, give intelligible reasons for what one does. Reasons are
thus constitutive of actions, and one of the most controversial claims of
this school is that they have no objective existence: that is, they can be
negotiated, and can be altered retrospectively. Accounts, as Shotter (1984)
puts it, are not the same as theories, and cannot aspire to the same sort of
objectivity. Shotter points out (1984, 24) that this puts a spanner in the
works for those who aim to reconcile *Naturwissenschaften* and *Geisteswissenschaften*.

On this view, psychology must abandon a long tradition of 'not taking
people seriously' as authorities on their own behaviour. Shotter proposes
that the basic task of developmental psychology is a *hermeneutic* one – the
study of meanings. One can equally well say, with Sheldon White (1983),
that it is a *moral* science – since morality and accountability have overlapping meanings.

This emphasis on accounting-systems goes some way towards meeting
the criticism that the neo-Meadians concern themselves too much with
interpersonal situations, at the expense of the 'generalized other'. Obviously, it has profound implications for developmental psychology, since it
puts paid to any behaviourist ambitions of 'objectively' categorizing
behaviour: what seems to be the same act can have very different significance in different accounting-systems. For example, a general theory of
'attachment' is doomed to failure, since the meaning of a caretaker's
comings and goings will vary greatly in different interpretative communities. The most fascinating implications of this viewpoint concern cultures
whose members do not account for themselves in ways commensurable
with contemporary Western notions about the boundary between self and
others, or between mind and body (see Heelas and Lock, 1981).

Yet the flaw in this approach is its rationalism – its axiomatic equation
of 'human' activity with conscious, rational conduct. Method and model
confirm each other in a tightly circular fashion. If we trust common-sense
accounts, we end up believing in the autonomy and rationality of their
authors: and if we believe in people's rationality, we must necessarily trust
their accounts. To the post-structuralists, as we shall see, this 'humanistic'
approach falls into the trap of accepting the contractual society's own

illusion about itself, namely that it is composed of rational agents: we are thus half-way back to Enlightenment individualism. We may not want to supplant people's accounts of themselves with a purely mechanistic alternative, as positivism sought to do. Yet if we take accounts *too* seriously, are we not in danger of imposing a false unity on the self, of crediting consciousness with too much authenticity, and assuming unlimited powers of self-control? Rationalist approaches such as ethnomethodology must turn their back on the Freudian vision of the disunity of the self, or the Marxian critique of 'false consciousness' – what Ricoeur (1970) calls 'the hermeneutics of suspicion'.

Analytic philosophy

Many of the ideas discussed so far correspond to central arguments within analytic philosophy, particularly in the work of Wittgenstein. Here again, language is seen as the vehicle of all thought, and as social in its very essence. Rules of signification and criteria for knowledge are essentially common, not private, property; so thinking and knowing cannot be seen as 'internal' processes (Coulter, 1979).

Russell (1978) has shown that this implies a view of development which is clearly at odds with cognitivism. Against Piaget's view of conservation abilities as developing independently of language, Light (1983) argues that 'children do not first learn what we mean by amount, weight and number and only later learn that these are conserved across certain kinds of transformations.' The disagreement with Piaget is even more pronounced in the case of mathematics. Mathematics may consist of 'operations', as Piaget says, but these operations are part of a system of social conventions: they can never be developed by the child directly out of his or her dealings with things (Venn and Walkerdine, 1978).

Soviet cultural-historical approaches

These approaches are built explicitly on the framework of Marxist philosophy, whose most significant tenet for psychology is perhaps the sixth thesis on Feuerbach: 'the human essence is no abstraction inherent in each individual. In its reality it is the ensemble of social relations.' Because these approaches also incorporate the genetic principle that phenomena should be understood in terms of how they come into being, they treat all psychology as, in effect, developmental.

Vygotsky recognized the split between human and natural sciences – indeed, as Wertsch (1985) points out, his background was more literary than natural-scientific. Yet a theory of mind divorced from the material sciences was as intellectually unsatisfactory to Vygotsky as it was politically unacceptable to the Soviet authorities. Vygotsky's well-known concept of 'interiorization' appears to resolve this dualism, by making the 'objective' the foundation of the 'subjective'. He states (1978, 57): 'Every function in the child's cultural development appears twice: first, on the social level, and later, on the individual level; first, *between* people (*inter-psychological*), and then *inside* the child (*intrapsychological*).' Vygotsky and Leontiev saw development as essentially the *appropriation* of a cultural heritage.

This school has directly influenced many English-speaking psychologists (e.g., Cole, Scribner, Wertsch, Bruner and Donaldson), as well as the 'critical psychologists' of the Berlin school (see Elbers, 1986). Vygotsky's influence on Margaret Donaldson, for example, can be seen in her emphasis on the practical, situated nature of reasoning; while Bronfenbrenner actually studied with Leontiev in Moscow during the 1960s. Under Van Parreren at Utrecht, Soviet approaches to learning have been firmly planted in the Netherlands.

This eager acceptance of Vygotsky's ideas by Western 'social constructionists' suggests a great deal of consensus in the underlying presuppositions of all the above four approaches. As an illustration of this, consider the way Wertsch (1979) uses Wittgenstein's concept of 'language games' to elaborate Vygotsky's notions about the co-operative nature of problem-solving. Another reason why Vygotsky's ideas may be so readily assimilated, however, may be that they are in fact very sketchy, and do not add up to a coherent theory of development. This is hardly surprising, considering that he died in 1934 at the age of 38! For instance, infant development and pre-verbal behaviour are hardly theorized at all by Vygotsky, and his distinction between 'higher' and 'lower' mental processes is unworkable and inappropriate (Van der Veer and van Ijzendoorn, 1985).

It is also not clear how successfully Vygotsky avoids the dualism of 'individual' and 'society'. The notion of 'interiorization' resolves the split between 'internal' and 'external' processes by saying that the former are based on the latter; yet the conceptual distinction between 'inside' and 'outside' is firmly maintained. Moreover, as Goudena (1984) shows, Vygotsky's account of the role of 'private speech' in interiorization may be quite inaccurate. In sum, this approach must also be regarded as an inadequate foundation for a 'social constructionist' paradigm.

The post-structuralist view

This is the most recent of the approaches I deal with here, and the one which poses most problems to the idea of a synthesis. The work of 'post-structuralists' such as Foucault, Donzelot, Derrida and Castel has to be seen as a reaction to the post-1968 disillusionment in France with the quasi-theological structuralism of Althusser. For the latter, subjects were merely 'the bearers of categories', but for Foucault, they were formed by structures of power or 'discursive practices'. These ideas were disseminated in Britain by the journal *Ideology and Consciousness*, after it abandoned Marxism, and a recent collection entitled *Changing the Subject* (Henriques et al., 1984) shows the dramatic impact they have had on psychological debate. Post-structuralism provides not only a view about subjectivity, but about psychology too, and its disagreements with the more traditional critics of psychology begin with the latter's understanding of that discipline. At this point, therefore, we must return to some of the themes of the critical movement, though by so doing we will come to appreciate better the post-structuralist approach to subjectivity.

According to the authors of *Changing the Subject*, the critical movement of the 1960s and 1970s was itself a prisoner of the Cartesian and rationalist framework it was trying to demolish. For that movement, power was inherently repressive, and 'emancipation' consisted in becoming liberated from it: yet the individuals who inflicted and suffered power were treated as already-existing *agents*. What post-structuralism asserted was that it was in the process through which agents were *created* that the real power resided. This is the essence of Foucault's (1980) distinction between 'repressive' and 'productive' power: he claims, moreover, that the hallmark of modern society is the predominance of the latter over the former.

The critical movement's way of handling the fact that power did not necessarily involve a 'clash of wills' was through the notion of ideology. By distorting reality, ideology persuaded people that their interests were, in fact, shared by those who dominated them: through ideology, oppression legitimated itself in generally acceptable terms. This notion of 'ideology' was categorically rejected by the post-structuralists. Discourses do not distort reality – they *create* it. Foucault's couple 'power/knowledge' expressed the idea that knowledge was essentially a codification of social practices (which American pragmatism, of course, had claimed a century before). 'Régimes of truth' regulated society by minting the very coinage in which their validity was assessed – by constructing the mentality, the aspirations, and the feelings of those they regulated.

Symbolic interactionism, as represented by the term 'social construction of reality', had argued something very similar – but despite this school's pragmatist origins, the creation of subjectivity was treated in predominately cognitive terms (e.g., 'definition of the situation'). The post-structuralists, by contrast, have insisted on studying the concrete social effects of a discourse. In the case of psychology, this means looking at the profession's administrative and managerial role. The system in which psychologists participate is much more than an *intellectual* framework: it pays out pensions, builds institutions, lays down procedures for every social contingency – in short, it is part of the running of society itself.

Theory does not determine these practices, nor does it simply provide rationalizations of them; it cannot be meaningfully studied apart from them. IQ-testing (Rose, 1985), child-centred pedagogy (Walkerdine, 1984), or welfare provisions (Donzelot, 1980) are practices that create a population *disciplined* in certain ways. Professionals are therefore, in a basic sense, socializers (Ingleby, 1985), and the environment they construct is every bit as crucial to the developmentalist as any other.

In that socialization has mainly been regarded as the task of the family, the 'psy complex' takes over many of the family's powers (hence the laments of such writers as Lasch (1977) over the decline of the family under the welfare state). What Donzelot insists, however, is that they do not always take over these functions by *supplanting* the family; they also work *via* the family, by regulating what goes on inside it.

This is particularly visible in developmental psychology, which, since it mostly concerns itself with childhood, is closely concerned with parental functions. External interventions – the actual take-over of parental functions by professionals paid or mandated by the state – could only expand up to a certain point, if they were not to threaten the sacred place of the family in capitalist society. Developmental psychology provided ways to increase the status of parents, while at the same time managing their activities.

Thus, mothers after the Second World War learned that they had a vital task in promoting optional emotional and cognitive development; but it was from the psychologists that they would have to learn to discharge this duty (see Jane Lewis, chapter 2). Parenthood became a skill – a valued one, perhaps, but one which must be monitored, theorized and refined by the experts. Whereas early forms of psychology were concerned with *excluding* the inadequate or defective (the 'sorting and grading' condemned by the critical movement), this has been superseded by *normalizing* practices – the promotion of 'healthy' growth. Developmental psychology thus illustrates clearly Foucault's notion of a shift from 'repressive' to 'productive' power.

Let us now consider how this theory about the productive effects of psychology functions at the same time *as* a psychology. According to Walkerdine (1984), the autonomous, self-regulating child celebrated by 'child-centred pedagogy' is actually *produced* within its discursive practices. The theory, as it were, creates its own truth. In an observation of nursery-school children playing in a Wendy house, Walkerdine (1981) further illustrates how children can shift between the different subject-positions which are available to them. Initially, the teacher sets up a game of 'doctors and nurses', with the children allocated conventional positions according to sex. One girl, however, manages to relocate herself in another discourse – that of domesticity – which affords her a more powerful position: she does this by redefining the Wendy house as a kitchen, and ordering her 'doctor' to eat up his food. It is hard to grasp what she is doing without using the notions of positioning and discourse. A further implication of this viewpoint is that overlapping discourses can create multiple subjectivity, which – as the above example shows – gives female identity a particular complexity (Selby, 1984).

There is a crucial difference between this approach and 'role theory', because 'roles' are essentially attributes which can be put on or cast off, rather like clothing, and can be distinguished from the person 'underneath' who plays them. Post-structuralists reject this Cartesian dichotomy, which they claim is also to be found in the 'humanist' or 'rationalist' approaches which presuppose a unitary self and give a privileged place to agency.

Yet this approach (like all the others) is not without its own problems. On the one hand, it rejects the idea of any essential human attributes existing outside of, or prior to, the social domain. On the other hand, it rejects the unitary, autonomous subject 'inscribed' in the discourse of bourgeois contractual society. Yet how can this form of subjectivity be rejected, if it exists as a subject-position? Post-structuralists cannot allow themselves to say 'because people aren't *really* like that'. One could turn their own argument against them by pointing out that the individual powers and responsibilities inscribed in the law of contract are not *hypotheses*: they are summoned into existence by the law itself. The unity of the self, for example, is intrinsic to selfhood itself: that is, it is not open to me to claim that it was somebody else who signed 'my' cheques yesterday. Child-centred pedagogy or client-centred therapy are therefore self-validating, in that they (and the culture in which they are situated) bring into being the autonomous, creative individual they describe: their only error is in seeing this form of subjectivity as coming from 'within' rather than 'without'.

From all this it will be apparent that the debate between post-structuralists and the other groups discussed here is likely to be an involved one, though as yet it has hardly begun. The fact is that Anglo-American thought has not yet decided what kind of a creature post-structuralism really *is*. To do this it would have to translate the new system into its own terms: yet it is precisely this possibility which is ruled out by the post-structuralists themselves, who adhere to Canguilhem's (1980) view of a 'radical break' between epistemological systems.

Conclusions

What, then, are the prospects for the 'broadly based debate' which would be necessary to construct a paradigm out of these divergent schools? Even from the cursory outline given above, it should be clear that there are basic areas of agreement between all of them. There are also obvious disagreements, most notably around the post-structuralist view – but as the philosopher Richard Rorty (1982) points out, even Foucault's pro-gramme shows points of convergence with that of the US pragmatists.

Let me make it clear that the goal of producing a social constructionist paradigm is not based on obsessional tidiness, or a grandiose desire for universality. Social constructionism insists that different historical con-texts and aims will necessarily entail different theories, and to assume that they must all be 'saying the same thing' can only produce a sort of flavour-less scientific Esperanto. But the motives for seeking common ground are, in my view, overwhelming. First, in order to increase the chances of sur-vival of this approach; secondly, to make available to each school the rich resources (empirical as well as theoretical) of the others: and thirdly, to offer a way out of the fundamental problems of each. Rather than seeing how many of the achivements of a school we can consign to the scrap-heap because of that school's shortcomings, the question must be how much we can salvage *despite* those shortcomings.

Unfortunately, even if I am right, such a debate is not guaranteed to get very far. History shows that, once people become psychologists of a particular school, they easily become imbued with an omnipotent sense of its ability to answer all questions; the fact that members of other schools share very similar preoccupations leads to more, not less, antagonism and professional rivalry. Again, the fact that psychologists do not often receive much training in social theory may make it hard for them to recognize what is being said in other theoretical languages. In this respect, it is clear that psychologists will have to become literate in other disciplines, notably philosophy and sociology. The panic that usually afflicts psychology whenever its carefully constructed disciplinary boundaries are threatened seems to me misguided: true, when a fence is taken down, your neighbour can move into your garden – but you, too, can move into his . . . .

A conspicuous lack in all the above theories, however, is that they tend to concentrate narrowly on cognitive development, abstracted (in a thoroughly traditional way) from affect or motivation. As Dunn (1984) pointed out, it is obvious to almost everyone except developmental psy-chologists that childhood is an extremely emotional period – both for adults and children: yet social development is predominately analysed in cognitive, not affective, terms. This schizoid attitude – for that is what dissociation of affect is – can be traced in large measure to the suppression of psychoanalytic contributions to developmental theory. Yet even if the traditional scientific prejudice against psychoanalysis can be overcome, it is not clear that its concepts can be easily utilized within a social-construc-tionist approach. Psychoanalysis tends to treat desire as constituted 'within' the psyche (Lichtman, 1982), and to see social relations as factors which merely speed up or slow down autonomous processes of develop-ment. In this respect, Freud and Piaget start from the same position (Ingleby, 1983).

Lacan's reformulation of psychoanalysis in structural-linguistic terms seems to offer a possible bridge, and Cathy Urwin's work (1984) shows how questions of power and desire in early childhood can be formulated in such terms.

These, then, are the challenges that the study of development in social context faces. To what extent they can be met will only become apparent when we review the *next* ten years; but in the meantime, I think that if the idea of progress in developmental psychology means anything at all, the social constructionist movement is at the leading edge of it.

References

Adlam, D., Henriques, J., Rose, N., Salfield, A., Venn, C. and Walkerdine, V. 1977. Psychology, ideology and the human subject. *Ideology and Consciousness*, **1**, 5–56.

Bernstein, R. J. 1976. *The Reconstruction of Social and Political Theory*. Oxford: Basil Blackwell.

Bronfenbrenner, U. 1979. *The Ecology of Human Development*. Cambridge, Mass.: Harvard University Press.

Bruner, J. 1976. The ontogenesis of speech acts. *Journal of Child Language*, **2**, 1–19.

Bruner, J. 1979. Psychology and the image of man, in *On Knowing: essays for the left hand*. Cambridge, Mass.: Harvard University Press.

Canguilhem, G. 1980. What is psychology? *Ideology and Consciousness* 7, 37–50.

Chomsky, N. 1959. Review of B. F. Skinner's 'Verbal Behavior'. *Language*, **35**, 26–58.

Coulter, J. 1979. *The Social Construction of Mind*. London: Macmillan.

Doise, W. 1978. *Groups and Individuals*. London: Cambridge University Press.

Doise, W. and Mugny, G. 1984. *The Social Development of the Intellect*. London: Academic Press.

Donaldson, M. 1978. *Children's Minds*. London: Fontana.

Donzelot, J. 1980. *The Policing of Families*. New York: Pantheon.

Dunn, J. 1984. Emotion and the development of social understanding (paper presented at British Psychological Society [Developmental Section] Annual Conference, University of Lancaster).

Dunn, J. and Kendrick, C. 1982. *Siblings: love, envy and understanding*. Oxford: Basil Blackwell.

Elbers, E. 1984. The social psychology of the conservation task (paper presented at British Psychological Society [Developmental Section] Annual Conference, University of Lancaster).

Elbers, E. 1986. The development of motivation as an historical process, in J. M. Broughton (ed.), *Critical Theories of Psychological Development*. New York: Plenum.

Erikson, E. H. 1950. *Childhood and Society*. New York: Alfred A. Knopf.

Foucault, M. 1980. Truth and power, in *Power/Knowledge: selected interviews and other writings 1972–1977*. Brighton: Harvester.

Gergen, K. 1985. The social constructionist movement in modern psychology. *American Psychologist*, **40**, 266–75.

Goudena, P. 1984. Private speech: an analysis of its social and self-regulatory functions (doctoral dissertation, University of Utrecht).

Harré, R. and Secord, P. F. 1972: *The Explanation of Social Behaviour*. Oxford: Basil Blackwell.

Haugeland, J. 1978. The nature and plausibility of cognitivism. *Behavioral and Brain Sciences*, **2**, 215–60.

Heelas, P. and Lock, A. 1981. *Indigenous Psychologies: the anthropology of the self*. London: Academic Press.

Henriques, J., Holloway, W., Urwin, C., Venn, C. and Walkerdine, V. 1984. *Changing the Subject: psychology, social regulation and subjectivity*. London: Methuen.

Heritage, J. 1976. Assessing people, in N. Armitage (ed.), *Reconstructing Social Psychology*. London: Penguin.

Hood, L. H. 1985. Pragmatism and dialectical materialism in language development, in K. E. Nelson (ed.), *Children's Language*, Vol. 5. Hillsdale, NJ: Erlbaum.

Ingleby, D. 1983. Freud and Piaget: the phoney war. *New Ideas in Psychology*, **1**, 123–44.

Ingleby, D. 1985. Professionals as socialisers: the 'Psy Complex', in A. Scull and S. Spitzer (eds), *Research in Law, Deviance and Social Control 7*. New York: Jai Press.

Kessel, F. S. and Siegel, A. W. (eds) 1983. *The Child and Other Cultural Inventions*. New York: Praeger.

Lasch, C. 1977. *Haven in a Heartless World: the family besieged*. New York: Basic Books.

Lichtman, R. 1982. *The Production of Desire*. New York: The Free Press.

Light, P. 1983. Social cognition in Piaget: a case of negative transfer?, in S. Modgil (ed.), *Jean Piaget: an interdisciplinary critique*. London: Routledge and Kegan Paul.

Lock, A. (ed.) 1982. *Action, Gesture and Symbol*. London: Academic Press.

Morss, J. in press. New Mead in old bottles. *New Ideas in Psychology*.

Perret-Clermont, A.-N. 1980. *Social Interaction and Cognitive Development in Children*. London: Academic Press.

Richards, M. P. M. (ed.) 1974. *The Integration of a Child into a Social World*. London: Cambridge University Press.

Ricoeur, P. 1970. *Freud and Philosophy*. New Haven: Yale University Press.

Rorty, R. 1982. *Consequences of Pragmatism*. Brighton: Harvester.

Rose, N. 1985. *The Psychological Complex: social regulation and the psychology of the individual*. London: Routledge and Kegan Paul.

Russell, J. 1978. *The Acquisition of Knowledge*. London: Macmillan.

Selby, J. 1984. Conflicting aspirations in female Ph.D. students (unpublished Ph.D. thesis, University of Cambridge).

Sève, L. 1975. *Marxism and the Theory of Human Personality*. London: Lawrence and Wishart.

Shotter, J. 1974. The development of personal powers, in M. P. M. Richards (ed.), *The Integration of a Child into a Social World*. London: Cambridge University Press.

Shotter, J. 1984. *Social Accountability and Selfhood.* Oxford: Basil Blackwell.

Sinha, C. 1985. A socio-naturalistic approach to human development, in M. W. Ho and P. Saunders (eds), *Beyond Neo-Darwinism.* London: Academic Press.

Taylor, C. 1985. Language and human nature, and theories of meaning, in *Human Agency and Language: philosophical papers.* Vol. 1. Cambridge: Cambridge University Press.

Trevarthen, C. 1979. Communication and cooperation in early infancy: a description of primary intersubjectivity, in M. Bullowa (ed.), *Before Speech: the beginnings of human cooperation.* Cambridge: Cambridge University Press.

Urwin, C. 1984. Power relations and the emergence of language, in J. Henriques et al., *Changing the Subject: psychology, social regulation and subjectivity.* London: Methuen.

Van der Veer, R. and van Ijzendoorn, M. H. 1985. Vygotsky's theory of the higher psychological processes: some criticisms. *Human Development,* **28,** 1-9.

Venn, C. and Walkerdine, V. 1978. The acquisition and production of knowledge: Piaget's theory reconsidered. *Ideology and Consciousness,* **3,** 67-94.

Vygotsky, L. S. 1978. *Mind in Society.* Cambridge, Mass.: Harvard University Press.

Walkerdine, V. 1981. Sex, power and pedagogy. *Screen Education,* **38,** 14-21.

Walkerdine, V. 1984. Developmental psychology and the child-centred pedagogy, in J. Henriques et al., *Changing the Subject: psychology, social regulation and subjectivity.* London: Methuen.

Wertsch, J. 1979. From social interaction to higher psychological processes: a clarification and application of Vygotsky's theory. *Human Development,* **22,** 1-22.

Wertsch, J. 1985. *Vygotsky and the Social Formation of Mind.* Cambridge, Mass.: Harvard University Press.

White, S. 1983. Psychology as a moral science, in F. S. Kessel and A. W. Siegel (eds), *The Child and Other Cultural Inventions.* New York: Praeger.

Index

environmentalism 299–301
Erikson, E. H. 301
Essen, J. and Wedge, P. 122, 126
ethnomethodology and developmental
    psychology 235, 304, 308–9
evolution, social 11, 14, 266–7, 273,
    293

Fagot, B. I. 139
family:
    as agent of modernization 47
    bourgeois ideal 8, 31–3, 35, 37–9,
        41–2, 47–50, 312
    in child development 8, 31–51, 96,
        98–113, 236
    disintegration of 32–4, 37
    as health care institution 86
    and law, *see* law and the family
    and motherhood 40, 80
    as natural unit 8, 12, 40–1
    post-war 40–7
    and reaction to external stress 234,
        236, 252–4
    and reaction to family stress 109–12,
        113, 130, 159
    relationships and child development
        99–104, 106, 107–12, 281
    reproductive function 12, 22–4,
        55–6, 69–70
    responsibility of 39, 312
    rules, and child development 104–6,
        112
    single-parent 22, 32, 38–9, 50, 152
    size 43
    as social construct 8, 12, 21–5, 27
    working class 33, 34–40, 43, 47–9
    see also father; household; mother-
        hood; privacy; state, intervention by
father:
    authority of 34, 42–3
    and child care 64
    and family relationships 99–101
    and gender-roles 150–1, 153–60
    role of 22, 31–2, 42, 47, 49, 78, 84,
        89–90, 267, 275
    see also motherhood; mothers;
        parents

feminism:
    and changes in developmental
        psychology 298
    and childbirth 87–8
    and fatherhood 90
    and femininity 78, 85–6, 90
    and Freud 81–2
    and Marxism 80–1
    and motherhood 9, 43, 74–91
    and motherhood as oppression
        77–9, 82
    origins of gender differences 13, 16,
        82–3
Ferenczi, S. 269, 270–1, 274
Feuerbach, L. 309
Firestone, Shulamith 77–9
Flavell, J. H. et al. 214
Fletcher, R. 32
Floud, J. E. et al. 116
Fogelman, K. 120
Fortes, M. 23–4
Foucault, M. 70, 277, 310–12, 314
Freeman, Derek 12, 59
Freud, A. 66, 268
Freud, S. 81–2, 83, 267–8, 269–71,
    273–4, 279–81, 283, 309, 314
    Oedipus Complex 275–7
functionalist views of family 32

Gallistel, C. 184
Garai, J. E. and Scheinfeld, A. 138
Garfinkel, 308
Garmezy, N. and Rutter, M. 109–10
Gelman, R. 174–5, 184
gender development 135–61, 243–4,
    276–7
    in behaviour 135, 136–43, 147–51,
        154–6, 161
    biological factors 136–7
    cognitive factors 97, 135, 143–50, 158
    and culture 16, 136
    and family 91, 96, 135, 150–61
    and stereotyping 136, 143–4, 147–8,
        150, 152, 158–9
    see also conservation; environment,
        influence of; identification
Gesell, A. 267
Gilmour, A. 182

Index by Meg Davies